FRANKLYNN PETERSON, a free-lance writer, is also
the author of *The Build-It-Yourself Furniture Catalog*
for Prentice-Hall, as well as other self-help books.

How to Fix Damn Near Everything

FRANKLYNN PETERSON

A SPECTRUM BOOK

PRENTICE-HALL, INC., Englewood Cliffs, New Jersey 07632

Library of Congress Cataloging in Publication Data

Peterson, Franklynn.
  How to fix damn near everything.

  (A Spectrum Book)
  Includes index.
   1. Repairing—Amateurs' manuals.   I. Title.
TT151.P47   643'.7   76-26007
ISBN 0-13-407213-8
ISBN 0-13-407205-7 pbk.

A Spectrum Book

10 9 8 7 6 5 4 3 2 1

Printed in the United States of America

Prentice-Hall International, Inc., *London*
Prentice-Hall of Australia Pty. Limited, *Sydney*
Prentice-Hall of Canada, Ltd., *Toronto*
Prentice-Hall of India Private Limited, *New Delhi*
Prentice-Hall of Japan, Inc., *Tokyo*
Prentice-Hall of Southeast Asia Pte. Ltd., *Singapore*
Whitehall Books Limited, *Wellington, New Zealand*

Dedicated to
DON FEITEL
Great friend, gifted writer and editor

Other books by Franklynn Peterson:

Handbook of Lawn Mower Repair
The Build-It-Yourself Furniture Catalog
Shop Smart!

Contents

1 The Fine Art of Troubleshooting

The reason that so many families call in high-priced professional repair people for simple household repairs has almost nothing to do with the average person's lack of mechanical abilities. It's largely psychological! Children who grow up with fathers and mothers who can't tune a television, won't rewire a lamp cord, and feel that they shouldn't open the back of a washing machine will probably grow up just like their parents. They will think of themselves as ungainly, unmechanical clods, and unable to cope with modern mechanical mayhem.

Men and women who can bowl a 200 game now and then, play golf in the 60s or 70s, turn out a handmade quilt, or paint a recognizable picture—even if by the numbers—suddenly lose their nerve when confronted by something so genuinely simple as an undertoasting toaster or a car that won't start in the deep of winter. But professional repair people probably don't have any greater natural dexterity than you do. They don't have many tools that you can't have. And they don't often have secret books and diagrams about the insides of those appliances you think are so mysterious.

1

The main difference between a professional repair person and you—no matter what your education, occupation, age, IQ, or handiness quotient might be right now—is only *one thing*. Once upon a time somebody took the pro aside and said, "Sure you can fix things. Here's how you get started."

This book is that arm around *your* shoulder, that voice saying, "You can do it. *Anybody* can fix things around the house with a little help."

How To Fix Damn Near Everything isn't a mechanical cookbook. You won't be able to turn to a page marked "Electric Peeler" and find a diagram of every electric peeler ever manufactured, followed by "1) Remove the box, 2) Unscrew the heater, 3) Unsolder the steamer," —because you may not know how to use a screwdriver, how to solder, or how to tell a shaft from a pin. Mechanical cookbooks like that—and there are dozens of them on the market—have to be aimed at men (mainly), who love to fix things and who would tinker with the electric peeler whether it needed fixing or not. They're also written for men who have basements full of exotic tools.

This mechanical noncookbook is for woman, man, or mature child who *doesn't want to fix anything but has to*. As the hourly rate of repair people gets steeper, as the scarcity of professional fix-its gets more drastic, as the sloppy workmanship of gadget and appliance manufacturers gets more distressing, more and more so-called unhandy people will become inspired to pick up a tool, overcome their psychological hangups, and unveil a malingering household helper. And they will probably be shocked to find that they can, indeed, fix it!

How To Fix Damn Near Everything is the collective knowledge and instincts passed on by a spunky father who could not afford the price of a house, so he built one himself from the foundation to the attic, and by his brash son, who gets miffed because manufacturers seem to make more profit by repairing asinine gadgets than by selling them in the first place, so he fixes everything in sight for everybody in the neighborhood as his personal revenge against sloppy corporate workmanship.

Ironically, professional repair people do not want or need a fix-it cookbook to tell them the steps they should take before collecting their fees. They have learned, we should hope, how to *think* about repairs systematically. Given a peeler made on the moon, a good repair person—and there still are some—would know how to begin fixing the moonmade gadget without waiting for a diagram to be flown in from out there.

You, too, can overcome your years of brainwashing. Even complicated-looking appliances actually are made up of very, very simple parts. The assembly line demands such simplicity. Read the early chapters of this repair book right now. Then, before starting a repair job, read each chapter pertinent to your particular home problem. After that, you too should be part of the now generation, the renaissance man and woman, a consciousness III person who refuses to sit around and complain about how bad things are. You will be doing something positive to make things better in your own house, apartment, trailer, barn, or tent.

Cliché aside, repairs really are as easy as that old 1, 2, 3:

1. Troubleshoot systematically, as this chapter will explain.
2. Use the right tool "right," which the next chapter will discuss.
3. Replace the bad parts with good ones, discussed in Chapter 3.

At the moment, you may think that *troubleshooting* is something experts do in return for a big fee. And that's right, of course. But non-experts can also practice the art of troubleshooting on practically any appliance or gadget in their homes to locate the source of trouble. A handful of very simple tools will suffice for troubleshooting even some complicated pieces of machinery. The important ingredient in this art is an appreciation for the *system* of troubleshooting.

Troubleshooting is no more—and no less—than finding the reason why an appliance such as a washing machine, a gadget such as a transistor radio, or even a toy such as a model airplane stopped running altogether or began operating erratically. A decision as to whether or not you are able to fix it, or even if you want to fix it, can be made later. If you first locate the probable source of trouble, you will save yourself the cost of replacing too many parts that actually may be in good condition. Or you will save the cost of having a repair pro come in to do the troubleshooting for you first, and then accomplish the actual repair second.

Economy aside, there is yet another reason why troubleshooting is a valuable skill for anyone to learn. Unscrupulous repair people are talked about very much, but very little is done about them. Here is your chance to do something! If you discover to your own satisfaction that the air conditioner, for example, has stopped cooling because a condenser on the compressor motor is faulty, you naturally would be very suspicious of a repair pro who insisted on taking the unit to the shop for a major, and very expensive, overhaul.

If the word "condenser" or any other technical sounding term is strange to you, fear not. They were strange to the most experienced repair pro at one time. For now, think of unfamiliar parts as "what-zits." Later chapters will offer simple meanings for almost any jargon you are likely to encounter.

Troubleshooting on a hit-and-miss basis *misses* more often than *hits*. To be both effective and simple, troubleshooting systematically

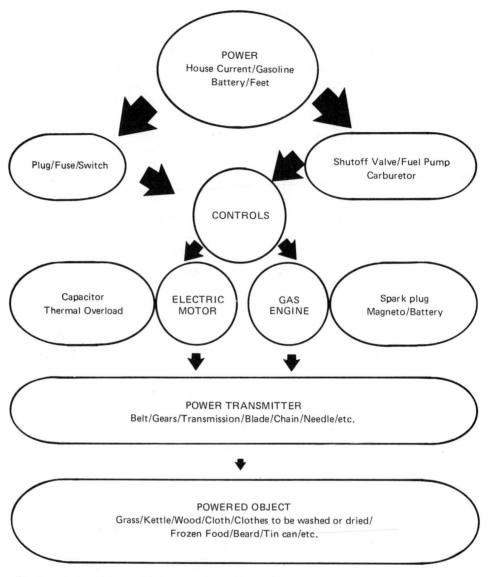

The fine art of troubleshooting abstracted into a block diagram to cover damn near every household appliance or gadget.

Figure 1 Troubleshooting anything goes easier with a system. Herewith a system for studying almost everything that can go wrong with household appliances and gadgets.

must trace the path of power from its source to its output, *no matter what kind of gadget is causing you trouble.* Figure 1 presents the entire step-by-step procedure for troubleshooting in a single generalized outline. The chart can work for practically anything, with the addition of just a bit of imagination.

4

POWER MUST BE AVAILABLE

Simpleminded as that sounds at first, TV repair pro's probably may retire earlier than most folks because of the unbelievable number of calls they get just to tell someone that the set is not plugged in. The same goes for washing machines, refrigerators, and just about every other plugged-in convenience. So, at the outset of troubleshooting, ask yourself, "Is the appliance plugged in?" Are you sure? Take a look anyway!

The power difficulty occasionally comes from using a wall outlet that is controlled by a switch. Such outlets were installed mainly as a convenience in connecting lamps, but after the lamp has been moved to another corner of the room, the TV or even a refrigerator might be plugged into the switched outlet. And with a refrigerator or freezer, you are really asking for serious trouble in such a case. What happens to all those steaks if somebody accidentally throws the switch off as you leave for a weekend trip?

It isn't enough that a plug is physically plugged into a wall outlet. It still may not be transmitting current from the house wiring to the appliance. Jiggle the plugs and various wires and connections on an ailing appliance—carefully. If the appliance jerks momentarily to life a few times during this test, it is probably suffering from a loose connection, a faulty plug, or a broken copper wire inside the rubber insulation. Don't overlook the possibility that *more than one* of these faults might be to blame.

Plugs and wires on almost any electrical or electronic device can be replaced with little money or effort (see Chapter 9).

FUSES AND CIRCUIT BREAKERS

Fuses must be good before electric power can do its job. Often there are more fuses in a particular circuit then at first meets the eye. The simplest fuse to check is the one that protects the house wiring. It should be well marked. If your house fuses are not marked well, why not do so now? Typically such fuses are hidden in a dark corner of the basement or high above the floor in some obscure hallway. You usually need a flashlight to locate which of the array of fuses actually protects the circuit in question and to make a quick check visually for the telltale signs of a blown fuse—melted wire, distorted spring, or darkened window area.

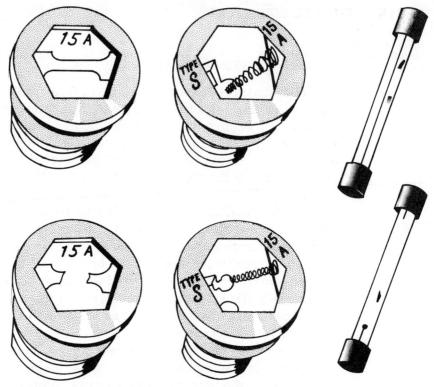

Figure 2　How to spot a blown fuse. The top view shows what the various types of fuses look like when they're OK. Bottom view shows it blown.

Don't be content with simply *looking* for an obviously blown fuse. Subtle changes within a fuse can interrupt the flow of current, too. Switch the questioned fuse with another one that you know to be working properly. But *never* walk away from the fuse box with a larger fuse screwed in than you found there. For instance, if a 15 amp fuse was protecting the circuit in question, it could be very dangerous to leave a 25 amp fuse in place of the smaller one.

Fuses have been replaced by circuit breakers in new installations or modernized homes. Typically the circuit breakers look very much like ordinary light switches, and they can function as an on-off switch. When a short circuit or an overload has taken place—a condition that would blow a fuse—the circuit breaker automatically stops the flow of electricity. When that happens, the breaker's handle in some models jumps to a position just above "on." Figure 3 shows what to look for when trying to locate possible open circuit breakers of that type. Other breakers simply kick the handle down to the "off" position when trouble occurs.

Many large appliances have a fuse or circuit breaker inside of them. Televisions, for instance, almost always have a simple circuit breaker. You can locate a TV circuit breaker by looking for an exposed button labeled (appropriately) "Circuit breaker" or (inappropriately) "Reset." If the trouble is caused by an electronic quirk, your problems will be over merely by pushing the button to reset it. However, if the circuit breaker opens again after only a short time, your problem apparently lies deeper inside the maze of wires and electronic components, a condition that calls for you to read Chapter 8.

For a radio, washer, air conditioner, or anything else that has an internal fuse, the location generally is conveniently marked on a wiring diagram. The diagram, however, is most often inconveniently hidden beneath some decoration or behind the back panel. It is well worth searching for the diagram and fuse before proceeding further down the line in your troubleshooting.

Fuses in your car are almost always hidden beneath the dashboard

Figure 3 Blown circuit breakers can either jump obviously out of line (bottom view) or only slightly out of line (top view).

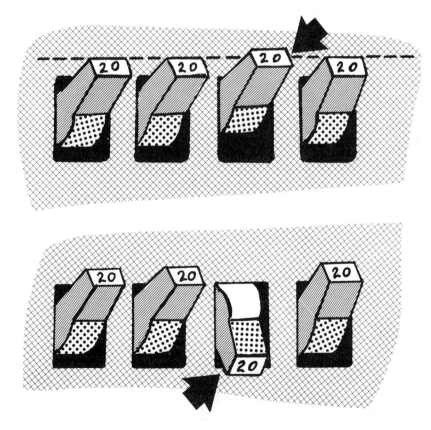

on the driver's side. The hiding place is easy to locate, assuming you can stand on your head backwards, letting your feet dangle out the front passenger door or over the front seat itself. Whatever your position, you will need a flashlight. Practically every light bulb and electrical device in the car is individually fused. And the dozen or more fuses are on both the front and back of each fuse holder. Some engineer has marked the fuse holder with cryptic notations that few people can fathom on their first several encounters. So you will probably resort to trial and error.

Even your trial and error efforts will be hindered by the fact that each member of the tight nest of thin glass fuses was intended to be removed with a *fuse puller*, a very inexpensive tool but one that few households have around. Don't despair, however; the glass fuses are actually pretty strong. You can pry them loose with a small screwdriver, and reinsert the fuses firmly with your fingers.

A blown fuse cannot always be spotted on sight. If you are in doubt about one in particular, temporarily replace it even if you have to borrow one from another electrical line that you know is working. Auto fuses range from 1 amp up to 20, so be very careful that you do not permanently leave a 20 amp fuse in a slot where 1 amp protection is called for.

BATTERIES

The battery is frequently the culprit when one of the dozen or so battery-powered gadgets around the house fails to function or performs erratically. Cleanliness, in the case of batteries, is all-important. The electrical power (voltage) inside a battery is so small that a tiny bit of corrosion or even some grease from your fingers can be a barrier to the flow of current to your radio, camera, or other small battery-powered equipment. If the cells inside your ailing appliance look off-colored or show any sign of flaking or corroding, get rid of them. Not only will they perform poorly, they can also damage electronic parts in short order.

Batteries that *look* clean may not be. If a battery-powered item won't work, and the batteries should be powerful enough to kick up at least a little noise, take them out and gently polish both ends of the battery and all of the contacts inside the battery holder. Figure 4 shows the polishing art for a variety of different battery types. A silver polishing cloth, pencil eraser, emery board, or fine sandpaper will clean the batteries and contacts nicely. In an emergency, some rougher treatment, such as a nail file, penknife, or even a penny can be used. Once the battery terminals and the contacts inside the appliance are

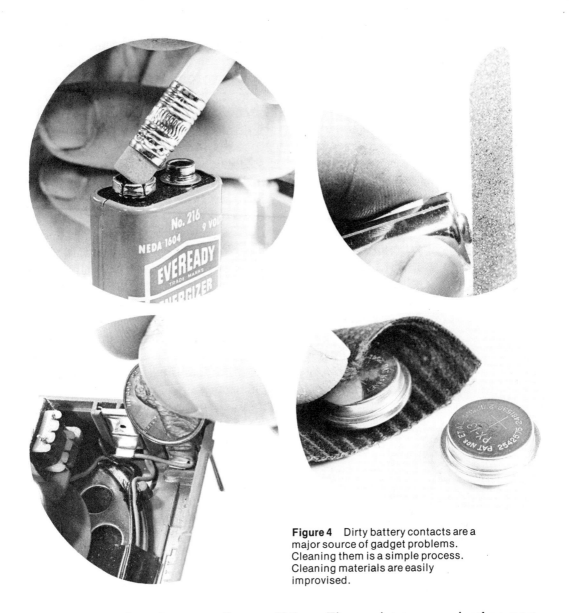

Figure 4 Dirty battery contacts are a major source of gadget problems. Cleaning them is a simple process. Cleaning materials are easily improvised.

clean, keep your fingers off them. Fingerprints are greasier than most people imagine.

The words *battery* and *cell*, incidentally, never did mean the same thing until the 1970s, when advertising obscured their original meanings. The makers of batteries and cells now use the words interchangeably, so presumably the rest of us can too.

It is a telling statistic that even in a nation so health-crazed as this one, people still spend many times more money buying batteries than even vitamin pills. U.S. consumers use over a billion small batteries every year without really knowing what they're buying.

As part of the research for this book, several hundred batteries of all types and prices were literally run to death in flashlights, radios, and toys. Some were operated continuously, some for only half an hour or an hour every day. Armed with the results of these tests, major battery manufacturers were offered the chance to explain why the test results were so much at odds with their advertising claims. As the discussions wore on, the companies brought out their engineering manuals. Ironically, what the engineers know about the life-span and recommended applications for batteries is considerably different than what the advertising copywriters would lead you to believe.

In general, for most applications *buy the cheapest batteries available* as long as you are reasonably sure they are fresh. Freshness is more important than price. Under ideal storage conditions (70°F. or less), the shelf life for penlight-size cells (AA size) is at most six months, even according to major battery manufacturers. Under the less than ideal conditions prevalent in warehouses and countertops, four to five months might be the maximum shelf life.

Batteries larger than the penlight size do have a shelf life longer than six months. Ordinary flashlight size (D cells) batteries theoretically can sit on a shelf for a year at 70° without losing more than 10 percent of their original life. Alkaline-manganese cells theoretically can hold on to 90 percent of their rated power for up to two years on a store

Figure 5 Author's son watching battery-powered train during extensive test of common batteries. Conclusion: it seldom pays to buy expensive batteries. Getting fresh ones is the most important aspect.

shelf, assuming they are protected from temperatures greater than 70°. (The so-called alkaline batteries and manganese power cells are one and the same product, by the way.) The problem is, how many stores keep their lighted displays and closed storerooms below 70°?

For one part of this study, brand name batteries were purchased in a wide variety of locations—downtown, suburban, and neighborhood stores in a metropolitan area. Assisted later by the manufacturer of the chosen cells, it was discovered that the freshest batteries bought in the test had left the factory two months earlier. The oldest on sale were four and one-half years old.

Despite the fact that batteries are a perishable commodity, manufacturers have long refused to make their dating codes available to the public. Most batteries made in the U.S. have a letter code stamped somewhere on them, on the side, bottom or top, which identifies the month and year of their manufacture, occasionally also the plant in which they were made.

What about cheap imported batteries? To quote the sales engineer at a major U.S. battery manufacturer, "There are great variations in how well they perform. But, admittedly, there are some pretty good batteries among them." Although that engineer's company does not like to identify foreign brand names in print, it does release a list of identifying codes to wholesale battery buyers.

One surprised department store buyer discovered that one obscure imported battery it was selling had been rated by the U.S. battery company as comparable in quality and performance to the U.S. company's higher priced, premium battery. Ironically, the department store was selling the imported product at retail for two cents less than it cost them to buy the comparable U.S. battery at wholesale prices.

In some situations, the alkaline-manganese cells *are* worth their premium price tag. Whenever a gadget such as a tape recorder, movie camera, or electronic flashgun is going to put an unusually heavy drain on the batteries and use up almost their full power capacity within a day or two, it pays to buy the alkaline-manganese cells. Toys also place a heavy drain on batteries, and you might consider the expensive alkaline cells either an economy or a nuisance—they will last longer if the kids play with toy dolls and racers for more than an hour a day.

There is value in using the expensive alkaline-manganese cells at the exact opposite end of the applications spectrum. If just a tiny amount of power is to be withdrawn from a battery, it must continue to function for a long period of time—perhaps a year—then the more costly products again become economical. This is largely a result of their superior shelf life characteristics.

Watches, clocks, hearing aids, and similar devices deserve batteries

Figure 6 Leaky batteries occur after stale ones have been allowed to sit around inside some equipment. Leaking chemicals can ruin sensitive devices, foul up anything else.

designed and marked for such special uses. Life-span, in this case, is not the only consideration. Batteries intended for use in expensive equipment are specially sealed to prevent leaks. Once the caustic materials inside a battery leak out, delicate electronic or mechanical parts can corrode very quickly. For this reason, toys, flashlights, radios, and any other gadget you value should never be stored very long with batteries left inside.

Rechargeable batteries and widely advertised rechargers, ostensibly for adding new life to old nonrechargeable batteries, can easily capture the economy-minded consumer's fancy. Very few systems that rely upon recharging batteries are feasible around the home, however. First of all, batteries not designed for recharging, *and marked that way*, should not be recharged. Some of the alkaline-manganese cells actually bear a printed warning that they may explode if recharged. That is overstated considerably, of course. It would take a very powerful battery charger to put so much pressure on the cell actually to generate an explosion. But they might *leak* if recharged, and they will not perform for very long after a recharge except in very specialized situations.

Nickel-cadmium batteries can be used for approximately half of their potential useful life before they must be recharged. They are also considerably more expensive than any other common battery product, and they must be recharged on equipment designed specifically for nickel-cadmium cells or their performance and overall life expectancy can be shortened.

If you have toys, flashlights, photographic electronic flash equipment, transistor radios, tape recorders, or similar devices that receive consistent use but for relatively short periods of time, the ni-cad batteries could prove economical. This assumes, of course, that you regiment yourself or your family to a regular ritual of recharging the nickel-cadmium cells before they are discharged beyond hope.

GASOLINE-POWERED EQUIPMENT

Such equipment as lawn mowers, snow blowers, go-carts, or snow-mobiles lend themselves to the same troubleshooting techniques as do electric appliances. Instead of tracing the flow of electric current, the flow of gasoline is traced, always watching for the point where it may be interrupted.

The gas tank should be your first check. Is it full? Is it full of *fuel* and not water? Someone in a hurry may grab an empty gasoline can and fill it with water for some project, then absent mindedly return the can half full of water to its usual place alongside the lawn mower. You can imagine the kind of mayhem that will take place the next time the lawn mower gets a tank full of something the owner forgets is not gasoline.

Because gasoline floats on top of water and fuel is pumped out of a gas tank from the bottom, you can't just sniff at the filler tube of the gas tank to find out if water has gotten inside. If you carefully use a straw to suck up a sample from the bottom of the tank, your nose can then determine if the tank really is filled with gasoline.

Gasoline flows through plastic or copper tubes from the tank to the fuel pump or directly to the carburetor. Along the way, however, there may be one or more shutoff valves that deserve a moment of your time to ensure that they are indeed open. Regardless of whether it is used to control gasoline, or water, when the handle of a simple shutoff valve is *parallel* to the line in which it is installed, the *valve is open. Perpendicular means closed* (see Figure 7).

Fuel pumps, carburetors, and other equipment necessary to the functioning of a gasoline engine are relatively easy to troubleshoot. Gasoline engines should be described as *surprisingly easy* to analyze, although most men and women regard the greasy world of mowers, carts, cycles, and outboards as untouchable. (Chapter 17 tackles

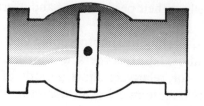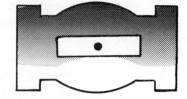

Figure 7 Gas valves, and most other shut-off devices, indicate whether they're open (on) or closed (off) by position of handle. Parallel to tubing means open, perpendicular means closed.

gasoline engines and their sundry applications in detail. Several chapters will be devoted to ailments common to specific electrical devices found in your home.)

POWER CONTROLS

Examine power controls in both electric-powered and gasoline-powered equipment after the power itself has been checked out. A second common cause of unnecessary calls to expensive service people is the fact that controls are often set improperly. This is especially true for washing machines, hi-fi sets, cameras, recorders, and practically every other fairly complicated gadget known to humans.

After you have made sure that power is reaching the balky appliance, but it still seems to be inoperative, take a quick survey among family members or neighbors. Can you get three people to agree that the controls really are set properly? It pays to keep the user manual that came with the machine in some easy to reach drawer for times like this. You may have used a washer for months without trouble, but a simple lapse of memory can lead you to overlook some important operating detail that will seem like a malfunction on the part of the machine instead of on the part of the user.

After checking that all knobs, buttons, dials, and switches are in their proper positions, try another test. Do they work in *some* positions but *not others*? On washing machines, for example, the controls do go bad just frequently enough to worry about. If the water level control will work for *medium* and *low* but not for *high*, the trouble might be in the control itself or in the various signaling devices hooked up to the control. (Chapter 12 deals with this problem and others in major appliances such as washing machines.)

In a hi-fi system, as another example, if a record plays but the tuner won't bring in radio programs in either mono or stereo settings, chances are the trouble is in the tuner, or more likely in wires connected to the tuner. The amplifier, according to our hypothetical troubleshooting findings here, would seem to be functioning properly.

On gasoline gadgets, the controls usually are limited to a throttle, a choke (although automatic chokes are replacing more and more manual controls), the shorting switch, which inactivates the spark plug on many devices when you want to stop the engine, and a clutch, which can be used to stop forward motion in a minibike or self-propelled lawn mower without stopping the engine itself.

When you carry your troubleshooting of gasoline engines to the stage of investigating the controls, keep in mind that one of the biggest single headaches in this area stems from a person trying to start an already *warm* engine when the controls have been set for starting a *cold* engine. Although the manufacturers of most gadgets incorporating gasoline engines label one setting "Start," what they really mean is "For Starting a *Cold* Engine" or "Choke." An engine that you have already warmed up by riding around the block a few times or by mowing a patch of front lawn should be started while the main control is near the position labeled "Idle." The clutch, the lever that generally decides whether the machine stops or goes, should be disengaged when the engine is started, so that the engine can start only itself without also having to turn some heavy machinery during its first few seconds of life.

THE POWERHOUSE

The powerhouse itself is the next logical step in a troubleshooting formula. Both gasoline engines and electric motors require a good deal more specific information to accomplish successful troubleshooting than was needed in the earlier, more generalized sections of this chapter on fuses, plugs, sockets, and controls. Chapter 17 gets into specifics on diagnosing gasoline engines. Electric motors are covered in such chapters such Chapter 12 on major appliances, Chapter 13 on air conditioners, refrigerators, and freezers, Chapter 14 on power tools, and Chapter 21 on toys.

THE POWER TRAIN

The various belts, pulleys, chains, and transmissions attached to the powerhouse suffer most often from lack of proper lubrication (covered here in a very general way). And second most often, they suffer from bent or damaged parts caused by lack of proper use (covered in specific chapters elsewhere). We are ignoring, of course, lack of proper engineering or construction, a malady about which you can do very little in a mechanical way after you have paid for the appliance. It is more than just an old wives' tale that if the warranty on a piece of equipment is good for five years, you will not start having trouble until five years and one day have passed.

If the power train doesn't seem to be turning as easily as it should, lubrication might be the answer. But since too much lubrication or the wrong kind can be as much of a problem as too little oil or grease, proceed cautiously. First, try to find out whether the balky pulley or gear originally was lubricated with oil—a thin, colorless, slippery liquid very much like cooking oil—, or grease—a thick, opaque, sticky substance very much like shortening or soft butter.

Before actually adding new oil or grease to an apparently under-lubricated shaft or gear, it is prudent to find out first if lack of lubrication is indeed the cause of trouble. A fast way to find out is by squirting a generous bit of penetrating oil on the suspect part. (Chapter 2 will explain penetrating oil.) If lubrication can cure what ails the appliance, penetrating oil will temporarily put the device back in service both by dissolving rust or old lubrication and by acting as a simple lubricant itself. If this test demonstrates that oil or grease can put the equipment back in operation, use it. But if not, the penetrating oil will evaporate harmlessly away as you proceed further down the troubleshooting path in search of the real cause.

If a belt that ought to be moving isn't, or if a belt is moving but one of the pulleys around which it moves is standing still, the problem might be *too much lubrication*. Oil or grease on a belt can make it so slippery that the belt slides right over a pulley without creating enough friction so that the pulley and belt can move in harmony. This condition is very often found in hi-fi turntables, especially after an eager handy person lubricated some nearby parts.

Small and inexpensive belts that have become oil choked are best replaced. For emergency repairs, and for larger or more expensive belts, the oil can be removed by vigorously wiping the entire length of belt and pulley with paper towels. Change to a clean towel frequently and continue wiping until you no longer find any obvious traces of oil or grease on the towels. A tube of *belt dressing* can cure many ailing belts. The sticky dressing contains particles that increase the friction between belt and pulley.

THE FINAL STAGE—HOW AILING EQUIPMENT IS USED

Improper or too vigorous use of a small motor-driven tool can often lead to *stalling* and *overheating*. The same two conditions also could be caused by internal disorders, such as faulty bearings, shorted starting windings on the motor, or worn brushes. It is important to find out whether the difficulty is in the tool itself or in the way the tool is used.

A badly dulled or broken needle, if used on hefty fabric, can cause slipping belts or a stalled motor on a sewing machine. And if a rotary saw with a dull blade is used for cutting plywood, not only will the resulting cut be smokey and wavy instead of straight and clean, but the motor can overheat, decompose the brushes, melt the insulation, and burn out the bearings.

Very often a person puts an appliance or tool to a use that the gadget can't handle, perhaps because it has not been used recently. Or, the device may be used frequently but on an entirely different kind of material than was employed at the time the trouble began showing up. Inadequate though many user manuals may be, they often do list various materials or techniques that require some out of the ordinary kind of treatment. Some manuals even warn about the limitations of a particular tool. For this reason, it is important that well-run households set aside one specific place as a depository of the dozens of user manuals large and small that otherwise quickly disappear.

The cost of buying a good quarter-inch electric drill is, believe it or not, about one fourth what it was 10 years ago, but the cost of repairing it is at least four times greater today. With that in mind, it might be easier also to keep in mind the five basic steps in logical troubleshooting, which are the keys to fixing damn near everything:

1. Source of power.
2. Power controls.
3. Powerhouse.
4. Power train.
5. Use.

Your Hero at the Hardware Store

2

Once you have successfully located the source of any household headache with the help of Chapter 1, you will of course, want to go to work on the ailing piece of furniture, appliance, tool, toy, or trinket. True, professional repair people may have some training to prepare them for such work—*but not necessarily*. Some of the best in the field picked up the repair business by rote, learning as they fixed. That is just what you're about to do.

There is a very simple, logical organization to virtually everything sold for home use today. The assembly line system requires that the entire complex TV set or washing machine be assembled in very simple bits and pieces. The repair person finds *which* bit or piece is malfunctioning (by troubleshooting) and generally replaces it. A repair pro may *appear* to repair a washing machine, but in essence he or she has repaired it by *replacing something*—a burned out solenoid, a belt, a broken wire.

There is no technical reason to prevent the average man or woman from replacing defective parts also. Aside from a certain psychological readiness to tackle an unfamiliar situation, such as the inside of a radio, only two ingredients are needed—the right part and the right tool. Buying and replacing the right part will be covered in detail in most of the following chapters. Right now, lets consider the right tool.

If you grew up sheltered by a parent who fixed everything from toy trains to toilets, you probably also have a virginal outlook on the price and complexity of tools. They are cheaper than you think! Having the right tool can save you the substantial cost of sending for a repair person, who happens to have the right tool when he or she comes to tighten a loose nut.

A good hammer costs only a few dollars. A screwdriver is less than a dollar. A good all-around wrench, pliers, and a hand saw will never break your budget.

Figures 8, 9, and 10 present lists and photographs of various collections of tools that the typical house and apartment dweller should

Figure 8 Basic tools. No home should be without most, if not all, of these tools and materials. Reading clockwise from plunger in middle: claw hammer, ruler, paste hand cleaner, flashlight, sandpaper, screwdrivers (large, small, 2 Phillips), pliers, combination saw, knife, crescent wrench (about 8"), combination wrench set, all-purpose lubricants (grease, graphite, light oil), all-purpose glues (contact cement, epoxy).

consider keeping close at hand. The first list is very basic. No well-run household should be without almost every item included in this collection.

As a novice fix-it person digs deeper into the internal workings of those once mysterious gadgets that break, the tools in the second list (Figure 9) will become more meaningful and considerably more valuable. These items can be added gradually to your collection, or as needed. For the man or woman who really gets involved in this home fix-it idea, or the rural home owner who can't always make it to a hardware or department store in 15 minutes, the third list (Figure 10) is worth looking at. The tools are more exotic or more expensive, often more specialized than those in the first two lists. Most people will put off buying items in the third category until they are actually needed, by which time you will find they are well worth their proverbial weight in gold.

The tools in the photos are not new. They are "working tools," straight from the author's toolbox.

Armed with a new awareness of your own skill in the mechanical area and with this book to help you tell the hardware or other storekeeper exactly what tool or replacement part you want, there is no telling how much money, time, and aggravation you can save yourself. And be sure to make friends at a good hardware store. The

---

Fig. 9   Intermediate Tool List

As your foray into the repair world gets more and more extensive, so will your collection of tools. The handy items listed here will prove to be very useful at odd moments of your life. Some of them you might want to buy only as needed. Others, like the quarter-inch drill, might make good presents (to give or receive).

#1. electric drill (¼ ")
    Accessories for electric drill
2. drill set
3. sanding wheel
4. wire brush
5. hole cutter set
6. countersinks
7. screw driving set
8. coping saw
9. brace and bits
10. pipe wrench (14")
11. needle nose pliers
12. files
13. vice grip pliers
14. test lamp
15. screw extractors
16. tool box
17. soldering iron

18. six foot rule
19. chisel (1" wood)
20. glass cutter
21. hand saw (cross cut)
22. small square
23. liquid wrench
24. plastic tape
25. silicone adhesive & caulking
26. heavy oil and oil can
27. silicone lubricant
28. 3-wire extension cord
29. step ladder
30. allen wrenches
31. more screw drivers
    a. very small slot
    b. #0 Phillips
    c. very large slot
32. putty knife

Fig. 10   Advanced Tool List

*When these tools are needed in your repertoire, they'll be worth their weight in gold—literally.
In the meantime, you'll find their use rather specialized. As was the case with Fig. 9, these tools
are arranged in very roughly the order of their usefulness around the average home.*

#1. saber saw	16. bent nose pliers
2. small circular saw	17. electricians pliers
3. belt sander	18. taps (⅛″, ³⁄₁₆″, ¼″)
4. strapping tape	19. feelers gage
5. socket wrench set	20. small sledge
6. propane torch	21. small ball peen hammer
7. small paint sprayer	22. star drill or masonry chisel
8. miniature screw drivers	23. trowel
9. miniature wrenches	24. paint scraper
10. chest for tools and parts	25. level
11. vice	26. micrometer
12. c-clamps	27. small plane
13. pipe clamps	28. large plane
14. multi-tester	29. offset screw drivers
15. chisel (¼″)	

local hardware dealer, after all, makes a living by selling tools and fix-it gadgets—his *advice* comes free. Sharper hardware peddlers realize that it is their advice that keeps many customers coming back. Consequently, they keep themselves up-to-date on what is new and what is good so they can lend a helpful hand to people like you in times of trouble.

If the advice offered by your hardware dealer—or anyone else for that matter—clashes with your own instincts, stick to your own hunches! The discrepancy may not come from ignorance or a conspiracy at all. *Communication*, or lack of it, is the cause of many failures in this field. Following are some basic tips on some basic tools.

BRACE AND BIT

Often called a "wood drill" by those who have no feel for the cultural aspects of the woodworking craft, a *brace* does exactly that—it braces a *bit* as the bit bores a hole through a piece of wood. The *auger bits* in Figure 11 commonly come in sizes from ¼″ to 1″ in diameter. Most bits are 7″ to 9″ long, but they are available, although not readily, in considerably shorter and longer sizes. A number is stamped on the *tang* of an auger bit to identify its size. Think of that number as a fraction over 16. In other words, a number 8 bit is ⁸⁄₁₆″ or ½″.

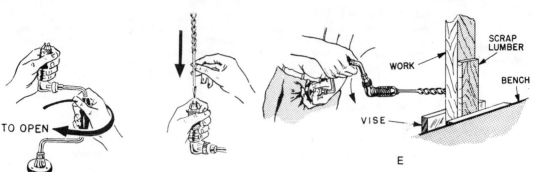

TO OPEN

A

B

SCRAP LUMBER

WORK

BENCH

VISE

E

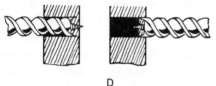

$\frac{3}{4}''$ 12 $\frac{12}{16}$

SQUARE TANG

$\frac{1}{2}''$ 8 $\frac{8}{16}$

$\frac{3}{8}''$ 6 $\frac{6}{16}$

C

D

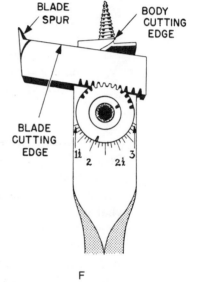

BLADE SPUR

BODY CUTTING EDGE

BLADE CUTTING EDGE

$1\frac{1}{2}$ 2 $2\frac{1}{2}$ 3

F

Figure 11 the brace and bit, commonly miscalled a wood drill, bores holes easily into wood. The brace opens (A) by a twisting motion so that the bit slips into the jaws where it is held firmly after twisting the jaws closed tightly. Sizes are indicated as a fraction over 16 (C). Bits tend to split wood at the end of cutting so as soon as point penetrates opposite end (D) of work, turn around and finish hole from other side. Alternately, (D), clamp a scrap piece of lumber to far side of wood. Expansive bit (F) allows you to cut holes of varying sizes.

For drilling holes larger than 1", an *expansive bit* is often used. It looks very much like a common bit, but the cutting edge is infinitely adjustable over the full range of this tool. Most can handle dimensions up to 2" or 3", but a few will go to 4". A circle cutting, sawlike attachment for electric drills is often used instead of an expansive bit for cutting larger holes.

The brace itself is a very simple, inexpensive tool. A ratchet feature on the bit is controlled by twisting the ring. If the ratchet is not in use, when you twist the handle to the left the bit moves to the left and when you twist the handle to the right the bit moves to the right. With the ring turned to the left, the bit will move if the handle is moved left but *not* if the handle is moved to the right. The converse situation applies when the ring is twisted to the right. The ratchet feature is ideal when the brace and bit have to turn in a limited space, such as for boring a hole near the floor or a corner.

CHISELS

There are wood chisels, metal chisels, masonry chisels, brick chisels, and more. Each is designed with a specific job to do. It does that job well but becomes a nuisance and even a hazard if used for any other type of work.

At one time wood chisels were meant to be struck by a wooden mallet. So many carpenters, pro or otherwise, used the common carpenter's hammer with a metal head on chisels that most manufacturers now have designed their wood chisels so that they can withstand the rigors of being hit by steel hammer heads. The mark of such a tool is an iron button at the end of the handle.

A flat chisel, which generally ranges in widths from ¼" up to 3", is used to remove relatively large amounts of wood to create a rough shape. More than likely you will find one to be quite handy when installing a lock or hinges.

The *gouge* is a wood chisel best suited to creating grooves or cleaning them out. If you feel quite handy, a gouge is the sort of chisel that wood-carvers most often use to chip away on statues. Figure 12 shows some of the varieties of wood chisels you can choose from.

The *cold chisel* is the major tool you will have occasion to use on metal. Like the wood chisel, the cold chisel comes in a variety of sizes and shapes, many of which you can see in Figure 13.

It is important that you wear glasses when using a cold chisel. Pieces of metal can fly off the work or the chisel itself. If you already wear glasses (assuming they were made after federal regulations required that all eyeglass lenses be hardened), *that* should be sufficient. If not, an inexpensive pair of protective goggles is needed.

Cold chisels must be struck with a hammer of the proper size. You cannot accomplish much by tapping at a big chisel with a tiny hammer. And at the opposite end of the weight spectrum, a tiny chisel slugged by a massive hammer is so uncontrollable that you will be inviting damage to your work or your body. The head of a

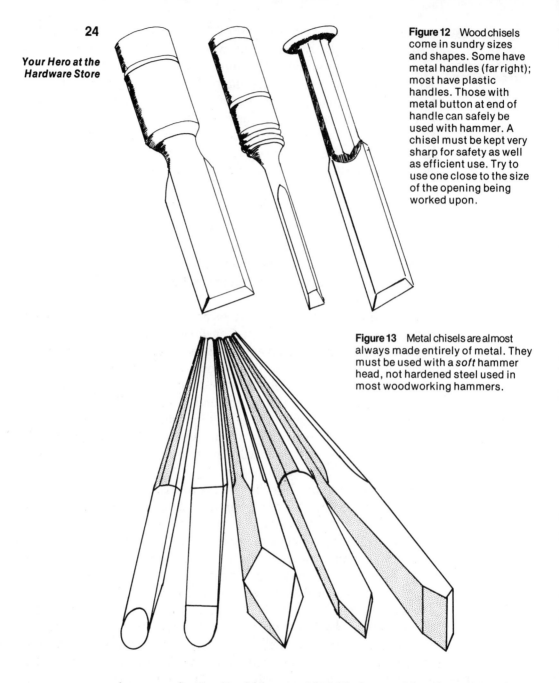

Figure 12 Wood chisels come in sundry sizes and shapes. Some have metal handles (far right); most have plastic handles. Those with metal button at end of handle can safely be used with hammer. A chisel must be kept very sharp for safety as well as efficient use. Try to use one close to the size of the opening being worked upon.

Figure 13 Metal chisels are almost always made entirely of metal. They must be used with a *soft* hammer head, not hardened steel used in most woodworking hammers.

hammer always should be considerably larger than the cold chisel it strikes. A ½ ″ chisel, for example, needs a hammer with at least a 1 ″ head.

Although the striking end of a hatchet is properly hardened so that it can be used for driving nails, it *cannot* be used against a cold chisel

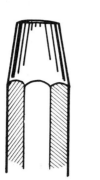
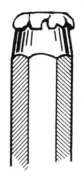

Figure 14 When head of a chisel mushrooms (right), odd ends of metal must be filed away or they may fly off when struck and lodge in eye or other sensitive area.

without the risk of splitting the hatchet head. Also, when the head of an all-metal chisel (whether intended for use on wood, metal, masonry, or brick) mushrooms over, the likelihood of its tossing off shards of sharp metal is very great. The mushroomed portion of the head must be ground away or the chisel replaced.

The typical man or woman around the house has to resist the temptation to say, "Hmmmmmm, a cold chisel cuts metal pretty easily. I'll bet it should cut through stone and concrete like butter." Not so! A chisel designed for cutting metal will do a very slow, tedious, and unpredictable job on concrete or stone. Besides, you will ruin the cutting edge of the cold chisel.

No chisel, whether for wood, masonry, or metal, is prohibitive in cost if you have some legitimate need for one. Among the various masonry chisels, the *star drill* is most often seen. The star drill is not a drill at all in the usual sense, but is a chisel designed to cut a round hole into a concrete floor or wall. One reference work put out by manufacturers says, "Popular sizes range from ¼" to 1-¾" in length," although "popular" is not the best choice of adjectives. Using a star drill cannot help but work up a hearty sweat.

First, locate the precise site for the hole you need through a piece of concrete. Then select a star drill that is close to the size required. If you are fluctuating between choosing one of two different sizes, you may be happier in the end to have picked the larger one. You will not enjoy going back over the hole to enlarge it. And should the hole come out a trifle too large, a bit of concrete, X-Pandotite, or epoxy glue will fill the void.

A star drill is struck with the largest hammer that is practical. The drill must be twisted slightly after each blow so that the four cutting edges create a round opening and not a four-pronged indentation.

Chisels can be, and should be, sharpened periodically, probably just before their next use (see Chapter 14).

Once there were little hand-powered drills on the market, well-machined pieces of equipment that looked and operated very much like a hand eggbeater. They could drill small holes (from ¼" down) in wood or soft metal. At the moment, however, mass production has brought the price of ¼" electric-powered drills down almost to the level of hand drills, so very few people want to drill by hand any more. Consequently, drills will be discussed in detail with other power tools in a later chapter.

HAMMERS

Pound for pound, the hammer is one of the most widely used tools in the home—and perhaps the most misused and abused. You may be surprised at how many different kinds of hammers there are. *Carpenter's hammer, nail hammer*, or *claw hammer*—common names for the same tool—generally come in sizes ranging from a head that weighs 7 ounces to one weighing in at a hefty 20 ounces. For home use, unless the muscles in your arms are as strong as iron bands, a hammer with a 13 or 16 ounce head is preferred.

The part of the hammer that pulls out nails is called the *claw* and comes either curved or straight. Novices generally find that the curved claw pulls better for them. The driving end of the head is labeled the *face*, and a *bell-faced hammer* is the one you are most likely to find in hardware or department stores (see Figure 15).

A carpenter's hammer is designed to hammer on soft steel items such as common nails, finishing nails, nail sets, and the soft metal cap on some wood chisels. It is dangerous to use the hardened head of a carpenter's hammer to pound on other hard steel, such as cold chisels, masonry nails, concrete nails, or on other hammers. Pounding hard steel against hard steel could crack the hammer head or cause pieces of it to fly off.

When you must pound against hard steel, a ball pein hammer is called for. The head on this tool can range in weight from about 4 ounces to 2-½ pounds. (The words "pein" and "peen" are interchangeable, although manufacturers now lean toward "pein." It simply means a striking surface opposite the face of a hammer.) Although not expensive, you are not likely to buy a handful of ball pein hammers. The 1 to 1-½ pound range is most suitable for simple home applications. If you buy two, a 12 ounce and a 1-½ pound hammer would be good choices.

Whenever you use a hammer to do any task other than driving soft nails, everybody is well advised to wear glasses as protection for your

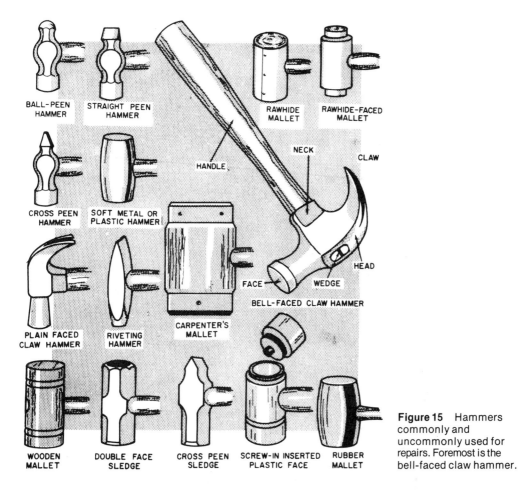

BALL-PEEN HAMMER

STRAIGHT PEEN HAMMER

RAWHIDE MALLET

RAWHIDE-FACED MALLET

CROSS PEEN HAMMER

SOFT METAL OR PLASTIC HAMMER

NECK

HANDLE

CLAW

PLAIN FACED CLAW HAMMER

RIVETING HAMMER

CARPENTER'S MALLET

FACE

WEDGE

HEAD

BELL-FACED CLAW HAMMER

WOODEN MALLET

DOUBLE FACE SLEDGE

CROSS PEEN SLEDGE

SCREW-IN INSERTED PLASTIC FACE

RUBBER MALLET

Figure 15 Hammers commonly and uncommonly used for repairs. Foremost is the bell-faced claw hammer.

eyes. Even the coated nails commonly used to install wood paneling will frequently split and send a sharp missile flying off in an unpredictable orbit.

To protect your hands, the nail, chisel, punch, or whatever other tool you may be hammering should be grasped only lightly. In that way, if you should accidentally miss the target, your fingers would slip quickly away—although not necessarily all the way out of the way—instead of absorbing the full blow. If the hammered-upon object is big enough, don't use fingers at all. Expose the fleshy part of your finger or hand to possible punishment as demonstrated by Figure 16.

A hammer's face and pein have been designed for hammering—*the side of the head has not.* And neither have the claws. Using these alternate surfaces probably *won't* accomplish whatever job you have set out to tackle and perhaps *will* damage the hammer.

27   *Hammer handles* come in a variety of materials. Unless you intend

Figure 16 Hold your hammer so the fleshy part of your hand, preferably, will be struck in the event you slip.

Figure 17 When pulling large nails, it often helps to slip a piece of scrap lumber under hammer.

to put a hammer to rugged or very frequent use, the plain wooden handle is perfectly satisfactory and priced very nominally. Fiber glass handles, despite their somewhat higher price, are becoming popular. And some deluxe models come with steel handles, either solid or tubular.

Hammer handles are priced so low that if one shows signs of wear, cracks, or in any other way is damaged, discard it. Hardware stores sell replacements. Removing the old head and installing it on a new handle is a five-minute job. Even if the handle is sound, it must fit into the head very solidly. Any shake or wobble, no matter how little, is too much. The amount of force in a steel hammer head that accidently flies off the handle as someone is pounding nails is sufficient to go all the way through a plate glass window—*or part way through a bony skull.*

To replace the wooden handle of a hammer, pry out the metal wedge using a chisel, punch or screwdriver to get it started. Pliers will help tug the wedge loose once it has been started on its way. With the wedge gone but not forgotten (it will be used later), tug, twist, or tap the handle or head until the hammer head separates from the hammer handle. The new handle fills the void just created, and the wedge must be firmly driven into the handle to expand the wood enough so that it will firmly grab the metal head.

PLIERS

Having a good pliers is almost like owning a third arm. Guide books dutifully tell the unwary that they must never, never use a pliers to loosen a nut—and it really *shouldn't* be done. But what if there isn't any wrench around able to tackle the particular nut in question? Almost every mechanic would whip out a pliers without a moment's hesitation. If the slot of a screw has been so badly chewed up that a screwdriver no longer works, a pliers saves the day. If you are going to tackle a plumbing job but have only one pipe wrench, a large pliers holds onto the pipe while your pipe wrench twists away on the fittings.

The granddaddy in this tool family is the *slipjoint pliers.* Like all types of pliers, this one comes in sizes ranging from a few inches up to a foot long. An 8″ model is good for all-around use. The frontmost part of the jaws are straight to accommodate flat pieces of work; the hind portion of the jaws are rounded to accept pipes or other circular shapes. The joint can be slipped into one of two positions depending upon the thickness of the material you want to hold onto.

A *slipjoint combination pliers* simply adds one refinement to the ordinary slipjoint pliers. Just ahead of the joint is a notch in each leg, which can be used to cut wire—not well and not heavy wire, but it can cut.

Also related to the slipjoint pliers is the *water pump pliers,* which grabs to the side instead of directly in front. And instead of only two positions in the jaws, this tool generally has about seven. The *channel-lock pliers* is a bit more refined. It may have more than seven positions and the handles are considerably longer than almost any other pliers, making them able to exert a very powerful grip.

Figure 18   Pliers are among the most versatile of home tools.
The most common types of pliers are shown here.

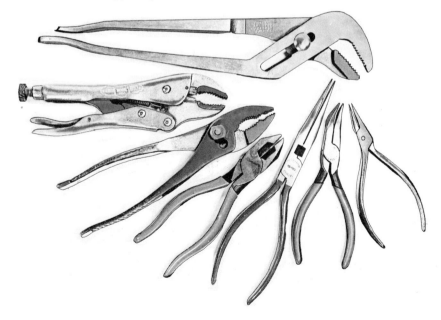

Second only to slipjoint pliers in popularity and usefulness is the *vise grip pliers*. Its jaws are hinged to multiply the pressure of your hand many times over, resulting in more leverage (squeezing power) than probably any other hand tool of this sort. That power is both a blessing and a curse. If someone accidentally twisted off a cup hook, for example, and wanted to screw out the broken-off stub, a vise grip pliers would grab firmly onto even the tiny remaining piece of hook. However, if the job called for twisting a thin, hollow chrome pipe, the vise grip pliers could very well squeeze too hard, collapsing or at least scratching and denting the pipe. (Vise grip pliers are often known as *lock grip pliers*.)

Electrician's pliers or *side-cutting pliers* are extremely handy for anyone undertaking some wiring or rewiring. The jaws form a small pliers, but a cutting surface on the side enables you to cut a small wire with ease and then to strip insulation off the wire (see Figures 20a, b, and c).

Anybody faced by some fine mechanical work will appreciate the delicate touch of one or more varieties of the *needle-nose pliers*. Actually, each of the variations on this basic miniature tool have

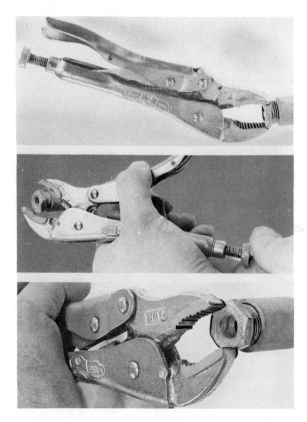

Figure 19 Vice grip pliers, when adjusted as in center photo, can lock onto most parts with a very sure grasp.

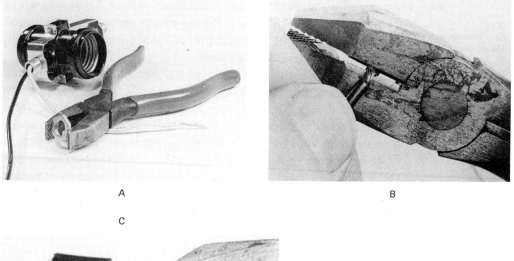

A

B

C

Figure 20   Electrician's pliers are useful (A) for grasping nuts and similar hardware, (B) cutting insulation off electrical wires, (C) twisting wires.

specific names, shown in Figure 18. Needle-nose pliers in general are valuable for retrieving parts that have slipped into a tiny space, for bending and locating wires in small electronic assemblies, or for holding nails too tiny for hands to steady while they are first being hammered into place. Some of their jaws are serrated for a rough grip, others are flat for gently holding onto delicate objects. And the needle-nose pliers themselves should be treated with a certain amount of delicacy. Their joints are small and precision-made (hopefully). If you try to squeeze too hard onto an unyielding object, the excess pressure can spring the joint or distort the jaws—and there is little hope of repairing such damage.

WOOD SAWS

Wood saws come in a practically unlimited number of variations, and they cut straight lines or circular patterns. A truly fine hand saw can cost you a great deal of money, but a saw that matches the expertise of a novice should cost no more than a few dollars.

The *crosscut saw* is designed for cutting across the grain of a board—generally that means across the width and not down the length of a piece of wood. A blade with 8 teeth per inch (or 8 points in wood-working jargon) is satisfactory for the coarse work that most home unhandy people will be undertaking. A finer crosscut saw generally will feature 11 points. It also is slower.

For cutting along the length of a board's grain, the *rip saw* is ideal because it typically has only 4 or 5 teeth per inch, and they are cut and sharpened to deal most directly with the mechanics of cutting with the grain. This refinement generally is not needed for home repairs unless you desire to turn out fancy woodworking projects.

Once it has been decided that the crosscut saw is the best single tool for all-around cutting, with or across the grain, the next problem is telling the two saws apart. Most often the designation is stamped on the saw blade, which is a good thing because it takes a well-trained eye

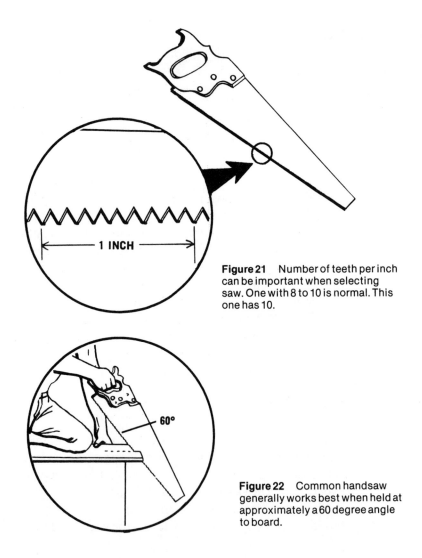

Figure 21   Number of teeth per inch can be important when selecting saw. One with 8 to 10 is normal. This one has 10.

Figure 22   Common handsaw generally works best when held at approximately a 60 degree angle to board.

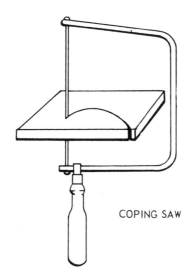

COPING SAW

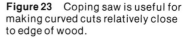

Figure 23 Coping saw is useful for making curved cuts relatively close to edge of wood.

to tell a rip saw from a crosscut saw just by looking at a blade.

For cutting rounded pieces, a *compass saw* (also known as a *keyhole saw*) and a *coping saw* do a fine job at a very small price. A coping saw is a bit more versatile, but it cannot reach farther than perhaps 12″ from the edge of a board.

A full-sized hand saw may be more than many homes need at the outset. A *combination saw* is little more than a handle that comes with two interchangeable blades, one for cutting small pieces of wood and one for cutting small pieces of metal. Even mechanics with big chests full of tools often carry one of these saws to use whenever the repair job really isn't big enough to require more equipment.

Small pieces of metal often can be cut by using only a *hacksaw blade*. Materials with the hardness and size of bolts can be handled nicely this way. And the blade itself, because a considerable amount of stiffness is built right into it, is ideal for cutting off nails or other hardware in a very confined space.

A hacksaw frame is relatively inexpensive. Many are fixed in length, about 10″ or 12″ long, but most are adjustable to hold blades 8″ to 16″ long. Hacksaw blades have a hole at each end, which fits a matching pin in the frame. A thumbscrew tightens the blade (see Figure 24). Also, notice that the blade is positioned so that the hacksaw teeth will be pointed away from you when the saw is used.

In general, the thinner the metal you are cutting, the more teeth a hacksaw blade should have. Thin tubing requires about 32 teeth per inch; big pieces of soft iron are best cut with a blade having about 14 teeth per inch. Figure 25 will guide your selection of blades. Coarser blades generally cut faster, but finer blades are required for thin materials.

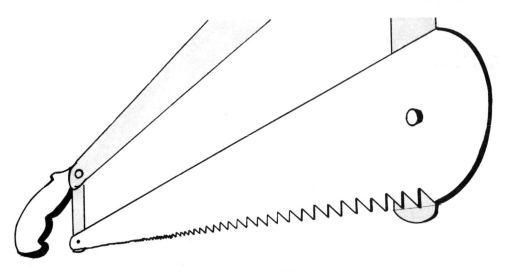

Figure 24 Hacksaw blade in its frame, in exaggerated view, shows how teeth should be pointed away from handle. Saw cuts when you push, coasts when you pull.

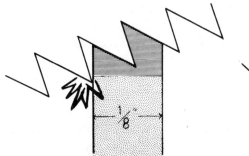

Figure 25 Why number of teeth is important in cutting thin metal. Left, with few teeth per inch of hacksaw blade, work strikes too deeply into tooth. At right, greater number of teeth (32 per inch) coast neatly and work smoothly.

There always should be a minimum of *two teeth* across the thickness of the material being sawed; that means a sheet of metal 1/16" thick requires a blade with at least 32 teeth per inch; 1/8" material can be cut with a hacksaw blade having only 16 teeth per inch—and cut faster.

Too many people grab a hacksaw and start to cut as if they were sawing through wood. A hacksaw blade, first of all, cuts only on the *push stroke*. Its teeth all point in that direction. On the *pull stroke*, you should be coasting. The teeth should stay in contact with your work but the pressure should be off.

Don't rush a hacksaw. About 40 or 50 strokes per minute is the ideal speed. A faster rate heats up the blade and dulls it, slowing down your performance. To end up with straighter cuts and to minimize the danger of breaking a hacksaw blade, the piece of metal that you want to cut should be held in place very firmly by a vise, clamps, vise grip pliers, or a similar tool.

The *rod saw* is a more recent addition to the cutting field. The "blade" actually is a heavy wire coated with thousands of supertough tungsten carbide particles. The rod saw will fit any adjustable hacksaw frame and many nonadjustable sizes as well. With a rod saw, you can cut through materials too hard even for a traditional hacksaw—hard steel, glass, tough plastics, and practically anything else short of diamonds. Like the hacksaw, this gadget must be used slowly, but it cuts on both the push stroke and the pull stroke. You'll be gumming up the works if you insist on using your rod saw on soft materials.

There are at least a dozen other kinds of saws available, although they are not always stocked at the local hardware store. Figure 27 shows what some of the more specialized saws look like and describes their use.

Figure 26   Much-advertised rod saw is sharp enough to cut glass. Unfortunately, it has relatively few normal uses around the home unless, as shown here, you need only half a cup but have a full cup measuring container!

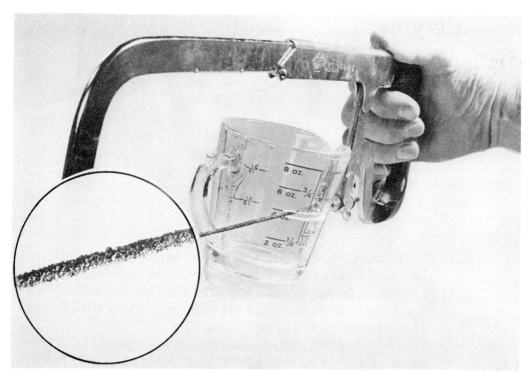

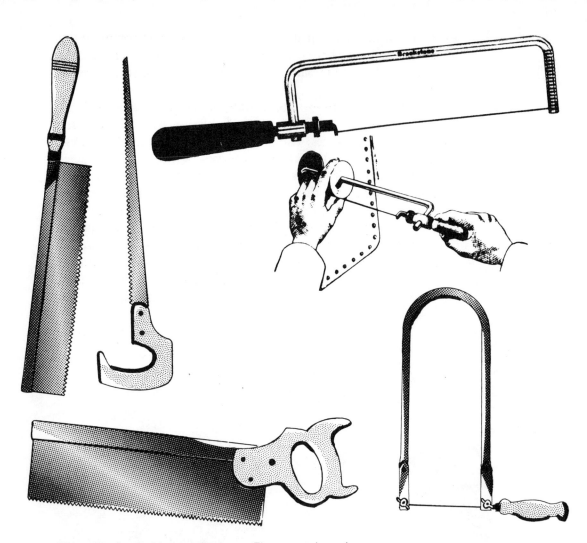

Figure 27 Saws with specialized uses. The average home has little use for these but when needed, they're worth their modest price. Top right cuts perfectly round holes and bottom left cuts perfectly straight mitered corners. Others are for reaching hard-to-work-in areas.

SCREWDRIVERS

This handy tool comes in a dizzying number of sizes, shapes, and descriptions. There are about a dozen types of screwheads that require their own particular screwdrivers. But out of that dozen, only two are common enough on household items that you will want to have screwdrivers on hand to match them.

The *standard* or *slotted* screwhead is most common. Into the round head of a screw or bolt, a rectangular slot is machined. The screwdriver blade must closely match both the thickness and length of that slot for optimum results. Anything less than a near perfect fit between slot and screwdriver can damage either the screwhead or the screwdriver, perhaps both.

Phillips head screws and bolts have a four-way slot recessed into the head. The slots are tapered, and it is impossible, therefore, to use a slotted screwdriver on a Phillips head without damaging the screw and the screwdriver.

Screwdrivers come in many standard sizes from about 2″ to 12″, plus a selection of specialized ones larger and smaller. Length is calculated by measuring the blade and shank but not the handle.

Supermarkets, drugstores, electronic stores—even hardware stores where they ought to know better—have taken up the practice of tossing an assortment of cheap screwdrivers into a small barrel and selling them at very, very low prices. For the average household, however, such cheapie screwdrivers are quite expensive in the long

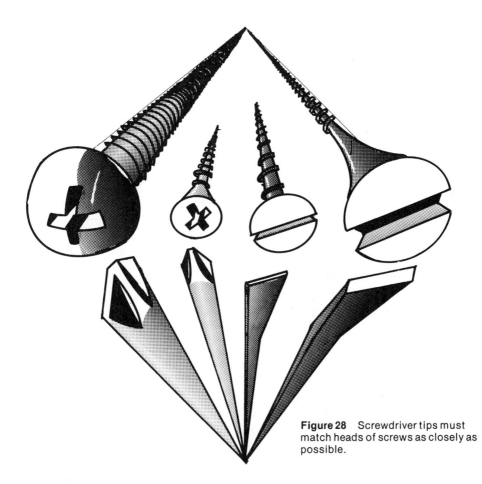

Figure 28 Screwdriver tips must match heads of screws as closely as possible.

run—except for a very specialized one that you expect to use gently only a few times.

The working end on a cheap screwdriver wears away or bends very quickly. When it is applied to an otherwise fine screwhead, the damaged screwdriver damages the slot or the Phillips recession. At that point, you will be buying screw extractors or trying to drill, pry, twist, or dynamite the damaged bolt or screw loose. And in the tedious process, you no doubt will cause at least some damage to the appliance or the cabinet housing the injured screwhead.

As you work your way deeper and deeper into home repairs, your collection of screwdrivers will grow bigger and bigger. Early in the game you should acquire at least two Phillips head screwdrivers and two or three slotted screwdrivers, all of decent quality. Phillips tools come in numbered sizes, commonly from 0 to 4. A 1 and a 3 should handle practically anything around most homes. Although slotted screwdrivers are manufactured by size, the dimensions are seldom stamped on the finished tool (they are on good Phillips screwdrivers). Your selection might include one with a wide, thick blade, one with a thin, narrow blade, and a third somewhere in between the two.

If you get into an original woodworking project that involves a frightening number of screws, it is possible to get an inexpensive screwdriver attachment for electric drills. Since a slow speed is preferred, the variable speed drills work best for power screwdriving. If you have a choice of head for screws that will be electrically driven into place, select the Phillips—it was designed with that function in mind.

WRENCHES

The word "wrench" makes most people think of a single tool that can be successfully adjusted to twist on everything from a peanut-sized nut to a bulky drainpipe. And that misconception has been the ruin of many of the best laid plans of men and women tackling what should be simple household repairs. Except for plumbing (discussed in Chapter 5), an adjustable wrench should be used only when nothing better is available. The most common of adjustable wrenches, the *crescent wrench*, is infinitely variable over the entire range for which it is designed. But it never quite fits perfectly. And if you try to loosen an especially tight nut or bolt with a wrench that doesn't fit well, the result may be a damaged bolt and a set of bruised knuckles as the wrench slips.

There is a fixed jaw and an adjustable jaw on crescent wrenches. The wrench always must be turned so that the fixed jaw receives the greatest share of the pressure (see Figure 30).

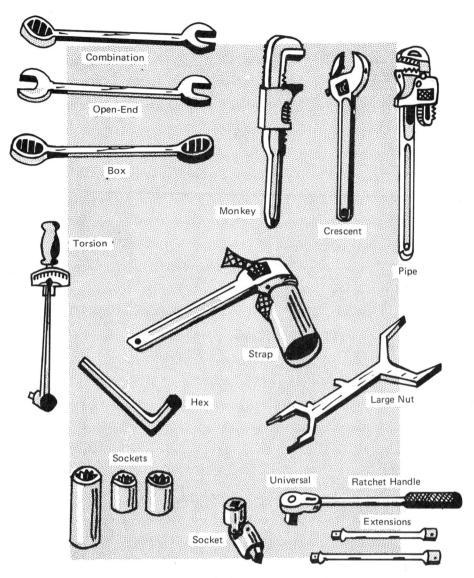

Figure 29 Wrenches that may prove useful for your own home repairs.

Crescent wrenches must be adjusted to fit as snugly as possible around any nut or bolt they are used on, and the head must be positioned as far back into the opening of the jaws as possible. That will bring the wrench and nut into firm contact on three of the nut's four sides. This three out of four rule also applies to nonadjustable wrenches.

When using either an adjustable or a nonadjustable wrench, it is

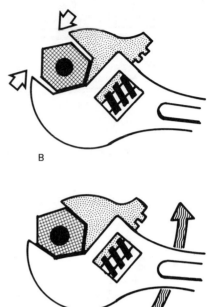

Figure 30 Adjustable crescent wrench has to be pointed properly for best use. Too tight (A) and too loose (B) cause trouble. Pushing so moveable jaw takes most pressure (C) causes wrench to slip. Properly pointed and adjusted (D) it works well.

highly advisable to *pull* on it and not to *push*. Your arm muscles are in much better control when you exert pressure toward your body. Should the wrench slip off the job you're working on, a pushing motion could send your hand into a nest of sharp nuts or edges of exposed metal. A pulling motion, on the other hand, would result in a tap on the tummy at worst. If you must push, do so with the palm of your opened hand.

For practically every repair application short of the big plumbing pipes, the *socket wrench* is nearly ideal. It is also expensive to buy a complete set of well-made socket wrenches. Instead of falling for some of the cheap but shiny socket wrench sets advertised, invest in a few pieces of well-made socket wrench equipment, which are described below.

A socket wrench set consists of sockets (they can be 6, 8, or 12 points), which slip snugly over a nut or bolt of one specific size. A variety of handles are available for the socket. Most common is the ratchet handle, ideal for quick work and for use in confined spaces. Extension bars in various lengths are available to reach out-of-the-way places, and a universal joint snaps into any part of the socket wrench system to provide turning power at odd angles.

One good way to overcome the cost of buying a full set of socket wrench equipment is to buy pieces as they become needed. The ratchet handle represents the most expensive single piece. Individual sockets are relatively inexpensive, varying with size. There are three standard sizes of drive ends for this tool, ¼", ⅜", and ½". The drive size is simply the standard-sized fitting on the handle, which slips into the back of each socket for your particular set. The smallest size is used almost exclusively for very small nuts and bolts. Of the two larger sizes, the ⅜" is a bit less expensive than the ½" and offers practically as much power and scope for household chores. You also can eventually buy an adapter so that ½" and ⅜" drive sockets can be used on the same handles.

Less versatile than the socket wrench but not less effective, the *box wrench* generally comes in sets that will encompass 8 or 10 common-sized nuts. Box wrenches can be brought with 6, 8, 12, or 16 points ground into the face. The 12 point is the most all-around adaptable.

Closely related to the box wrench is the *open-end wrench*, which is faster to use than the box wrench and occasionally can reach into more inaccessible areas. Trying to combine the best of both worlds results in the *combination wrench,* a box wrench at one end, open-end at the other.

A single open-end or box wrench has a wrench at each end of its handle and thereby covers two sizes of bolts. Each individual combination wrench works on one size only because it has a box wrench on one extremity, an open-end wrench of the same size on the other.

Open-end wrenches generally are not laid out in a straight line. Their ends are displaced by 10°, 15°, 45°, and even 90° for a purpose. A 15° *displacement* is common. In very tight quarters, it is often impossible to twist a nut more than maybe ⅛ of a turn. But with a hex nut (six-sided) or a square nut, a full ⅙ or ¼ of a turn is necessary before the wrench can grab the next set of faces. With a 15° displacement, however, the wrench is simply turned over after every twist (see Figure 31).

Some wrenches, aside from featuring a displacement, also offer an angled arrangement from top to bottom, an *offset*. Here again, 15° is typical. Figure 32 shows how a 15° offset in a wrench is useful for clearing nearby obstructions that otherwise would make twisting on a nut very difficult.

There is only one other wrench out of all those pictured in Figure 29 that is of some importance to home handy people—the *allen wrench.* Some refer to this tool as a *hex wrench* because it has six sides, which

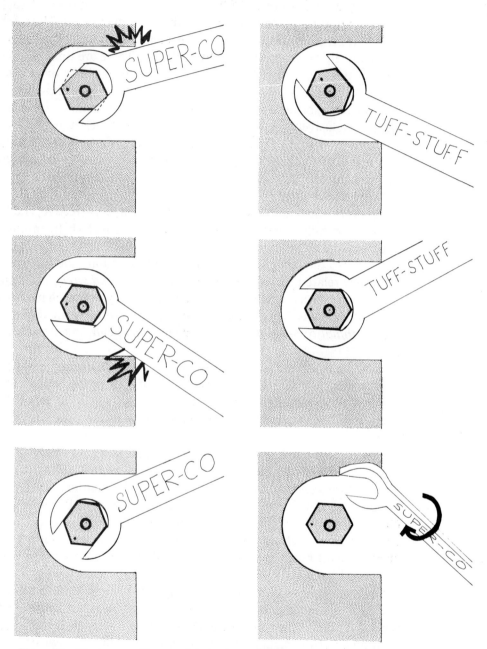

Figure 31 Displacement in wrench helps to reach tight corners.

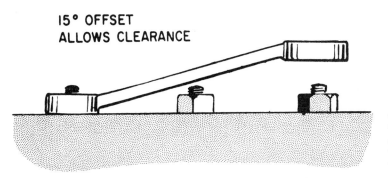

**15° OFFSET
ALLOWS CLEARANCE**

Figure 32 When end of wrench is offset, you can work in cramped quarters. Watch for this feature when buying wrenches.

makes it a hexagon. For less than $1 you can buy a set of imported allen wrenches in a plastic case, usually clear on one side and red on the other for some reason. People always seem to lose one or two pieces from the set, however, and always the most used ones, of course. So be smart; spend a little extra change on a set of allen wrenches mounted permanently in a single case.

It is hard to predict where you may encounter a hex head next. They are used to hold pulleys onto shafts, knobs on TV or hi-fi sets, fan blades onto motor shafts. Even the mirror in your car may have a bolt with an allen head. Using a screwdriver in the recessed space of an allen head will do no good to the bolt or to the screwdriver—or to the job you're doing.

After all, consider the philosophy underlying the technical aspects of this and other chapters. A good tool, a good mental outlook on your ability to cope with modern pseudo-technology, and this book are worth many expensive service calls to a company that would like to sell repairs instead of workable merchandise.

Making
Space Age Hardware
Work for You

A great many people, probably you too, find that they could easily lick some of the household headaches that plague them if only they knew the name of a certain nut, bolt, screw, fastener, or clip. And if they knew where to buy one just like it. This chapter will give you that information.

You also will learn the nontechnical purposes for such technical sounds as resin, knob, nipple, elbow, pin, belt, lever, shaft, male, female, ratchet, and so on. The words of repairs, repair people, and repair supply stores stymie many of the best plans of home fix-it people. Now let's try to take the mystery out of the major materials of the repair world, the glues, lubricants, and hardware of fixing things.

Not every item of value in the home repair area is available at every well-stocked hardware and department store. Occasionally an industrial supplier, electrical or plumbing supply house, or a big manufacturer will be called on to sell you a piece of equipment or a tube of something. And *then* you'll really have to know the precise name of what you're looking for. Those people don't particularly want to deal with the home fix-it crowd, but they will if you can talk their language so that the transaction takes only a short time. And therein lies the fundamental reason why so much of this book is devoted to graphics and charts, which give commonsense meaning to otherwise uncommon objects, terms, and techniques.

ADHESIVES

There are a dozen or more different chemical types of *glues* and *cements*. Whatever difference there was between a glue and a cement is all but nonexistent now. Many different forms of adhesives are commonplace today—liquids, pastes, tapes, and even sprays. And so many varied formulations have been created for certain specific sticky jobs that organizing the subject of adhesives in a logical fashion is nearly impossible. Nevertheless, this section will cover general gluing technology and the general types of glues available. Later chapters will deal with specific applications.

GLUES

"Curing method" is the technical term that most people know simply as a glue getting hard. In selecting the right glue for a particular job, it is important to know whether it sets because water or solvents evaporate or because of a purely internal chemical reaction.

In bonding two pieces of metal or nonporous ceramics, for example, you would want to avoid a glue that depends on the evaporation of solvents or water to set. If the two pieces to be glued were held tightly together, there would be no room for the solvent or water to evaporate. In other words, the glue could not get hard. Porous materials such as wood or nonglazed ceramics can be bonded successfully with a solvent or water-based adhesive because the material itself absorbs the solvent or water, allowing the glue to set in a reasonable length of time.

Environmental factors also must be weighed when choosing an adhesive. Patching the broken arm on a piece of outdoor furniture requires a waterproof glue. Mending the handle on a cooking pot demands a heat-resistant glue. Anything near a bar should receive an alcohol-resistant glue, of course. And a workbench repair demands chemicals and heat-resistant adhesives.

For repairs in the bathroom or basement, stick to an adhesive that is resistant to moisture, mold, and mildew. Not only is the growth of mold and mildew unsightly, it also can weaken the glued or sealed joint.

45

Adhesives that are most susceptible to organic growths include silicone rubber and casein products, although chemicals can be added to resist mold and mildew, so check the labels. If it is a casein or silicone rubber adhesive, the label should specifically state that the product will resist mold and mildew if you intend to apply it near moist areas.

Flexibility must be considered. In general, glues intended specifically for wood are very strong but not especially flexible. Rubber adhesives, as you might expect, are rubbery and flexible. Many of the other adhesive formulations can be created with flexibility in mind. So if you are stuck with a broken item that flexes and bends a lot, make sure that the label on the glue specifically mentions the product's flexible qualities.

Whenever two items to be joined are made of different materials—such as wood to glass or glass to rubber—a flexible adhesive is very necessary. Dissimilar substances expand and contract at different rates when heated or cooled. An inflexible glue would be unable to absorb the slight variations and would soon crack or break. Silicone rubber and cyanoacrylate glues are especially flexible, although rather expensive.

Glue line, in simple terms, means the amount of glue that must or can be applied between the two pieces being bonded. Most glues specifically intended for use with wood require a thin glue line for maximum strength; rubber adhesive compounds do best with a fairly thick glue line. When gluing wood with a glue requiring a thin glue line, therefore, it is important that both surfaces to be bonded should be smooth so that a thin layer of glue will successfully grab onto as much of the surface area as possible. In repairing a *broken* piece of wood where it may be impossible to obtain a truly thin glue line, your needs might best be served by choosing an adhesive that reaches maximum strength with a wider glue line.

The repaired items themselves may dictate what types of adhesives should be used. A solvent-based cement could chemically attack many thin plastics. And water-based glues will cause photographs to swell until the water dries up. A very thin, fluidy adhesive might be absorbed into a porous material, leaving too little glue in the glue line to hold the two parts together successfully.

Set time is the length of time it takes the adhesive to become hard enough to support the glued joint. This term is almost synonomous with "drying time" or "cure time." An instant-setting material, if you stop to think about it, really is not ideal at all for most applications. If you are trying to line up two matching pieces of wood or crockery, an instant-setting glue would hold the pieces together immediately upon your first try. For that purpose, you would want to select a glue that sets slowly enough to give you time to line up the pieces after they are initially pushed together. On the other hand, if you are using adhesives to stop a badly leaking pipe, the faster setting the better.

Travel is linked closely with set time. Some adhesives such as contact cements clamp the glued materials tightly in place after the two pieces are laid together. Other materials allow for movement up until a certain percentage of the set time has elapsed. If alignment of two objects is important, you will want an adhesive with plenty of travel. If you are gluing heavy handles onto an erect piece of glass, however, more than likely you would choose a material with very little travel, or you would have to support the handles in some way until the glue finished setting.

Tack is almost synonymous with "sticky." Thin, watery glues may end up forming a powerful joint by the time they are hardened, maybe the next morning. But if you are forced to hold tile, cork, or wall covering onto a wall while the thin glue sets, next time you will look for an adhesive with lots of tack. A tacky adhesive, such as the bituminous, silicone, rubber, and some epoxies, can hold even relatively heavy materials in place before the glue has had time to set completely.

Figure 33 sums up the major attributes of popular glues on the market. Not all of them are found on all markets, however. Captions to the photographs elaborate on specific features of readily available glues, which make some glues more popular or useful around the home, barn, and shop.

SEALANTS AND CAULKING AGENTS

For the most part there is little basic chemical difference between the glues just described and sealants and caulkers. Only the way you apply them is different, and that means there must be subtle alterations in the specific formulations.

A glue does the best it can to hold together two pieces of something. Sealants and caulkers however, generally don't have to provide any holding power. All they must do is grab firmly onto one or two surfaces, such as at a crack or joint, and provide a seal against weather, water, chemicals, air, sound, or whatever other undesirables are to be sealed in or sealed out.

In this area, no two manufacturers seem to use the same words for otherwise similar materials. *Caulk* and *sealant* are two very common words for the same material, and *sealer* is a close third although it also can be used when referring to materials that seal the entire surface of a wooden or concrete floor.

Fig. 33 Types of Glues

	Bituminous & Mastics	Cyanoacrylate	Epoxy	Hot Melt Glues	Plastic Cements
Ingredients	Tarry chemicals, and sticky plastics.	Powerful chemicals	Powerful chemicals.	Synthetic resins, often phenoxy plastics.	Plastics dissolved in volatile solvents.
Available	Cans. Caulking tubes.	Small tubes. Small bottles.	Tubes. Cans.	Sticks sized to fit heater.	Generally in small tubes.
Form	Paste.	Liquid.	Liquids or pastes, mixed at time of application.	Solid. Melts inside the heater compartment.	Liquid.
Strength	Low, but adequate for specified jobs.	Very high.	Very high.	Moderate.	Moderate at best.
Flexibility	Moderate, but adequate for specified jobs.	High.	Very low.	Low.	Moderate.
Set time	Slow (hours or days).	Few seconds.	Moderate (hours).	Very fast.	Very fast (minutes).
Setting method	Loss of solvents.	Internal chemical reaction.	Internal chemical reactions.	Cooling of glue resins.	Evaporation of solvents.
Travel permitted	Very high.	Low.	High.	Low.	Moderate.
Amount of tack	High.	None (but not vital due to very rapid set time).	Very high for pastes. High to moderate for liquids.	High.	Moderate.
Preferred glue line	Thick (1/16 - 1/8").	Very thin.	Thin for liquids. Thick for pastes.	Thin.	Thin, but can be made thicker by repeated applications.
RESISTANCE TO: Moisture	Low except for special formulations.	High.	Very high.	Moderate.	Moderate.
Mold & Mildew	Low, except for special formulations.	Very high.	Very high.	Moderate.	High.
Chemicals & solvents	Low.	High.	High.	High.	Low.
Heat	Low.	Very high.	Very high.	Low.	Moderate.
Clamping required?	No.	No.	Very seldom.	No.	Very seldom.
Relative cost	Very low.	Very high.	High.	High.	Low.
Applications	Used for sticking floor tile to floor. Also for holding wall panels onto wall. See: Chap. 23.	Repairs on smooth surfaces. Small constructions which require fast set time and high strength.	Repairs to wood, glass, tile, pottery, metal, most plastic, leather, fiberglas, etc.	Assembling wood, leather, some plastics, metal, paper, cardboard.	Light repairs or construction such as models, textiles, paper, etc.

	Polyvinyl Acetate	Resorcinol	Rubber Cement	Silicone Rubber	Urea-Formaldehyde Resins
Ingredients	Plastics suspended in watery solvent.	Industrial chemicals.	Natural or synthetic rubbers dissolved in solvents.	Industrial chemicals.	Industrial chemicals.
Available	Bottles of many sizes.	Bottles. Cans.	Cans. Tubes. Jars.	Tubes. Caulking tubes.	Cans.
Form	Liquid (milky, white).	Liquids; two parts mixed at time of application.	Liquid.	Paste.	Powder which is mixed with water at time of application.
Strength	Moderate.	High.	Low.	High to very high, depending upon items bonded.	Excellent.
Flexibility	High.	Moderate.	Very high.	Very high.	Low.
Set time	Moderate (hours).	Slow.	Fast (generally in minutes).	Moderate (hours).	Slow (hours to days).
Setting method	Evaporation of solvent and water.	Internal chemical reactions.	Evaporation of solvents.	Chemical reaction set off by moisture in the air.	Internal chemical reactions.
Travel permitted	High.	High.	Very high.	Very high.	Very high.
Amount of tack	Moderate.	Moderate.	High.	Very high.	Moderate to low.
Preferred glue line	Thin to moderate.	Thin.	Thin, but specific products can use heavier glue lines.	Thick ($\frac{1}{8}$ - $\frac{1}{4}$").	Thin.
RESISTANCE TO: Moisture	Moderate.	Excellent.	Fair.	Excellent.	Poor.
Mold & Mildew	High.	Excellent.	Low.	Poor unless label specifies additives are present.	Good.
Chemicals & solvents	Moderate.	Good.	Very low.	Good.	Excellent.
Heat	Moderate.	Excellent.	Low.	Excellent.	Excellent.
Clamping required?	Often, when used for wood projects.	Yes.	No.	No.	Yes.
Relative cost	Low.	Moderate.	Low to moderate.	High.	Moderate.
Applications	Excellent for crafts since it dries colorless. Good for paper, textiles, some plastic, wood, photographs, etc. Most non-toxic of popular household adhesives.	Outdoor furniture, boats, toys, etc.	Used to bond flexible materials to other flexible materials or solids such as textiles or plastics to metal, wood, rigid plastic. Also rubber or leather to wood or metal. Can be used as one-shot glue or as contact cement.	Can bond most materials including glass and metal. Especially good for two solids of different composition subjected to heat, vibration and similar environmental abuses.	Indoor wood, furniture.

Figure 34 Cyanoacrylate glues, billed as "super glues,"
require only a drop to hold most moderately heavy jobs. Glass
slides in foreground were glued with cyanocrylate being used
here to mend plastic car.

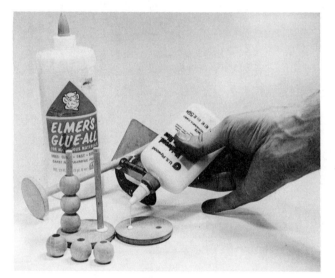

Figure 35 Very popular glue available from several manufacturers,
white polyvinyl glue dries colorless
in short time on most jobs.

Many sealants available at hardware or paint stores are variations
of polyvinyl, rubber, or silicone rubber glues described earlier. Some
can be used interchangeably as glues and as sealants. The principal
requirement for calling a glue a sealant is that it have a high enough
viscosity to bridge a gap of ⅛″ or more without sagging or running off.
To give them added surface strength, more internal thickness and
color, many caulking materials have fillers such as powdered aluminum
added to them.

A second general type of caulking compound has been around

since before chemists ever heard of silicone or synthetic rubber. Closely related to common putty, common caulking has a base of linseed oil or related natural vegetable oils. The body of this caulking agent can be any number of minerals—most of them chemically and physically similar to the chalk that kids use in school.

Common caulking materials are cheap and easy to use. But *permanence* is not one of their virtues. Ordinary caulking compounds on the commercial market generally have been available only in professional sizes, large cans, or caulking gun cartridges. Oil-based caulking compounds are intended principally for exterior use around windows, doors, eaves, and such. As long as enough oil stays in the compound to keep it from drying out and cracking, the seal is okay. However, if you plan to stay in your house for a long time, your laziest and most economical alternative over the long range is one of the more expensive synthetic products of rubber or silicone rubber.

There is a natural latex rubber sealant on the market. Most, however, are made from one of the synthetic rubbers—neoprene, nitrile, butyl, polysulfide, or silicone rubber. Some product descriptions mention "elastomer," simply a synonym for synthetic rubber.

Sealants must be flexible enough to withstand the slight motion or vibration that accompanies their bridging a gap between two walls or a tub and a wall or a window frame and a wall. Most of them are waterproof, and some can be applied underwater or to wet surfaces—but don't do it if you can use a dry application instead.

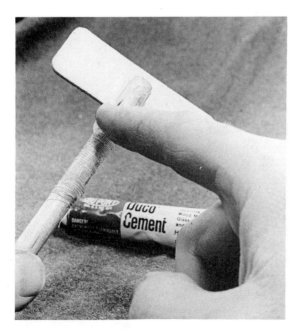

Figure 36 Plastic cements work best for holding some plastics, craft projects, and similar applications requiring fast drying time with only modest strength.

Drying times for most ordinary sealants is quite slow. In as short a time as 10 minutes, they may skin over and get tough at the very surface but remain unset underneath. Most will require a day or more of relatively unmolested drying time. If the caulking around a bathtub has skinned over, chances are you will be able to take a bath and splash water onto the new seam. But if you want to take a stinging shower less than a day after the new seal has been squeezed into the cracks, better read the instructions carefully, especially the fine print. If in doubt, take a bath instead.

Colors are limited for most caulking materials. Generally you will have to settle for white, clear, black, or aluminum, although some companies are now offering colors such as tan and pink. Whether or not smaller hardware stores feel they can stock a complete rainbow of colored caulking products is yet another hurdle.

Some sealants can be painted over with good results. If this is important, make sure you select one that specifically says it will accept

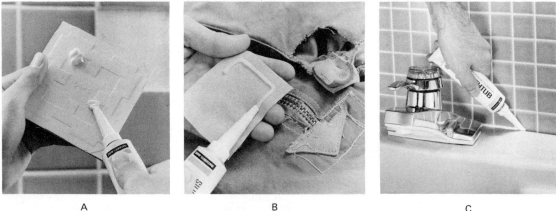

A   B   C

D   E

Figure 37 Silicone adhesive is very versatile. It glues glass and ceramics (A), fabrics (B) and most other materials. It seals cracks in bathrooms (C), outdoor hardware (D) and elsewhere. It can even form a gasket for vacuum cleaners and cushion for ashtrays (E).

a coat or two of paint. The silicone rubber sealers in general cannot be covered over with much of anything except more silicone rubber. There is an unwritten rule that the cheaper the sealant, which probably is an indicator of its having the least amount of rubber compounds, the easier it is to paint over.

For home use, sealants generally come packed in tubes, often with a spout that can be cut to varied dimensions to create a bead of caulking material from about $\frac{1}{16}$" to $\frac{1}{4}$" wide. The size you select should be big enough to bridge whatever crack has to be filled with some extra to adhere to solid tile or enamel. For economy, you don't want to squirt a $\frac{1}{4}$" bead when $\frac{1}{8}$" would have done just as well. Conversely, it will take more material still to use too miserly a bead and have to redo the entire job.

Instinct seems to make folks use caulking tubes or caulking guns *backward.* The sealant should not be squeezed out and allowed to fall free as you do with a tube of toothpaste. The nozzle of the tube must force the oozing, sticky stuff firmly back onto the corner or crack, an art illustrated in parts of Figure 37.

Small tubes (about 4 ounces) will handle a patch-up job around a tub or sink, renew putty around a window or two, or reseal a drain spout. For bigger jobs, a bigger squeeze tube would be handy. Not every rubber sealant comes packaged that way, however. The next size above 4 ounces often is a cartridge for caulking guns holding $\frac{1}{10}$th gallon. Such a cartridge cannot be used by hand. Fortunately, the price of a gun designed to hold caulking cartridges is so reasonable that the reuseable gun and disposable cartridge often can be purchased for the same price as a comparable amount of material in smaller tubes.

TAPES

Most of us had our first contact with tape adhesives when we fell off a swing or tricycle. That particular adhesive tape product has been improved drastically, and hundreds of other pressure sensitive adhesives, which is what industry labels what we call sticky tape, have been developed.

The chemistry of tapes is of little real importance, especially when compared with glues. For the most part, tapes are strips of paper or plastic coated with specially formulated synthetic rubber or vinyl plastic adhesives. On top of the backing material, the manufacturer might also fasten metals, foamed plastics, or rubber sealing materials. When compared with a glue, the adhesive properties of the active materials in tape are quite poor. But for the applications they are intended to tackle, tapes can be a valuable time saver.

It's an old concept, technologically speaking, but if you will think of tapes as a big strip of tiny suction cups, their proper use should become more clear. Inexpensive, light-duty tapes, such as paper-backed *masking tape* used to confine paint to a given area, are made with very small, easily destroyed suction cups. In use, masking tape does not have to produce tremendous adhesion to the walls and windows it is protecting. And since the painter will soon want to remove the tape without pulling part of the woodwork with it, the tiny suction cups have to surrender their grip without much of a fight.

Tapes designed for jobs such as holding up a mirror have to exert a very strong adhesive force to the wall and to the mirror, in addition to which the suction cups have to hold their shape (and thus their adhesion) almost permanently. Cheap masking tape products will dry out and grow brittle if left in place very long. That is no problem because they are not intended to be left on the job for more than a few hours or at most a few days. Mirror tapes, however, may have to last many years. Therefore, the adhesives that make up the working surfaces have to retain their softness.

A good point to remember about glue and tape adhesives is: although some glues seem qualified to handle a hundred different varied applications with ease, there is no comparable all-purpose tape adhesive. Broken down according to their strong points, here is a list of some of the major tapes that are of some value in and near the home.

1. Temporary Tapes—paperbacked. For years after it was introduced, *masking tape,* available single-coated or coated on both sides, was used principally to provide a sharp cutoff line when painting. "Auto-Pak" by 3M Company is a variation on the masking tape idea for auto nuts who want to paint racing stripes. The tape automatically creates a mask for both sides of a thin stripe, a feat that is hard to accomplish with your unaided hand and patience.

The double-faced tape is used best for holding paper or similar materials in place. On a horizontal surface, paper or cardboard can be held temporarily with double-sided masking tape to practically any nonoily, dry surface. This technique works on vertical surfaces only for very lightweight objects such as unmounted photographs, maps, and so forth.

Packaging tape features a hopefully high-strength paper with a heavy coating of an adhesive that bonds tightly with paper and cardboard. Its main advantage over gummed wrapping tape is that your tongue doesn't have to endure that awful aftertaste when you lick the gummed tape. Some of the packaging tapes are reinforced with rope fibers. But for maximum packaging strength, plastic tapes are preferred.

Labeling tape is just a shiny paper tape that makes a neat looking label when you write or type on it. Some of these products come in the traditional long, narrow roll; others are available in precut sizes. There is at least one precut paper label on the market coated with an adhesive that makes it practically permanent.

A less formal use for the paper tapes designed for labels is in identifying parts. A mechanic or home handy person who thoroughly disassembles a complicated device such as a tape recorder would do well to use labels instead of memory to ensure that the parts are put back in the same order they came out. At the outset, write 1, 2, 3, 4, 5, and so on onto the labels. As each new part is removed, tack one of the labels onto some noncritical surface. A tiny bit of the adhesive material might cling to the part, so the label should not, if possible, be stuck onto the working face of pulleys and shafts. And as a final precaution, a bit of alcohol on a rag or paper towel will remove traces of the adhesive just before the part is reassembled.

2. Temporary Tapes—fabric backed. Colorful as a rainbow and stronger than paper tapes, fabric-backed adhesive products are without much use beyond decoration. The adhesive substance on the sticky side of cloth tapes is at best only slightly tackier than the coating on paper tapes. Cloth tapes stick well to paper, cloth, and themselves. If you want to make a rough mend in a torn cushion, a cloth tape of the appropriate color will fill the need. And if you want to create a new handle by wrapping tape around a tool, that also will work because the tape actually will be sticking not to the tool but to part of the layer of

Figure 38 Plastic or fabric-backed tapes fill many household
needs such as (A) refinishing tool handles, (B) repairing
books, (C) patching together playpens.

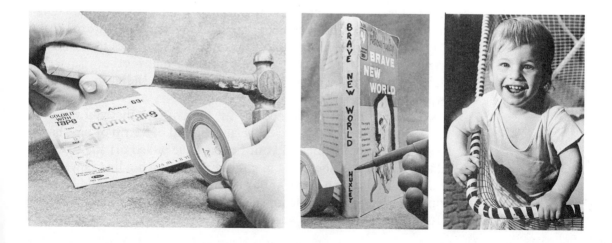

tape immediately beneath. And another nondecorative use is in mending or enhancing the binding on books.

Because fabric-backed tapes cling well to other fabrics or to plastics that don't have a shiny or oily surface, they can be used for repairing inflatable toys or furniture.

3. Temporary Tapes—plastic backed. There are many colorful tapes in this category that are nearly identical to the cloth-backed ones described above. And they are just about as useful. Their application is the same also. Other plastic tapes do have something more to offer.

Strapping tape is made of plastic reinforced with fiberglass filaments, which is why it is called *filament tape* when sold to some industrial users. The backing on this tough tape, generally sold in ½″ widths for home use, can support 140 pounds. But the adhesive material applied to the backing can't!

The strapping tape adhesive seems to stick best to dull, slightly porous surfaces such as paper, cardboard, and fiberboards. It also has a strong affection for its own plastic surface. The product is advertised by its principal manufacturers (Borden and 3M) as being valuable for wrapping heavy packages. And it is. When using such tape, however, make sure that the ends of at least several strips overlap onto a layer of tape below.

Electrical tape sticks best to itself and to rubber or plastic insulation, which is exactly what the product is intended to do. It creates a great insulating covering over frayed wires, splices, and any other exposed electrical connections. But don't count on plastic electrical tape to *support* much of anything, including a set of heavy wires. It is blended to be extremely flexible so it can conform to the shape of wires and connectors. But if subjected to the burden of carrying a weight, it will begin to sag. Sharp edges bearing down on this tape also will cut it.

When using any kind of plastic tape, it is important that you resist the urge to jerk it apart. Use a scissors or knife when trimming it to size. Plastic tape often possesses an uncanny "memory." After being stretched out of shape by someone applying excessive pressure to break it or to finish an electrical splice, the tape gradually tries to regain its original shape, and in the process it mars many otherwise well-executed projects by coming loose at the ends or sliding far enough away to expose hot wires.

Keep your fingers off the ends of any kind of tape that you want to stick well. The beginning and especially the end of a strip of tape have the most demanding jobs. If your fingers have pulled off some of the adhesive materials, there just might not be enough holding power left to do the kind of job you want or need. The inside end could lose its grip on a wire, pipe, handle, or stick, and then slide out of place. If the outside end works loose, wear and tear generally will lift more of the tape, exposing its sticky materials to the air and drying it out, causing more and more of the tape to work loose.

4. Permanent Tapes—for sealing. The type of backing material for the more or less permanent tapes is often of less importance than their intended application. For the most part, they have a synthetic rubber, plastic, or foamed plastic body coated with an adhesive chemical, which generally is tougher than the sticky part of temporary tapes.

Duct tape is a very flexible plastic tape generally sold in 2″ widths; it can conform to odd shapes very well. Its principal purpose is to repair or seal heat ducts, to patch damaged or leaky clothes dryer exhaust vents, to fasten loose asbestos or fiberglass insulation back onto pipes, and sundry related tasks. It is somewhat more adhesive than electrical tape, holding onto clean, shiny surfaces quite well. It resists heat amazingly well and can keep a firm grip even under very cold conditions if it does not have to remain highly flexible in the cold.

Weatherstripping tapes, in general, consist of a foamed plastic backed with an adhesive that sticks well to metal and painted surfaces but only fairly well to unpainted wood. They come in many widths and lengths. Most of these tapes that you buy at the hardware or department stores were not actually manufactured by the company on the fancy colored labels but by only two or three large adhesive manufacturers, such as Avery Products Corporation and Morgan Adhesives Company.

The 3M Company of Scotch Tape fame makes another weather proofing product they call Weatherban Brand Sealant Tape. It is a hefty, very flexible rubber-based tape with cloth reinforcing and a tough adhesive formulated especially for grabbing onto glass and metal surfaces. Apparently it was first designed for heavy duty automotive use, judging by the company's preponderance of pictures showing it in use making gaskets for truck and trailer windows. The Yellow Pages should help you to find this product under "Tapes, Adhesive." If you have to apply this tape during cold weather (3M considers "cold" to be down to 40°F. for these purposes), there is a cold weather version available.

5. Permanent Tapes—for mounting horizontally. A tape that holds two objects together, whether one be a tile and the other a floor or if both objects are movable, such as a book and a book cover, must have enough gripping power to stay in place even in the midst of the normal pressures applied against it. In the case of a floor, the rug or tile is held to the floor by gravity; the tape need only prevent them from sliding out of place. These tapes can, as a rule, be relatively thin and the adhesive less tacky than required by tapes that have to hold an object such as a tile or a mirror to a vertical wall.

Most mounting tapes have an adhesive coating—usually a synthetic rubber or an acrylic formulation—on both sides of what is generally a thin plastic backing. This is a general-purpose type product, formulated to stick to glass, wood, metal, tile, and often to fabrics and some of the less slippery plastics. Although it can be used vertically to display unmounted photos and lightweight objects in that category, its thin adhesive coating prohibits heavier use.

Carpets can be held in place by a quick application of doublesided tape. This is especially handy in patio areas or bathrooms where the carpet is often removed for cleaning. If the carpet is rubber backed, it is generally possible to re-lay the rug without having to lay down a new strip of tape every time.

6. Permanent Tapes—for mounting vertically. Today there are almost uncountable ways to use permanent tapes. But most of them are inferior to the older ways of doing the same jobs. Instead of driving a tiny nail into the wall for mounting a picture, the consumer can slap a couple of square inches of permanent tape onto the wall. Instead of squeezing some tile adhesive out of a tube when bathroom tiles work loose, or when another towel rack is needed, modern man or woman cuts off some tape, and then spends a day or two wondering if it is going to hold such a heavy, ornamental towel bar to the soapy, greasy tile. There is nothing wrong, of course, with having some fun with the double-sided tape products on display at your hardware or novelty store, as long as you realize that you are just having fun and not being practical.

There are, however, some very practical and valuable applications for the permanent double-sided tapes powerful enough to support heavy objects to the side of a wall. For one, if you have ever tried to drill the holes necessary to mount shelves or pictures on a brick or concrete wall, you will appreciate being able to accomplish the same end with a few square inches of tape. And if for some reason you think that some day you might like to remove all of those mirror tiles mounted to a wall, the tape is considerably easier to remove than a cement—although taking off the permanent tape cannot be called "easy" by a long shot. Industrial users make creative application of these same tape products by affixing strips of tape to the back of objects they sell you to hang up—paper cup dispensers, towel racks, tiles, small mirrors, and such.

For permanent tapes intended for either horizontal or vertical applications, don't look for bargains. Buy the best there is. This is one time to stick with a store or a brand name you can trust. After a mirror has toppled off the wall or a picture crashed to the floor, nothing will convince you that your cheap package of tape was a bargain.

Pressure-sensitive adhesives are also sensitive to oil, grease, dirt, and moisture that may be hiding on your walls. Press though you might, the tape still cannot successfully adhere to a wall on which the surface is not spotlessly clean and dry. Somewhat the same problem occurs with glues, of course, but since there can be a chemical reaction between the liquid or paste glue and whatever impurities may be lodged on a wall, the chemical adhesives stand a better chance of grabbing onto the surface of a wall that is less than 100 percent clean and dry—which is most walls.

Pressure-sensitive adhesives are also sensitive to heat and age—adversely so. If you have some tape left over from one job, chances are you will not find another big use for it before the active surface of the tape becomes hardened and discolored, signs that its effective days are over. And when shopping for tapes, keep your eyes open for the same signs of deterioration. Aging can occur on the shelf in a sealed package just as surely as in your drawer at home.

SPRAY ADHESIVES

It sounds like a good idea to be able to spray sticky stuff from a can. And industrially, where the materials and working conditions are carefully controlled, spray adhesives do work nicely. The gooey stuff that gets blown from the spout of some common aerosol cans of glue, however, is seldom as tacky as some of the spray paints.

LUBRICATION

Now let's discuss the opposite end of the household spectrum—the lubricants, the oils, greases, powders, and potions that keep moving parts moving. Try to count the moving parts in your home some day—electric motors on the blender, mixer, washing machine, dryer, phonograph, and vacuum cleaner, cylinders and tumblers and bolts inside the locks. Windows and drawers are moving parts too, and so are the hinges on doors. Your car is full of moving parts and so is the lawn mower. Whenever two pieces of anything rub against each other, if the moving parts are to keep moving well, they need oil or something else slippery.

OIL

Oil is the most common lubricant. Simple bearings and high-speed motors benefit from oil. The gasoline engine in your car, lawn mower, or go-cart are obvious examples. A constantly circulating supply of oil bathes moving parts in a fresh film to lubricate the moving parts and to cool them as well. But if the oil isn't fresh, the lubricating and cooling powers both will be dampened by impurities, which oil gradually dissolves or suspends.

The single most important maintenance chore for gasoline engines is a frequent change of oil. Follow the manual if you have it; if not, follow the rules in later chapters.

Electric motors may have permanently lubricated and sealed bearings in them. Most, however, require a drop or two of oil periodically. Despite all of the space age chemistry we've been exposed to, oil is still the preferred lubrication for motors on sewing machines, drills, saws, fish tank pumps, and on and on and on.

Ball bearings on roller skates benefit from a small soaking with oil periodically, as do bicycle bearings. You can silence squeaks in strollers, shopping carts, wheelbarrows and other rolling stock with simple bearings by applying a few drops of oil where it counts. Even the simple bearings on drive mechanisms in tape recorders and phonograph turntables benefit from a drop of oil now and then, but read Chapter 7 first—too much oil in the wrong place can cause major headaches.

The easiest way to apply oil around the home is with that familiar little squirt can. Only don't squirt too much. A common misconception seems to say that if two drops are good, four must be twice as good. But the excess drips onto motor brushes, belt, carpets, or all over the polished teak tabletop.

Figure 39 Most common forms of oil for use around the home. Most economical is to buy a quart at a filling station and keep filling a flexible oil can. Tiny needled oil vial is for reaching out-of-way places or miniature equipment. Spray can is good for dousing large items or preventing rust.

For large users of oil, a cheap oil can with a flexible spout is the answer. A quart of light oil—usually SAE 10 motor oil—costs less than a loaf of bread. The long flexible spout on an oil can is ideal for reaching out-of-the-way places. For miniaturized equipment, there is a disposable oil can available with a spout as fine as a hypodermic needle.

Like just about every other substance known to humans, oil also is available in an aerosol can. Its use for internal lubrication purposes is quite limited, as you might expect. But a generous squirt of oil forms a good protective coating over metal parts. Tools that will be stored over the winter should be sprayed generously with oil, likewise for sleds and skates to be stored over the summer. Additional handy uses will be mentioned in appropriate chapters.

Like peas, meat, and fine paintings, oil comes in several different grades (see Chapter 19).

GREASE

Grease is the hefty big daddy of lubricants. It is used principally on slow-moving devices and inside gearboxes. Grease generally has to be used inside enclosed housings for a number of reasons. For one, it has to be packed solidly around the moving parts it protects. When grease gets hot, it can become quite thin and can drip away from the gears or shafts. A large glob of grease packed around the moving parts, however, helps the grease to hold its cool.

A second reason for keeping grease in enclosed areas is that although it may seem slippery to moving parts, it is a tremendously sticky dust trap. Grease left exposed to the open air traps so much debris that it very quickly upsets whatever benefit the lubricant might have provided.

Power tools such as saber saws and drills have grease packed around the speed reduction gears and eccentrics. It is a good idea to replace the grease every couple of years. Beyond those items, grease is not all that common around the home except for the lawn mower or car. A lot of people who go to the trouble of changing oil in their cars, even those who dutifully replace the oil filter and clean the air filter, often over-look the grease fittings. The ball joints and bearings need some attention too. If you want to maintain your own car, invest in an inexpensive grease gun and some lithium grease.

Except for automotive use, the type of grease you buy for around the home is not of critical importance. Various firms have tubes of varying types of grease on the market—silicone grease, lithium grease, white grease. Whichever happens to catch your fancy should do whatever job you have in mind unless some user manuals specifically advise otherwise.

There is one use for grease that passes almost unnoticed. It is great for damping noise. The knob and bolt on your doors, for instance, can be packed with a liberal quantity of grease since all of the mechanism is enclosed and practically dust-free. The grease will make the parts move easier and will make them virtually silent. The noise damping qualities of grease also can be put to good use in the controls of recorders or other music systems, the gears of a noisy electric can opener, and other items.

GRAPHITE

The preferred lubricant for slow-moving parts exposed to dust is graphite. Unfortunately, few people remember graphite when they're looking for a way out of sticky problems. The most commonly known use for graphite is in the tumbler section of a lock. One graphite product comes in a squirt can like oil and consists of powdered graphite suspended in a volatile solvent. You squirt it into a lock or any other crevice and wait for the solvent to evaporate, leaving behind a film of powdered graphite. Trouble is, it is hard to squirt liquid very far horizontally, such as deep into a lock tumbler. And once the liquid gets there, it can take a long time for the solvent to evaporate because air does not circulate very freely inside a tumbler.

Graphite also comes in flexible plastic or rubber tubes and jars with narrow points for spouts. One squeeze of the tube or jar will send a cloud of pure powdered graphite into the air, or into the lock. Aside from convenience, buying powdered graphite is also the cheapest way; you pay only for the works and not for the extraneous solvent too. Treat the small, transparent plastic tube of graphite with a bit of care, however. If you store it in your toolbox and toss a wrench on top of the tube, it's graphite all over forever!

The slow-moving arms of your record changer should be doused with graphite instead of grease or oil. And, unless you keep returning it to the case faithfully, your typewriter also. The dry graphite gets the job done without quickly attracting a competing film of dust. If you must lubricate moving parts in a camera, graphite is the traditional lubricant, but carefully blow away all excess particles before they lodge on the film, leaving an artsy-craftsy abstract speckled design. Can openers and similarly exposed kitchen levers will be better treated with graphite than with oil or grease, which attracts food particles, and they in turn attract bacteria.

Your pliers and wrenches are a little stiff, you think, so you grab for the oil can to loosen them up—for a while. But dust and sand begin collecting on the tool, and maybe within only an hour the joints are more arthritic than ever. Then you will have to clean off the joints with penetrating oil or some other solvent, dry them well, and then start all over again—using graphite the next time.

PENETRATING OIL

This isn't oil at all. It is a potent solvent that does a great job of soaking out rust, corrosion, dried up films of oil or grease, and just about anything else that "freezes" moving parts. If you can't budge a nut or pipe thread, rest for five minutes while a generous outpouring of penetrating oil tries to dissolve the deposit. True to its purpose, one firm has adopted the name *Liquid Wrench* for its brand of penetrating oil, and that name is popularly used for anybody's brand of penetrating oil.

Not every stuck thread can be soaked loose after a five-minute application. Sometimes more than one squirt is needed. Leaving the project overnight is often sound advice. After a salty winter of driving, penetrating oil may be needed to free the stuck nuts on your auto tires. If you are changing the valves on a steam radiator, better squirt some penetrating oil onto the threads a day in advance and some more just as you start to unlimber your pipe wrench.

Penetrating oil is beneficial for other sticky problems too. If you've

Figure 40 Other lubrication handy for home use. "Liquid Wrench" loosens stuck hardware. "Lock Mate" and "Lock Ease" are forms of graphite useful for lubricating locks and other devices. "Lubriplate" is a form of white grease. Spray can contains a silicone dry lubricant. And when all else is unavailable, try the old standby, Vaseline.

had a small motor tucked away in the basement for a year or two, chances are the bearings are going to be stiff from the old oil and possibly some corrosion as well. Squirt just a drop or two of penetrating oil into the bearings to loosen them up. Follow the treatment with a squirt of light oil or whatever happens to be your preferred lubricant.

SILICONE LUBRICANT

This glamorous slippery stuff of the space age does have a few important uses. However, what we now do with a relatively expensive can of silicone spray used to be done with a bar of soap or a hunk of wax. And, frankly, for practically every household use, the soap works just as well.

If you are straining hard to twist wood screws into hardwood or deep into softwood, a squirt of silicone lubricant on the threads before putting in the screw will make your chore easier. But so will a dab of soap. The same treatment helps to take the spunk out of large nails being driven into hardwood or tough softwood, and silicone can help stuck zippers too. Once the zipper shows signs of aging due to repeated laundering, squirt some silicone lubricant on it.

Silicone sprays, soap, and wax are valuable whenever two flat surfaces have to slide over each other. Windows and drawers come immediately to mind. Skis and sleds will slide over the snow faster after lubrication. The same goes for snow shovels. Even lawn mower blades can benefit by an occasional spray of silicone—they'll be less likely to choke on grass that otherwise tends to stick to the rotary or reel blades.

Aside from its lubricating powers, silicone has one other interesting characteristic—it is more resistant to water than light oil. If your wooden boats become water-logged every time you take a bath, silicone lubricating spray may solve the dilemma. Under the hood of your car, a heavy spray of silicone lubricant can help to waterproof the ignition wires.

THE HARDWARE OF FIXING THINGS

BOLTS

Bolts come in many different varieties. Since the assumption here is that you won't often be designing new mechanical equipment, but merely replacing bolts that have become mangled or lost, we will skip a technical discussion of the respective merits of each kind of bolt. Figure 41 names the basic parts of a bolt, the types of bolts that generally are threaded into *nuts* to secure two pieces of metal, plastic, or wood together, or to hold a piece of equipment onto wood, metal, or plastic. Several types of heads can be found on bolts of most general varieties (see Figure 41).

In heavy machinery—such as a car or a washing machine—vibration can work the nuts loose off a bolt, setting up a situation where something vital could drop out of place. Figure 41 shows how engineers decide what portion of a bolt should be *threaded* and what portion should be reserved for the unthreaded *grip*, all with the intent of slowing down the ravages of vibration.

Ideally, no more than one thread should be in the metal held in place by a heavy bolt. Expressed another way, the grip length should equal

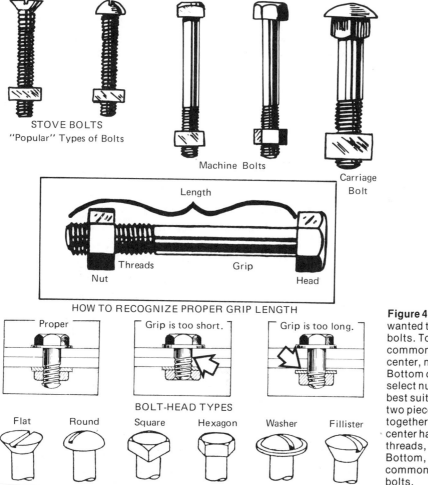

STOVE BOLTS
"Popular" Types of Bolts

Machine Bolts

Carriage Bolt

Length

Threads   Grip

Nut   Head

HOW TO RECOGNIZE PROPER GRIP LENGTH

Proper   Grip is too short.   Grip is too long.

BOLT-HEAD TYPES

Flat   Round   Square   Hexagon   Washer   Fillister

Figure 41 All you ever wanted to know about bolts. Top, various common types. Top center, nomenclature. Bottom center, how to select number of threads best suited for holding two pieces of work together. (Left is ideal, center has too many threads, right too few.) Bottom, names of common heads found on bolts.

the width of the metal or machinery to be held in place. On the other hand, the threads must come all the way up to the bottom surface of the metal or the nut will not be able to turn up tightly. Even a well-stocked hardware store or industrial supplier may not have a bolt of precisely the same configuration as the one you must replace, so if a compromise is necessary, you must of course select a bolt with more threads on it than the original even if that leaves you holding a bolt with a shorter grip length.

"Screws" and "bolts" are confusing terms, and there's little that can be done to clear up the confusion. Technically speaking, a bolt needs a nut before it can be called a bolt. Otherwise, it's a screw. You can refer to the screws that look like bolts without nuts as *machine screws.* That will separate them from other objects such as wood screws and sheet metal screws. A machine screw fits into the threads of some machinery. A bolt fits through a hole and fastens onto its own nut. But you can call a machine screw a bolt in most hardware stores.

Another variety of bolt is the *setscrew,* which, like the machine screw, is used without a nut. As a rule, setscrews do not have a head, although a few do. A setscrew is threaded through some metal portion of items such as pulleys, gears, and clamps, to secure them to a shaft. On large machinery or precision-made small equipment, a slot or indentation in the shaft receives the point of a setscrew to form a rigid union.

Closely related to the setscrew is the popular *thumbscrew.* It is designed to be tightened or loosened by hand in such applications as music stands, light stands, tabletop vises or meat grinders, appliance covers, and hundreds of other devices that must be tightened or loosened without the assistance of tools (see Figure 42).

At one time, every bolt manufacturer turned as many threads per inch into his product as he wanted to. Therefore, a handy person needed to know not only the type and size of bolt he or she wanted to replace, but also who manufactured it. Standardization has arrived, fortunately, but there are several different categories within that system of bolt standards.

NC (National Coarse) threads are used in most common applications; *NF* (National Fine) threads appear in fine machinery as a rule. *EF* (Extra Fine) thread is used in a few automotive and engineering items. These threads are not interchangeable. When in doubt, either buy one of each available type or count the number of threads per inch.

Figure 43 also shows the standard sizes for bolts of all types. From ¼" up, bolts are stocked by their actual dimensions. Below ¼", gauge numbers from 0 through 12 are the standard for size. Actually,

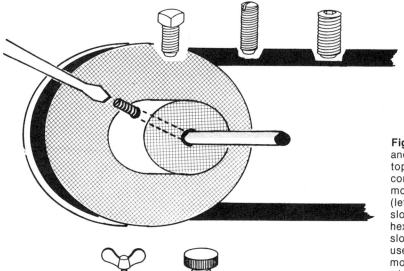

Figure 42 Setscrews and thumbscrews. At top, 3 types of setscrews commonly used to hold moving parts in place: (left to right) square, slotted and recessed hex heads. Center, how slotted setscrew is often used to hold pulley onto motor shaft. Bottom, winged thumbscrew and knurled thumbscrew.

Fig. 43 Bolt and Machine Screw Sizes

	DIAMETER		THREADS PER INCH		
No.	*Inch.*	*Equivalent Decimal*	*NC*	*NF*	*EF*
0	1/16*	.0600	—	80	—
1	5/64*	.0730	64	72	—
2	3/32*	.0860	56	64	—
3	3/32*	.0990	48	56	—
4	7/64*	.1120	40	48	—
5	1/8*	.1250	40	44	—
6	9/64*	.1380	32	40	—
8	5/32*	.1640	32	36	—
10	3/16*	.1900	24	32	40
12	7/32*	.2160	24	28	—
	1/4	.2500	20	28	36
	5/16	.3125	18	24	32
	3/8	.3750	16	24	32
	7/16	.4375	14	20	28
	1/2	.5000	13	20	28
	9/16	.5625	12	18	24
	5/8	.6250	11	18	24
	3/4	.7500	10	16	20

*Approximate size only. Small bolts and screws are identified by their gauge numbers.

miniature bolts do exist, 00, 000, and so on, but it is unlikely that you'll meet them except in a jeweler's shop.

When drilling a hole to accommodate a bolt that must slip all the way through a piece of metal or wood, select a drill one size larger than the given diameter. If you intend to machine a set of threads into the hole, however, a smaller sized hole is required.

TAPS

Although taps actually belong in the earlier chapter on tools, they will make more sense now that you are more acquainted with bolts and threads. A tap is an ingenious little gadget that gets twisted through a plain hole in a piece of soft metal or plastic, and, with the expenditure of very little energy, threads appear so that a bolt can then be threaded into the metal or plastic.

It is foolish for the average household to invest in a full set of good taps since their use, fortunately, is very limited. It is equally unwise to invest in a set of very cheap taps. When the need does arise, a tap of the proper size can be bought at most well-stocked hardware outlets for very little money. Tap size designations exactly match the screw thread numbers shown in Figure 43.

One common tap is the ¼"-N.C., or a one-fourth inch National Coarse thread tap, a tool that will convert a 7/32" hole into a set of threads to accommodate a ¼" bolt. You will often see ¼"-N.C. written as ¼-20, meaning that there are 20 threads per inch on the ¼" National Coarse thread bolt or tap.

Smaller sized bolts are almost universally referred to by the gauge numbers given in Figure 52. You should never see something reading ⅛"-N.C. A bolt or tap of that type would be written as 5-40. By the same rule, what a novice might write as ⅛"-N.F. should be 5-44. Knowing a relatively unimportant procedure such as this improves your chances of getting satisfaction at a hardware store or especially at an industrial supplier.

If existing threads that are part of some machinery you are laboring over have become worn or damaged—"stripped" is the common trade word—you can probably overcome the difficulty by buying a tap and matching bolt of the next larger size. With a bit of lubrication, the tap will quickly put a new, although larger, set of threads into the existing hole.

Should you want to create a hole and set of thread where none existed before, the hole you drill before applying a tap is very important. The proper drill size to use with any tap is usually engraved right on the tap. If it is impossible to use the proper drill size, start with the next *smallest* size available. Selecting a larger size could result in very thin, fragile threads. If you have had to rely upon a smaller drill size, lubricate the tap thoroughly and often during the tapping, a simple process. However, should the drill chosen to make the initial hole be more than 10 percent smaller than the size specified, enlarge the hole slightly with a round file.

For the technical minded, the size of a drill chosen for the initial hole to be tapped will produce what is known as a ''75 percent thread.'' Only 75 percent of the maximum thread diameter the tap *can* cut will be utilized. At 100 percent, or close to it, the friction between thread and tap or between thread and bolt will be too great, leading to awkward working conditions. Less than 75 percent results in weaker threads than most jobs can tolerate.

Some confusion inevitably results when people start looking at pipe sizes alongside bolt sizes. Both are threaded. Both seem to be done according to the same system. But they're not! Pipes are sized according to the inside diameter of some very ancient thick-walled iron pipes. In other words, when someone in the know refers to a ¼ " pipe, the inside of that pipe is slightly larger than ¼ ". And the outside, threaded portion actually is slightly over ½ ". There is yet another difference between pipe threads and bolt threads. To make a watertight or airtight seal between the inside and outside threads, the pipe thread system includes a built-in standardized taper of ¾ " for every foot of pipe thread. Consequently, bolt threads and pipe threads are not interchangeable *in any way*.

Fig. 44   Pipe Sizes (in inches)

"Official" size	*Actual Outside Diameter*
⅛	$^{13}/_{32}$
¼	$^{17}/_{32}$
⅜	$^{11}/_{16}$
½	$^{27}/_{32}$
¾	$1^{1}/_{16}$
1	$1^{5}/_{16}$
1¼	$1^{21}/_{32}$
1½	$1^{29}/_{32}$
2	$2^{3}/_{8}$
2½	$2^{7}/_{8}$
3	$3^{1}/_{2}$

Screws function in much the same way as do bolts. Their nomenclature and size designations are somewhat similar. But, as we know, a bolt must be turned into an already existing set of threads; a screw makes its own threads as it is used.

There are two basic types of screws you are likely to encounter when fixing things—the *wood screw*, most common, and the *sheet metal screw*. Since wood screws are used almost exclusively in wood, as their name implies, they will be discussed at some length in the chapter on wood repairs, along with nails.

Sheet metal screws are found most often in radios, TVs, refrigerators, and similar appliances that have metal chassis parts to hold together. They resemble a bolt except that the threads are so coarse and so spread out that once you see Figure 45 there should be little room for confusing them in the future.

A sheet metal screw is designed principally for mass assembly techniques. It requires only a hole of the appropriate size to hold itself and two or more pieces of metal tightly into place. You will have to deal with sheet metal screws whenever vibration or frequent repairs wear the screw's appointed hole so large that the threads not longer can grab onto enough metal to hold securely. Then you take the old screw to a hardware store and select the next larger size, maybe even two sizes larger to be safe. The bigger version will screw comfortably into the enlarged hole and solve the problem instantly.

There is an alternate solution to the problem of a sheet metal screw in an enlarged hole. Substitute a bolt and nut for the old screw. It costs you no more and is far stronger. The reason that the manufacturer of

Figure 45   Sheetmetal screw (left) and wood screw placed side by side so you can compare them. Sheetmetal variety is very straight; wood screw tapers.

your ailing gadget did not use a bolt in the first place is that a bolt is a fraction of a cent more expensive than a sheet metal screw and requires a second or two longer to install as the assembly line goes whizzing by.

WASHERS

Here is another major category of industrial hardware that finds its way into your home via manufactured items—although fewer and fewer are now used as assembly lines seem to find more ways to leave out any part that can possibly be considered extraneous to the initial operation of an appliance.

Washers are round pieces of metal with holes in the middle, very much like flat, metallic donuts (see Figure 46) for three of the most common varieties). They come in literally hundreds of sizes. The split washer and the lock washer both are used to hold nuts onto bolts whenever vibration is a factor.

Common flat washers cover a variety of sins. But you can be sure that if a manufacturer included such a washer, it is a vital part of the machine. If the hole through which a bolt has to slip is a trifle over-sized, and there is a resultant danger that the head of the bolt might eventually enlarge the hole further and slip through, a washer under the head will eliminate the problem. If the threaded portion of a machine bolt is too short for the nut to twist tightly against the body of your appliance, one or more flat washers either under the head or under the nut—perhaps in both place—will take up the slack with almost no loss of mechanical performance.

In simple motor-driven gadgets, washers often serve as a buffer between a rotating shaft or pulley and some bolt. Without the washers, the constant rotation might twist off the nut or bolt—or at least twist it off sooner than generally happens anyway.

Hardware stores of all sizes should have washers of many sizes. Better stocked ones will have more of the odd ball varieties and sizes. If you can't get the size you want, try to select a washer with the center hole close to the correct diameter and the outside dimension larger

Figure 46 Three common washers. Left to right—flat, split, and locking washers.

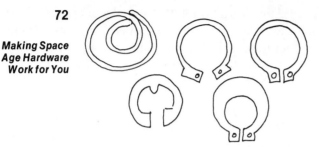

Figure 47 Sampling of retaining rings, often used to hold small pieces of equipment together. Lost or damaged rings must be replaced by one of almost identical size and shape. Fortunately, many hardware stores have bins full of them.

than the original. Put another way, keep the center circle close to size but let the outside circle get larger.

RETAINING RINGS

Often called *snap rings* or *snap retaining rings,* these items are used to hold moving parts onto a shaft of some sort. They are common in phonograph turntables and tape recorders where a retaining ring often holds each of the pulleys and levers onto its shaft. They have a nasty tendency to get lost because people who snap a snap ring off a shaft often forget that the ring is under tension and usually jumps several feet once the tension is released. (See Figure 47.)

Retaining rings come in many sizes and several shapes. Although you might get one style to work in place of another, it is generally impossible to get satisfactory results from a retaining ring of the wrong size. So if one of them gets lost, better buy several replacements of varying sizes.

RIVETS

The main reason for the popularity of rivets is that one company has developed an ingenious and relatively low-priced riveting tool that does away with much of the drudgery once a part of riveting. However, there is little practical application for rivets around the home.

If the rivet in some applicance goes bad, it is far simpler to replace it with a healthy nut and bolt than to attempt to use the amateur riveting for that job. The so-called pop riveter does a splendid job for certain craft projects such as leather working, but beyond that don't get carried away by promises of a tool for all rooms and all purposes.

There must be a thousand or so specific bits of hardware, one or more of which may some day become tremendously important to you, more than likely, when you least expect it. If you can come up with the name of the oddity and a rough approximation of its important dimensions, you will no doubt be able to find a reasonable facsimile at a hardware store, how-to-do-it center, hobby shop, industrial supplier, or similar outlet. Figure 48 displays much of the less common hardware you may face some day when a vital appliance breaks down or you set off on a new mechanical project. The caption for Figure 48 lists the key facts or figures you will want to have on your shopping list as you go in search of the items shown there.

Learning of the existence of once-strange mechanical things, and then finding out what to call them is one of the most fundamental ways to overcome all of the blocks that stand between you and successful repairs of your gadgets and appliances. More important still is to get it through your head that, contrary to popular opinion, average people *can* look after their own household ailments.

Figure 48 Miscellaneous hardware of use to home repair people. Left to right: top—U-bolt, turn buckle; center row— cable support, cotter pin, snap cap, insulated staple; bottom—shelf bracket, repair plate, L-plate.

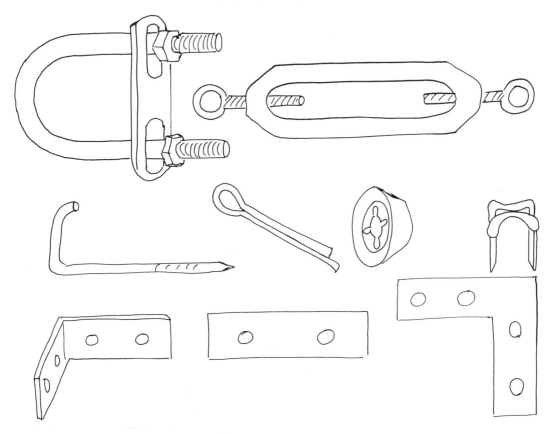

4 The Aesthetics of Home Repairs

Maybe you can't see anything beautiful about having to fix an ailing electric percolator—especially if you're waiting for the first cup of coffee in the morning. Agreed! But there should be something beautiful about the coffee pot when you've finished restoring it to like new condition—or better than new if the manufacturer goofed somewhere along the assembly line.

Tackle the common or even the uncommon household repairs with the thought that you are performing something more important than merely rejuvenating an old electric toaster. What can you say is so beautiful, so important about household repairs? For one, you stand to save a bundle of money. For another, you're fighting back against the rip-off repair system, if that interests you. And it's ecologically unsound to toss out useable appliances just because nobody thought to repair them. Perhaps most important of all, however, is the fact that you are taking charge of your own life again.

Here are some step-by-step battle plans to use when attacking the strange world of fixing things. Keep them in mind, at least during your early tries, and you will soon be surprising yourself at how easily the average woman or man can fix damn near everything.

First, find a well-lit, flat place to work. A desk of the kitchen table is fine. Then give yourself some added protection against those annoying little parts that jump off the table—work on a cookie sheet. It's big, flat, and versatile. And the turned up sides do wonders at confining screws, bolts, nuts, and just about anything else that has a tendency to roll away.

If for some reason you have to put the repair job away before it's finished—maybe you have to run downtown to pick up a new part—don't assume that you'll be back in a few minutes to resume where you left off. If a multitude of small parts are involved, find a bottle or jar, maybe a small box, anything with a cover, and put the whole collection of loose odds and ends inside, close the top, mark it well, and put it safely away from unauthorized hands both big and small.

A second important part of your personal work plan is that *you must save all user manuals,* warranties, sales slips, and similar documents that accompany everything you buy. In the first place, manufacturers occasionally put some valuable information into their manuals. Besides, you might try to perform some strange job with an appliance and get the idea that it's not working, when in truth you may have been using an incorrect dial setting or making some similar annoying error. The user manual should be consulted before plunging into a repair job.

The user manual also can provide the addresses of local or regional repair stations where you can buy replacement parts. Although local hardware stores or similar suppliers might be able to sell you such items as nuts, bolts, belts, wires, glues, and standardized replacement handles, it will take a manufacturer's agent to supply one-of-a-kind items.

Unfortunately, most warranties, guarantees, and similar pieces of paper not worth the paper they are printed on. The warranty, in case after case, has proven to be little more than an extension of a manufacturer's sales pitch.

Here is a close look at a typical warranty, this one on an expensive electric portable typewriter. Along with the bright, red type that says "Guarantee" and "Congratulations" is finer type adivisng that if your typewriter requires service *during the guarantee period* . . ." it should be sent to the company in the following manner: "Please be certain that it is securely wrapped, preferably in its original shipping carton with the foam blocks." Once the typewriter's warranty period has elapsed, however, the same firm advises tht the machine be treated thus: "Please be certain that it is securely wrapped...." Period.

Typical of most warranties, the typewriter manufacturer pays for no more than the cost of the defective part. You have to pay the company for the *labor* it requires to replace a part, for the postage and insurance required to mail the ailing machine *both ways*, plus sales tax in many cities or states. Since the cost of a replacement part is typically about 10 percent or less of the overall cost of a repair, all the manufacturer does when making repairs during a warranty period is to do so at a slight discount for you. A very slight discount!

Most companies who sell you everything from gadgets to life-saving equipment also enclose a card of some sort in the box, generally labeled "Owner Registration Certificate" or "Purchase Registration Card." Implicit in the language is the thought that if you fail to return the card, your warranty will be invalid. In most cases it is not legally essential that you return the card.

Most of the self-proclaimed registration cards are, in fact, a market survey. They are designed to help the manufacturer create a profile of what kind of people are buying what it has to sell. Which is the reason for such otherwise irrelevant questions as your age, profession, why you bought the gadget, or why you selected this brand.

Since warranties for the greatest number of consumer goods on the market are practically worthless, you may as well treat them that way. Once you become reasonably adept at making simple repairs around your home, you will more than likely dispense with the nuisance and money, not to mention danger to the item, of mailing the broken gadget back to some factory repair center. You will, instead, call or write for the spare part and put it in yourself.

There are other ways to attack the matter of nearly worthless warranties. After you've had a guaranteed item repaired by the *alleged guarantor,* sue him. This may not be practical in every community, but it is in cities that have a small claims court. In return for a few dollars, you will have the satisfaction of getting a lawyer for the company into the courtroom to explain to the judge and the spectators that the firm's guarantee isn't really a guarantee at all even though it does say so.

By suing for a refund of the money you had to pay for repairs—or even just the price of buying a new part to replace a defective one—you will also put some pressure on the local retailer from whom you bought the item because that store's name should be included as a codefendent. At the very least, a copy of the actions should be mailed to your local store, which would be sure to discuss the matter of warranties with the manufacturer's sales people.

Copies of all your letters and legal papers about defective merchandise covered by defective warranties should be scattered around town very liberally. Be sure to mail copies to the local newspapers and radio stations. Your Better Business Bureau might be convinced to step in if enough people complain seriously enough about a particular company or product.

REPAIRING WITH BEAUTY

There's a good deal more to the aesthetic side of making repairs than shouting and screaming, however. Nobody likes to use a coffee pot, toothbrush, phonograph, or even a garbage can that doesn't look reasonably attractive. Aside from the purely mechanical aspects of twisting, turning, hammering, or soldering a gadget back to its proper working condition, you also should pay some attention to how the finished repair job looks.

Chrome finishes should be protected with tape during a repair if there is any chance that you will scratch them. The same advice holds true for any delicate painted or wooden surface. We have already discussed sound mechanical reasons for selecting the right kind of wrench or screwdriver. But there is also an aesthetic side. The wrong-sized tool is likely to ruin the appearance of even some not so delicate household items. It's bad enough having to stand at a sink to wash dishes, but if the sink and accompanying pipes or faucets look dreadful, the chore becomes all the more dreary.

As we discuss each of the various repair sections, the care and feeding of specific beautiful household objects will be covered in some detail. At the moment, however, you might remember one set of paints found in most art stores that should have a great deal of value around the well-repaired home.

ACRYLIC PAINTS

Acrylics are a synthetic plastic material designed to give the beauty, versatility, and texture of oil paints but the durability of rugged plastic. They dry quickly—too quickly at times—and can be mixed to match practically any color you are likely to want to duplicate around the home. Even gloss or matte surfaces can be matched with amazing ease.

An artist's full set of acrylic paints is a significant investment but not a vital one. Once you have bought a very inexpensive color chart (or talked the store into giving you one), you can determine which two, three, or four tubes of color pigments will handle your present job. Add other colors later. A one ounce tube of each required color is virtually a lifetime supply for a household of repair people.

Small chips on the edge of laminated plastic countertops (Formica is the popular name) can be repaired with acrylic paints. Despite the fact that this art medium is water soluble when you use it, and brushes or hands can be cleaned in soap and water, once acrylics dry they are just as tough as many of the surfaces you apply them to. And they dry literally within minutes.

For especially big chips out of countertops and any other area that gets plenty of use, such as tile floors, porcelain sinks, brightly colored enamelware pots and pans, and so on try mixing the acrylic pigments with an epoxy glue. The combination is at times slightly weaker than epoxy resins alone, but it is many, many times stronger than an epoxy patch covered over even with a tough decorative acrylic finish later on.

For patching purposes, you will want to use what pros refer to as a "filled epoxy glue." In other words, the resin is blended with a material such as powdered iron or powdered aluminum, which adds some body and some structural strength to the glue. Since the epoxy compound will be grey in color, you will have to consult the color mixing chart that shows what the particular acrylics look like after being mixed with white and then with black pigments. And work quickly. Both the acrylics and the epoxies harden extremely fast.

If you have to patch a rather large area with the epoxy-acrylic combination, do some experimenting first. Using fairly precise measurements, mix up a small batch. Your recipe might read something like this: One teaspoon of epoxy resin and one teaspoon of epoxy hardener. Add ⅛th teaspoon cadmium red-light acrylic paint, ⅛th teaspoon cadmium yellow-light acrylic paint, and ¼th teaspoon burnt siena acrylic paint. Stir well. If your trial recipe results in a color combination that looks right and is tough enough upon drying, multiply the proportions, using the same accuracy, and go after that big patch.

Acrylics can also modify the colors of other popular patching or mending materials, including those hard-to-mix-with silicones. The addition of foreign substances like the acrylic paint might alter the basic properties of the glue or sealant, but it won't necessarily affect it for the worst. The acrylic polymers and many of the synthetic glues and sealants in popular use are quite compatible with each other.

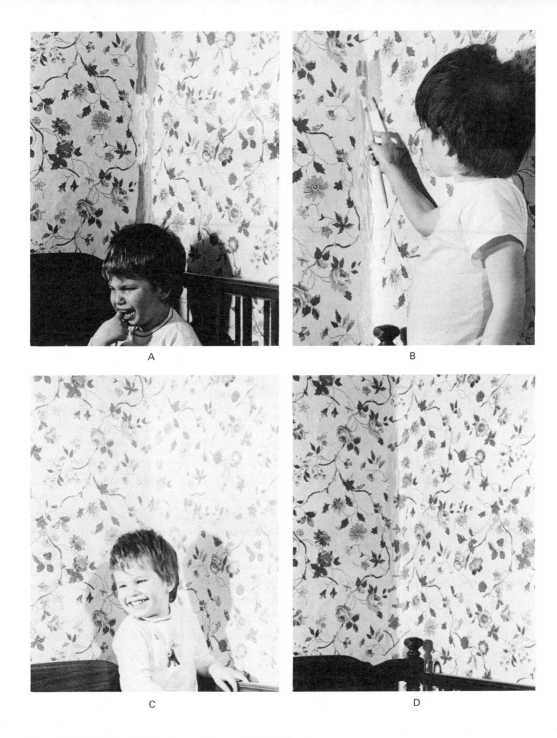

Figure 49 Little Brother's unhappy because Big Brother tore wall paper from corner (A). So, (B) Big Brother is sent to work with brush to paint corner the same color as wall paper's background. Daddy then paints something vaguely resembling the original pattern with acrylic paints close to the original colors. And (C) it fools Little Brother and all other viewers. In closeup (D), you can still see the deception only on close examination. This camouflage works for all similar problems.

Since we are discussing aesthetics, we might mention a product called X-Pandotite, which is manufactured in a family factory in New York City. X-Pandotite comes in a can and mixes with water, resembling plaster or mortar in that state. It contains no plaster, however, and exhibits a most uncanny property—as it dries, X-Pandotite expands. (Most mortar products tend to shrink a bit.)

Compared with epoxy or silicone glues and sealants, X-Pandotite is relatively inexpensive, although it costs more than conventional plaster or cement patching materials. For really large areas, or for special applications such as a big room full of cracks in tiles and bathroom accessories, it might be worthwhile and economical to experiment with X-Pandotite. It can be colored after you have mixed water with the powdered product. The acrylic polymer pigments are perfectly compatible with the mortar product, but the X-Pandotite family has traditionally recommended that users color X-Pandotite with one of the powdered dyes sold principally for dying fabrics.

X-Pandotite dries slowly. This can be a virtue, particularly if you are working on large areas or with unwieldy objects.

If you are patching a broken marble floor, the X-Pandotite or epoxy patch can't be limited to a single color because marble is marbled in its coloration. The same applies to wood-grained Formica, plastic, and wood. In such a situation, you generally will patch the main area with a color that matches the background of the wood or marble. In the case of X-Pandotite, the darker colors can be added later on with an appropriately colored, penetrating oil wood stain.

For large chips in wood-grained surfaces such as a Formica countertop where the endurance and heat resistance of epoxy is needed, the easiest way to duplicate the grain is first to apply a patch colored to match the background color. When the main epoxy material has hardened sufficiently, mix a new batch colored to match the grain. Apply that rather delicately with a fine brush. After the whole thing has set, you will be able to file and buff the patched surface secure in the knowledge that your Formica's renewed beauty is more than just skin deep.

Sometimes it doesn't pay to repaint or clean a surface one more time. The bureau has had it, the phonograph plays well but has such a shabby case you wouldn't dream of passing it down to the next child in line. Maybe you once liked shocking tangerine on the bookcase, but now you like a wood-grained home for your library again. The answer to all of these complaints is a new skin of self-adhesive vinyl (often known by one of its early trade names, Con-Tact.)

In case you can't find a convenient way to disguise a nasty looking repair job into something that vaguely resembles a work of art, perhaps you can redesign the entire appearance. If a young member of your household has battered her trike, but it's still in great mechanical condition, a paint job is easy. But what about the chrome handlebars? Forget the chrome! Go colorful! Wind a strip of colored plastic tape around the handlebars, being sure to leave a gap between consecutive windings. Then wrap a matching or contrasting layer of a different colored tape evenly around the blank spaces. The result is a two-toned set of handlebars on the "new" trike, now the envy of the block.

Using gimmicky items such as colored tapes can redesign other implements you thought were beyond repair. The major misuse of this technique comes in getting carried away—a little colored tape redesign work is clever and creative; too much becomes obvious and gaudy. Specific jobs that might benefit from a mixture of tape and cleverness are covered in following chapters.

If you want to keep your hands from looking like a grease monkey's, while making repairs make one of your first repair investments a can of paste hand cleaner. Auto mechanics swear by it because it works even in filling stations that have only cold running water. Just smear on the paste cleaner, rub thoroughly, then wipe off the paste and dirt with a paper towel or rag.

Keep a can of the paste hand cleaner in your toolbox, junk drawer, or basement workbench. Keep a spare can in the trunk of your car. You never know when a dirty job will come up—it's also great for dry cleaning messy little boys and girls.

MEASURING

The art of measuring is one of the biggest mental blocks in the repair field. More grief and sloppy work have resulted from people who could and wanted to do better but did not because of bad measurements. When measuring a board, belt, bolt, or bauble, if you say "That looks like 3¼ " *and a little more*," you'll never get past the "*hammmer it till the damn thing fits*" stage.

Even when working with nonprecision things, an error of 2 percent generally is the absolute maximum you should tolerate if your repairs or constructions are to hold their own. And in a 1 ′ long piece of wood or steel, that 2 percent tolerance comes out to a mere ¼ ″ your measurements can be off. And to attain the kind of precision that ensures your cutting will be no more than ¼ ″ off the mark, you must measure with an accuracy not of ¼ ″ but of ⅛ ″. In other words, you should use the ⅛ ″ gradations on whatever ruler you use.

Items in the under 2″ bracket require the precision of measurements read on the ⅟₁₆″ portion of a ruler. Above 10′, the ¼″ rulings are okay. Figure 63 provides a convenient rule of thumb for this area. For rough woodworking jobs, especially if sawing is involved, measurements finer than ⅟₁₆″ are practically meaningless since the precise thickness of a saw cut is tough to predict in advance.

There is a measuring shorthand taught in most math classes, but somehow only during nap time. The quick abbreviation for *foot* is ′. And *inch* is abbreviated ″. Thus, 8′ translates to eight feet whereas 4″ becomes four inches.

On the face of it, a ruler seems one of the most logically laid out pieces of apparatus in the world. In truth, rulers, as they are sold today, are one of the most *illogical* of inventions. Whenever someone goes near a ruler, save for those engineers or designers who use one everyday, he has to calculate all over again, "These are the ¼″, those the ⅛″ markings, and so on. A large share of the blame has to be laid on our English measurement system of inches, feet, and yards, 12 inches to a foot, 3 feet to a yard. The metric system, which will

Figure 50 Collection of rulers for use around home. Left to right—level with ruled scale on top, square, stainless steel ruler, folding carpenter's ruler and rectractable rule.

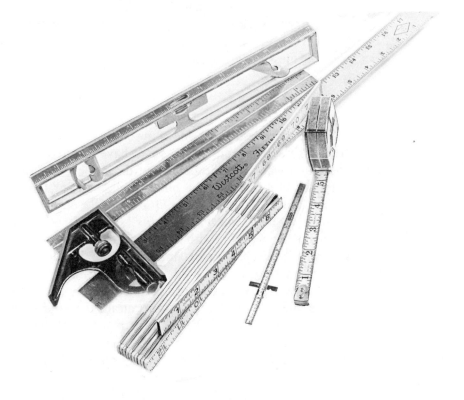

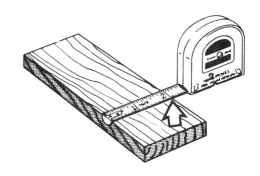
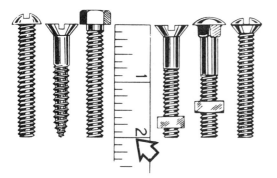
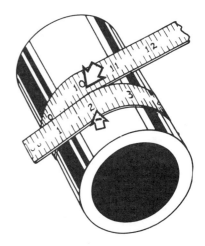
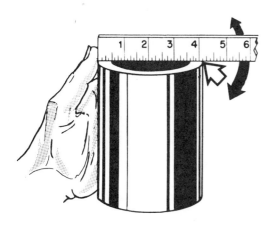
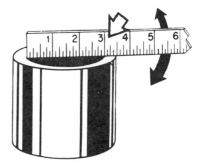

Figure 51 How to measure various home repair articles.

eventually be in use in the United States, doesn't have to be divided up so arbitrarily. Everything you see is in 10s, just one more decimal place to consider when you use such a ruler.

Figure 50 shows some available measuring tools. The *tape rule* is most widely used; its case is fairly accurately made to be 2″ wide. With that concept in mind, a pro or novice carpenter can measure the inside of a window, for example, by using the tape rule *case* as part of the overall length, then adding 2″ to whatever figure is displayed on the rule. Since the case is not *exactly* precise, you should not use it as part of your measurement for readings that have to be more accurate than ⅛″. (Figure 51 gives some hints about how various materials best can be measured.)

There once was a manual arts teacher in Port Edwards, Wisconsin, whose loud voice could often be heard up and down the halls as he yelled at beginning students making their first wooden bread boards. "Make it precisely something. Make it exactly 10″ or exactly 10 ⅛″, but make it exactly something!" He knew, of course, that beauty and simplicity stem from having an appreciation for the value that accuracy has around the home and workshop. (This collection of ways to beat the repair system is compiled by a once-reluctant student of that Wisconsin shop teacher.)

Accuracy is not in the cards for a great many carpenters, plumbers, repair people, and homemakers. All that expensive molding and trim nailed or glued around the bottom of walls, the top of walls, the middle of walls, the sides of sinks, and all over everything else is not only put there to add beauty to a job well done. It is also a way to hide big gaps caused, for the most part, by bad measurements.

If you find a really practical use for or some beauty in a strip of decoration, tack it up. But if you and the decorative gimmicks are not truly compatible, spend a few extra seconds measuring and cutting just a bit more accurately. Besides the fact that your job will look better, it is one more way of helping to stamp out the "*repair people mentality.*"

5 How to Keep the Plumber Away

Economy isn't the only reason for a household to keep on top of its own plumbing repairs. You've no doubt already heard those chilling words from your dedicated good old family doctor. So brace yourself. Any day now local plumbers may attain the same status and, when you yell "help" into the telephone as the broken sink is overflowing down the stairs, the plumber will calmly advise you, "Bring the patient to my office. I don't make house calls." It is already hard to get a plumber when you want one.

As is true with most household repairs, the best way to handle plumbing fix-it problems is to *avoid them*. Preventive medicine of pipes and drains is not difficult. But it does require people to reconsider some well-entrenched habits.

KITCHEN PROBLEMS

The kitchen is probably a plumber's greatest bailiwick. The family cook fries hamburgers and chops carefully to get rid of the grease, knowing that it's no good for a stomach. Then he pours all the grease down the sink, not knowing that grease is no good for the drain either.

Grease floats on top of water, and all of those greasy discards don't always get beyond the S-shaped trap beneath the sink. That trap is carefully designed to retain some water in the pipes to keep sewer gasses from blowing into your kitchen. But the trap also can keep grease floating there until it cools and sticks to your pipes. Eventually, the accumulation of solidified grease results in hardening of the sink arteries, and the water will not drain at all or only very, very slowly.

The best way to keep the kitchen drain clear is to pour the grease into an old tin can. Once it cools and hardens, the grease and can can be tossed out with the garbage.

Suppose you have a garbage disposal unit or the cook still insists on pouring the grease down the sink. Then squirt a hearty dose of liquid detergent into the greasy pan first. Detergent makes grease temporarily water soluble. And if plenty of hot water follows the soap and grease into the drain, the sink stands a better than average chance of recovering from the shock.

A second common kitchen sink ailment comes from food solids. Peeling potatoes, carrots, apples, onions, and grapes is usually done while standing over a sink. But plumbers don't do it that way. The chrome strainer that doubles as a sink stopper lets plenty of peels slip by. Some of them get washed away, but enough sink to the bottom of the trap and stay there. Eventually, the collection in the trap gets big enough to slow down and to stop the flow of drain water. Once a significant pile of debris is lodged in the trap, more and more will be trapped quickly because the speed of draining water will be slowed down by the dam, allowing additional peels to be dropped off on the way.

If you insist on peeling vegetables over the sink, there are some tricks that will help to ward off troubles. Pull the strainer-stopper out and look down the drainpipe. If there is a set of additional supports only an inch or two beneath the strainer, cut a piece of stainless steel or plastic screen big enough to cover the opening completely. The hardware store should have some small, inexpensive pieces of screen or mesh. That second line of defense will have to be pulled out and cleaned periodically—maybe as often as every week in a busy kitchen—but cleaning it is a lot easier than tackling a major drain blockage.

At the bottom of the S trap beneath your sink, you should find a screw cap about 1″ in diameter. Every few months, unscrew it with a wrench or screwdriver (turn counterclockwise when facing the screw cap). Loosen the accumulation inside the trap with an old bottle brush or a reasonable facsimile. After replacing the screw cap firmly, flush plenty of hot water through the sink.

Some landlords or plumbers save a few pennies by putting in traps without a removable clean-out plug. If blocked drains are a habitual problem for you, you might consider investing a few dollars for a new trap that does have a removable plug.

Figure 52 shows the common types of traps and other drain fittings you will find in sinks. When buying replacement traps or other tubes in a drain system, keep in mind that they come in two popular sizes— 1¼ " and 1½ ". The smaller size is generally found only in the bathroom sink; the larger is used in the kitchen, the bathroom tub, and elsewhere.

Preventive sink maintenance has usually meant dumping the proper amount of Drano into every drain on Saturday mornings. No doubt such treatment, with its modified lye, does help to ward off a few plumbing difficulties—it can also cause problems. Lye is also called caustic soda or sodium hydroxide. By whatever name, it can blind, burn, maim, and kill if it gets onto or into a human being. If too many of the harmless looking crystals are dumped into a badly blocked drain, or if very hot water is still sitting above the trap, the reaction between the lye crystals and the water can make the water boil and sputter violently, perhaps tossing one or more of the crystals out of the drain and onto the one who is only doing what the ads seem to advise.

You pay your money and take your choice, or take your chance. If you want to make lye a permanent part of your household, please do so with the full knowledge that it has to be treated with great respect. Without the weekly dose of lye, your drains might slow down and require special attention every year or two instead of once every three years. But you won't find out for yourself unless you start to skip the periodic doses of industrial chemicals.

Lye and the products containing it as their major ingredient are most effective for eating out the chronic accumulations of grease that plague kitchen drains. It doesn't do very much to the hardened soap that accumulates in bathroom drains and does practically nothing to hair that gets into plumbing. There is a safer, cheaper alternative to using lye products for preventive maintenance in the kitchen sink— *plain old boiling water*. Ironically, one reason that boiling water is safer than chemicals is that people have developed a healthy respect for it and handle it with care—not so with dangerous chemicals.

If you pour a couple of quarts of boiling water into the kitchen sink and elsewhere once a week, then flush it 10 minutes later with about a

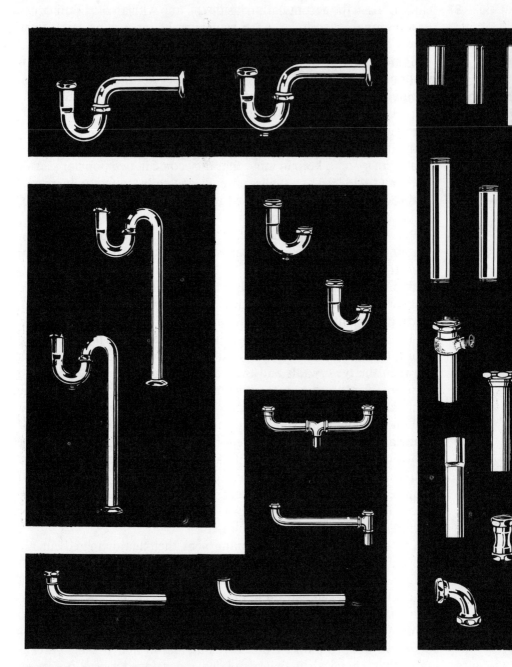

Figure 52 Traps and similar under-the-sink pipes you're likely to encounter around your home. Compare this page with your problem item and take this book with you to buy a replacement—even many hardware store clerks don't know the names.

minute's worth of hot water from the tap, the drain should be kept just about as free of grease and debris as if you store a can of deadly poisons under the sink and dump it into the plumbing periodically.

BATHROOM TROUBLES

Bathroom drains are mainly a problem of hair. If the long-haired men and women in your family brush their locks over the bathroom sink, and then forget to scoop up the loose strands that fall into the bowl, better open the trap under the sink and clean it out every few months. Hot water and lye won't do much to get rid of hair in the trap.

Those tiny, annoying pieces of soap that clutter up the soap dish don't belong in sink drains or toilets either. Believe it or not, those leftover ends from bars of soap can build up to quite an obstruction.

There are many common bathroom items that don't belong in a toilet—cotton, sanitary napkins or tampons, cellophane, paper cores from toilet tissue rolls, and baby's toys. Paper diapers are another unwelcome addition.

Antique car buffs who know how well a 1930 Chevy runs, won't be surprised, but the noisy old toilets can flush paper diapers away with hardly a whimper. It's those shiny, new, so-called quiet models that run into problems. To avoid as many hangups as possible, faithfully follow the instructions packed with disposable diapers. Remove the plastic backing and synthetic tissue liner. And then bounce the paper filler up and down in the toilet bowl several times to speed up its disintegration. Then, given a sufficient rush of water, the pulp will vanish and keep on going.

When a diaper is good and soaked before it gets changed, the entire waterlogged mass often plops into the toilet bowl in one piece. If you reach for the flush lever right away, you will jam up the plumbing for sure. Assuming you don't mind leaving the diaper in the toilet bowl for five minutes, a short soaking will give the paper a chance to disintegrate into a loose pulp on its own. But if you prefer not to wait, you will have to stir up the situation. And what better implement is there for the job than a *plunger*. Any family that flushes disposable diapers should have such a tool standing by. But don't ever flush more than one disposable diaper at a time. It isn't even a good idea to flush two of them in a row unless you have a toilet that is old (and probably noisy) but very powerful.

Check the water level in the flush tank to make sure that it is filling up to the waterline that is generally marked inside. You can adjust the

89

water level by carefully bending the rod that supports the float—that big copper or plastic ball. Bending it *upward will raise* the water level. To preserve our natural water supply, some ecology buffs have adjusted their tanks to flush with less water, occasionally by tossing a brick into the tank, thus saving almost a quart of water with every flush. However, you can't flush paper diapers and preserve water too. And wrapping them in individual plastic bags—one of the few good alternatives to flushing them—isn't exactly good ecological sense either. So again, you have to choose the alternative that is most tasteful to you personally.

For any plugged up drains, the old plunger is your best first line of attack. Fill the sink or tub or toilet with enough *hot* water to cover the plunger's rubber cup, unless quite a bit of waste water is already standing there. Fit the rubber cup over the drain, and then jerk the stick up and down. If at first you don't succeed, try again.

If your double sink (mainly in the kitchen) is in trouble, have someone hold a cover over one side as you work on the other. If you don't, the plunger will be idly blowing air into the air without forcing torrents of cleansing hot water against whatever hidden obstruction ails the sick drain pipe.

Assuming that water is able to trickle at least slowly through the drain, take a breather while the sink or tub or toilet empties. Then pour in boiling water and give it a chance to seep down to where the obstruction probably lies. Then go to work with the plunger again.

Snakes should be your second weapon against a stopped drain. Most people believe that those coils of stiff wire and springs that professional plumbers twist down the plugged pipe are terribly expensive. They're not, only a couple of dollars a small snake. A supersnake, ideal for home owners, will cost only a few dollars more. Sometimes what we call a snake is sold as an *auger*. A drain auger is designed with sinks in mind; a closet auger is for the toilet.

Snakes come in many sizes and shapes, but their essential function is similar. The coiled wire is gradually fed into the blocked drain. If there is a mesh over the drain, it may snap out of place or be held by a single screw. (The movable drain covers—pop ups—common to bathroom sinks and tubs will be discussed in some detail later in this chapter.) Most smaller snakes can be shoved right around or through practically any drain cover, however.

While the snake is being pushed progressively into the drainpipe, it should be rotated almost continuously. The end of the snake is designed to dislodge—hopefully—any and all obstructions or, in some products, to grab hold of certain solid obstructions (such as toothbrushes, toys, combs, and so forth) and retrieve them. The rotating motion not only aids in shoving aside blockages, but it helps

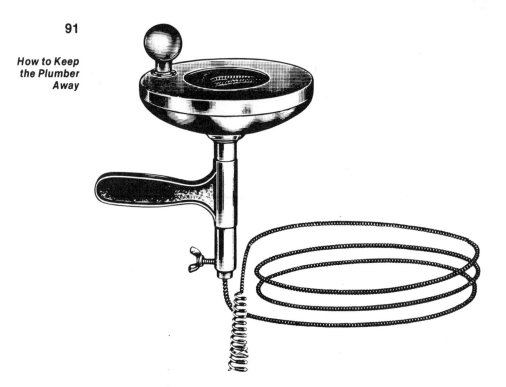

Figure 53   One popular, inexpensive type of plumber's snake
useful around the home.

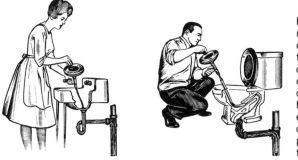

Figure 54   A snake,
unlike a plunger or
chemicals, goes directly
to the cause of a blocked
drain and generally
cures the problem
quickly. While the
handle is twisted, coiled
end is threaded through
drain and down into
pipe. In toilet, hose has
to protect the inner bowl.

the coiled wire to snake through the pipe, which often twists and bends
at traps, elbows, joints, and couplings. At least one snake on the
market is designed to be driven by an electric drill. What the ads for
this tool don't always point out, however, is that a variable speed drill,
preferably reversible, is required for efficient and safe performance.

Even after water seems to be flowing through the drain again, don't
stop using the snake or plunger immediately. If at first you dislodged
only a small part of a big obstruction, the rest may come back to haunt
you again very soon.

A bit of special care is required when you use a snake in the toilet bowl. For efficiency and to prevent damage to the porcelain bowl, a specially shaped hollow tube encircles the closet auger wire between the upper lip of the toilet bowl (the part on which the seat rests) and the throat through which waste water passes. Some snakes are specifically designed to fulfil this function with a foot or two of hollow tube built as an integral part of the entire snake. This specialized version works best only on toilet bowls, however. Others have an optional tube you can slip into place at will. But there is nothing wrong with improvising. A couple of feet of old garden hose or washing machine drain hose will accomplish much the same effect. And if you are just plain careful, you can use any common snake in your toilet.

If you do insist on using some of those powerful chemical drain cleaners, which cost as much as a good snake but are consumed in one day, handle the stuff as if you were in a chemical laboratory—because you will be! *Read all of the fine print first.*

In five seconds, the concentrated sulfuric acid, which is the active ingredient in many drain openers, can blind you, give you second degree burns, or eat completely through most synthetic and natural fiber clothing. If swallowed, it will burn away your throat and part of your stomach. Nevertheless, plastic bottles of it are sold across the counter and are nationally advertised for use in the home. If you feel that you must use such a chemical, buy only enough to handle the job you have in mind. Don't tempt fate by storing some of it for use at a future date.

The sulfuric acid chemicals are best suited for burning loose deposits of food, paper, hair, and similar organic wastes. A second common variety of chemical drain openers uses a solution of lye, which is best adapted for dissolving solidified grease and helps a bit on hardened soap.

Never, never, never attempt to mix the acid and the lye varieties of drain openers! Manufacturers of both types of product are very negligent about posting such a warning prominently on every bottle. The chemical reaction that could result from the acid and lye meeting inside a drainpipe would be so violent that boiling corrosive chemicals might bubble into your face. Weak pipes very well could be blown apart by the rapid increase in pressure caused by the reaction. This warning is not hypothetical—it has happened!

When using acid type drain cleaners, start slowly. Acid eats away at some iron pipes as well as it does organic solids. Weak joints or thin pipes might actually develop leaks because of the acid. If you have to use acids inside pipes that are not fully exposed so you can watch them, keep your eyes and nose alert for acid leaks, which would quickly destroy furniture, rugs, clothing, and almost anything else beneath the leak.

If all of your efforts to unblock the drain in a sink or tub have been for naught, it may be necessary to begin uncoupling the drainpipes at intervals. Later in this chapter, the actual technique for opening and closing pipe joints will be covered. For the moment, let's concentrate on *where* to look.

Guided by how long a piece of snake you have been able to twist down a drain, you should be able to measure to the most distant point along the drainpipe to which the passageway apparently is open. This time guided by the maximum length to which your snake will extend, find the next most distant coupling you can open and run your snake through the drainpipe first in one direction and then in the other. Meeting no obvious obstacles, you can proceed to the next plateau, dictated by the length of your snake and the location of convenient couplings in the drainpipes.

It is unlikely that you will be able to follow the suggestions of the above two paragraphs exactly. Life just isn't that simple. Couplings may be few and far between, they may be of types that do not lend themselves to opening unless the entire drain system is dismantled, plus the fact that age and corrosion can seal many joints so securely as to make them impractical to tamper with.

An alternate test to help you isolate the drain blockage with some precision is to pour water down the sink or tub after one selected pipe has been opened. If much of your drainpipe is concealed in walls and floors, for example, but you can find an easy coupling to open in the basement, have someone pour a pail of water into the balky drain. If the water runs out of your open drainpipe, obviously the blockage is farther down the line. Make certain that the *pitching* pail of water is smaller than the *catching* pail.

A second way to detect with some precision the location of drain blocks is to study where the pipes from working drains join the pipes from nonworking drains. Obviously the trouble should lie *above* the junction *or at that joint*. Your first suspicions should be directed against any spots where pipes change directions, bending to the left, right, up, or down.

If all of your efforts to remove some obstruction in the toilet itself have failed, it may be necessary to remove the appliance and work on the blockage from underneath. Figure 55 gives a cutaway side view of how a typical toilet is installed over a pipe, which is generally 4″ in diameter. The toilet and pipe connect via a hole cut into the bathroom floor, a hole you probably never realized was there.

First, turn off the water that fills the toilet tank. Then, all

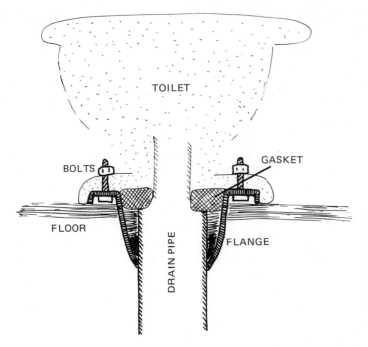

TOILET

BOLTS

GASKET

FLOOR

DRAIN PIPE

FLANGE

Figure 55 Cross-section of your toilet and how it is fastened to the floor. When removing it, bolts are unfastened and the ceramic bowl is pried up from floor. New wax gasket has to be installed when resecuring the bowl to floor.

connections between the tank and bowl must be disconnected with a pipe wrench.

There are seldom more than four bolts holding the bowl to the floor. With them removed, the bowl can be jiggled from side to side to break the seal that has kept water from leaking out until now. To keep water from leaking out once the bowl is loosened, it is advisable to bail out as much water as possible with a sponge or siphon (Figure 56).

The toilet bowl is much heavier than you might expect and quite fragile. So turn it onto one side or onto its top with care. If the toilet seat would be endangered by this, remove it first.

Once the obstruction has been removed, the bowl can be set back into place. A new wax gasket or seal should be used, available at hardware stores and plumbing suppliers, and the bottom of the bowl must be cleaned thoroughly to ensure a tight, leak-free operation again. Then bolt the bowl to the floor, being careful not to overtighten any of the nuts. When reinstalled, the bowl should not wobble even a little, but the nuts must not be tightened beyond what it takes to prevent that wobble.

For most efficient performance, the toilet bowl must be exactly level, which can be accomplished through the use of a carpenter's level laid across the top of the bowl with the seat raised (the seat or its hardware might be uneven even though the bowl itself is level). Be sure to check both for side-to-side and front-to-back levelness. A small amount of correction to the level can be accomplished by selectively tightening some nuts more than others. Large amounts of unevenness will require you to slip *shims* of thin wood, plastic, or tile under the low side.

If you take the toilet off the floor carefully in the first place, you will be able to watch for any shims that the original installer had to use. More than likely, you will have to duplicate that handiwork. When the bowl and tank are back in place, and all of the connecting plumbing and hardware reinstalled, you should have perfectly working equipment.

Both the toilet bowl and the water tank are definitely on the delicate side. But once they are installed well, neither is in danger of breaking or cracking with careful use. Hazards to them include dropping bottles or similar heavy objects on them; shoving, twisting, or banging against the tank or its cover; allowing water to freeze inside either the tank or the bowl; using a snake in the bowl that does not have

Figure 56 How to siphon water out of sink or other area. Find a hose long enough to reach from water to floor or chair at a level lower than water. Fill hose completely with water and hold fingers over ends. Keeping one end in water, lower other end to pail and release both fingers at once.

protective tubing, in which case the snake often becomes tangled in the bowl's passageways and requires excessive force to free.

A crack in either bowl or the tank can be remedied with ease. If a piece has been knocked loose *above the waterline,* that too is a relatively simple repair matter. If a piece has been broken out *beneath the waterline,* it's a tough repair headache, but you will probably prefer to try a patch job before investing the considerable amount of time and money required to make a complete replacement.

The key to repairing ceramic bathroom fixtures is to dry the damaged spot thoroughly. After the water seems to have all evaporated, aided by a heater or heat lamp, clean the spot with a solvent such as rubbing alcohol, which not only removes grease but helps to draw out additional moisture.

A filled epoxy glue makes the toughest repair material for a job such as broken toilets, but you will have to color it later with acrylic paints (see Chapter 4). If the original color of the tank or bowl matches one of the available silicone rubber adhesives (generally white, black,

Figure 57   Inside view of toilet tank. Trip lever raises flush ball and water runs into bowl, lowering float. Lowered float opens valve in ball cock so water flows through filler tube until float reaches top of water level once more.

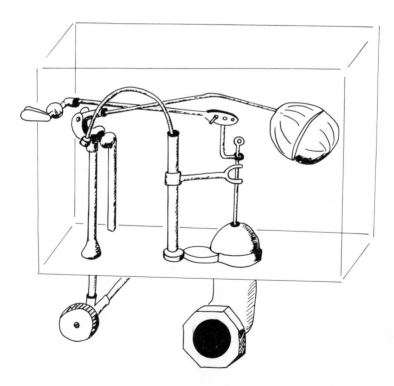

pink, tan, silver), that is a totally acceptable second choice. For a crack on the tank, the ideal job is done with epoxy on the dull surface inside and colored silicone rubber on the glossy outside. In that way you will be using the adhesive properties of both materials to the maximum and giving yourself insurance as well.

If you have no choice but to apply either the silicone or epoxy adhesive to a glossy surface, get rid of the gloss first. Sandpaper or emory cloth wrapped around your finger can wipe away the gloss for about ¼ " on each side of the crack.

Don't hurry the drying time for any repairs to toilet bowls or tanks. The adhesives must be thoroughly set before the surge of cold water is allowed back in. A heater or heat lamp can speed things up, but give the repair a chance to cool down before the first plunge into the cold water.

You can't expect to make a totally invisible repair on a ceramic bowl or tank. To do so, you would have to grind away enough of the material at the break so that a sufficient quantity of epoxy or silicone glue could be applied without causing a bulge. Ceramics are so brittle, however, that your grinding efforts could very well result in even worse damage. If your repair is on the tank, department stores already stock the ideal camouflage for you—a cotton shag cover, which comes in colors to match or contrast with rugs.

FAUCET LEAKS

A small leak in a faucet can keep some people awake all night. Much ado has been made about the faucet washer, the villain responsible for most leaky faucets. But instead of simply showing people how quickly they can insert a three-for-a-nickel new washer to stop the leak, companies market superwashers and super-superwashers, all of which do a better job to be sure.

Your faucet is a surprisingly uncomplicated device, as Figure 58 hopefully proves. A leaky faucet almost always stems from the fact that water can force its way past the bibb washer even when the appliance is fully turned off. This may be the fault of the washer itself, which is the case in most new, well-built faucets. On faucets that have seen plenty of wear and water, or on cheap newer ones, the seat into which the washer fits is often at fault. Leaks will appear most often in the hot water faucet because the washers do not hold their own as well under heat.

Take the leaky faucet apart to prove to yourself that you really can do it. First locate a shutoff value on the hot or cold waterline

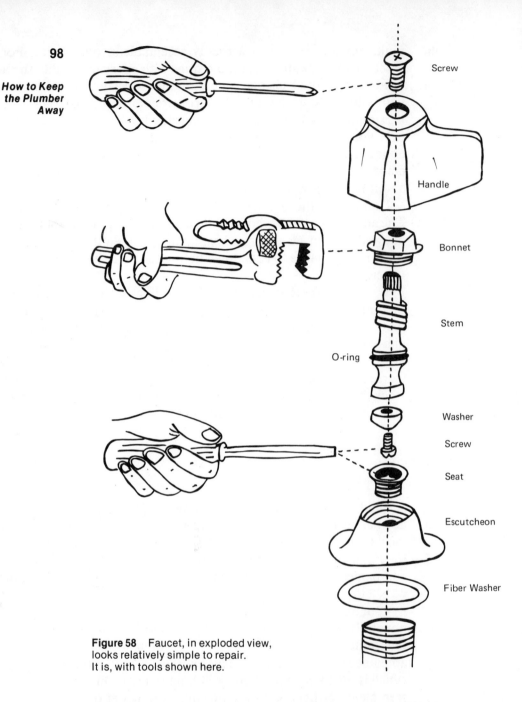

Screw

Handle

Bonnet

Stem

O-ring

Washer

Screw

Seat

Escutcheon

Fiber Washer

Figure 58 Faucet, in exploded view,
looks relatively simple to repair.
It is, with tools shown here.

connecting to the faucet. There should be a set of shutoff values within
a few feet of every sink, tub, or toilet, but that depends upon local
plumbing codes and the craftsmanship of the plumbing contractor in
charge of your original installation. Turn the value fully clockwise to
shut off the water.

Valve and *faucet* are not completely interchangeable words. The word "valve" covers all controls for liquids, gas, or other materials moving *through pipes.* A "faucet" is the *end control,* the regulator of how much liquid flows out of a pipe. So if the valve has pipes on both sides of it, it's truly a valve. If it has a pipe on only one side of it and discharges water or another liquid on the other side, the correct word is faucet.

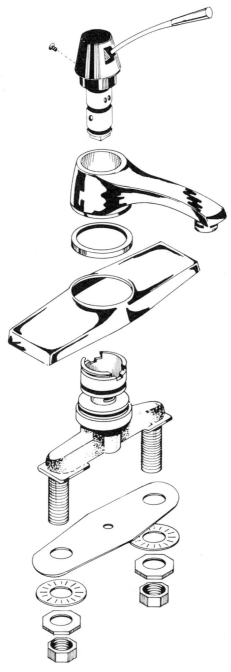

Figure 59 One-hand faucet, in exploded view, seems even easier to repair than traditional types. It is, assuming you can find the manufacturer's exact replacement parts.

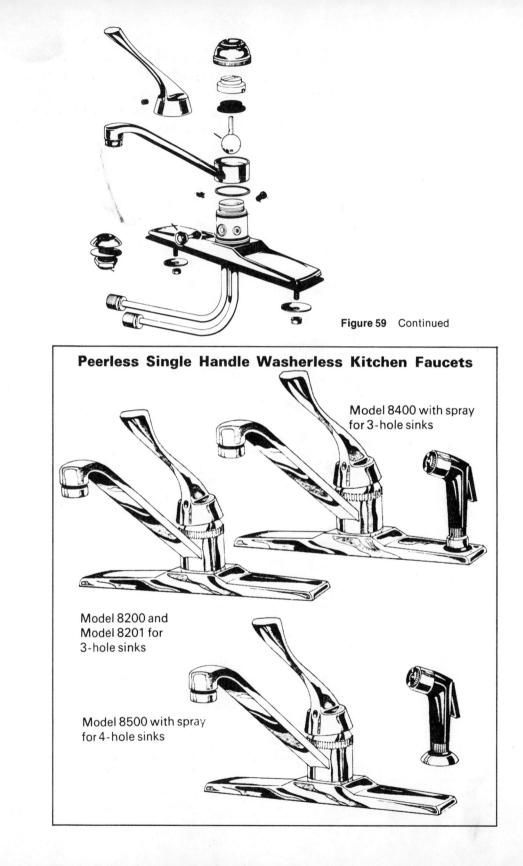

Figure 59 Continued

Peerless Single Handle Washerless Kitchen Faucets

Model 8400 with spray
for 3-hole sinks

Model 8200 and
Model 8201 for
3-hole sinks

Model 8500 with spray
for 4-hole sinks

Should any maintenance ever be necessary on this faucet, you can do that yourself, too. Three basic repair kits are available in store plumbing departments.

1. If you should have a leak under handle—follow steps A, N, O, and P.

2. If you should have a leak from spout—follow steps A, B, C, D and J, K, L, M, N, O. and P.

3. If you should have a leak from around spout collar—follow steps A, B, E, F and I, M, N, O, and P.

4. If you should have diverter failure on spray models—follow steps A, B, E, G and H, M, N, O, and P.

Shut off water supply

A. Loosen set screw and lift off handle.

B. Unscrew cap assembly and lift off.

C. Remove cam assembly and ball by lifting up on ball stem.

D. Lift both seats and springs out of sockets in body.

E. Gently rotate spout and lift off.

F. Cut "O" rings and remove from body.

Figure 59 Continued

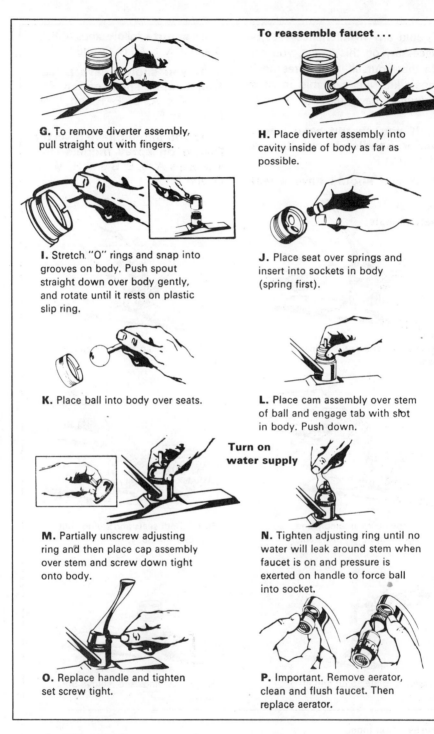

To reassemble faucet ...

G. To remove diverter assembly, pull straight out with fingers.

H. Place diverter assembly into cavity inside of body as far as possible.

I. Stretch "O" rings and snap into grooves on body. Push spout straight down over body gently, and rotate until it rests on plastic slip ring.

J. Place seat over springs and insert into sockets in body (spring first).

K. Place ball into body over seats.

L. Place cam assembly over stem of ball and engage tab with slot in body. Push down.

Turn on water supply

M. Partially unscrew adjusting ring and then place cap assembly over stem and screw down tight onto body.

N. Tighten adjusting ring until no water will leak around stem when faucet is on and pressure is exerted on handle to force ball into socket.

O. Replace handle and tighten set screw tight.

P. Important. Remove aerator, clean and flush faucet. Then replace aerator.

Figure 59 Concluded

A small pipe wrench is the preferred tool for disassembling a faucet. However, a vice grip pliers, a large crescent wrench, or even one of the larger common pliers or channel lock pliers will do. (Chapter 2 explained these tools.) In any case, if you want to protect the finish on your faucets, wrap several layers of tape around any surfaces that the wrench or pliers will grab.

The *handle* of a faucet often comes off only after considerable muscle is applied to it. Part of the reason is due to the fact that the handle is too often made of a different metal than the stem onto which it fits. Whenever two different metals are in contact, particularly in the presence of water, an electrochemical reaction similar to that powering a battery takes place, generally forming corrosion as a by-product. You may have to tap the handle gently with a hammer (protecting the polished surface with wood or tape) or pry at it.

Next comes the *packing nut*. Again, protect the item against scratches if it is exposed. And finally you can take out the working, moving part, the *stem*. Often it will be necessary to slip the handle back in place to turn out the stem. To remove it, simply turn the stem as if you were turning the water on. Generally, the cold water turns on clockwise and the hot water counterclockwise (at least, in the United States).

Although the ribbed top of the stem is almost always standardized so that replacement handles by dozens of different manufacturers will fit, the stem itself is anything but standard. If you must replace one, the fastest and surest way is to leave the water turned off (both hot and cold if the faucet is part of a mixer where two handles control the flow out of a single pipe as in the kitchen sink or bathtub). Take the broken stem with you to a plumbing supply outlet. Hardware stores do not always stock replacement stems unless they specialize in selling to professional plumbers, although larger stores will stock some of the more popular brands used locally.

There is a universal replacement stem on the market, however. It is billed as being able to duplicate almost any stem ever made. And maybe it can. Although it may not do the job 100 percent as well as the exact replacement, it is bound to work better than no stem at all! And the universal stem is on sale at most local hardware shops.

At the bottom of the stem you remove from a drippy faucet, you may still find the remnants of the faulty rubber washer. At the very least, the brass screw that held the washer in place should still be there. These valve washers (still called bibb washers by some) generally are cone-shaped today, in which case a cone-shaped replacement should be fitted into place and attached either with the original brass screw or with one of the new ones that often come with a hardware store replacement kit. If your faucet had a flat washer, or it seems from

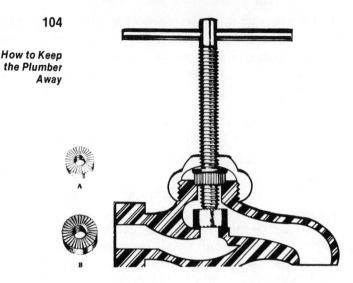

Figure 60 Seat dresser simply hones the rough edges off faucet's seat, making sure the faucet stops leaking and stops chewing up rubber washers so quickly.

whatever evidence remains that the original washer was flat, try to replace it with a flat one.

The rim around the stem is important to good faucet operation. It should be cleaned and inspected before a new washer is installed. If minor blemishes are present on the bottom edge, they can be removed with a small file. But if serious dents are present, or if part of the rim has vanished, you should buy a replacement stem, not as large an investment as you might imagine.

Replacement washers should be screwed into place firmly but not with so much pressure as to compact them. They should retain their original shape on the bottom of the stem.

Before inserting the stem, examine the valve seat that will still be inside the faucet. A flashlight often permits visual inspection, but a finger rubbed around the seat is sufficient. It should feel smooth to the touch. Roughness will cause leaking at once and lead to the premature end of your new washer. Unless you happen to have a valve seat reamer in your toolbox, you will want to put the faucet back together, faulty seat and all, until you can make a trip to the hardware store for another inexpensive tool or two.

A *valve seat reamer* is sold under various odd names such as "drip stopper reseater kit" and "faucet fixer kit." The kit, among sundry other hardware it includes, has a hardened steel cutting disk (or more than one, each intended for a particular size of faucet seat). With the disk in place, plus attached rods and threads, the roughness on a brass faucet seat is shaved away. The resulting smooth seat meshes firmly with a new washer and provides leakless sinks again. If the seat is beyond such a simple cure, however, heavier medicine is called for.

Many valve seats are replaceable. A large screwdriver inserted deeply into the opening in the brass seat might be able to twist it loose (the threads turn counterclockwise). Even on some replaceable seats, age and corrosion have allied to freeze them in place. In that event, as well as with faucets made without replaceable seats, a combination reamer and threader tool accomplishes a repair with relative ease.

The inexpensive *reseating tool* is attached to a disassembled faucet according to the manufacturer's instructions (see Figure 60). The *reamer* part of this tool is twisted until it has gouged out the old seat, at which time the *tap* portion cuts new threads into the remaining metal. Along with most reseating tools comes a selection of threaded brass replacement seats. The seats, as well as the cutting ends of this tool, come in sizes matched to the size of your faucet seat, generally ¼ " or ⅜ ", both requiring a ⅜ " reseating tool, or a larger size that receives its own tool, ½ ", ⅝ ", and ¾ ". If you measure the size of the washer or rim at the bottom of the faucet stem, you'll know how large a reamer and threader tool you should buy or borrow. The same size factor applies to the valve seat reamer described above and to replacement seats or washers. Washer sizes are as irrational as pipe sizes. Figure 61 compares dimensions with trade nomenclature.

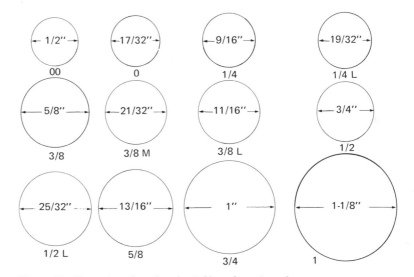

Figure 61 Faucet washer size chart. Since faucet washers come in so many sizes, and people often pull them out of faucets after they're deteriorated to the point where their markings are gone, you can use this chart to find the trade name for whatever size washer your faucet takes. Simply lay old washer on the circle that matches its size and that's its trade name. Numbers below the circles are "trade-size" names. Numbers inside the circles are the actual dimensions of the washers.

When smoothing or reaming and threading a seat, it is important that you remove as much of the waste metal as possible to avoid clogging the threaded portion of the valve stem or slicing your new washer. Ideally, you should open the shutoff valve momentarily to let the gush of water wash the metal out of the faucet area.

The replacement brass seat, treated first with grease or vaseline for protection and lubrication, is slipped onto the blade end of a screwdriver and carefully lowered into place, then screwed in securely (turning clockwise). Then you can replace the stem by turning it in exactly as if you were turning off the water. Tighten snugly with a wrench.

Replace the packing nut and tighten it securely but not vengefully. The packing nut prevents water from leaking over the top of the stem when the faucet is turned off, but if you overtighten the packing nut, it becomes too difficult to turn on the faucet. Beneath the packing nut is a fibrous substance of some sort—it's called *packing* in the trade— which combines with just a moderate amount of pressure from the packing nut to seal in the water.

If water persists in leaking under the packing nut unless you tighten it excessively, invest in some faucet packing. Sometimes a faucet repair kit includes some. Most of the faucet packing material looks like ordinary string or twine, although it does (or is supposed to) contain some sealing aids. The best packing for home use is made of Teflon and comes in a shiny white cord. In a pinch, however, ordinary string or twine can be pressed into service.

Packing material plays an important leak-preventing role in many places besides faucets around your home. The swiveling outlet on your kitchen sink, for instance, depends on the fact that packing and the compression nut combine to hold water inside the apparatus. Even the various drainpipe connections discussed earlier require packing. It is generally a good idea to have fresh packing materials on hand whenever such a connection has to be disconnected and then reassembled.

For those of you delighted by the notion that humankind has finally found an alternate solution to the faucet drip—an alternate, that is, besides the simple remedy of just replacing the washer, a five-minute job after you've sweated through it the first time—there are super-washer, super-superwashers, and no washers at all.

Traditional rubber faucet washers last a minimum of several months even on a busy hot water faucet, much longer on cold water taps. But now that plastics have been developed to tackle the same job in a tougher fashion, it is possible to extend the time between washer changes. Superwashers come in bright colors, usually red and baby blue, and bear such colorful names as Grizzly and Pignose.

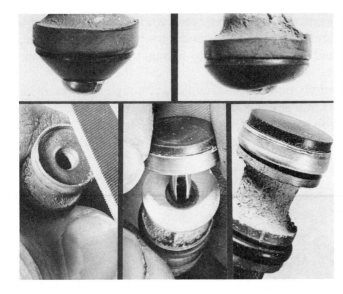

Figure 62 Super washers compete with old-fashioned rubber washers in the nickel and dime faucet repair business. Top left—old fashioned washer screwed in properly. Top right—it's screwed in too tightly and will wear out prematurely. Center—to use No-Rotate washers, you have to file away rim from faucet's stem (left), shove prongs of washer into screw hole (center), and then insert stem with new washer back into faucet. Bottom, view of what's available in faucet washer field: left—washerless stem; center top—No-Rotate washers and one of them inserted on old stem; center bottom—old-fashioned washers above hard rubber replacement washers reputed to last longer; right—old-fashioned washer on stem above replacement brass seat that will help all kinds of washers last longer.

An even more novel twist to the faucet washer is a nonrotating washer. Much of the wear and tear on faucet washers comes from the fact that they twist against the brass seat. So a washer is now available that does not rotate. If you buy some, however, you had better be confident of the results because the installation instructions call for ruining an otherwise good rim at the bottom of your faucet stem. If for some reason this super-superwasher doesn't work for you, you will have a hard time going back to a more conventional type washer (but then maybe that's the idea).

107   If you have a yen to replace an old faucet with a washerless faucet or other new one for practical or aesthetic reasons, it can be done easily. However, there are so many fancy replacement handles available, even in 24 karat gold and platinum, that you might want to stop at that level.

Installing an entirely new faucet assembly, although it represents a significant investment, is not a difficult job. If you've successfully read this far, the job should come easily. Even the fanciest single lever or double faucet sets for bathroom or kitchen sinks seldom require

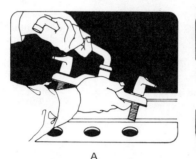
A

B

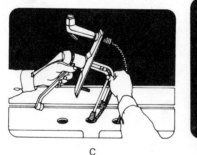
C

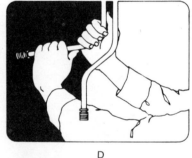
D

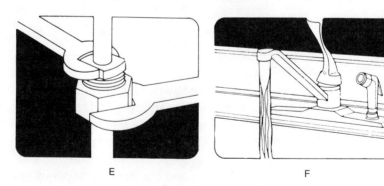

E   F

Figure 63   Installing new faucet: (A) requires that you remove old one first. Then put gaskets or other hardware into place on new one (B). Slip new faucet into old holes (C) and bend pipes (D) to meet up with ends of old ones. Tighten connections (E) and then turn on water (F) for new faucet.

more than two nuts to hold them in place. New faucets and handles usually are sold as an integral part of an entire set.

Before rushing to the store to select a shiny new superfaucet, there are several items to be checked in advance. Measure the distance between the center of the faucets. Faucets commonly come in what trade users call 4″ centers, 6″ centers, 8″ centers, and so on. Some standardization has taken place, however. Bathrooms now use a 4″ center faucet set on sinks and 8″ center layouts for showers. Kitchen sinks most often have 8″ centers.

Count the number of holes in the kitchen sink before buying a new set of faucets. This is not as obvious as it seems. If a deck covers the top of the sink, you may not be able to see for sure whether there is one hole for the hot water, one hole for the cold water, plus a third hole for the spout through which runs the mixture of hot and cold. With a flashlight, peer under the sink if a deck hides the top.

Kitchen sinks can be two hole, three hole, or four hole, and the number determine what kind of faucet set you must buy. Two holes require what is called an exposed deck faucet. Hot water runs through one hole, cold through the other, and the two streams are mixed within the deck itself before moving into the spout.

With three holes, you have the option of buying either a concealed deck faucet set (which means that the porcelain of the sink will be seen between handles and spout) or an exposed deck. Four hole sinks are designed for use with a spray attachment. If someone once decided to do without the spray, a snap-in cover may partially conceal the fourth hole. some single handle kitchen faucet sets are able to include the spray attachment on the deck, thus using a three hole sink for four holes worth of convenience.

Bathroom sinks have traditionally been two hole designs, although a small hole in the center accommodates the pop up handle. A few very fancy models have widespread handles—up to 16″—with a third hold in the center for a mixer spout.

Plan for the installation of new faucets in advance. Study the old connection. If you're extremely lucky, it will have a flexible tube linking the faucet itself with the solid plumbing farther down the line. If not, plan to add the flexible connector. Determine where the next closest coupling in the pipe has been placed; it might be at the shutoff valve if they were stuck under the sink. If there isn't a shutoff valve on the hot and cold waterlines immediately beneath the sink, you might want to install one. In the plumbing trade, those small shutoff valves are known as *stops.*

If your pipes to the sink run out of the floor, you will want a *straight stop.* And if the pipes come out of the wall, an *angle stop* will not only give you the convenience of a shutoff valve, it will at the same time make the right-angle bend necessary to link the horizontal pipes of the faucets with the vertical pipes sticking out of the way. The flexible supply tubes conveniently connect directly to the stops.

Stops, both the straight and angled variety, are commonly available for use with pipes measuring either ½ " or ⅜ " in the threaded iron types or for ½ " copper tubing that is soldered into place. Supply tubes come most often in 12 " and 20 " lengths, although longer sizes are available if you are willing to shop to find them. In case you need extra fittings to adapt your own sink and plumbing into an integrated system again, attachments to the flexible supply tubes are called *compression fittings* and are either brass or chrome plated.

The comprehensive pictorial manual displayed in Figure 8 should show about all you need to begin installing new faucets. That and courage or confidence.

One faucet company in Indiana has built its business around do-it-yourself faucet installers. Its ad says, "Install this washerless two handle faucet over the weekend." Like most ads, it exaggerates— you should be able to do it in an afternoon even if you must stop to do other things.

Now that you have mastered the techniques for getting water out of faucets and into tubs, sinks, and toilets, then out again through cloggable drains, let's give some attention to how the drains themselves are hooked to the sinks and tubs. Sometime you may be in the market for some new drains due to old age or new faucet sets. Since the water draining out of your kitchen and bathroom appliances is under

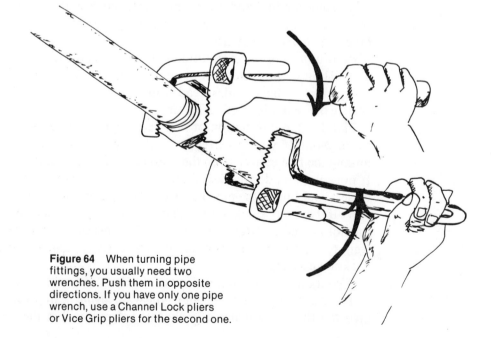

Figure 64 When turning pipe fittings, you usually need two wrenches. Push them in opposite directions. If you have only one pipe wrench, use a Channel Lock pliers or Vice Grip pliers for the second one.

no pressure except what gravity gives it, the pipes have to be many times larger than the water supply pipes from which the water squirts with a pressure of perhaps 25 pounds per square inch.

In older original plumbing installations, the various traps were made from the same heavy type of iron as were the supply pipes. Since rigid pipes were used all the way from the sink drain outlet to the street, the entire system had to be lined up carefully every inch of the way. Today's plumbers prefer to use a more flexible system.

The opening at the bottom of the sink is fitted with a *plug top*, a *flange,* and *lock nut*, all of which are sealed by one rubber washer under the flange and another one generally under the lock nut. Plumbers putty is used instead of washers in some installations, but you will be happier to use the washers instead of putty unless all else fails. Some stores refer to the plug top as a *sink strainer assembly* if it goes into the kitchen sink and as a *pop up assembly* for the bathroom sink or tub (see Figure 65).

In a bathroom sink, which usually has an overflow vent, a *vented plug top* is employed as shown in Figure 65. The overflow drain, which is built into the body of the sink itself, matches the vent opening in the plug top; both are quite well standardized. In your kitchen, where there is no overflow—unfortunately—if you accidentally bought a *vented* plug top instead of an *unvented* one, drain water would pour through the vent because kitchen sinks do not match up any overflow drain to the vent.

You will seldom encounter a leak in the plug top itself. The rubber washers or putty in the apparatus may deteriorate, but corrosion and other debris accumulate fast enough and permanently enough to block any drips. Most strainer assemblies in the kitchen are replaced because they have become unsightly or part has broken away. In the bathroom, a broken pop up is the added excuse for investing in a whole new plug top.

Plug tops have threads about 4″ in diameter, larger than most wrenches found in a home. So you have two alternatives for removing a plug top: (1) spend a few dollars to buy a wrench designed specifically for working with large nuts found in such plumbing installations, or (2) dig out your hammer and a small block of wood. Instead of replacing the strainer assembly in your kitchen sink with a traditional model, at least one company sells a plug top made especially for home repair people. It requires only a screwdriver to accomplish successful installation.

By employing a series of *slip joints*—joints that slip together and are secured by *slip nuts*—both the length and vertical position of drainpipes can be varied to match the location of the sink drain with the location of your home's original drainpipe. In case the drainpipe goes

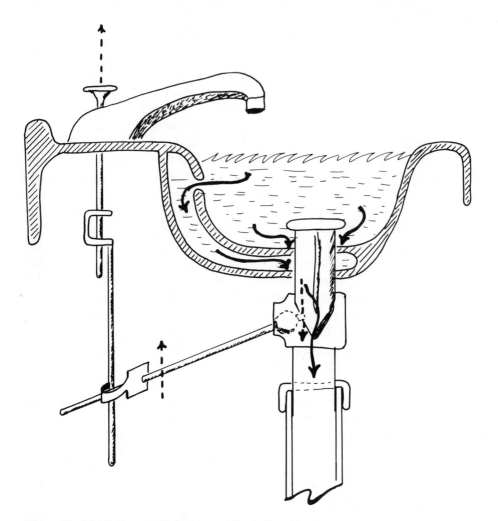

Figure 65 Sink drains usually have a vent (for bathroom models) that allows water to overflow rather than run onto floor. Pop-up is usual way to open and close drain.

through the bathroom or kitchen wall behind the sink instead of through the floor, the trap ends up moving horizontally instead of vertically, and plumbers then call it a P-trap instead of an S-trap. The first half of both a P-trap and an S-trap is a J-bend.

The tubes that connect the sink or tub to a trap and that connect the trap to the main drainpipes are called *tailpieces*. Some are threaded like ordinary pipes, but now most are held in place by simply being slipped inside of a threaded plug top, trap, or main drainpipe and secured by a slip nut (also called a *slip joint nut* or a *lock nut*). It is important that washers be fitted underneath the slip nuts to make the connections watertight.

Those handy mechanical drain openers and closers that start to need adjustment after a few years of use in a bathroom sink are called *pop ups* in the plumbing trade. Think of the gadget as a seesaw. At the heart of almost every pop up is a seesaw called the *operating lever*. A large, solid ball on the lever provides the fulcrum for the seesaw to seesaw on, and a lever extends in both directions from the ball. One end of the operating lever is attached to the stopper, which moves up and down to empty or retain water. The other end of the operating lever is attached to the *operating rod*, which in turn is capped by the knob extending from the top of your sink (see Figure 66).

If the knob seems to move up much too far before the stopper closes tightly, or if the stopper won't close tightly enough no matter how far the knob is pulled, chances are the *connector* must be adjusted upward. Loosen the set screw, which holds the connector to the operating rod, and close the stopper tightly by hand. Now move the knob to about where you would like it to be when the drain is fully stoppered—about ¾ " to 1 " above its lowest resting place. With both the stopper and the knob held in place, tighten the set screw again. If the apparatus works properly once more, you've done it. If not, move on deeper.

Dirt, corrosion, or worse may be clinging to the bottom of the stop-

Figure 66   Exploded view of typical pop-up drain assembly which can be bought at hardware or plumbing supply stores to replace old one.

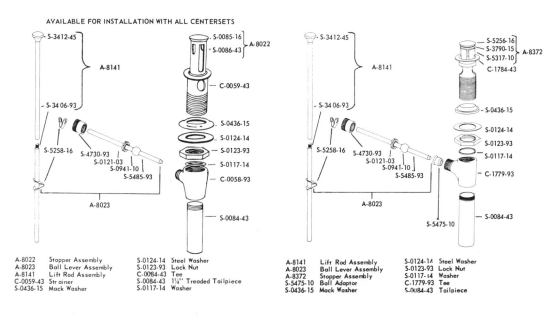

AVAILABLE FOR INSTALLATION WITH ALL CENTERSETS

A-8022	Stopper Assembly
A-8023	Ball Lever Assembly
A-8141	Lift Rod Assembly
C-0059-43	Strainer
S-0436-15	Mack Washer

S-0124-14	Steel Washer
S-0123-93	Lock Nut
C-0084-43	Tee
S-0084-43	1¼" Treaded Tailpiece
S-0117-14	Washer

A-8141	Lift Rod Assembly
A-8023	Ball Lever Assembly
A-8372	Stopper Assembly
S-5475-10	Ball Adaptor
S-0436-15	Mack Washer

S-0124-14	Steel Washer
S-0123-93	Lock Nut
S-0117-14	Washer
C-1779-93	Tee
S-0084-43	Tailpiece

per, like barnacles on a well-worn ship. Loosen the set screw again and slide the operating rod up and out of the connector. The preferred tool is a small box wrench. A pipe wrench is used to loosen the *stuffing box nut*. The nut should be removed carefully because a large (although harmless) spring is housed inside the stuffing box. With the operating lever pulled out, the stopper can be lifted up and out. All parts, including the spring, should be cleaned well with scouring powder or something heavier.

Invest in a new gasket for the stuffing box nut. Alternately, you can make one with faucet packing cord or even silicone sealant (see Chapter 3). If the spring is broken or if corrosion has left it damaged or lifeless, replace it. Once you have all parts back in place and the apparatus has been adjusted in the manner described earlier, the pop up should "pop up" just right again.

The spring in a pop up can be replaced with a standard one from the collection a large hardware store should have. And if the set screw on the connector becomes too worn, the old hole can be rethreaded. Choose a tap (see Chapter 3) a size or two larger than the old hole, and also a size that fits whatever new set screw you can buy. Beyond those two items, replacement parts for an ailing pop up assembly are hard to come by largely due to a lack of standardization of sizes and shapes. Try to locate a good plumbing supplier who handles parts for the original manufacturer of your sink or pop up, but don't count too heavily on much success. By the time a pop up is beyond repair, let's hope the faucets themselves are so old that you will be willing to replace the entire faucet and pop up set.

Leaks in any of the pipes already mentioned and those yet to come are very rare except in brand new installations or where pipes have been abused by frequent baths of drain opener chemicals. The effects of slow corrosion and particles left behind by hard water tend to seal pipes together more firmly with every year they remain in use. When leaks do occur, most often they will appear at joints, and then principally after some part of the pipe system has been disturbed.

If you think that you have found a leak somewhere between the joints of a pipe, look carefully. The leak itself might actually be at the nearest union or coupling, but the water may be flowing almost unnoticed along the pipe until, for some reason, the leak suddenly drips downward. Wrap your fingers about the pipe both upstream and downstream of the leak. The flow of water generally will stop and start dripping from the moist hand if it originates from a nearby joint. A leak in the midst of a length of pipe, unless it has been caused by some specific malady, can be a signal that the entire system of pipes is growing old and may need replacing soon. When copper tubing or plastic pipe has been used for a plumbing job, however, it will occasionally spring a leak where the tube once had to endure an inept bend or excessive strain.

Leaks in drainpipes and water supply pipes can be stopped with epoxy glues. If the water supply can be shut off, clean the area around the leak and allow it to dry thoroughly before applying the epoxy. Even if pressure on the leaky pipe cannot be removed, most epoxy glues will work anyway since they depend on their own internal chemical reaction to set.

Mix the two-part epoxy glue thoroughly and hold it onto the leaky pipe with some absorbent material such as a strip of cotton or fiberglass. If you use ordinary epoxy resins, several wrappings of the cloth soaked in plenty of the glue is best. With the thicker aluminum or iron-filled epoxies, one or two layers work best. If water pressure is still forcing on the leak, the wrapping is particularly critical. You must wrap the pipe thoroughly enough to stop the leak until the glue has had time to set.

With particularly ornery leaks, it may be necessary to add a C-clamp. The clamp exerts more pressure against the leaky spot than your cloth bindings can. Protect the clamp from the epoxy glue, however, with a piece of rubber or some other nonporous material. Otherwise the clamp may become a permanent part of the repair.

Should you find a leaky joint in the pipe system, it is doubtful whether sealing it with an epoxy glue is the best alternative. Once the durable epoxy patch has set, there will be almost no practical way for you to ever separate the pipes at that particular sealed junction. Most leaks that occur at a joint come from faulty use of the fitting.

Two lengths of pipe should line up well *before* a fitting is used to join them. If the union, tee, coupling, elbow, or any other fitting has not only to *unite* the pipes but *align* them as well, there probably is so much sideways pressure on the fitting threads that water is seeping through.

Most people do not realize that the threads on a pipe are *tapered*. The thread at the end of a pipe fits less snugly into a fitting than the final thread at the inside portion. Therefore, the pipe and its matching fitting have to be threaded together far enough to result in a tight fit.

Pipes and pipe fittings are not designed to create leakproof unions by themselves. It is necessary to apply a substance that plumbers call *pipe dope.* The dope not only helps to form a watertight seal, but it hopefully keeps the joined threads from freezing together, a condition that makes for very tough removal later. Dope comes in tubes or cans of varying sizes. Don't scrimp on this important, inexpensive substance.

Pipe size is expressed by measuring the *approximate inside diameter.* What is called a 1″ iron pipe has an inside that actually measures

1.049" in diameter and some 1.315" outside (about 1 5/16") (see Figure 67). There is no real need to understand the long history that has led to such an apparently irrational numbering system. You will simply have to live with it if you expect to buy a few pieces of pipe or fittings. Figure 67 also will help you to identify the size of a particular pipe you may have to replace (or a fitting that goes with it) in case you prefer to uncouple it only after a replacement is at hand. Fittings, by the way, are identified by the size of pipe on which they fit.

Figure 68 spells out the names for various fittings that are used to join, bend, split, or change the size of pipes throughout plumbing systems. The ones you purchase should be made of the same material as your home's existing pipes—iron, brass, or plastic. Mixing brass pipes with iron can cause premature corrosion, and mixing plastic fittings into the midst of metal pipes is often impractical.

Much has been written about some conspiracy between the plumbers' union and plumbing contractors and plumbing pipe suppliers to keep plastic plumbing material off the general market. There may be some amount of truth in the tales, but plastic pipes were

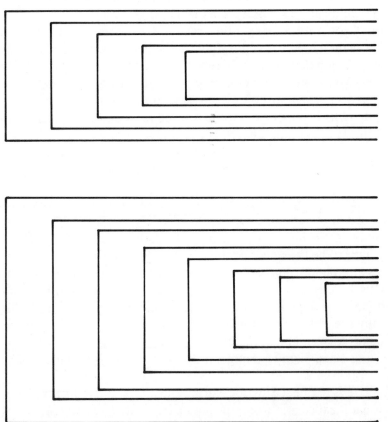

Figure 67 Pipe sizes seem irrational to novice fix-it people. Match up old piece of pipe to these drawings, and you'll know instantly what size to ask for. (Size does not match actual measurements of pipe due to old tradition.)

Fig. 67 Actual Size of Pipes Compared to Trade Name Sizes

Iron Pipe (in inches)

Trade Name Size	Inside Diameter		Outside Diameter		Circumference		No. of Threads per Inch
¼ inch	.364	⅜	.540	⁹⁄₁₆	1.696	1¹¹⁄₁₆	18
⅜ inch	.493	½	.675	¹¹⁄₁₆	2.121	2⅛	18
½ inch	.622	⅝	.840	¹³⁄₁₆	2.639	2⅝	14
¾ inch	.824	¹³⁄₁₆	1.050	1¹⁄₁₆	3.299	3⁵⁄₁₆	14
1 inch	1.049	1¹⁄₁₆	1.315	1⁵⁄₁₆	4.131	4⅛	11½
1¼ inch	1.380	1⅜	1.660	1¹¹⁄₁₆	5.215	5³⁄₁₆	11½
1½ inch	1.610	1⅝	1.900	1⅞	5.969	6	11½
2 inch	2.067	2¹⁄₁₆	2.375	2⅜	7.461	7⁷⁄₁₆	11½
2½ inch	2.469	2½	2.875	2⅞	9.032	9¹⁄₁₆	8

Copper Tubing, Type "L" (in inches)

⅜ inch	.430	⁷⁄₁₆	.500	½	1.571	1⁹⁄₁₆	
½ inch	.545	⁹⁄₁₆	.625	⅝	1.964	1¹⁵⁄₁₆	
¾ inch	.785	¹³⁄₁₆	.875	⅞	2.749	2¾	
1 inch	1.025	1	1.125	1⅛	3.534	3⁹⁄₁₆	
1¼ inch	1.265	1⅞	1.375	1⅜	4.320	4⁵⁄₁₆	
1½ inch	1.505	1½	1.625	1⅝	5.105	5⅛	

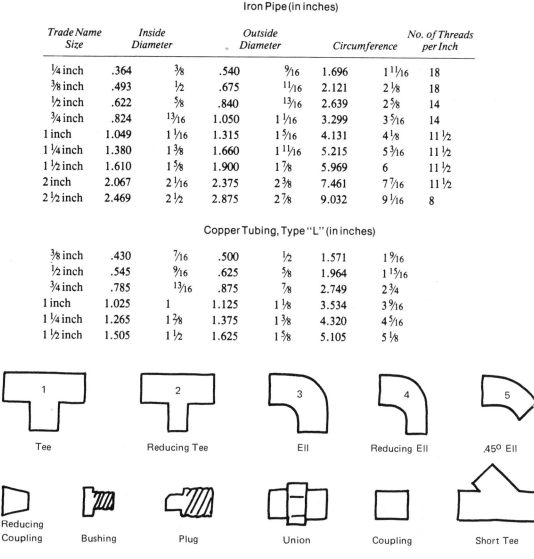

1 Tee

2 Reducing Tee

3 Ell

4 Reducing Ell

5 .45° Ell

Reducing Coupling

Bushing

Plug

Union

Coupling

Short Tee

Figure 68 Fittings for plumbing work are easier to get if you know their trade name.

only recently highly enough developed to be trusted as an across the board replacement for the older, heavier brass or iron pipes. This is particularly true in the case of hot water systems.

Plastic pipe comes in many different chemical types. Most of the products in use for home plumbing are joined by fittings fastened together with solvents that melt part of both the pipe and the fitting, leaving a solid connection when the solvent evaporates. *Chemical welding* is the trade jargon for this procedure.

117

Cut rigid plastic pipes to size with a fine toothed saw such as a hacksaw. Try on the fitting to make sure that a good exists. Then dab the proper solvent onto the *outside of the pipe* and *inside of the fitting*. The pipe and fitting are shoved together quickly and firmly, then twisted to ensure that the solvent is uniformly spread. The weld dries in minutes. Each chemical variety of pipe requires its own solvent.

Once a chemical weld is finished, the fitting can never be removed, unlike plumbing procedures for brass or iron pipe. The pipe will have to be sawed apart, a very easy thing to accomplish. Rigid plastic pipe is relatively flexible. But it is not flexible enough to bend around corners. Elbows must be used. It is flaccid enough that minor corrections in direction and layout over the length of a long stretch of pipe are quite feasible.

Polyethylene plastic pipe is highly flexible but is seldom used inside of a house. If it is used for drinking water supplies, make certain that the product carries a seal from the National Sanitation Foundation, which indicates that the pipe is approved for use with drinking water. Polyethylene can be bent around corners and over obstructions. Fittings such as tees are added by cutting the pipe with a sharp knife or a fine-toothed hacksaw. The fitting slips *inside* the pipe, then a metal clamp secures the joint from the outside. Polyethylene can be left in place and filled with water during freezing weather, but it cannot be used for hot water. Plastic pipes able to withstand the temperatures of hot water are generally very clearly marked because their price is substantially above other plastic pipes.

Plastic pipes are proving most valuable for home drain systems because both temperature and pressure there are moderate. Before plastic pipe, the iron materials were so heavy and so hard to work with that they eluded the skills of all but the most rugged amateurs. Even a 6″ plastic pipe can be carried and erected with ease, but a 6″ cast iron drainpipe requires the muscles of two strong people. Since plastic often replaces only a portion of existing drain systems, you will find a bevy of fittings designed to link the plastic part of your system to the older metal portion.

Most of the manufacturers of plastic pipes, knowing that their product is relatively new to most people, include illustrated instructions about how to work with their specific brand. They will mail details to you in advance also. The chemistry of pipes and solvents varies extensively, so your best information will be from a manufacturer or local supplier of plastic pipes.

Because the plastic materials that go into pipes are considerably softer than their brass or iron counterparts, most manufacturers recommend that you do not use a pipe wrench on plastic pipes. Fortunately, there is practically no reason to use a wrench of any kind, but if the need should arise, a strap wrench is the preferred implement. A strap wrench also can be used if you have to assemble or disassemble any of those shiny chrome drainpipes under the sink if the bottom of the sink is exposed to view. Figure 29 in Chapter 2 shows what a strap wrench looks like.

The pipe wrench is a much misunderstood kind of tool. It is designed to do a wonderful job of tightening or loosening lengths of *round* pipe. The surface on its jaws is machined with teeth that grab firmly into the somewhat soft pipe metal. And the jaws are subtly angled to provide maximum grabbing power on round surfaces, but at the same time allowing for limited use on squared-off fittings too. The jaws are also hinged so the pipe wrench can be moved backward without pulling the jaws loose from the pipe, twisted hard, then backed off again, and twisted some more. The net effect is very similar to the ratchet action on a socket wrench. Some people still refer to the pipe wrench as a Stillson wrench.

Pipe wrenches come in sizes so small they will fit into your pocket up to sizes so large they will scarcely fit into the family station wagon. Size is determined by the length of the handle. A pipe wrench of about 14″ or 16″ is best for most home applications. Plumbers generally carry at least two pipe wrenches because one is often needed to hold a straight length of pipe still while the other wrench twists off some fitting at the end of the pipe. Since a pipe wrench is not exactly a minor investment, a vice grip pliers or channel lock pliers generally can take the place of that second pipe wrench (see Figure 64).

The aesthetics of plumbing appliances is quite simple. The porcelain or ceramic finishes are able to hold their own against many years of corrosives and abrasives. Chrome fittings, assuming they are well made (expensive), also can outlast one generation of children. The one abuse that neither the porcelain (typical of metal tubs and sinks) nor the ceramic (generally found on toilets and some sinks) can tolerate is hard knocks.

For those unsightly chips in porcelain sinks, buy a tiny bottle of paint made specifically for covering them up. In this day of rainbow-hued porcelain, rainbow-hued paints are available also. And when the label on that paint says to clean the damaged area thoroughly, it does indeed mean *thoroughly*. Steel wool and much detergent should be applied first, and then plenty of clean water. The area must be thoroughly dried before the paint is applied. Use a volatile solvent such as alcohol to help draw out the moisture, and it wouldn't hurt to direct some heat on the damaged spot to ensure good drying. Porcelain repair paints that are given a chance to adhere to clean porcelain or steel will last for years. If applied over grease or moisture, the same patch will do well to hold out for months.

The white grout between the wall and tub or between the tile and tub never seems to stay white for long. Mildew is one of the principal reasons for the discoloration, and second is a deposit of minerals or dirt. The particular mineral coloration depends on what part of the country you live in.

A silicone rubber caulking agent is one of the most permanent ways to patch the gap between tub and tile, and also one of the more expensive. There are similar, although less expensive and less permanent, substances also available in handy tubes. Slightly fancier, and slightly more expensive too, is a ceramic tile edging. Installed like tiles, the edging forms a convex-shaped molding in the corner where tub meets tiles and thus helps to repel dirt.

Mildew, being generally dark green, black, or blue bits of live vegetation, shows up best against light-colored backgrounds such as the white grout between tiles. Scouring powder and conventional cleansers remove the mildew with the addition of some elbow grease. There are a few fancy spray cans of potions designed specifically to lick the dirty tile gremlin. The aerosol cans also contain a fungicide chemical put there to retard the growth of mildew. Typical chemicals include n-alkyl dimethyl benzyl ammonium chloride or tetrasodium ethylenediamine tetraacetate or both.

Tests made of several tile cleansing products with antifungus chemicals revealed that they did indeed remove the usual blend of stains and mildew somewhat easier than chloride scouring powders. But no difference at all could be found between the length of time the scouring powder and the aerosol kept mildew from reappearing. The aerosol product, by the way, contains this warning: "Causes eye irritation. In case of contact, flush with plenty of water. Do not use on painted surfaces."

As towel bars and other supporting hardware wear out or break, you can add bronze, brass, gold, or silver bars, rings, faucets, and handles. If they have to go onto tile, unless you relish using a masonry drill for 15 to 20 minutes per hole, you will probably be happy to use some foamed plastic mounting tapes to hold up the fancy new devices. On the walls, sheet metal screws or small anchor bolts of some description provide adequate support (see Chapter 3).

Unsightly floors and tubs, the result of too much or too little cleaning over the years, often cause needlessly high replacement bills. Instead, a little creativity with the use of carpet can cover up an eyesore bathroom floor and tub, maybe more. Buy the washable carpet large enough so that it not only covers the floor but also extends up the side of the bathtub. A strip of good double-sided carpet tape holds the carpet in place between washings. Not only does the carpet lend a plush, neat, modern look, but it is practical and easy to maintain.

Electronic Hangups in Listening Equipment

6

WIRE CONNECTIONS AND PROBLEMS

The single most common ailment in listening systems of all sorts—transistor radios, portable phonographs, high fidelity radio-type recorder-phonograph-amplifier component systems, even many consoles and TVs—is a bad connection caused by corrosion, loose wires, or wear.

Correcting a loose wire is relatively simple. However, finding it often represents a Sherlock Holmes kind of challenge because gadgets have not been invented yet to help even the pros track down a wicked wire.

For symptoms such as no sound, weak volume, bad sound quality, or intermittent performance, the loose wire or bad connection should be the prime suspect until it has been eliminated absolutely from contention. Following the generalized troubleshooting formula in Chapter 1, you can trace the network of exposed wires from the power to the powered. And don't forget to check the fuse early in the routine.

The fuse on components such as amplifiers and tuners generally is located in the rear and inside a screw-out receptacle (see Figure 69). Although these glass fuses may look like the ones that protect the wires in your car, there are important differences. Fuses in most listening equipment are built for use on 120 volt house current; the auto variety are designed for 12 volt operation. They are not interchangeable.

It is unlikely that you will have spare fuses for the various home entertainment equipment you own. And you can be sure that the manufacturer didn't pack a set of spares. So if a fuse is at fault, before trotting off to an electronic supply store for a replacement, pull out the fuse holder in all similar equipment and jot down the appropriate size so that you can buy a full set of extra fuses for everything in your home.

All fuses of the same size and similar outward appearance may not be the same inside. There are three basic types of fuses, and any of the three are likely to be found in your home. *Quick-blow* fuses open at even a momentary overload and are used mainly to protect delicate or sensitive instruments. *Common* fuses will open a few seconds after a substantial overload begins; if the overload is just temporary, therefore, the fuse will not blow. *Slow-blow* fuses are designed to protect equipment where heavy, periodic demands for current would blow a common fuse even though the apparatus was operating normally.

Large amplifiers—tube or transistor—draw much more electric current when they are first turned on than during normal operation, and motors place heavier loads on a circuit when they start than during their ordinary, full speed use. In both kinds of equipment, you are likely to find slow-blow fuses. The best rule is to replace fuses with exactly the same size and type of fuse that the manufac-

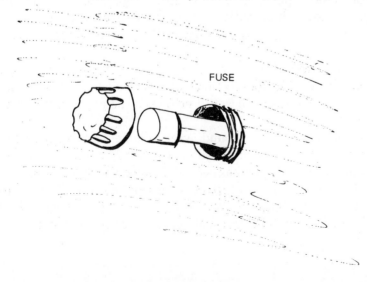

FUSE

Figure 69 Fuses on
hi-fi and similar equip-
ment are often located in
small screw on opening
in rear.

turer installed. And once a fuse has been either vindicated or replaced, resume your tracking through the web of wires.

Even that little package of sound dynamite, the transistor radio, is subject to loose wires in several locations. The models that have battery holders, which fall out and spill batteries all over the floor, can pull a wire loose after only two or three loading attempts. One or both of the tiny wires carrying the battery current to the on-off switch will snap or pull loose and have to be reconnected.

The FM antenna on small radios is often mounted on the removable back and fastened to the other half of the radio by a fragile wire. If the antenna wire jerks loose from the main radio mechanism, chances are you will not be able to spot where it was originally fastened. Later in this chapter, a short lesson in reading electronic language will show you how to interpret a schematic diagram so you can find where the antenna was in the first place. The art of soldering the wires back in place also will be dealt with.

After the battery or antenna, the input section of radios, phonographs, and hi-fis is the next most common location of bad connections. Gently manipulate each of the wires and each of the plugs on the wires. The important word here is *gentle*. Wires inside some of the cords are quite fragile and tiny. Connections between the wires and plugs are equally delicate. By lifting or easily twisting the cords that link your tuner, phonograph, and tape deck to the amplifier, for example, or the cords that link the TV antenna to the back of your television, the trouble may clear up, even if only for a moment. By handling one cord at a time, you will know which one to dig into deeper.

If your set's trouble clears up permanently after one particular input plug is twisted more tightly into place, stop there for now. Don't look for extra trouble, assuming the sound or picture or noise is fully up to your expectations, because you can easily create bad connections by twisting or jerking excessively on the plugs and wires.

In certain situations, it will be possible to test the condition of cords by substituting those you know to be good for ones in doubt. Let's assume the tape deck and the phonograph turntable work fine when connected to your hi-fi amplifier but the tuner (radio) does not. If the amplifier or preamp has both a "tuner-mono" and a "tuner-stereo" setting, try the tuner in both settings first to test for the possibility of a bad switch. Remove the cord (or one of the cords) that links the tuner to the amplifier and replace it with a cord you know to be working, such as the one linking the tape deck to the amplifier. If the trouble goes away, you can conclude that you're probably holding a faulty cord in your hand. If it doesn't go away, there are still some simple remedies (later we'll discuss the signal tracing section).

When very long wires are involved, the chore of switching around wires and plugs would be needlessly involved. In the case of an intercom system, for instance, you might find two units that work and temporarily plug one into each end of the suspect line. If they work, then the line is okay; the trouble evidently lies inside one of the intercoms or in its plug.

As an alternate to hooking on two working intercom units—which aren't quite standard equipment in every home yet—what pros call a *continuity tester* is valuable. A tester that tests for the continuity of wires can be nearly anything that will generate an electrical signal to let you hear or see whether the wires in question are unbroken.

Assuming your transistor radio is working, it can double as a continuity tester, and a doubly convenient one if the intercom giving you trouble is one that comes with miniature plugs on both ends of the wire. Using a small cord with a male miniature plug at both ends, connect the headphone socket of your radio to one end of the intercom wire and turn the volume up high. At the other end of the wire, plug in the earphone from your radio. If you hear music coming through, loud or soft, you can be sure that the wires are sound. If silence should prevail, however, first check your continuity tester connections before assuming that there is a break in the long wire. Figure 70 shows how to use this handy gadget. The plugs, cords, and sockets you may have to assemble to use a small radio as a continuity tester are available at most electronics stores. (*Male plugs* are shaped to protrude and fit snugly into the *female plugs.* The plug at the end

Figure 70 Continuity tester made from transistor radio's headphone fastens onto both ends of suspect wires. If music comes through, wires presumably are OK.

Figure 71 A flashlight can double as continuity tester if simply converted this way. A cardboard disc separates batteries from spring. One alligator clamp (available at almost all electronics stores) is wired to flashlight's spring; another is stripped and taped to upper side of cardboard disc.

of your toaster cord, for instance, also could be called a male connector, and the wall outlet into which the toaster is plugged could be labeled a female connector.)

There is a second kind of continuity tester, a more traditional one, which resembles a flashlight with two wires sticking out of the back. You can buy one at many stores or you can convert just about any flashlight into a continuity tester in five minutes. Figure 71 shows such a tester being made.

In a flashlight, the spring at the bottom normally makes contact with the battery's negative pole (the bottom of the battery). Interrupt the contact there by putting a cardboard disk over the spring. The inside end of one wire for your continuity tester is stripped of insulation for about 2″ and coiled around the top side of the cardboard disk, then secured with tape. The end of your second wire is fastened securely to the spring. Both wires are fed through a hole in the end cap of the flashlight *before you fasten them* in place. You can punch the hole with a can opener, nail, nutpick, or such. For maximum convenience, the two wires can have what electricians call *alligator clips* on the working end, but plain wires will do. (Alligator clips are sold at electronic shops.)

To use a battery continuity tester on something like long intercom wires, one end of the wire has to be shorted. If there is no plug on the wire, simply twist the two uninsulated ends together securely. A plug can be shorted by wrapping aluminum foil around it tightly, being sure that the conductive foil makes good contact with both parts of the plug. At the other end of the wires, turn on the flashlight switch; it should not light up, however. Touch the testing wires together to make sure that the light and batteries are working; the light should come on when the test leads touch each other. Then touch one test lead to each of the two suspect wires. If the bulb lights, the wires more than likely are good.

There is still a chance that the two intercom wires are shorted somewhere along their length. That is, insulation from both sides of the pair may have been worn or knocked loose, and the two wires are touching. To test for that condition with a flashlight continuity tester, unshort the end you earlier shorted—remove the aluminum foil or untwist the ends. Now repeat the continuity test. If there is *no short,* the flashlight *should not light up* because there is no point along the entire length of wire where the two sides touch.

Even the miserly quality wire included with inexpensive intercoms and similar devices does not break without cause. More often than not, a break or a short in the midst of a long run of any wire occurs at some obstruction—where you tied the wire to a water pipe, where it runs through a hole in the floor or wall, where a closing window

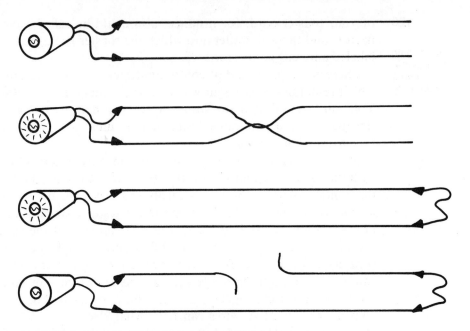

Figure 72 In using continuity tester, here are four major possibilities you may encounter. Top, bulb unlit when fastened to one end indicates no short between wires. Second, bulb lit when fastened to one end shows short between two wires. Third, bulb lit when fastened to one end but other end shorted with extra wire, shows that wires are unbroken their full length. Bottom, bulb unlit when fastened to one end while other end deliberately shorted, shows broken wire(s) along the way.

slams on it every time somebody gets chilly. It is virtually impossible visually to spot shorts or breaks in fine wires unless physical damage has occurred to the outside. With heavy wires, such as TV antenna leads, it is possible to flex the wire every foot or so. A clean break in the copper wire beneath the covering of insulation would cause the flexed wire to kink instead of flex gracefully. Once that point has been located, you can cut out the damaged section and carefully splice in a new length of wire at least as big in diameter as the one removed. Ask yourself at this point if repairing the wire is better in terms of cost and time than replacing it with new cable entirely. Wire splicing is demonstrated in Figure 73.

In hi-fi sets composed of separate units for the amplifier, tuner, phonograph turntable, tape deck, and maybe even a separate preamp, there is often a legitimate question about *which* of the many cabinets houses the ailing parts. Just because the tape deck and tuner play and the turntable switch generates only silence is not a positive indication that the fault lies with the turntable itself. The problem

126

might be with the control on the amplifier, which switches signals from phonograph records into the amplifier sections, assuming you have already checked the wires linking various components in the setup.

If the amplifier (or preamp if there is a separate one in the system) has a selector switch for "phono-mono," "phono-stereo," "tuner-mono," "tuner-stereo," and such, switching between the monophonic and stereophonic mode could show whether the trouble lies in the actual unit that produces no sound or within the amplifier. Alternately, run a substitution test by plugging a tape deck or tuner you know to work into the input connector for the turntable. We're still assuming for the sake of this example that the phonograph is not working. If the tape recorder or radio plays through the hi-fi system even if the selector switch is set at one of the "phono" modes, the trouble more than likely does lie somewhere within the phonograph portion.

Figure 73 If you isolate parts in your mind, you'll have less problem in finding what you're after. Here, for example, if you're looking for faulty transistors, try to find a picture of them first, and then block out the other components as has been done in this photo. Then you'll find only transistors and soon the faulty one.

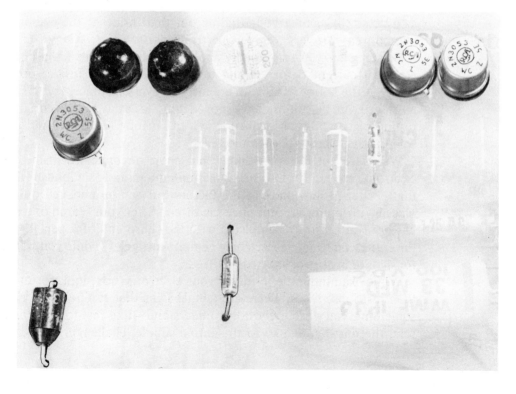

Even a small transistor radio can be connected to your amplifier for a substitution test, assuming you have the proper adapter plugs on hand or buy them. The sound quality may be poor if a tuner is plugged into the phonograph input. Each of these signals requires special treatment inside of the preamp section, which is why the selector switch is carefully labeled instead of simply marked "input 1," "input 2," and so on. But poor sound or good, this substitution method will help you to isolate more precisely where the trouble is located.

Broken wires don't always occur *outside* an electronic marvel. They can occur anywhere, especially inside anything that gets moved about or vibrated, such as an intercom sitting unattached on a shelf. (Why not attach it to the shelf to avoid the problem and annoyance of knocking it over?) Walkie talkies, portable radios, portable phonographs, and portable-anything-else invite broken wires inside.

The outside cases of most gadgets are simply held together by several small sheet metal screws, generally with a Phillips head. On some small, inexpensive electronic gadgets, there will be a warning decal that says something like: "There are no user serviceable parts inside this case. Only experienced service personnel should open to avoid serious electrical shock." In most instances, you can ignore the notice if you exercise reasonable caution. It appears to be there more as a deterrent against your finding out that inside of the elaborate intercom case are very, very few electronic parts.

Be sure that you unplug any appliance that operates from house electrical current before taking off the cover. Once inside, probe gently at the major wires with a pencil. In every instance, try to spot any loose wire before you have shoved it too far away from its original resting place. Otherwise you face an exhausting search to find out where the wire has to be reconnected.

Wires are not the only things that come unconnected inside the electronic boxes. For instance, one small intercom has a loudspeaker that is clipped into place at the factory but can be knocked out of place by dropping the unit once too often. After your search of wires has been successfully completed with the sharp end of a pencil, use the eraser end to jiggle electronic components gently while you watch for signs of broken or shorted wire leads.

While examining the inside of your electronic box, look for more than just loose wires. There are telltale signs that can help you turn something you absolutely don't understand—like resistors, transistors, thermistors, and so forth—into a simple, challenging detective game.

Corrosion comes most from leaky batteries or excessive humidity. It is most likely to affect metal contacts inside your ailing gadget, such as the plug for an earphone, the on-off and volume controls, the contacts in the battery holders themselves, relay contacts in tape recorders that automatically change direction or operate off both house current and batteries, and dozens more. An eraser makes an effective tool for rubbing away the corrosion from many accessible metal parts. A small file or emory board can be used on heftier spots.

Dirty internal metal mechanisms of switches and controls will have to be cleaned with chemicals available at most electronic suppliers and some hardware stores. Instructions that come with the particular bottle or spray can are quite good, with one important exception—they don't always warn that you must give the cleaning solvents time to dry thoroughly before finally evaluating whether you have succeeded in cleaning a control or not.

Dirt and moisture, once they get inside the case, can cause small but significant amounts of electricity to become misdirected. The result could be loss of power or total silence. Evaporate the moisture in a warm, dry place. Brush or blow any dirt away, but gently.

Heat, too much of it, kills electronic parts even faster than too much rough treatment. When an electronic component becomes overheated, it can be the result of a breakdown inside the same device that overheats, *or,* a fault or breakdown in a part connected to the overheated part.

A hot resistor (the resistor is discussed in more detail later) usually becomes quite severely charred on the outside. You can spot such a condition with your naked eye. Transistors that overheat don't show such graphic signs. The set must be turned on while you test each large transistor with a finger for signs of excess heat. Power transistors and power transformers should be no warmer than toast. Smaller transistors, output transformers, and coils should give almost no sensation of heat at all.

When you're sticking fingers into any electrical appliance that plugs into house current, make sure that the 120 volts stay in one place and your finger in another. With the important exception of television sets, there should be no dangerous amounts of electricity inside small radios, amplifiers, phonographs, intercoms and the like,

129 *except* at two points: (1) where the line that plugs into the house current enters the appliance and fastens generally onto a trans-former, and (2) where the house current line connects to the on-off switch, which often is an integral part of the volume or a tone con-trol. In small music and sound makers except TV sets, once the 120 volt current reaches the power transformer, it is reduced to only a small level, generally from 6 to 48 volts.

If you first locate the two (or more) spots where 120 volt current exists and you feel that your fingers will definitely avoid them, carry on your tests with the plug plugged in. If not, you can still test for hot electronic components in a less direct fashion. Turn on the set for 5 to 10 minutes. Hopefully you can have the cover removed so you will see obvious indications of overheating, such as smoke. After you unplug the device, run the finger test for heat. What you do after dis-covering a hot spot, which part you will replace first, is not exactly complicated. But it does require that you know something about electronic parts.

THE INGREDIENTS OF ELECTRONIC CIRCUITS

Despite beliefs to the contrary, electronic circuits are simple to understand. If you can understand the difference between mixing and beating cake batter or between hooking and slicing a golf ball, you can understand the electronic circuit.

SWITCHES

In electronic gadgets, switches perform exactly the same function as the switches that turn your lights on and off. They either *make* or *break* connections between two or more wires. In technical jargon, to make means to *turn on*, to break means to *turn off* a switch or relay contact. That little "click" sound as you turn on the volume control of your transistor radio is actually from a tiny on-off switch built into the volume control itself. On some fancier pieces of equipment, the volume control and the on-off switch are separate.

If you are playing a record on the hi-fi set and then decide to listen to the news, you twist a knob that turns the amplifier or preamp sec-tion of the hi-fi away from "phono" and over to "tuner." Actually, you are twisting a switch, a very complicated-looking kind of switch. There are more than a dozen sets of wires running to the selector switch, and every one of the couple dozen contacts within the switch have to be clean and soundly wired for your set to give maximum performance. Unfortunately, the complicated selector switch is one of the most frequent bugaboos in any home music system.

Switches deserve periodic maintenance due, first of all, to their relatively delicate disposition. And second, tracking audio troubles down to a faulty switch is a brutal kind of detective work at times. There are chemical switch and control cleaners that should be applied according to instructions about once a year. And if you've been able to track down some distorted sound—or no sound at all— to particular sections of controls or selector switches, the cleaner also might help them.

By the time audio troubles are so bad that you can hear them, the chemicals might not be tough enough to remedy the headache. Many radio repair outlets sell a tiny burnisher that polishes away corrosion, dirt, and other undesirables from the tiny switch contacts. Since you no doubt don't have a switch burnisher (also called a relay burnisher) around the house, make do with an emory board or a piece of one— the finer the better. Carefully blow away any dust left behind after using either the burnisher or the emory board.

If some of the contacts on the selector switch are beyond solid and foolproof repair, prepare to replace the entire switch. Buy a replacement or order one from a supplier who handles the wares of the particular manufacturer involved. When the new one arrives, don't immediately snip off the old wires because you'll never find where they go on the new one.

Most selector switches have a numbering system. The contact numbers may be tiny, but most often they are there if you look for them. Since most selector switches have more than one layer, arbitrarily call the one closest to the front "A," the next one back "B" and so on. With a generous supply of marking tape or labels, identify every wire attached to the old switch with a totally unique code. Example: if that purple and white wire is fastened to the #3 contact on the first layer, mark it "3A."

Don't be too easily misled. There often are two entirely separate sets of contacts fastened to a single plastic wafer in some switches. The front layer should be designated "A" for marking purposes and the rear layer "B."

Simple toggle switches or slide switches perform simple functions, such as turning the power on or off, turning the tuner from stereo to mono, or switching various filters or loudness circuits into or out of the operation. If one of them becomes noisy or balky, and if chemicals aren't tough enough to remedy the situation, replacement is the simplest and surest solution. If the switches in your equipment resemble the switches in Figure 74 in the name-the-component section,

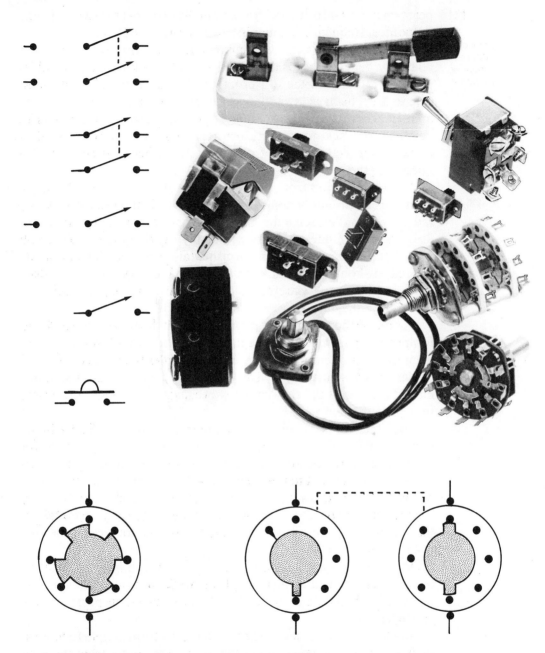

Figure 74 Switches come in dozens of varieties. Pictorially, you can find the faulty one and order a replacement. Most simpler switches have a four-letter designation. The first two letters tell how many incoming lines switch handles (SP = single pole, DP = double pole, TP = triple pole. Beyond that, use number such as 4P = 4 poles). The second two letters tell how many different outgoing positions the switch handles (-ST = single throw, -DT = double throw).

you will more than likely be able to buy almost any standard replacement slide or toggle switch regardless of who made your set and who made the switch. Just pay attention to details, such as single pole, double pole, single throw, double throw, and such.

A switch that regulates only a single wire is called a *single pole* switch. If it handles two wires, keeping the current from each one separate within the switch, the component is called a *double pole* switch. Three separate wires into a switch would lead to a *three pole* switch.

There is yet another characteristic of switches to be considered. If the particular switch in question either passes the electricity through or stops it, the switch is labeled a *single throw* device. In other words, it can either be *thrown off* or *thrown on,* and that *thrown on* mode is where the term "single throw" comes from.

It is possible for a switch to take the electricity from its input pole and direct it either to a red light or a green light, for instance. Such a device receives the label *double throw* switch.

Now let us put the pole and throw designations together. A switch designed to handle one electrical line and only for on-off modes is, or course, a *single pole, single throw* switch, shortened to SPST in the trade. If we add facilities for a second separate line to a simple on-off switch, it becomes a *double pole, single throw* switch. or DPST. A third or fourth line would be written as 3PST or 4PST. It is also possible, in fact common, to have a *double pole, double throw* switch, shortened to DPDT, and a *single pole, double throw* switch, SPDT.

To be absolutely complete in describing a replacement switch, you should say something like this when ordering it: "May I have a double pole, single throw slide switch." And in the case of many toggle type switches, you have the additional choice of how long the threaded stem portion will be. Both $\frac{11}{32}$" and $\frac{15}{32}$" are standard lengths. It is unlikely that $\frac{1}{8}$" ($\frac{4}{32}$") will seem to be of much consequence to you, but if a replacement switch won't clear some part of a panel, that may be the reason. For special applications, the threaded stems do come in considerably longer and shorter lengths.

When the rotary switches, such as in hi-fi selector units, are described, the designation "throw" is dropped in favor of the word *position.* And each wafer layer in the switch is called a *gang,* although some use the word *section.*

RESISTORS

Resistors function in an electronic circuit very much like valves in a set of pipes, except that this valve is never completely shut off. A resistor is used in an electronic device for a variety of good reasons. It lowers the voltage (or electrical pressure, if you want to think of it that way) at which an electric signal passes through a circuit. It can reduce the overall quantity of electric current passing through wires. A resistor also is used at times to let signals pass harmlessly out of the way, acting in that function almost like an overflow valve.

Most common resistors consist of a composition of carbon and bonding chemicals. Other types are made of resistive wire wrapped around a hollow ceramic core or resistive wire encapsuled in a heat dissipating material.

The quantity of resistance is measured and expressed in terms of *ohms.* It is not important to know exactly what an ohm is, only that it refers to how much resistance a resistor or other electronic device offers against the flow of an electric current. Resistors commonly come in sizes ranging from 1 ohm to 22 million ohms. For many applications, the precise value of a resistor is not critical. A variation of 20 percent or more above or below the specified value is accurate enough for most jobs. A resistor with a 20 percent tolerance (± 20) percent) was standard for all but very specialized applications until the advent of transistors. Many transistor circuits require greater accuracy for dependable performance, so 10 percent tolerance (± 20 percent) is becoming standard, and specialized circuits employ resistors made to a 5 percent tolerance (± 5 percent).

The more expensive wire-wound resistors have their actual values stamped on the outside of their cases. The letter "K" in electronics means *thousands* and "M" means *millions.* In other words, a resistor stamped "27K" is 27,000 ohms. One marked "2M" is 2 million ohms. And "4.7M" means 4,700,000 ohms ($4.7 \times 1,000,000 = 4,700,000$). In shopping for a replacement resistor, however, simply tell the counter person, for example, "I need a 4.7K, ½ watt resistor."

Values for the more common carbon resistors are marked in color coded bands as shown in Figure 75. Example: You discover an overheated resistor and want to replace it. You carefully clean off the dirt without destroying the code too. Examining the resistor you find four color bands, *red, green, orange,* and *silver* (reading from the outside toward the center). Consulting the chart in Figure 106, the consumer finds that red means 2, green is 5, and orange equals 3. The first two bands provide the actual real numbers in any resistor's value, and the third band designates how many zeros follow. In our example, then, the resistor is 25,000 ohms, usually shortened to 25K. The silver fourth band means a 10 percent tolerance.

More examples: The 4.7M resistor mentioned earlier would have a yellow band for the 4, a violet band for the 7, and a green band signi-

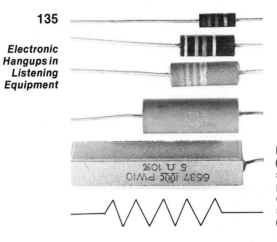

Figure 75 Resistor nomenclature: (top to bottom) ¼-watt, ½-watt, 1-watt sizes. Bottom two are wire-wound precision resistors. Color bands designate amount of resistance; simply jot down colors in proper order (edge toward center).

fying 5 zeros; 4,700,000. If you encountered a resistor with bands of red, violet, and orange only, no fourth band, here is what you would have: 2 for the red, 7 for the violet, and 000 for the orange; hence a resistor of 27K ohms. The absence of a fourth band indicates a tolerance of 20 percent.

It is perfectly fine to replace a resistor having a 20 percent tolerance with one having 10 or 5 percent tolerance. Going in the other direction should be avoided if possible. It is unlikely that any real harm will come to you or your electronic equipment by using a 20 percent resistor instead of a 10 percent version. Sound quality in radios or amplifiers *may* suffer, accuracy in meters *will* be less precise. And then again, you might not be able to notice the difference at all.

Aside from ratings in ohms, resistors also are manufactured according to how much power they must be able to handle. Power is expressed in terms of *watts*. The most common power ratings for resistors are ¼ watt, ½ watt, 1 watt, and 2 watts. They are also found, although less frequently, in bigger sizes such as 5 watts, 10 watts, and up. The physical size of a resistor identifies its power rating as a rule, a fact made clear in Figure 75. For the most part, replacement resistors are very inexpensive, except for those in the over 2 watt size.

Jobs such as controlling volume or regulating treble or bass tone balance are handled by a breed of variable resistor called a *potentiometer,* "pot" for short (see Figure 76). Like the nonvariable types, potentiometers are rated according to how many watts of electrical power they can handle, typically 1 watt, 3 watts, 5 watts, and so on. They are also rated according to the maximum number of ohms resistance they provide. Most begin at zero. Typical sizes are 100 ohms,

Figure 76 Potentiometers, called "pots" for short, have to be replaced with exact duplicate for proper performance.

1K ohms, 50K ohms, even as high as 1 meg. For some reason unexplained except that there is more writing space on a pot than on a small resistor, manufacturers often abbreviate the one million ohm rating with a "meg" standing for megohm instead of a simple "M" also standing for megohm.

There is yet another variation in pots beyond even the refinements of wattage and ohmage—_taper_. In going from 0 ohms to 1000 ohms, for instance, it is possible to move very quickly at first and then slower and slower toward the upper regions, or it can be done slower at first and faster at the end. It even can be accomplished by moving uniformly from 0 to 1000. For applications in music and voice systems, the choice is in favor of a potentiometer that moves slowly upward at the lower end and rapidly upward in value at the maximum end.

When buying a replacement control, unless you buy one at the original manufacturer's dealer, specify _audio taper_ for volume controls, _linear taper_ for tone controls and most other applications. To ensure an exact replacement for an ailing pot, therefore, the enlightened consumer would ask for something like this: "A 3 watt, 100K, audio taper pot."

Almost all of those tiny transistor radios use only a couple of standardized types of volume controls. This is extremely fortunate because they become noisy and temperamental relatively easy, particularly if someone persists in dropping them or twisting volume controls with wet hands. Later in this chapter we discuss how to replace electronic components, including a new volume control for your transistor radio.

CAPACITORS

Capacitors, the next big category of electronic components, store electrical energy in some applications. And capacitors (occasionally still called condensers) are widely used in audio circuitry to filter out or separate various types of signals.

The standard unit to capacitance is the *farad*, which is much too large for practical electronic applications. Capacitor size, therefore, is expressed in tiny fractions of farads. The *microfarad* (one-thousandth of a whole farad) is used to measure large capacitors and is generally abbreviated *mfd*, although occasionally you will find it written simply *mf*. Smaller capacitors are marked in a unit called micro-microfarads (millionths of a whole farad), abbreviated as *mmf* or *uf*. (The "u" isn't really intended to be a "u" at all but the Greek letter *mu*, μ.) Some capacitors used in small transistor radios are so tiny that there isn't room to write a value such as ".005 mmf", so the manufacturer stamps it simply ".005." If the mmf, and mfd. notation is omitted, assume that it is mmf. in everything smaller than a walnut.

There is a second value to consider when buying replacement capacitors. For both economy and size, they are built to withstand voltages only up to various levels. In the early stages of a TV set, voltages never go over 50 volts or so; consequently capacitors used there are rated at 150 volts, allowing a factor of three as a margin for error, abuse, and safety. As TV circuits get closer and closer to the picture tube, voltages reach several thousand volts, and capacitors in that area have to be rated accordingly. For small transistor radios, walkie talkies, and most battery-powered gadgets, voltages never top 10 volts. To identify a common capacitor completely, therefore, you would have to say, "20 mfd. rated at 50 volts." To be technically correct, many capacitors state "150 volts *DC*," but the DC is all but redundant.

One more variation of capacitor is the *electrolytic capacitor*. Certain circuits require a polarized capacitor so that the positive current is kept on one side of the device, negative current on the other. Electrolytic capacitors are generally large relative to the other components inside electronic equipment. They also had a + and − sign marked on them, hopefully conspicuously. When installing a new electrolytic capacitor, it is vital that you orient it so that new + side is wired to the same part of the circuit as the old + . Likewise for the − terminal. To be doubly safe, before removing an old electrolytic capacitor, mark a + and − on a nearby space with a pen or pencil. If any capacitors are likely to need replacing just for reasons of old age, it will be the electrolytics due to their more fragile disposition.

Variable capacitors are used principally in radios and tuners. Fortunately, there is very little that goes wrong with the component itself. It can get dirty, which causes noise or similar difficulties, but that ailment can be remedied with a good control cleaner chemical. And connections to the variable capacitors can be broken. The cure for that should be obvious—resolder it. If a variable capacitor does need replacing, you will almost inevitably have to replace it with one

Figure 77 Capacitors store and filter electricity in electronic instruments. Most have clear markings on them and can be replaced easily (A). Electrolytic capacitors (B) are larger, more expensive, and have to be wired into place with plus and minus signs in same position as original equipment.

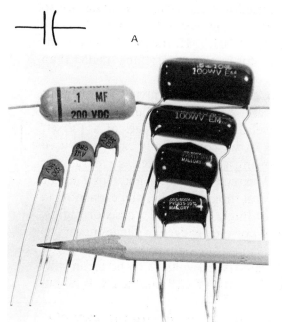

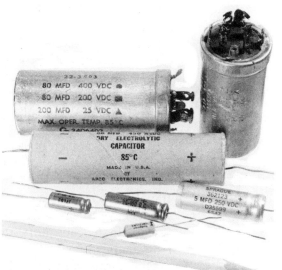

Figure 78 Variable capacitors are generally used for tuning purposes in radios. They're large in large ones, tiny in transistor sets. Shown here is a large one, but tiny ones, although often enclosed in clear plastic case, are similar. There are two different ways of drawing symbol for variable capacitor. They have to be replaced with exact replacement, often a tough job. Fortunately they seldom need replacing.

from the original manufacturer. Variable capacitors come in such a variety of sizes, shapes, compositions, and dispositions that little short of a miracle will help you to find one listed in a catalog that will exactly fit the one you must replace (see Figure 78).

THE TRANSFORMER

As its name might imply, the transformer transforms electric current from high voltage into low or, conversely, low voltage into high. Any radio, phonograph, TV, intercom, or other music and sound-making gadget that plugs into house current will inevitably have one or more transformers to transform the 120 volts into something like 12 or 20 volts in radios and amplifiers or into something like 2000 or more volts in a TV. Warning: The 120 volt side of a power transformer can give you the same kind of shock as if you stuck your finger into a live light socket. Don't be scared away! Just be scared.

You might still encounter at least one exception to this rule about a transformer for every 120 volt gadget. If you have held onto a small table model radio made between the end of World War II and the beginning of the 1960s, you may be amazed to find that there is no

transformer. Through clever electronic calculations, radio engineers

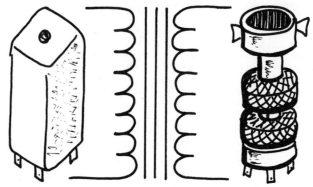

Figure 79 Transformers and coils look similar at times. You don't have to tell them apart, however, as long as you find exact replacements. In all cases, you may find more wires shown on drawings and hanging from transformers than are pictured here. Top items are generally called transformers; bottom items are coils.

found a way to dispense with the then relatively expensive transformer by wiring tubes and resistors into series with each other. Current from one tube passed directly through the next. But like the old-fashioned Christmas tree lights, when one tube failed, they all went dark. Replacement tubes for radios like this are becoming hard to find, but they can be recognized by their high initial numbers—examples, 50HK6, 35C5, 26HU5, 17JZ8, 12JQ6. In the nomenclature system for tubes in the United States, the first number identifies the voltage needed to operate the tube.

Replacement transformers in abundance are *not* likely to be stocked by a neighborhood electronic gadget shop. Many mail order supplies also stock precious few. Start searching for a replacement by jotting down both the manufacturer and part number from the transformer case. You may be lucky and find out that it is a standard item that good electronics houses carry in stock or have an exact substitute for on hand. Beyond that you will have to locate an authorized distributor for either the manufacturer of the transformer or the manufacturer of your ailing electronic gadget. If the Yellow Pages can't help you find a new transformer, the local dealer who sold it to you should be willing to help. And if not, keep that in mind next time you go shopping! If all else fails, call collect to the main office of the company who manufactured the crippled device.

When a transformer is burning out, you may immediately recognize the fact by the smell of burning insulation, smoke from the singeing wire insulation pouring out of the transformer, an the extremely hot metal exterior. If the transformer dies more quietly, you may find out about it through a blown fuse, which blows again as soon as you replace it.

There is a simple way to track down the transformer that died quietly; the signal tracing pages just ahead will discuss it and the continuity tests earlier discussed it. If the wires inside have parted company, the signal will not go through the transformer, a feat any healthy specimen accomplishes with ease.

The *power transformer* is the one connected to the house current. Generally, it is the largest and most expensive single component in music systems. For the sake of producing a system with an attractive price, the power transformer often is selected with just enough of a power rating to handle the load the various components will put upon it.

If the manufacturer chooses a transformer with too marginal a power rating, even normal use, simple abuses, or operating variations can overload it, cause it to overheat, and perhaps burn it out or short its internal wiring when excessive heat compromises the insulation. Unless your own meddling led to the transformer's end, if a power transformer burns out on a major item such as a hi-fi amplifier, expensive radio-phonograph console, TV, or a good radio, you should become heated too. With very few exceptions—assuming they are not abused—power transformers should last for the lifetime of the appliances in which they were installed.

Another kind of transformer inside many audio gadgets is an *output transformer*, which is used in many high quality sets because the electronic characteristics (impedance, for those in the know) of the amplifier does not match the electronic characteristics of the line into which the signal will be fed. An output transformer is a simple remedy for the condition. Like the power transformer, it should not need replacing unless badly abused.

Since output transformers are handling relatively small amounts of current, they need not be approached with the same kind of caution as the 120 volt side of power transformers. But how does a novice tell which transformer is which? The power transformer may be located very close to the spot where the 120 volt cord enters the chassis. And the output transformer, or transformers in stereo sets, is located very close to where the output lines connect to speakers or to other noise-making units.

Other types of coils, inside radios in particular, are very similar in outward appearance to transformers. Only a highly technical fact or two actually separates a coil from a transformer. Most often they are used to convert signals from one wavelength band into another. Fortunately they do not wear out, although some will deteriorate after many years. Since each manufacturer designs equipment to operate on a particular set of coils, replacements must come from original manufacturers or their dealers. Because they require accurate tuning, replacing the coils in FM radios is beyond the scope of anyone outside a well-equipped radio repair shop.

LIGHT BULBS

Ironically, light bulbs are a frequent source of annoyance in many electronic appliances. They are used to signal on—off, record on tape recorders, and just to shed light on some dark areas. Manufacturers of equipment often assume that pilot lights never need replacing, which is close to true under ideal conditions.

If it is possible to offer any kind of generalization in an area so filled with diverse styles and sizes of lamps, it could be said that the most common pilot and signal light in use to indicate on, record, stereo station, and so on is the *neon glow tube*. The neon lamp is wired right into some part of a circuit since its life expectancy is given as "in excess of 5000 hours." *Light emitting diodes* (LED) as pilot lights are becoming popular despite their cost, more because of their gimmick appeal than the fact that their life expectancy is 100,000 hours. If you play a radio 100 hours a week without stop, the LED should last for 20 years!

Ordinary incandescent pilot lamps, similar to flashlight bulbs and Christmas tree lights, come with at least 10 different bases and more than 10 possible configurations of glass. Whereas most neon glow tubes operate on ordinary household current (due in part to a resistor built into their plastic case), incandescent pilot lamps may operate at 120 volts but also can be rated from 2 to 28 volts. If your new pilot lamp is to last as long as the one it replaces, matching the proper voltage is important.

Very few lamps actually have their rated voltage stamped on them. The manufacturers generally prefer to use the limited writing space for indicating their own model number. The simplest way to replace a burned out lamp is to remove it and take it to a well-stocked electronic supply store or to the pages of a mail order electronics catalog. To demonstrate the complexity of the new pilot light issue, a typical mail order catalog has to devote two pages of fine print to the hundreds of varied lamps available and in use.

Since pilot lamps are generally very inexpensive, it is possible to experiment if you are unable to determine immediately the proper replacement for your particular needs. With screw-in or bayonet base bulbs, the variation between the highest and lowest voltages available in that specific base is relatively limited, so experimentation should not take forever.

If you have bad luck locating a wire-in replacement, try to improvise. Buy several inexpensive NE-2 neon glow lamps and wire one into the space left vacant by the old one. If it works right off, you're all set. Should the bulb appear to glow too brightly compared with what was there before, or if it burns out well short of 5000 hours in use—perhaps instantly—wire a ¼ watt, 100K ohms resistor to one lead of the glow lamp. The free side of the resistor is then soldered to one of the two wires left vacant when you snipped out the old lamp. And the second NE-2 wire lead is soldered onto the second of the old wires. (Soldering is covered in pages ahead.) If bulb brightness is of some critical concern to you, it is possible to vary the size of the resistor. A 50K ohm version would make a somewhat brighter output, and a 250K ohm resistor should create a slightly dimmer glow. Going into too high a resistance will result in no glow at all.

TUBES AND TRANSISTORS

Tubes are not altogether obsolete for a number of good reasons. One is that some tube radios and TVs were built at a time when manufacturers still felt that their reputations depended on building long-lasting products. The sets made during that time last on and on and on. Tubes also are still used in some specialized high power applications, for which they are better suited than the more modern transistor.

Tubes and transistors both perform the same kinds of functions. They turn alternating current into direct current for power supplies. They can generate vibrations of a given frequency, which can be used to measure the pitch from unknown sources such as a TV or radio station, or the fixed vibrations can be used as a timer. Tubes and transistors also can appear to amplify the strength of an electrical

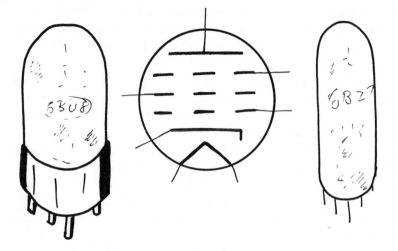

Figure 80 Tubes are still used in many electronic applications. The drawing of a tube diagram is just one of dozens of variations, all of them within circles or ovals, however. Tubes come in sundry sizes and may be concealed beneath a metal shield.

signal, one of their most widely used attributes today. Without tubes or transistors used as amplifiers, the tiny bits of electricity that make up radio, phonograph, or TV signals would never be able to drive a small headphone, let along a hefty 15″ woofer loudspeaker.

Tubes are encased in glass, but don't be misled. Occasionally the radio or TV manufacturer slips a thin metal shield over the glass. Tubes are big, at least bigger than 1″ long in the places you are likely to find them. Transistors are housed in metal or plastic and are in the ½″ or under range except for the broad, flat power transistors. Figure 80 shows tubes and their graphic symbol.

Although tube testers are becoming less and less common in places such as drugstores, they are still found in many electronic supply houses. Before pulling out a set of suspect tubes, however, make sure that you will be able to put them back in the proper place. If the manufacturer hasn't supplied a tube diagram, which is generally glued to the cabinet or metal chassis inside the set, draw one yourself.

All tubes are not alike. In fact, chances are pretty good that no more than two or three of a set of maybe a dozen tubes in a major electronic device have the same number. Tube types in the United States feature a one or two digit number, then one or two letters, followed by another number of two. Here are some typical tube types: 6CD7, 6B6, 12AU6. Tubes for hi-fi applications often are sold by their European numbering system. The 6CD7 tube, for example, also could be called an EM34. Your electronic supplier can quickly look up interchangeable tube numbers for you, or you can do it yourself with a mail order catalog.

Tubes used in other than hi-fi equipment are easy to obtain. For hi-fi sets, however, a better grade of tube is preferred. Be sure that you

144

tell the clerk you want *hi-fi grade tubes*. And don't listen to any lecture that "there isn't any difference" if you are any sort of critical music listener. If two tubes in a stereo hi-fi amplifier bear the same type numbers (such as 12AU7 or ECC82), they probably are the power output tubes and always should be kept as closely matched as possible. Therefore, if one tests bad and will be replaced, replace both of them at the same time. For the *real* music buff willing to pay a premium price, hi-fi grade tubes can be bought in pairs that have been precisely matched by their manufacturer. Matched tubes are identified by an "MP" after their usual nomenclature, such as EL84MP or 6BQ5MP.

Tubes or transistors are the brains and muscles of most electronic circuits. Novices can best understand their job by thinking of both tubes and transistors as electronic valves. When employed as a power rectifier, for instance, the electronic valve opens only for electricity flowing in one direction.

When a tube or transistor is used as an amplifier, a small electric signal, such as the unamplified music signal from a phonograph needle, acts like a superquick hand on the valve control knob. As the

Figure 81 Tubes and transistors operate like electronic valves. Here, a tiny electronic signal from the phonograph "turns the handle" so a larger amount of electricity is given exactly the same properties as the phonograph record. That signal in turn operates "the handle" on a larger transistor which admits a larger electronic supply to be converted by "the value" into an exact duplicate of the original signal, this time powerful enough to drive a large loudspeaker.

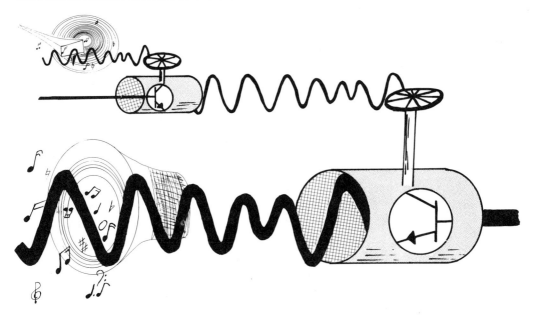

faint signal gets louder and softer or vibrates faster and slower, that hand on the valve opens and shuts so the signal, which in our analogy is flowing through the valve, also gets louder and softer or vibrates faster and slower exactly like the weak signal controlling the valve handle. As a result, the signal that flows out of the valve is exactly like the signal on the handle, except that it is many, many times stronger. It has been *amplified*, we say.

The stronger signal that flows out of the electronic valve then can be wired directly to a small loudspeaker. But for even greater electronic power, the first amplified signal can be sent to a second valve just like the first one in our analogy, only larger. The strengthened signal acts like the hand on this second valve, thus duplicating the original weak signal in a still more powerful reproduction.

Transistors are not so easily tested by novice fix-it people—pros either! The corner drugstore does not sport a transistor tester next to its tube tester. In any event, it is not so simple to pull most transistors out of their moorings deep inside the amplifier or radio. But don't despair because there are a number of surprisingly simple ways to find out if transistors are not doing their job.

When you are looking for overheated components according to suggestions earlier in this chapter, any transistors connected directly to the heat damaged part also may be disturbed. This is especially true if the charred or melted component is a resistor. If the transistor went bad first, it could short out or draw too much electric current and cause the resistor to overheat. And conversely, if something happened to the resistor, it could fail to protect the transistor, allow too much current to pass through it, and destroy the innards. An electrolytic capacitor that reached the age of retirement unnoticed also could lead to a damaged transistor.

In stereo amplifiers, the broad, flat power transistors (shown in Figure 82) come in pairs. Often there are four or more of them, generally arranged two by two. If one of a pair is warm to the touch and the other is very hot or not warm at all, there appears to be trouble with the latter transistor or its nearby circuitry. This condition will be found most often when one channel of a stereo set is functioning well, the second channel is malfunctioning. The same holds for larger self-contained tape recorders or phonographs that have their own speakers and thus also must have their own built-in amplifiers. Intercoms, walkie talkies, and similar miniature sound makers seldom generate a powerful enough output ever to warm up their low powered transistors.

Small transistors generally are fastened into circuits with three separate leads. In the large power transistors, however, there are but

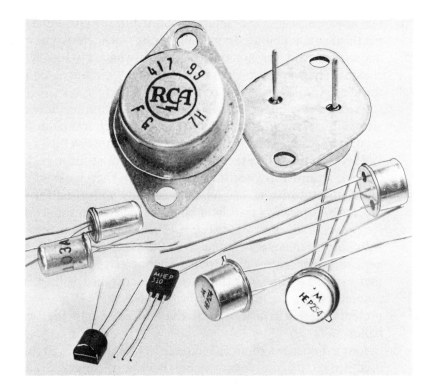

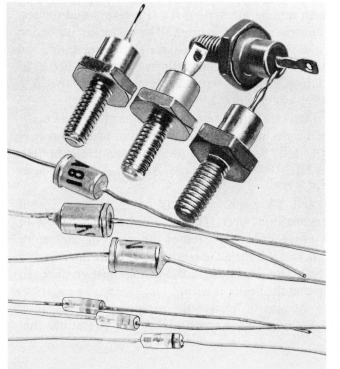

Figure 82 Transistor and diode nomenclature. In schematic, left is transistor of PNP variety; center, NPN transistor; right, diode (often called rectifier in some circuits). Top, transistors have three leads (the case is often the third lead in large power transistors). Bottom, diodes have two leads (case is second lead in some).

two apparent leads; the metal case bolted to the metal chassis acts as the third contact point. To save on wiring, most electronic equipment manufacturered for home use employs what pros call a grounded chassis. That is, the negative side of many circuits is connected to the metal chassis instead of to wires.

Sometimes a manufacturer builds two or more individual transistors into a single housing, in which case *each* transistor get its own set of wire leads. This is not a common item, however.

There is another member of the broad semiconductor family (diodes, transistors, rectifiers, and such) that most of us would mislabel a transistor. The *diode* is actually *almost* half a transistor, or, more correctly, a transistor could be called two connected diodes. Anyway a diode has two leads (see Figure 82). Small diodes are coded with color bands very similar to resistors. The small diodes seldom need replacing unless a component connected to them has failed. In that event, be sure that the new one is installed with positive lead pointed in the same direction as the old one. If a + sign is not present, the positive lead is at the end closest to the set of color bands.

Large diodes are often called rectifiers because they are most often used to rectify the forward and backward surges of alternating current into forward-only direct current. Typically they are mounted in a metal case, and the case itself acts as the negative lead when bolted onto a grounded chassis.

There is a uniform numbering system for transistors and diodes, just as there is a uniform system for tubes. The classical numbering system for diodes and transistors is a one digit number, a letter, and then a multidigit number. Diodes begin with "1," such as 1N916. In specialized applications, it may be possible to find a 1N916A. Transistors most often begin with "2," such as 2N190.

Transistor manufacturers force their own systems upon us in many cases. General Electric begins many of its consumer-oriented diodes and transistors with "GE," such as GE-10. Motorola uses a preface of "HEP", such as HEP159, for its devices. And RCA typically uses "SK," such as an SK 3037.

No sane radio and TV supply shop is going to stock semiconductors by every manufacturer. They do, however, have one or more replacement guide books distributed by each of the major manufacturers. So if you ask for a General Electric part number and the dealer hands you a Motorola part, don't assume just on the basis of that information that the dealer is wrong.

If you enjoy the thought of being able to repair and understand transistor circuits, you might have some interest in publications that will take you deeper into the subject than this chapter can go. Motorola has a replacement guide (less than $1) with several priceless pages of graphic, practical repair information. Both RCA and General Electric publish huge, low-priced volumes in paperback to lead you though the theory, diversities, adversities, and applications of nearly every semiconductor known to exist. Some of the contents will be within your grasp no matter how much or how little schooling you have in electronics.

On the subject of transistors and diodes, there are some very practical things to remember. Manufacturers know which parts will need replacing most often under normal use. With an eye on the fact that the cost of hiring a person to repair an ailing music maker is much greater than the cost of letting a machine grind out transistors, company engineers usually try to hold dispensible parts in place with only a bolt or two. So when looking for the source of electronic troubles, take a tip from the manufacturer—first consider the parts that seem to be the easiest to remove.

In amplifiers or the amplifier section of tuners, phonographs, or recorders, the power transistors can need replacing relatively often—perhaps every two or three years in a good machine. Therefore, most power transistors are held in place by two small bolts, occasionally by only one.

Power transistors are also smeared with a top quality silicone grease before being fastened into place. The grease helps to conduct heat away from the transistor and is much more important than you might imagine. So if a large transistor needs replacing, buy a small tube of silicone grease from the same electronics dealer who stocks the appropriate transistor.

In stereo equipment, it is often possible to pinpoint a burned out power transistor without spending a penny. Figure 82 will help you pick out the rather obvious power transistors from others. Aside from their size, they also require constant cooling, which means they are either bolted firmly to an uncluttered part of the metal chassis or, even more likely, enclosed by a set of aluminum cooling fins, known in the trade as a *heat sink*.

If the one good stereo channel stops playing after one of the pair of identical power transistors is removed, no doubt you are holding a *good* component in your hand. Unbolt the matching transistor—in stereo devices they almost always are arranged in pairs—and put the known good transistor in its place. If the once quiet channel now works, you can buy a replacement for the dead transistor. However, if you are a critical hi-fi listener, replace *both* power transistors in any pair at the same time.

Large amplifiers probably will have more than one pair of power transistors. Proceed systematically, switching one piece at a time from the known good channel to the bad channel until you isolate the bad one. Replace it or that particular pair with new ones.

If both channels in a stereo appliance are silent or jammed with weird noises you know aren't music, your problem probably is not in the power output section at all. If so, switching around the transistors should not help, not just yet anyway. Start looking for large diodes like the ones shown in Figure 82. Near the power transformer you should find four diodes hooked together as well as linked to the transformer output wires and to the rest of the electronic circuitry. Occasionally cheaper sets will use only two diodes in this capacity. Modern sets can have four diodes worked into a single case, however.

All of these diode collections convert the pulsating alternating current in your home into the steady direct current needed by electronic components. If you buy or build the flashlight type continuity tester described in the troubleshooting section early in this chapter, you can test all four of the rectifier diodes (or all two) in less than five minutes.

There are two wire leads on each diode, one positive and the other negative. Your flashlight continuity tester also has a + and a − lead. But it is not important for this test that you know in advance which leads are − and which are +. With the + test lead on one diode + wire and the − test lead on the same diode − wire, the continuity tester lamp should light up. Conversely, with the test leads *reversed* (+ to − and − to +), the test lamp should not light up.

Test each rectifier diode in turn and replace any that fail. Failure means not lighting the lamp in either of the two test positions or lighting it in both. This test *cannot* be performed with a transistor radio adapted for use as a continuity tester.

Diodes serve functions other than to rectify house alternating current in power supplies. For most diodes you will encounter in household applications, the simple flashlight test will suffice, however.

Except for the rectifier diodes and the power output transistors at the other end of the circuitry, small diodes and small transistors almost never fail during normal use. After the device has been in service long enough for you to find out conclusively that your gadget does indeed work, only serious physical damage, such as dropping or the failure of a nearby resistor, electrolytic capacitor, larger transistor, or occasionally a transformer, will destroy a small transistor or diode. Unlike electronic tubes, transistors almost never get weak or go bad slowly. They either work completely or don't work at all.

All of those squizzles and jerky lines you may have seen glued to the inside of hi-fi and TV sets, or reproduced in books and magazines aimed at fix-it nuts, really do have some meaning. Earlier in this chapter, alongside the pictures of various components such as resistors, capacitors, transistors, and the like, a drawing was included to show how the item looks in what pros call a *schematic diagram.*

To make electronic design and repair simpler, a graphic shorthand has evolved. The schematic symbols not only identify a particular bit of gadgetry, but they demonstrate the function of components within the circuit. It is not necessary that you understand every obscure facet of reading schematics, but the next page or so will give you all the electronic knowledge necessary to tackle fully 75 percent or more of all the repair jobs on household electronic noise makers.

In addition to the symbols already given, Figure 83 gives a picture and symbol for other important ingredients in electronic equipment. Don't memorize them, and don't even worry about whether you understand what any of the electronic parts do. It's not important. All you really want to know is how to spot a piece of hardware that isn't doing its job so you can replace it, no matter what the electronic engineers might say its job has been.

Get ready for the shock of looking at Figure 84A. It's the full schematic drawing for the amplifier in a simple portable phonograph. But before get too confused, look at Figure 84B, which is a small portion of the big, complicated drawing. If you recognize the circles with arrows and lines inside them as shorthand that says "transistor," you can isolate the transistors and the two 8.2 ohm resistors between them. Isolate them both in your mind and in your work.

If one of those two 2N1415 transistors from Figure 84 badly overheats, the trouble could be within the transistor itself, but more likely is within the resistor attached directly to it. All other leads from the transistor in question attach directly to coils, which seldom cause such troubles. Your first effort, therefore, should be to replace one or both of the very cheap 8.2 ohm resistors. If that fails to clear up the trouble, then the low-priced transistors also should be replaced. If you value fine sound, you will replace the transistors eventually anyway. Once they have been abused by something such as heat or a faulty resistor, which should be guarding the delicate component, quality probably is a thing of the past.

151   Move on to less directly connected parts if neither of the above

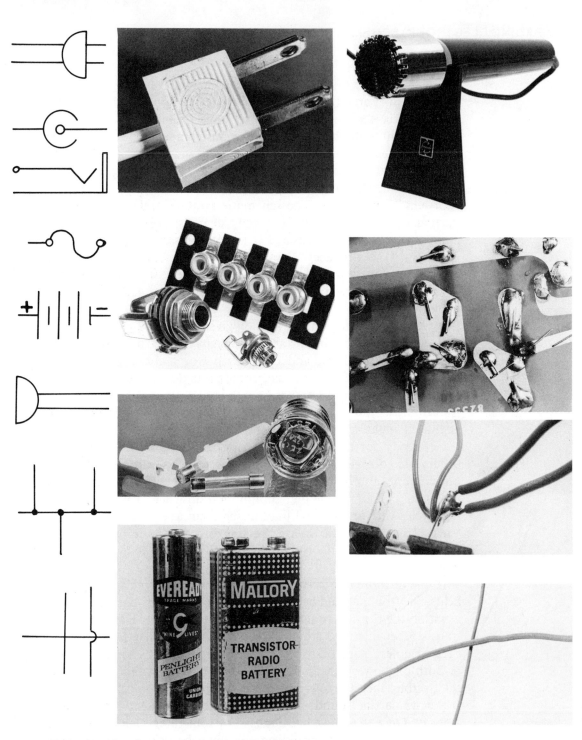

Figure 83 Miscellaneous electronic components you may encounter. A, power plug. B, phono jack (top) and phone jack (bottom), C, fuse. D, battery. E, microphone. F, connected wires. G, unconnected wires.

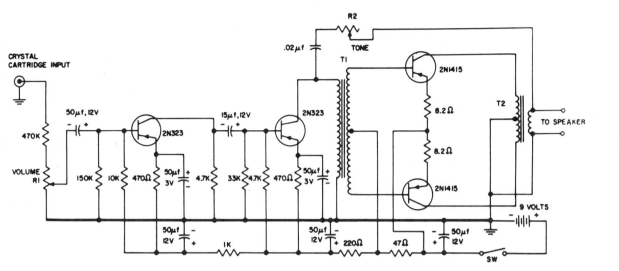

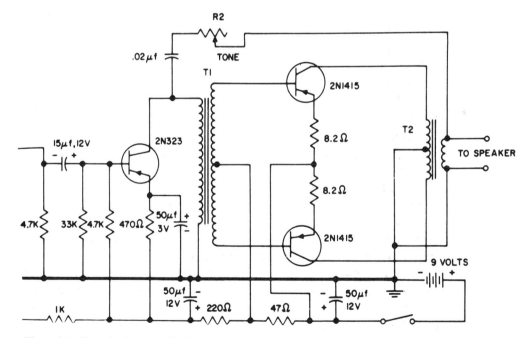

Figure 84 If you look at overall schematic view of inside works of hi-fi equipment, you'll get confused (A). But (B) by zeroing in on small areas, you can make sense of what's happening.

remedies clears up the problem. We are assuming that you have isolated this one area as the probable site of problems by such evidence as an overheated component right there or through signal tracing, which will be covered shortly. In our example, the 47 ohm resistor would be a logical next choice for replacement.

Since the 50 mfd. capacitors are electrolytics, which you can spot by their + and − signs, it is possible that they have become aged or defective. They are not all that expensive, so replace them and find out.

But how do you isolate the approximate site of trouble if nothing so physically telling as overheating is present? By *signal tracing*. First, however, you will need a signal injector, which you can buy in kit form for a few dollars. It will pay for itself in one successful repair. The ready-made versions generally are about the size of a fountain pen. Kits fit together into a package slightly smaller than a pack of cigarettes.

Don't be frightened at the thought of assembling a signal injector kit. It will be good experience for any novice or near-novice. A typical kit includes 1 transistor, 4 resistors, 1 capacitor, a switch, a battery, a few pieces of wire and plenty of diagrams. You need absolutely no electrical expertise or knowledge to assemble such a gadget. Sometimes the less you know the better. Most kits come with a picture, so all you do is lay the seven or eight parts in two rows, solder them together (a skill soon to be taught), and start using it.

You can buy an assembled signal injector or a kit at most consumer-oriented electronics shops and in catalogs.

In short, the signal injector enables you to run troubleshooting methods backward. It requires expensive test equipment and some training to measure values like volts, milliamps, and ohms all the way through a complex circuit. With a signal injector, however, you let your ears do much of the work. The injector sends a very broad signal into the circuit, which would come out the loudspeaker or headphone if all worked well. You simply trace the amplifier, intercom, radio, or other gadget's inside wiring *backward* from the speaker until you find out where the noise injector noise *begins*. And that's where the trouble probably also begins.

For an example, let's assume that your little transistor radio stopped making noise. If you want to fix it, after checking obvious things on our troubleshooting scheme, turn on the set even though no noise may be present. Attach the signal injector as instructed. Generally that will mean clipping one lead to a grounded part, such as the battery clip or earphone socket. If the signal immediately charges through a radio loudspeaker no matter where you try to clip the first lead, work only with one lead instead of two. Radios often pick up the signal from that number two lead via the air, just like they pick up the radio signal via their antennas.

A few words of caution are in order. If the appliance you are checking with a signal injector plugs into the 120 volt house current, please keep in mind where your fingers and the tester *should not go.*

In the silent transistor radio, begin roughly at the output and touch the test lead to each exposed wire or component lead in turn. At some point along the path, the signal suddenly may stop buzzing in the loudspeaker or headphone or, if has been quiet thus far, it may suddenly start buzzing. Note that point, but continue your probe until you have picked up as many similar points as possible.

Simply because two or more individual parts are not plugged side by side into an electronic device does not mean that they are not in fact wired together. Because of what pros call *printed circuit boards,* two parts on almost opposite sides of a chassis actually may be directly connected. Get at the bottom of a circuit board some day soon, and look at the copper channels etched there. Photographically mass-produced, the channels take the place of wires.

After isolating several dead spots during your signal tracing, study the printed circuit channels. You will probably find that some of the dead areas are interconnected. If you also have access to the schematic drawing for your troublesome appliance, life would be much simpler. Unfortunately, not many manufacturers supply such diagrams with every item they sell. Once the bad area of a circuit has been isolated, procede with parts substitution just as with our earlier suggestions. Following signal tracing, however, begin by first being suspicious of capacitors that may be malingering, then transistors, and resistors last of all.

Signal tracing is not limited to radios. It will work on nearly anything electronic. If you want to use it to analyze troubles something like one of those old UHF TV converters, you will have to fasten a headphone of some sort to the end of the electronic line. Even the tiny earplug type of headphone included in the price of a transistor radio will do. The headphone goes at the output as you probe toward the input.

On TV sets, keep the dial turned toward the lower numbered channels. On FM tuners, the lower end of the dial again works best. Phonographs can be traced from the needle (clamp one lead to any metal part on the tone arm, then touch the test lead to the needle, to the contacts on the cartridge that encases the needle, to the plugs, and on through the entire circuit).

Stay away from the power supply portions of appliances that operate on house current for a number of reasons. First, you would not want to shove a finger into a live wire. Second, the rectifiers that change the alternating house current into direct current will do the same thing to the buzzing sound of your signal tracer. It will turn the buzz into at most a faint click every time you touch the probe to a rectified contact point.

SOLDERING

Electronic parts transmit such delicate quantities of power that they must be joined very thoroughly. Consequently, virtually every connection inside electronic machines are joined with solder, a combination of lead and tin that melts at a very low temperature and is a good conductor of electricity.

First, you will need a soldering iron, a very inexpensive tool but a very important one. A cheap electric soldering iron with a 40 watt heating unit is ideal. An iron with more than a 100 watt heating element is not only more expensive than you need, but can be downright dangerous to delicate electronic parts. Buy a small tube or spool of very thin *resin core* solder. The equally popular acid core solder should not be popular for electronic uses; it will corrode your transistors, plugs, and chassis.

Presumably you will be repairing an already assembled item, so we'll start with *unsoldering*. Transistors must be protected from heat if you plan to reinstall them. A needlenosed pliers or similar tool, used according to Figure 85B will absorb enough heat to keep the transistor from getting scorched internally while you solder near it, unless you take excessive time. Other components are more rugged, although they also should receive as little heat as possible.

After the soldering iron is up to its operating temperature, touch the tip to the connector being unsoldered. Just as soon as the solder shows signs of melting, grab the appropriate lead with a small pliers and pull it away from the connector. In the case of a transistor, the pliers would be on the lead all the while, soaking up dangerous amounts of heat. If the first gentle tug does not loosen the wire fully, apply more heat and then another firm jerk.

If a component is being discarded anyway, there is seldom any need to unsolder it at all unless the particular connector to which it is fastened is already too cluttered to tolerate a bit of additional wire. Simply snip off the leads of a soon-to-be-junked component.

Most new components come with longer leads than you will actually need. Trim them with a wire cutter, snippers, or cutting pliers to a length just about ¼ " or ½ " longer than the old leads. If the old connector point has been well desoldered, there should be an opening through which the new lead can pass. If not, wrap the end of the new lead about the connector once or twice. Here, and everywhere else, make sure that the uninsulated leads do not touch each other except where they are supposed to. If necessary, add some electrical tape or insulation removed from a large wire to a troublesome area.

When soldering electronic parts—or anything else for that matter—it is important to remember that the solder preferably should not be melted directly by the soldering iron but by the heat of the connector. That heat, of course, is put there by the soldering iron. Therefore, hold the heated soldering iron onto the connection

Figure 85 Soldering requires hot iron to melt a tiny piece of solder quickly and allow it to flow into crevices between wire and connector (A). The iron must be kept clean. When soldering or unsoldering delicate parts such as transistors, clamp jaws of needlenose pliers (or similar tool) between part and hot soldering iron to absorb as much heat as possible (B).

point until it becomes hot enough so that solder touched against it can melt. Occasionally the soldering process is speeded along by touching the tip of the new solder to the tip of the iron itself, but the joint on which you are working must be hot enough to sustain the melting.

Once you become adept at the simple art of soldering, the entire process should not require that the hot soldering iron touch the leads of any component for more than a very few seconds. Plugs are no different than other electrical connections except that insulation has to be stripped from wires before they can be soldered.

As more and more modern people abandon their books for electronic boxes, the preceding chapter will not only save a lot of money. It will help put *you* more firmly back in control of that part of your life which you have unwittingly surrendered to some stranger who just happened to read up on electronics before you did.

Figure 86 All these plugs were taken apart and resoldered to make sure their connections were not the cause of sound troubles. If your soldered joints look this good, your sound will be good too.

Mechanical Hangups in Listening Equipment

7

The mechanical problems that plague all kinds of electronic gadgets can be as devastating and frustrating as all of those electronic problems discussed in Chapter 6. But just like electronic problems, mechanical hangups can be solved too.

DIALS AND ANTENNAS

Radios, hi-fi tuners, and UHF TV tuners often feature a foot or so of cord wrapped around a tuner knob, a dial that shows you the stations, and then around a variable capacitor that tunes in the selected stations. Age and gremlins play havoc with one or more parts of the dial cord set up.

If the dial cord has broken, carefully sketch the path it followed before touching anything. Some dial cords meander like the Mississippi River, crossing three or four pulleys in addition to the essential parts. It could take an evening of trial and error or logical deduction **159** to reconstruct a complete, complicated dial cord system.

Fortunately, most problems with dials come from slipping, not breaking cords. The *dial marker*, the part that actually points to the frequency number of a station, typically is held onto the dial cord by three small metal prongs. Dust, corrosion, or other impediments gradually may build up so much friction against the marker or the slide on which it rests that the cord begins slipping through the prongs. The logical solution is to clean away the resistance-causing dirt. If that fails, perhaps the center prong can be bent so that it grabs more firmly onto the cord.

Before making the dial indicator fully secure, tune the radio to an easy-to-identify station. Then set the marker at the appropriate frequency on the dial without moving the variable capacitor that tunes in the stations. In other words, the station should come through loud and clear all the while you are making this adjustment.

Once the dial marker is at the right setting for the selected station, tighten down the prongs. It would not hurt to test the setting by turning carefully to another station or two to make sure that their published frequencies match the numbers shown on your dial.

If a slipping problem becomes chronic, and all of your bending, cleaning, and tightening doesn't seem to help, a drop or two of plastic cement will hold the cord and dial marker together. A few drops of solvent will loosen it again if that ever becomes necessary.

On the big pulley, which most often is connected to the tuning variable capacitor, there is a spring that applies tension to the cord. In the good old days, manufacturers provided a series of holes that could be used to adjust the spring as the years rolled by. Today, however, those handy adjusting holes are not always included.

With your finger resting on the dial cord at some spot not directly in line with the pulley itself, apply extra tension and see if that resolves whatever problem has been annoying you. If it does, you must either drill your own adjusting hole in the pulley—probably ½ " away from the original one—or shorten the cord itself. Drilling the new hole is by far the easier solution.

There is yet another possible hangup along the dial cord path, where it wraps around the inside end of the tuning knob. If that shaft seems to be letting the dial cord slip, it is possible that the surface of the shaft has become so slick that it not longer generates sufficient friction to turn the cord. In that case, the cord can be shoved to one side while you roughen the surface with a file, sandpaper, or similar implement.

In the event you decide to replace the cord altogether, radio supply houses sell spools of replacement cord. Fishing line, however, is a good substitute, the old black fabric kind, not monofilament.

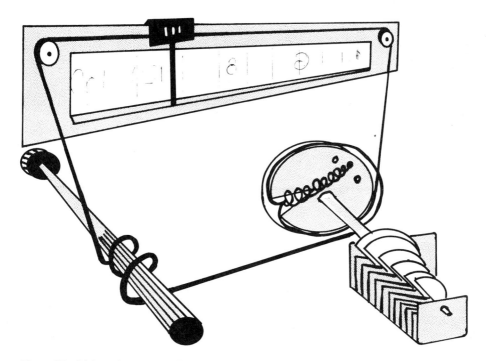

Figure 87   Dial cords are assembled in this general fashion.

The FM antenna on many small radios has the nasty habit of snapping off. You might bear in mind that the long, slender, collapsible tube of an antenna is intended for FM use only on most radios. The AM reception is handled through an iron-cored coil built into the set itself. Fortunately for those of us who habitually bend and break the flimsy FM antenna, most electronic shops sell replacements at very reasonable prices. Most often, two screws come off, the new antenna slips into place, and the two screws go back on. The electrical connection is usually made by a slip-off, slip-on-again terminal inside the radio case.

Instead of actually replacing a frequently broken external antenna, you might try a shortcut, which works fine except in areas too distant from FM stations. Find where the wire from the broken external FM antenna enters the inside of the plastic case. Then connect approximately 3 ' of some thin single conductor electrical wire. (If you never had 3 ' of wire waiting in a drawer before reading this book, lets hope from now on you will.) For optimum results, solder the connection. Then wind the wire into a loop that will fit comfortably on the outside or inside of the case and tape it into place. This is one antenna that will never snap off.

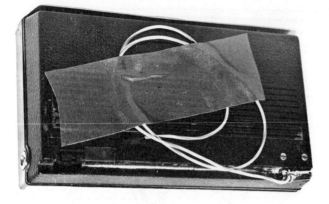

Figure 88 The FM antenna on small transistor radios breaks off too often. Taped on, soldered replacement such as this is makeshift but effective. Experiment with the length of wire until optimum results are obtained.

INTERCOMS AND WALKIE TALKIES

When something goes haywire with an intercom or a walkie talkie, chances are pretty good that a switch is at fault. And most of them are anything but standard replacement items. That is the *bad* news. The *good* news is that you can improvise due to the fact that although the switches may not look like standard items, the *function* they perform *is* standard. For example, if that fancy rocking double pole, double throw switch on your intercom wears out or breaks, you might have to phone around for a long time to find a replacement made by the original manufacturer. But if you are willing to compromise a bit on appearance, you should find a standard double pole, double throw switch on the shelf of every radio and TV supply shop in town.

Here's another example of how the knowledge you have picked up in one chapter applies to other areas. Many small intercom systems, especially the imported ones, use a volume control identical with the one we spoke of when discussing transistor radios in Chapter 6.

Since intercoms sometimes get knocked around and shifted more than they can stand, wires have a habit of coming loose—and not always just at the ends inserted into the gadget itself. At least one of the intercom models that requires no special wiring because the sound travels over house wires has a four-conductor wire between the intercom proper and the transformer box, which plugs into the wall. If something happens to that wire, you need only remove one screw to open up the main part of the intercom.

The small power unit of the intercom plugged into the wall often seems to be sealed into a solid and the wires along with it. Don't be misled. The small plastic case is hollow, held together with little more than some plastic cement. And inside you will generally find a tiny transformer and an electrolytic capacitor or two. You will also find the ends of those wires, which may need replacing. Note carefully the location of each old wire before starting to install the new.

POWER CONVERTERS

Much the same layout is used for the very popular power converters on gadgets such as tape recorders, small computers, and electronic flash guns, along with many other gadgets that allow you to run a battery-powered device on a/c house current. To open such a case, liberally apply some solvent such as lacquer thinner or nail polish remover around the seam. Never give the solvent a chance to evaporate completely. Keep applying more periodically until the case is fully opened. Such solvents are flammable, so if you soak, don't smoke. It will probably be necessary to pry the plastic halves apart in the end with a screwdriver, putty knife, or some other tool not intended specifically for such use.

The beautiful part about these superminiature power supplies—beautiful, that is, for the manufacturer—is that should the electrolytic capacitor become defective, you would get poor recording quality or the flash batteries would need recharging and replacing more often than before, but you might never suspect a defective capacitor.

Replacing an electrolytic capacitor you suspect to be over the hill is relatively inexpensive and easy, as we saw in the last chapter. The diodes in power supplies of this sort likewise are very inexpensive and easy to buy. *However,* they are often fastened right into the protective upper layer of the transformer. Finding a replacement transformer in small power converters promises to be more of a problem. The original manufacturer has to be contacted. By that point, unless you persevere in matters like these more than the average timid soul, you will buy an entirely new appliance.

TAPE RECORDERS

Tape recorders in general suffer from hardening or softening of their rubber arteries that power the tape drive. Power is not always transmitted directly from the motor to the little capstan that spins around to move the tape. *It could be*, however, if you and your tape recorder manufacturer were willing to invest a few more dollars at the outset.

163

The soft, tacky kind of rubber that is best for friction drive mechanisms has a habit of losing its good qualities rather easily. Age, heat, cold, ozone from electrical discharges, oil, chemicals, and excessive pressure all can combine to turn the rubber drive wheels into hard, almost brittle cookies or into spongy, sticky, practically formless gums. Consequently, it is important that you protect your recorder drive wheels.

Once a recorder drive section has deteriorated to the point where your ear notices obvious distortions, the trouble is already far advanced. For the more discerning listeners or fanatic recording buffs, inexpensive equipment is available to spot troubles before they become advanced enough for tin ears to detect. Inexpensive but generally reliable equipment for home maintenance, test, repair, and cleaning are carried by most mail order electronic supply houses.

A good machine that is over one year old, regardless how much use it has received, probably needs some internal maintenance. And any machine that gets constant use can benefit by tests and cleaning several times a year. By the way, once you have taken a tape recorder out of the showroom and played it for some time, you have lost any chance to run a concrete test to determine if the recorder *ever did* play at precisely the right speed. Before any recorder is taken home, the salesperson should demonstrate with a strobe test device that the machine is performing perfectly—or at least as perfectly as it can.

To ensure that a recorder is moving tape at precisely the proper speed, a test reel, cassette, cartridge, or just a loop is "played" while a small strobe light is held near the tape. The test tape actually has a network of lines printed on it that correspond to the speed of the fluctuating strobe. House current is 60 hertz (formerly known as "60 cycle" and abbreviated as "60 Hz"). And since the light flashes bright every time the current changes direction, the light puts out 120 pulses of light every second. With tape moving at precisely 3¾ ips (inches per second), the tape pattern of 32 lines per second (120 divided by 3¾) is calculated to seem as if it were standing still. Should the speed be off, however, the pattern of lines would appear to be moving forward for excess speed and backward for too little speed.

Once you have determined that your recorder is not operating at its proper speed, the problem becomes *why*. If the machine is operated by batteries and is priced below several hundred dollars, you may have to live with minor inaccuracies. Low cost d/c motors cannot operate on battery power with the precision equal to even some low priced a/c motors. And running a battery-powered recorder on its a/c converter will not change the situation. Bad inaccuracies should not develop, however. So if batteries are not to blame, perhaps the problem can be corrected by cleaning and adjusting all parts that take power from the small motor.

There are plenty of ways to clean the rubber drive wheels, to revitalize them, to check whether they have worn down or been compacted by a few thousanths of a inch. But there really is no need to go through so much puttering when a set of brand new wheels costs very little. This assumes, of course, that you have access to a local distributor of parts for the brand name you need. If not, write or call directly to the head office of the manufacturer. Your local public library should be able to supply the address or telephone number. If you call, the manufacturer should take your name and address and promise to mail you replacement parts COD or tell you precisely where to obtain the necessary parts and for how much. If you write, the same response should be received within 10 days.

If you are unable to obtain replacement parts with ease, phone or write again—this time directly to the president of the firm. And mail a copy of your communications to a local Better Business Bureau, your county district attorney, and to any consumer protection agencies in your city or state. The time is long past when consumers have to accept whatever maintenance crumbs manufacturers offer them. But let this be a warning to you too—catch up with minor maintenance matters before they deteriorate into major problems.

Since oil is such an enemy of rubber drive surfaces, lubrication should be taken care of *before* recorder housecleaning. The object is to get oil into the bearing and shaft but not onto the surface of any drive wheels. One drop from most oil cans is too much. Unless you are quite handy at the art of letting a too-big drop of oil slide down an exposed shaft and catching most of it with a dry swab before it oozes all over, you should invest in an oiling device made for miniaturized equipment.

The standard cleaning agent for recorders is alcohol. If you don't already have some in the medicine cabinet, buy a bottle of rubbing alcohol with the highest percentage of alcohol your druggist stocks. Cotton swabs soaked in alcohol can rub away oil, grease, dirt, and a film of magnetic oxides, plus other foreign matter, from all of the drive wheels whether they be rubber, metal, or plastic. You must be careful if you do this while the motor is running. First of all, don't touch any live a/c wires, which would be hard to do even if you wanted to in most recorders. Hold the swab well away from any area where two wheels meet. If the swab gets into the upstream part of such a power transfer point, the cotton can be pulled loose and wrapped around the wheels. It is not a disaster by any means, but picking cotton out of the works can get annoying.

After cleaning all of the drive wheels with alcohol, give them a chance to dry off before starting the recorder again. If you clean the wheels while the motor is running, don't try to change the speed or direction. Wet drive wheels can spin, just like wet wheels on your car. And once they begin to spin, they stay that way *even after the alcohol dries.*

While you are probing beneath the cover of your tape recorder, take a look at the various springs there. They should look clean, and both ends should be fastened onto something that looks like a proper home for the spring. In both the relaxed and tensed posture, a spring should be almost uniformly spaced throughout its entire length.

If you are sending away for any parts to rejuvenate an ailing recorder, it would not hurt to include a set of replacement springs on your shopping list. Because springs do not often retain their original shape and tension after any sizeable amount of use, they are not often used in important drive portions of better engineered recorders.

Well-stocked hardware stores have many springs. With luck you might find some the right length, width, and power.

Although the capstan, the metal wheel that spins the tape, actually controls the critical speed at which your recorder operates, the take-up and feed reels can adversely affect the capstan's performance if they are not functioning reasonably well. The capstan moves at a fixed speed, hopefully, but the take-up reel must move faster at the start of a reel and slower at the conclusion.

At the start there is little tape wound around the reel hub so a 5″ reel, which has a hub measuring approximately 1.75″, takes up almost 5.5″ of tape in each revolution. To handle 3¾ ips, the take-up reel must turn about 38 rpm. As the end of a 5″ reel draws near, due to the fact that almost a full reel of tape has increased the actual dimensions of the reel windup surface, the reel need make only 13 or 14 rpm to handle the 3¾ ips flow of tape. Cassettes, despite their much smaller overall size, offer the same extremes in how the take-up reels must perform.

To handle the diverse speeds required of a take-up reel, most recorder engineers employ one of two basic systems in a one-motor recorder: 1) a *clutch* that allows the take-up reel to begin slipping once it no longer has to turn at full speed; 2) a *pulley and belt* system, which does the same. In both instances, the mechanism should be cleaned occasionally, at least every time it gives you trouble, and must be kept free of oil or grease.

Most clutch mechanisms offer little chance for adjustment. In the pulley system, a new belt cures most problems that cleaning and lubrication of bearings hasn't already remedied. With the clutch mechanism, a felt pad that separates the two disks in the clutch is the most common cause of grief, and it merits replacement every time you have occasion to disassemble your recorder that far. The belts and pads are the sort of nickle and dime spare parts you should order at the same time any other parts are required; then you'll have them on hand.

There is a *brake* somewhere within the array of parts on most tape recorders. It prevents tape from unraveling off the reels every time you push the stop button. On most simple machines, the brake is little more than a spring or two coupled to crucial moving parts. When you push the play or record buttons, the spring is deactivated, relaxed. But as soon as you push the recorder stop button, the springs jump into life and halt the tape reels. If your tape is piling up after you push the stop button, check for broken, missing, or distorted springs.

On more expensive machines, the brake is often electrical, accomplished within the internal windings of motors on the take-up and feed reels. Alternately a magnetic brake may be triggered by the stop button. In any event, trouble in an electrical brake system has to be traced by troubleshooting from power to powered, from the switch to the pads on a magnetic brake. Fortunately, a machine built well enough to include electric brakes is also built well enough that the brake seldom goes awry.

There is almost no standardization among tape recorder manufacturers beyond agreeing upon what speeds ought to be used. In general, however, the connecting levers, rods, bars, and buttons require little care except that they be cleaned occasionally and lubricated with a tiny bit of white grease to help the sliding members slide easily.

It is a race right down to the wire to decide whether worn and dirty drive wheels contribute more bad tape performances or whether dirty tape heads do. The head is that part of the recorder that actually imposes a magnetic signal onto your tape or that reads the magentic signal there and converts it into pleasant sounds—hopefully. As mile after mile of tape feeds past the heads, traces of the oxide coating accumulate on the head. The oxides, generally rust colored, interfere with both the electrical and mechanical performances of any recorder. Electrical signals in a playback head generally are below 1/1000 volt, so even a tiny metal oxide covering over the head represents a sizeable inteference.

Alcohol cleans off the oxide deposits on the head—with a bit of elbow grease. Do not, however, use anything abrasive to clean the heads. A tape recorder head is a precision piece of equipment even in very inexpensive recorders.

There is yet another kind of dirt that accumulates in a recorder head—magnetism. Since the metal parts inside and surrounding a tape head are subjected to constant magnetic fields, they are bound to become magnetized. And this residue of unwanted magnetism interferes with the sensitivity of even very good tape heads. For a reasonable price, you can invest in a tape head demagnetizer, which should be used according to the manufacturer's own instructions after every 10 or 15 hours of tape recording or playing.

The tape recorder heads themselves should provide fine service for many thousands of hours of use, assuming they are not dropped, battered, cleaned with abrasives, or subjected to excessive pressure from the pressure pads that hold the tape into contact with the head. Many sound distortion problems that may seem to be caused *inside* the head actually have to do with its improper *alignment*, a purely external problem. Check periodically that the screws holding the head into place are not loose. If they are, tighten them very carefully to avoid any pressures that might force the head out of its proper location.

Especially with four-channel and eight-track machines, even a tiny change in position can lead to distortion and a loss of high frequency sounds. The bad sound will be noticed most easily on prerecorded tapes. Tapes you record at any time after the misalignment will appear to be properly aligned when played back on the same machine, unless the maladjustment is so bad that one track falls almost completely off the head.

There are several prerecorded tapes available that can help you determine if the heads on your machine are in proper alignment (see Figure 90). Do not confuse the rather expensive *alignment test tapes* with the more commonplace tapes intended to help you balance the stereo separation, and take an educated guess as to the frequency range either your recorder can reproduce or your ears can hear.

Armed with an alignment tape, you can make fine adjustments in head alignment by first loosening whatever setscrews or nuts lock the head into position, and then very slowly raising or lowering the head via whatever screws are put there for that purpose. This is a job guaranteed to fill most of an evening.

If you have realigned your tape heads but still suffer from bad sound, what then? Assuming you're convinced that the distortion does not originate within the amplifier portion of the machine (a job for the preceding chapter), or in the tapes themselves (which you can check on a friend's machine), you can replace the heads. They are relatively simple to replace although new ones are not cheap. Order them in advance from a mail order house or an over-the-counter electronics supplier.

There are fewer basic heads than you might at first imagine. The supplier will have to know the manufacturer and model number of

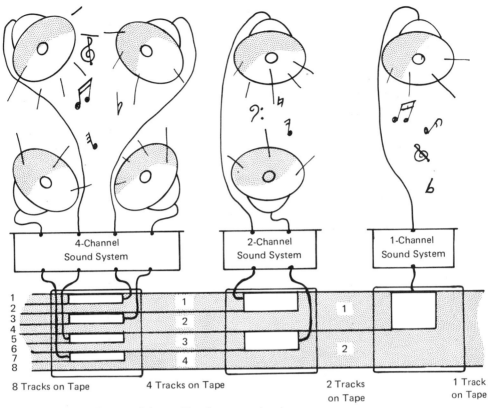

Figure 89 "Track" versus "channel" on tape recorders is graphically explained here.

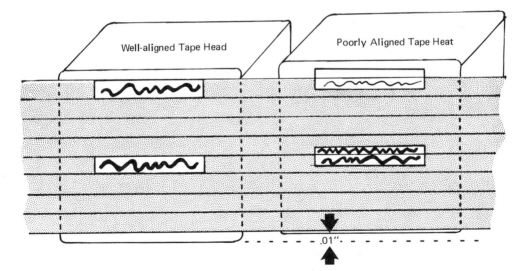

Figure 90 When tracks on tape and head of tape recorder are not properly aligned, poor sound results. Special tape can indicate state of alignment. Screws generally can correct alignment.

your recorder. On a recorder that plays stereo music, alignment with a set of test tapes is almost an inevitable part of the head replacement routine.

The pads that hold tape onto the heads deserve periodic cleaning with alcohol. And if they show any signs of wear, they should have been replaced a long time ago. Self-adhesive replacement pads of varying sizes are available for a very nominal price.

On many machines, the arm on which the pressure pad moves is controlled by a spring. These springs ought to be checked or replaced periodically. Do not underestimate the importance of that *pressure pad* and its support system. *Too little pressure* will result in bad recordings and bad playback sound. *Too much pressure* wears out recording heads and tape prematurely.

Now lets concentrate on what the person behind the controls of the recorder often does wrong. In truth, the manufacturer ought to

Figure 91   Block diagram of how the typical tape recorder works.

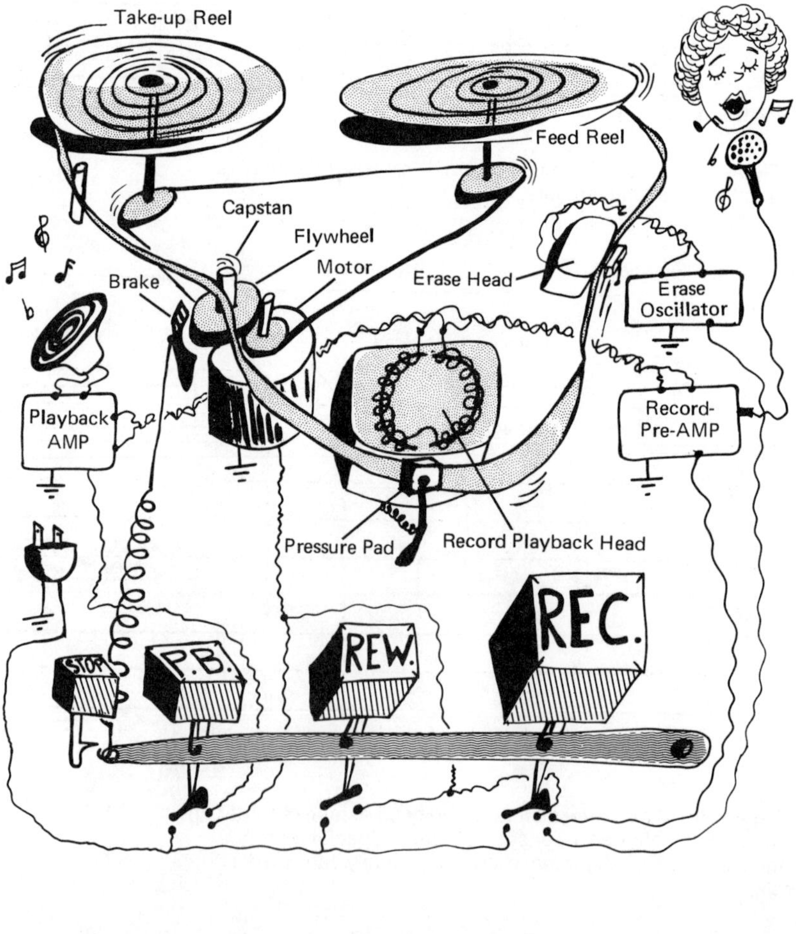

include comprehensive instructions with every machine sold. Either out of economy or a desire to make its product seem supersimple, the page or two of how-to-record literature barely covers the fundamentals.

The major problem with tape recording is *noise*—noise inherent to the technological aspects of magnetizing tape; noise from microphone cables that are too long; noise generated by feeding the wrong signals into your recorder. How many user manuals have you seen that go even this deeply into the how-to of recording, or the how-not-to?

Except in the automatic level setting machines, you must set the recording level quite accurately. The object is to get as loud a signal on the tape as possible to overpower tape and recorder noise while avoiding that excessive amount that will distort the sound. The meters or lights that accompany records can help. Your user manual no doubt tells you that the sound level should make the needle bounce below the red area. That's true, except that the needle should become *into* the red area fairly often. When you record music, those loud drumbeats or trumpet blasts should tilt the needle into the red. For speech, emphasized words and syllables should chase the needle well into the red.

Level indicators are notoriously inaccurate, especially on lower priced machines. If your sound is coming out distorted despite your care in setting the dial to what seems like a proper recording range, try a significantly lower recording level next time. And conversely, if you hear an objectionable amount of hiss in the background, perhaps your recording level should be raised. This assumes you used *new tape* and there is no hiss present when a radio or other quality source is played *through* the recorder, not onto its tape. Set the recording level meter well into the red next time and see if the ratio of good sound to the objectionable background hissing noise is improved. That is what pros refer to as the "sound-to-noise-ratio." Very good machines have internal adjustments for the level indicator, but your brain, the best machine of all, can compensate on any machine without every a screwdriver.

Tape generally is priced according to quality. You get what you pay for. If you pay little, you may pay a lot in listening quality. Newer machines have settings that allow for the use of chromium oxide recording tapes. The chromium tapes generally result in a more favorable sound-to-noise-ratio, but they cannot be used on a recorder designed exclusively for the older iron oxide tapes.

Recorders are designed to accept input signals from only very narrowly specific sources. If you plugged the relatively high voltage output from a radio into the microphone input designed for very low voltage sources, the results would be very distorted. And if you tried the reverse, your sound would be barely audible.

More subtle complications reside in the microphones themselves. Less expensive recorders are very often designed to use *low impedance* microphones. And finer pieces of equipment may prefer the *high impedance* microphones or provide input connections for either type.

Microphones often are marked with a rating such as "50 ohm impedance" (low) or "10,000 ohm impedance" (high). Some recorder user manuals list the preferred impedance of their circuits. If you run into recording hangups when using anything but the microphones that come with a recorder, and other complications have already been ruled out, investigate whether impedance ratings are mismatched.

If impedance or voltage input is the problem, a *mixer* probably can resolve it. The device, which can be relatively inexpensive, electronically copes with mismated impedance and voltage ratings between equipment such as recorders and microphones, radios, or other sources of sound.

If Junior stands on one side of the room and recites his poem while Dad sits across the room holding a microphone, don't blame your recorder for the resulting weak, tinny sound. If Junior stands right in front of Dad, then the sound has a chance to come through very clear. In general, the microphone should be as close as possible to the voice or instrument being recorded. With a piano, of course, the sound comes from so many different individual sources scattered over the five feet of sounding board that you will have to move back far enough to avoid one side overbalancing the other, unless you record the piano in stereo with one microphone close to each end of the instrument.

Other tape recorder noise and distortion problems come from the same reasons as similar electronic ailments in other home music makers.

PHONOGRAPH TROUBLES AND USE

PHONOGRAPH TURNTABLES

The mechanisms of phonograph turntables bear a striking resemblance to tape recorder mechanisms once the exterior has been stripped off both. Two principal ailments befall the record players—*speed* that goes wrong or fluctuates and *needles* that are worn out or improperly adjusted.

Speed can be checked with a low budget stroboscopic tester identical in principal to the one used for checking tape recorder speeds. If your phonograph has an automatic record changer instead of a manual turntable in which you have to put one record into play after another manually, test the speed with varying numbers of records on the platter. Since the motor in all but very cheap, very old, or very abused players is seldom directly at fault, the first place to check as the cause of fluctuating or incorrect speed is the network of rubber drive wheels and an occasional small rubber belt.

Since there is less diversity among record players than tape recorders, you stand a good chance of finding replacement wheels and belts in a local shop. Change them often, keep them clean, don't spill oil on them, and speed problems should be rare in good machines.

You will probably find at least one spring in your turntable mechanism, connected to what is called an *idler wheel*. In changers you might find a handful of springs. They can stand a checkup periodically and replacement whenever the coils become uneven, stretched, or weak. And when lubricating moving parts, don't overlook the main bearing at the very bottom of the turntable.

There are several products on the market for making improvised drive wheel repairs. They are of a certain amount of value for both tape recorder and phonograph systems, mainly in a pinch. Essentially they are chemicals that are spread onto the drive wheels or portions contacting the drive wheels to increase their friction. The most effective of such materials is a mixture of carbide granules and synthetic rubber in a solvent. It is not the cheapest, but once the rubber has bonded to metal drive surfaces, the carbide particles noticeably increase the friction between the metal and rubber. Carbide potions are most valuable for emergency, stopgap repairs when oily or aged rubber drive wheels cannot be cleaned or replaced easily.

Changer mechanisms have become simplified over the years. A device that can sense when a record has finished playing, lift the tone arm, move it back to the beginning, trip a new record onto the turntable, and then lower the tone arm at approximately the proper starting point—that sounds fairly complicated. But in truth it isn't.

At the heart of many changer mechanisms is a small gear that protrudes from the bottom of the turntable and is, in a sense, built right around the hole in the center of the turntable through which the spindle passes. A much larger gear is positioned so it would mesh permanently with the small gear except that several teeth have been deliberately omitted in the large gear.

The larger gear is spun around by the smaller one whenever the changer mechanism is tripped. This can be done manually, such as when you push the reject lever. The changer does it automatically whenever the tone arm has reached the end of a record. In either event, a small arm attached to the big gear reaches out and catches onto teeth of the small gear. The lever is able to hang into the groove just long enough so that the large gear is moved around far enough for its teeth to engage the small gear's teeth.

Once the large gear begins to turn, it moves a large, flat, odd shaped metal plate first forward and then backward. In moving toward its forward position, the rear portion of the plate lifts the tone arm. Then via a mechanical coupling, it moves the tone arm back to the outside. In its full forward position again, the plate shoves against a lever, which delicately bumps the lowest record off the remaining pile. It bumps only one record because the top of the record-bumping lever protudes up into the spindle the precise distance for one record. Gravity slides the new record down the spindle and onto the still revolving turntable. If you have installed the spindle improperly, too many or too few records may be bumped during the automatic cycling. On some machines, it is even necessary to insert the spindle only after the machine has finished its automatic cycle. If you try to force it in while the changing mechanism is somewhere in the midst of a cycle, it won't fit.

On a backward moving stroke of the changer plate, the tone arm is lowered again and moved to a position just inland of the edge of the new record. When the insides of automatic record players looked very complicated, there was a separate adjustment for where the tone arm would hit the outside of the record as well as where it would trip the reject mechanism at the inside. Today engineers have dispensed with the separate inside and outside adjustments on most machines. Consequently, if the inside and outside settings don't fall precisely where you would like them to, you may have to settle on a compromise unless your particular changer still has the double changing routine—there is an adjustment screw to compensate for that. Here again, the exact location varies from maker to maker and even model to model. You probably will have to raise the plunger that lifts the tone arm into its highest position to reach the adjusting screw. Whenever you tamper with the tone arm lifting adjustments, be certain to check later that the tone arm is able to move without restriction into its lowest position. The apparent weight a tone arm exerts on the single record and pile of records is quite important.

Lubrication of all the moving levers, plates, arms, and other pieces inside a record changer is not critical, but some grease now and then is helpful. All of the gadgets connected directly to the tone arm, however, must be oiled, and carefully. If the inside of your changer shows that obvious quantities of dust accumulate in a relatively short period, you would do better to use graphite instead of grease. Continue to *oil* the tone arm mechanisms, however, due to their delicate nature.

All parts attaching the tone arm to the engaging lever also must be designed with sensitivity in mind. The tone arm itself cannot exert more than a microscopic amount of pressure in any direction, up, down or sideways. Consequently, all of the pivot points on levers in this area must be kept meticulously clean, and a light oil—not grease or graphite—must be used regularly. If the tripping system fails to operate, or if it operates too soon and cuts off a record before the music is over, an adjustment screw remedies the complaint. Like everything else on phonographs, its location varies.

The adjustment of a tone arm on your hi-fi phonograph is probably the most critical and frequently performed adjustment of all. Fortunately, the test equipment necessary to make such delicate tune-ups is readily available and very inexpensive. Anybody interested in fine music or fine machinery should be able to adjust the weight of a tone arm. The alternatives are to put up with second-rate performance or to lug the turntable to a competent repair person once a year, pay a good deal of money, and then pray that the adjustment doesn't come apart as you cart the turntable home again.

You'll need a mirror—any small, shiny piece of metal works better than a looking glass type mirror because it reflects from its front surface. And you'll need a turntable balancing scale, which every electronic shop or catalog should sell.

Today's records feature such microscopically proportioned grooves that the stylus (mostly still called a "needle"), which reproduces the music, is measured in fractions of *mils*. A mil is 1/1000 of a inch. A stylus of 0.7 mil (.007″ or 7/10,000″) is common. Generally a replaceable part of the cartridge, the stylus, must be positioned very precisely if it is accurately to reproduce the notes pressed into the record grooves via ridges and depressions.

At one time hi-fi buffs and hi-fi stores bought small microscopes to help determine whether a stylus was in good shape, literally. The demands of stereo, and more so the demands of "quad" sound, have made stylus shapes so complicated that microscopes are about useless. So we are better off simply replacing a stylus every year or after 400 hours of use for *diamond* styli. Sapphire styli require replacement twice as frequently.

Once the stylus is placed into the cartridge, put a tone arm balance into position to find out how much pressure the tone arm is exerting. Instructions that come with each balance will explain the proper use of the specific tool you own.

The actual total weight of a tone arm, of course, is considerably

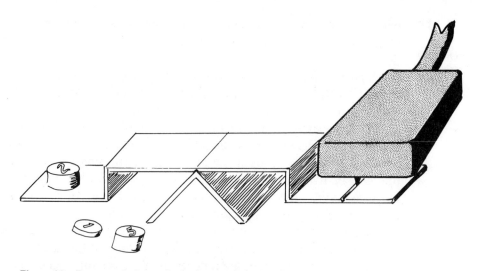

Figure 92 Tone arm balance device in use. For long-lasting records plus optimum sound quality, the apparent weight of the phonograph tone arm should be carefully checked and adjusted on quality machines. Various balances are on sale; all operate like a scale.

more than the few grams recorded on the tone arm balancing scale. However, any tone arm worthy of the hi-fi label has a spring or counterbalance weight that limits the apparent force on a stylus to just a few grams. And the amount of force should be adjustable.

Some cartridges require relatively heavy *tracking forces,* others can reproduce sound with only tiny amounts. For years, avid record fans were convinced that cartridges with heavier tracking forces would wear out their records in months if not in days. Plastic technology, however, has produced record materials tough enough to withstand most moderate tracking forces without appreciable wear even after many years of normal use.

The tracking force adjustment should be set to match the approximate value recommended by your cartridge manufacturer. If you can't remember what that figure was, if you lost any literature that may have accompanied the new cartridge, leaf through a mail order electronics catalog and find the tracking force for the same or similar cartridge.

Automatic changers require a heavier tracking force (2 to 7 grams) than do manual machines (½ to 3 grams). Cheaper tone arms also require heavier tracking forces than better built mechanisms. But if you have any doubts about what force to use, try one slightly toward the heavier side of the stated high and low range. Example: A super-Hi-Fi-273XKE cartridge maker recommends a tracking force of from **176** 2 to 4 grams. Try 3 or so at first, and gradually decrease it a bit until the performance becomes erratic. Then add ¼ or ½ gram to that setting and sit back to listen in peace. If the needle gets stuck or if it jumps out of the groove during noisy passages, increase the tracking force by ½ gram increments until the problem goes away. However, if you end up with a tracking force more than one gram over the recommended figure, you either have an inaccurate tone arm balance or there are other problems you have missed.

Some changers or turntables have what is called an *antiskate device*. It is supposed to keep the stylus from skipping across the somewhat sensitive grooves in case somebody bumps the machine. Generally it has a dial that has to be set to a figure about matching the tracking force you have on the cartridge. So, after adjusting the tone arm force, also make any called for adjustments on your antiskate device. But as with any adjustment on any machine, you are not compelled to set it only at some prescribed figure. If it works for you, it is the right setting no matter what anyone says.

Once the cartridge part of the tone arm has been set to some proper sort of weight, you must ascertain that the stylus is aimed very straight at the record grooves. The cutting needle in the recording studio is held very precisely at right angles to the record master. If your own little stylus is a few degrees off to the right or left, the output from one side of every groove will be emphasized more than the other, and distorted as well. The left half of a stylus reproduces sound based on vibrations given it by the left half of every groove, and the right half does likewise for the right side of every groove.

Lay a small mirrorlike piece of metal or front surface mirror on the turntable where a record ought to be. Then gently place the tone arm onto the mirror. Crouch down and stare at the stylus and its mirror image straight on. The stylus and its reflection should appear to form a straight line. If they seem to make an angle, the stylus itself may be bent slightly out of line or the entire tone arm may be misaligned.

Figure 93 If you lay a mirror beneath stylus on phonograph cartridge, you can check if stylus is precisely vertical (stylus and mirrored image in straight line) or askew (style and image form definite angle). Askew stylus should be corrected.

Bad news: very few turntables have adjustments for such a condition. Good news: unless the stylus is very obviously out of line, you can live with the condition.

When trying to correct a tilted stylus, check the connection between the tone arm and the cartridge holder. Is it tight? Can you twist it a bit to the right or left as a way to adjust the stylus angle? Is the cartridge mounted properly? Is there a washer under both of the two cartridge mounting bolts? You can add makeshift paper washers to one side as a way to adjust a tilted stylus.

USING YOUR HI-FI CORRECTLY

You say you already know how to use your hi-fi. Let's find out.

The almost ideal position for the various level and volume control knobs on your amplifier or control preamp is just about halfway around the dial. At very low levels, most circuits clip off the high notes and the low notes (or the bass and treble). And very high levels of sound generally result in distortion, to say nothing of unhappy neighbors. For instance, if your treble and bass settings are both midway between maximum and minimum, you can push the volume control up well beyond the halfway point without annoying distortion. But if your personal taste runs to plenty of those thumping bass sounds, you probably have the bass control turned up well beyond the midpoint. Then, should you want to really sock it to the sound level, the treble notes would stand a good chance of coming through undistorted, but the bass sounds would not.

Long wires are noisy wires in the hi-fi business. This is especially true at the input side of an amplifier. If the wire between your tuner, turntable, or tape deck and amplifier is very long, you are probably losing sound quality and you may be gaining something else undesirable. Audio wires running alongside power cords pick up a low frequency hum from the alternating house current. And if you really feel that the hi-fi wires and the power cords must be in the same area, be certain that you don't try to be overly neat. A rolled up power cord is about 10 times better at producing a 60 Hz hum in your sound system. that a cord tossed aimlessly about. And if the excess cord linking the tuner with the amplifier is neatly rolled up, it makes a 10 times better receiver of stray hum.

In the days, not long ago, when stereo sound was exciting enough for everybody, many people went through life not realizing that they had their two speakers hooked up incorrectly. One was pushing sound when the other was pulling it—literally. The vibrations that cause beautiful sounds to come gently from your speakers depend upon a vibrating current sent out from the amplifier. The vibrations

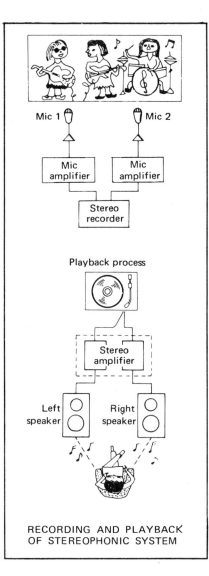

RECORDING AND PLAYBACK
OF STEREOPHONIC SYSTEM

Figure 94 The stereo process in simplified graphic form. Quadraphonic is simple—2 more microphones, 2 more speakers.

from both speakers of a stereo setup (and with quadraphonic, all four speakers) should take place at the same instant. If they don't, the vibrations actually will cancel each other out, not totally but enough that you would notice a diminished sound if only you knew how.

What determines that the + vibration in the right speaker takes place at the same time as the + vibration in the left speaker (*in phase*) instead of at the same time as the − vibration (*out of phase*)? Answer: The way you hook up the wires. There are plenty of tests and plenty of words about why this effect takes place. One simple test is simply to listen carefully to the loudspeakers just the way they

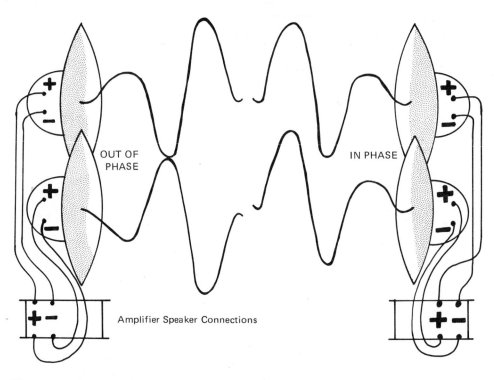

Figure 95 Why speaker phase can influence both quality and amount of sound your hi fi produces. When out of phase, sound waves battle each other. In phase, they work together.

are. Then reverse the position of the wires on *just one* speaker. If you can detect a difference in sound that way, either louder or softer, make sure that the wires go into whichever position gives the loudest sound.

Some amplifiers and some speaker systems have a + and a − position clearly marked, or a red and a black terminal. But with long two-conductor speaker wire, sometimes it is difficult to keep track of the separate halves. One popular kind of speaker wire, however, has transparent insulation plus one copper wire and one aluminum wire. In that way, if the copper is hooked onto + or red all along the way and aluminum hooked onto − or black, everything should come out *in phase*. But it never hurts to check.

If you can't tell the difference between *in phase* and *out of phase* when you switch your own wires around, the logical question would be, what difference does it make? But if you tend to be fanatic about such things when it comes to your listening pleasure, the next simplest test for phase is a stereo test record, which includes what hi-fi devotees call *phase testing bands*. The record itself *tries* to explain how to run such a test.

8 TV First Aid

Some television sets run neck and neck with the car as a family's or home's most expensive luxury to maintain. Many people are already convinced that one way to avoid frequent and expensive auto repairs is to buy a make and model that has demonstrated mechanical worthiness. And the same kind of advice holds true for TVs, although less attention has been given to this item by vocal consumer advocates.

But how do you find out what kind of TV set is good in the repair department? For one, you can ask a good repair person. Assuming you have located a TV repair shop that has proven to be honest and competent, ask them what kind of TV sets are lemons these days and which ones are the plums. A good department store should be able to separate the junk from the gems too.

Whenever you buy any major piece of equipment today, don't make the mistake of assuming that it will work just because it's new. A reputable store should check out every major item it sells *before* it leaves the warehouse. Some of them will, but only after you ask if the salesperson knows for a fact that the item is in good working order.

Some stores get the item out of the warehouse as fast as they can, then a different department comes to pick it up again after you call to point out that it didn't work from the minute it was unpacked.

The moral to all of these warnings is to simplify your potential repair and maintenance headaches by making sure that, at least when you start out, the appliances you buy are in good working order. Insist on it! Scream at the salesperson if you have to, call the district attorney if you must, notify the Better Business Bureau and consumer protection agencies too. And most powerful of all—take your money elsewhere. But don't settle for anything less than the very best.

No color TV should be sent home with a paying customer until the store has checked it out themselves. No large TV set should be delivered to a home unless arrangements are made to send a competent technician along a bit later. During transit, the various magnets and coils that focus the color signals can become loosened and misaligned. Printed circuit boards can be twisted and snap component leads or break one of the printed "wires."

There is one way by which stores escape their responsibility to inspect what they sell. "We don't have to check the set right now; it's covered by a warranty," the clerk will protest. If that's how the store wants to do business, you may have to play along. But just as soon as the set is delivered or unpacked, turn it on and *try to find something wrong.* Then call up the store and complain. In the process of looking for what might be wrong, the technician will more than likely give your magic box a thorough physical exam and tune-up, the kind it should have had in the first place!

Getting into the repair and maintenance of a television set is no different than every rule, suggestion, and warning you've read thus far. Troubleshooting proceeds from the power (the house current or the antenna) to the powered (the picture tube). But don't start unscrewing the protective back cover of the TV until a good many steps have been examined first. There is a good deal inside the set that can go wrong, but fortunately many troubles are external and, therefore, easy to reach.

POWER PROBLEMS

Don't forget to check the plug and fuses if no picture and no sound appear. There is a circuit breaker built right into most TVs. Generally it is a narrow shaft protruding from a hole labeled "Reset." It can open just on a rare quirk, in which case you simply push it in to remedy the matter. If it opens frequently, however, begin to suspect deeper maladies or a malfunctioning circuit breaker.

In case the on-off switch on the TV itself is faulty, you should be able to notice a change in how it feels when you turn the tube on or off. If it no longer snaps into place, or if it snaps only after a good bit of exertion on your part, the cause of an obvious lack of power could be that switch. Then you will have to open the back and locate where the on-off switch is hidden. Often it's an integral part of the volume control.

The volume control portion of the potentiometer (see Chapter 6) most often has three prongs sticking out of the top, bottom, or side. The on-off portion can be sticking out the rear and will inevitably be only two prongs. With the power cord unplugged from the wall (which it should be whenever going into the insides of a TV), short out the on-off switch by a wire with an alligator clip on each end. Then plug in the set, and if the power surges through, congratulate yourself. You have already located the problem and saved repair money too. The replacement part should be available from any reasonably well-stocked TV and radio parts supplier. If necessary, unsolder the old connections and carefully solder in the replacement. However, most of them are hooked up with solderless push-on connectors.

Not all TV problems stem from *no* power. Often *too little* power generates annoying symptoms too. If the usual load on the house wiring circuits that supply power to your TV is greater than 1000 watts, chances are pretty good that your viewing gets interrupted by sporadic picture disturbances. The picture may slip off the top of the screen and flip over a few times. The sides of an indoor arena may collapse or bulge inward. Green Astroturf or the blue Pacific may dim for a few seconds every now and then. Any and all of these ailments can come from overloaded power lines.

A TV draws from one to three amps of power continuously. If there is another 8 or 9 amp continuous draw on the same power line, which is what a load of approximately 1000 watts would demand, there would be scant power to spare for the increased demand of starting a refrigerator or furnace blower motor. Every time some heavy appliance like that kicks in, the TV picture will suffer. The answer to this problem is obvious. Change the TV to a less loaded line, assuming you can find one within easy reach. Or, switch one heavy appliance to another circuit.

Motors can generate yet another annoyance for TV viewers. If your favorite program is disturbed by occasional outbursts of noise through the speakers and weird patterns on the screen, that also might be caused by motors. If a motor is getting worn, or if it never was properly grounded or shielded in the first place, it may send high frequency interference through the house wiring. The TV picks up the interference and broadcasts it for you to see and hear. Shortwave radio transmitters, X-ray equipment, and similar gadgetry can also kick up interference signals. Although it is possible to ward off the interference with what pros call a minor rewiring at the source of the trouble, you will no doubt find it much simpler—and probably equally as economical—to invest in a low cost filter, which plugs into the wall between your TV and the source of interference.

Some TV filters are used where the annoyance-generating appliance is plugged in. They should be selected specifically for the kind of interference you hope to eliminate. Others are broader in their filtering span and work reasonably well at the TV set itself. In any event, when you buy a filter such as these, tell the clerk exactly what kind of interference you hope to eliminate and get some assurance that if the particular filter you are carrying home *does not* do the job, you can return it. But play fair! Unwrap the item carefully and don't abuse it so the store can be confident that some other customer selecting that same piece of merchandise will not get a dud.

If your TV picture never quite fills the entire screen, and maybe doesn't look quite as brilliant as the picture enjoyed by the family next door with a set as old as yours, *low voltage* may be the culprit. A picture that is perfectly proportioned during the midmorning quiz shows, but becomes scanty about the time the 5 or 6 o'clock news comes on, may stem from voltage problems from your power company. If they haven't recently updated their transformer serving your block, the line voltage may be below normal during times of

Figure 96 Interference from electrical source.

Figure 97 Low voltage shrinks picture.

heavy use, such as just as the sun goes down and the stoves and house lights go on. The power company should be willing to check the voltage for you at various times of the day. And if their equipment is at fault, they should update it within a reasonably short time.

Conscientious TV manufacturers are fairly careful to make sure that the sets they ship to specific locations are matched to local voltage standards. Normal house voltage does vary from town to town; 110, 115, 120 are fairly common standard voltages. Most American-made TV sets are designed for 120 volt operation. Many Japanese sets are pegged at 117 volts. That 3 volt variation is negligable, but the 10 volt difference that would occur if you moved a set designed for 120 volts into a 110 volt city could be enough to shrink your picture noticeably. Conversely, operating a 110 volt set in a 120 volt city could increase the picture size right off your screen so you would be missing a few locks of hair or a few teeth at the bottom of every smile.

Some better built solid state TVs are designed to operate from 110 to 130 volts. Their circuitry contains a built-in voltage regulator. The power requirements of all electrical equipment, televisions included, should be marked on a label that is not too impossible to find, generally at the rear of a TV cabinet. If you belong to one of those families who keeps getting shifted from the Topeka office to the Green Bay office to the New Orleans office, it would not be a bad investment to make your next TV one that handles a broad range of voltages. The same advice goes to rural residents who still see occasional long periods of voltage drops. Even some big city residents in "brown out" areas would do well to consider the 110 to 130 volt sets to tide them over a long, hot, powerless summer.

Once you have already invested in a TV, however, it's not likely you will be anxious to trade it in just for the sake of a few volts here and there. The least expensive solution to a voltage insufficiency then is an *auxiliary booster*. These devices consist of a small transformer that boosts the house current by approximately 5 or 10 percent.

Power boosters come in several basic types, but all of them connect between the power outlet and the power plug. The kind of booster that hooks into the picture tube circuit is for another purpose entirely and will be discussed a bit later.

The easiest booster of all for the typical busy household is a fully automatic, solid state regulator, which keeps its output to the TV set constant regardless of gradual fluctuations in house voltage. Some less effective variations will add 10 volts to the output whenever the house power drops below a predetermined level, often 110 volts. Other varieties feature a small voltage meter, which the TV viewer must watch periodically; if the voltage is above or below whatever you decide to call "normal," the booster is manually adjusted.

Some boosters, generally the least expensive, simply boost the voltage by a fixed, unvarying amount no matter what the house voltage may be at the moment. If your particular situation gives proper voltage in the morning, low voltage in the early evening, a booster with a fixed stepup would be just as bad as no booster at all unless you put it into the line only when needed.

When investing in a power booster, you must make sure that whatever gadget you buy is able to handle the power requirements of your set. Some of the advertisements for boosters say, "400 Watt Capacity," but if you get into the finer print, the ad may admit something to the effect that it is actually only "400-watt intermittent, 300-watt continuous." And since TV viewing is a *continuous* thing, the 300 watt capacity would be too low if your set draws 330 watts or more.

ANTENNA PROBLEMS

The antenna wire is an often overlooked trouble spot when the TV tunes itself out. A broken, disconnected, or missing antenna wire causes very weak pictures—if any come through at all—or more snow than a blizzard. Through all of these sundry interference patterns, however, you will still be able to see a *raster* on the blank screen. A raster is a faint, lined pattern traced by the electron beam of the picture tube whenever its electronic circuits are working well

Figure 98 Missing antenna wire results in very weak picture or none at all.

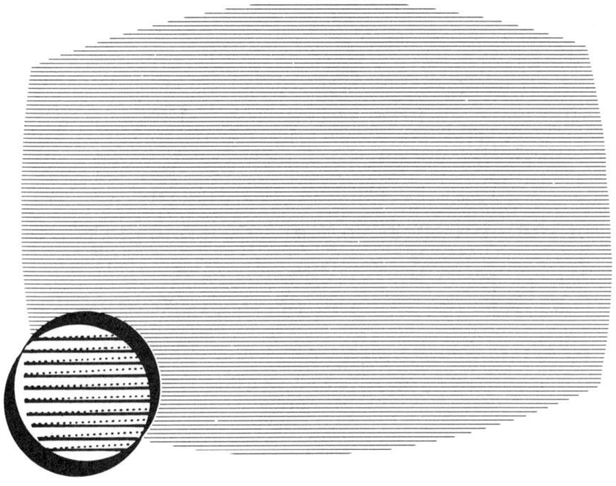

Figure 99 Raster of set is the electronic pattern for scanning. It is seen when no signal is being sent to tube but most other high voltage and sync circuits are operating.

but there is nothing coming through for the circuits to beam onto the picture tube (see Figure 99).

Where the wire meets the antenna, and where the wire meets the set itself, are two of the most logical places to check for broken antenna wires. However, if the antenna is on the roof or up a tall mast, you may be inclined to leave a check of that spot until later in the troubleshooting game.

If people are prone to trip over your antenna wire, it's possible that a stiff lead inside the insulation is broken. After first moving the wire away from where it can attract feet, flex the antenna lead every inch or two it see if you can spot a break. Antenna wire is pretty stiff, so if your troubleshooting detects a limp spot, chances are it is a sign of a broken wire or two.

In case you are not able to determine immediately whether or not a broken antenna wire might be the cause of interruption, unscrew the wires and hook up the old rabbit ears. If you are in a fringe area, the reception will be a long way from good, of course, but if there is reception with the indoor antenna, then you will at least be inspired to look harder for where the break in the outside antenna may have occurred. Signal tracing, as described in the intercom wire section earlier, can be a help in tracking down the site of a snapped lead inside the insulation.

You might want to modify the technique by first deliberately shorting the antenna at one end, simply by disconnecting the two leads from the TV set and wrapping them together. Then move progressively along the wire with two stick pins or hat pins. Poke one pin through the insulation of each of the two leads until you feel it contact the copper wire. Then hook the continuity tester or signal tracing device to the pins. If the buzzer buzzes or the light lights, that means the break is farther away from the set.

A *ghost* from your antenna is a beast to contend with. TV signals that reflect off obstacles like large metal buildings, mountains, or occasionally even clouds reach your antenna just a fraction of a second behind the signal that comes directly from the transmitter. The reflected signal gets beamed onto the TV tube a fraction of a signal later than the original and forms the ghost.

If you live in a local reception area where the common rabbit ears are about all the antenna you need, ghost hunting is tough. The one or two slender poles are open to signals from every direction, and the ghost signal stands as good a chance of getting screened as does the authentic signal.

With luck, the reflection may be coming at you from a large natural or man-made object far away from the local TV transmission towers and not closely lined up with your house and the towers. In that event, some of those fancy looking, TV-top rabbit ears with a dial or two may be able to screen out the ghost, as their advertisements promise. There are so many different kinds of ghosts and so many different kinds of ghost-trapping rabbit ear antennas that it's almost impossible to recommend one design over another. Your best protection, as with most purchases, is to choose a reputable dealer who will first recommend which one might solve your ghost problem and, second, take back the item within a reasonable length of time if it doesn't work out.

You also might be able to block the ghost with something as simple as aluminum foil or chicken wire. Pull off a good-sized piece of kitchen aluminum foil and hold it between both hands. Stand near the rabbit ears and gradually move the foil around. If the makeshift ghost screen manages to eliminate the ghost pattern in one particular position, try to concoct a more permanent but less unsightly death trap for ghosts. One alternative might be to replace the foil with chicken wire or screen. The wire, if painted black or the same color as your walls, might be camouflaged.

It is also possible that a bookcase or large piece of furniture will be positioned or can be moved around to just the right spot. Then the foil or wire could be concealed behind the furniture, but it should be just about as effective as if it were out in plain view. Ghost traps generally work best if they are grounded by a thin wire running from the trap to a water pipe, steam pipe, or even the screw that holds the decorative cover onto an electrical outlet.

Larger antennas and outdoor antennas often can be repositioned or aimed to eliminate or at least mollify a ghost. And when you are just about to erect an antenna, it's the ideal time to start thinking about reception, ghosts, and other potential maladies before they occur. Chat with neighbors about their experience with TV reception. Do likewise with a good TV repair shop or antenna installer.

Almost any catalog, brochure, chart, or sales person will break down an array of antennas into categories such as "far-fringe," "fringe," "near-fringe," "suburban," and on down the line. The differences in the product, however, encompass more than merely how far away from it you can pull in a useable signal.

TV and radio antennas have directional qualities. Some of them, such as simple rabbit ears, will pick up signals equally well from virtually any direction. Its sensitivity, thus, is expressed by pros as being 360° (360 degrees), there being 360 degrees in a full circle.

Directional antennas, however, concentrate on only a small portion of a circle. The portion of a very directional TV antenna, which receives signals for channels 7 through 13, can be sensitive only to signals within about 22°, almost $\frac{1}{16}$th of a circle. Lower channels and UHF signals generally cover a somewhat wider area of sensitivity for complicated electronic reasons.

In an area where you have found ghosts and other forms of interference—such as radio stations, electronics labs, X-ray equipment, radar devices at airports—to be a problem, it might be worthwhile to invest in a far-fringe type antenna even if the neighborhood in which you reside is closer to the transmitters than far-fringe.

Experience is the best resource for you to rely on when it comes to antennas. But if none of your neighbors have tried a very selective antenna, you might be able to predict what kind of success you will enjoy by dragging out a good map, a ruler, and a protractor, the kind you used for measuring angles in high school geometry class.

On the map, plot your house and the location of the TV towers.

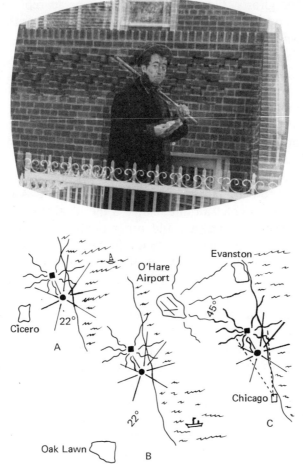

Figure 100 Ghosts are caused by reflected signals arriving split seconds behind original signal (A). Text tells how map exercise (B) can help to correct ghost problem.

Then put an "X" on any natural or man-made barriers that local people blame for their bad reception. (In New York City, for example, the massive World Trade Center gets blamed—rightfully so—for most ghost reflections. Chicago viewers blame Sears corporate headquarters.) Then, on your map, see whether a 22° or a 45° spread could take in the TV tower but leave out the suspected ghost house. Several instances of hypothetical map exercises from Chicago are shown in Figure 100.

Even though TV viewers in both the Chicago and New York areas need only a local, or at most a suburban type, antenna system to bring in a strong enough signal, they could benefit by the keener focusing qualities of the 22° or even 45° fringe antennas.

Using a fringe antenna in local areas could present just one more problem to cope with. The signal might be *too strong*—yes, it is possible to have too strong an incoming signal for your TV.

Distortion and smeary looking pictures are the result. But it is easily remedied. An *attenuator*, a relatively inexpensive gadget, reduces the overall strength of an incoming signal without reducing its clarity.

CONTROL TROUBLES

Assuming your set has been working well from its purchase date, quality can deteriorate anyway. Various components change with age, which is not necessarily a sign of bad quality. To compensate for gradual changes in picture quality, TV manufacturers put a variety of controls into various circuits so that repair people, professional or amateur, can bring a malfunctioning TV back to normal.

Not every manufacturer offers the same complement of controls, and their location is even less standardized. Some are found under a decorative panel of some sort in the front of a TV, some are located behind the back of the set but can be adjusted with a fine screwdriver. Others are in the back or side of the TV but extend outside the cover via small knobs.

Contrast, brightness, and vertical hold are the three most common controls, aside from whatever color-regulating knobs and buttons protrude from the box. Less easy to find, as a rule, are controls such as horizontal hold, horizontal size, and vertical size. All of these controls are essentially black and white adjustments. Good color reception, in fact, is dependent upon good black and white reception most of all.

There is not one signal for black and white beamed to your house, plus another one for each of the three primary colors. One signal, and one alone, brings reception to you. On that very complex electronic signal, the black and white portion is the controlling element. The sound and the color signals are little more than subvibrations within the big vibration, which brings in the black and white picture.

No amount of fiddling is going to bring in good color reception if the black and white picture is scrambled. So we will try to find whatever can be dealt with by only the external controls. And that encompasses a lot.

Contrast, oversimplified a bit, controls the amount of black in your TV picture. It regulates the relative percentage of time that the beam of electrons, which produces a TV picture, should be turned off.

Brightness, closely related to contrast in screen appearance and function, regulates the relative intensity of that beam of electrons regardless how much the contrast control decides that it will be on or

Figure 101 Contrast and brightness controls can result in flat, too-dark picture (A) or flat too-light picture (B), or a picture with too much contrast.

off. With a high brightness and high contrast setting, there would be plenty of dark regions on the screen, but the light portions should be very, very bright. There is no critical electronic performance that is linked to these two controls. They should be adjusted to the most comfortable picture, period.

When tampering with any of the controls discussed from here on, make careful note of the position each knob is in when you find it. If twisting a particular control does not clear up the problem, you must return it to its original setting or you may actually *increase* the complexity of your repair problem.

If the TV image is broken horizontally across the middle or even across only the upper or lower regions, or if a black bar or series of bars moves up and down through the picture, locate the *vertical hold* adjustment. After studying its present location—even if you have to mark the knob with a pencil—twist it gently to see if the bars are affected. Generally only a slight compensation of this control is ever called for.

Once you have managed to restore your picture by adjusting the vertical hold control, move it just a trifle farther in the same direction. This will allow for localized variations and for a bit of future aging of whatever parts brought on the malady in the first place.

The classic way of describing to pros what a picture looks like if the *horizontal hold* control needs tuning is to say that the picture looks as if someone hit it with a machete three or four times at an angle. However, often you will detect a poor horizontal hold adjustment by watching type moving across the TV picture. If it waves up and down a few times, try to adjust the horizontal hold knob gently.

The variations and subtleties to all of these adjustments are enormous. Study the figures on the following pages and try to digest

Figure 102 Vertical hold maladjustment or problem results in divided picture that often travels up and down.

Figure 103 Horizontal hold problems break picture up wildly.

the various word pictures presented. Then see which adjustment seems to fit the combination. And as long as you carefully return every control to its original setting, even a trial and error approach should not do any lasting harm. You just might stumble onto the solution to a problem without first figuring out exactly what is wrong. That happens more than most repair people care to admit!

And here is a neck-saving tip. Get out a mirror when you are trying to adjust a TV control in the back of the set. That way you can see what is happening continuously instead of sneaking a peek at the picture after every gentle twist.

Vertical size adjustment will restore the missing top and bottom of your picture; *horizontal size* control is for restoring the left and right of your picture. All of these projections, of course, assume that you have already taken the precaution of making sure that the picture problem does indeed lie within your own set. TV stations themselves have transmission problems too. And some of them can seem to fit

Figure 104 Vertical size problems mimic voltage problems (Figure 97) in some ways.

Figure 105 Horizontal size control problems mimic low voltage (Figure 97) in only some ways.

Figure 106 AGC (automatic gain control) problems cause washed out, erratic picture.

the symptoms for various control maladjustments. Switch channels somewhat before doing much serious knob turning.

To keep airplanes and such from upsetting the picture when they pass between you and the TV tower, an *automatic gain control* (AGC) has been worked into the circuitry of most sets. Like almost everything that calls itself automatic, it needs some nonautomatic adjusting now and then. If the picture in general becomes bleached out or distorted, a condition that neither the contrast nor the brightness control seems to fix, try twisting the AGC control gently to one side or the other. In more extreme cases, an AGC maladjustment results in a very broken up picture. But it is unlikely that you will ever see a broken up picture caused by a faulty AGC adjustment unless you have moved the AGC knob yourself while searching for solutions to some other problem.

The AGC can be a relatively sensitive kind of adjustment. So turn it slowly. And be sure to restore the AGC screw or knob to its original place again if twisting it does not clear up your washed out picture.

Age begins creeping up on even the biggest component in your TV set, the picture tube itself. From hours and hours of bombardment by the tube electron gun, scum develops inside the tube, leading to loss of sharpness and overall grey tinges. Age also can lead to short circuits between internal wiring networks, and that generally causes excessive contrast, which even the contrast control cannot compensate for completely. The relatively inexpensive answer is a *picture tube booster.*

The picture tube booster generally fits like an extension cord between the socket of your picture tube and the plug that normally slips into that socket. The booster is little more than a small transformer, which boosts the picture tube filament voltage from a normal of about 6.8 volts up to 8.5 or 9 volts, thus bombarding the tube with more electrons to compensate for the dulling effects of scum.

The booster offers yet another benefit. It isolates the various tube circuits that might have become shorted and thereby reduces the excessive contrast brought on by aging.

Picture tube boosters work well on either black and white or color sets and should prolong the useable life of your tube by about one year. There are many cheapies advertised in magazines and many good ones on sale at reputable electronic outlets. You should pick a good one, of course, and it should indicate somewhere on the package or on a label that it is intended for use with your set design. A *parallel* tube booster is for tube type TV sets in which the tubes are wired in parallel; you will be able to spot such a fact by noting the tube type numbers. If all of the initial numbers are identical, it is a parallel circuit—example: 6BC7, 6AD9, 6BQ4.

Series wired tubes have different beginning numbers. And for such a set you would want to purchase a series type picture tube booster—example: 3BC7, 7AD9, 9BQ4, 27UL3, 50AL6.

There can be even a picture tube booster made specifically for the transistorized TV sets, although most will be marketed as combinations for two or more different basic design types. If you do install a picture tube booster—or *rejuvenator,* as some literature prefers—but find the tube performance is not improved, you would be well advised to remove the booster. Used on a picture tube that hasn't yet reached old age, a booster will only hasten it on its way. It is best you look elsewhere for the cause of your failing picture.

A *noisy tuner* is a common TV malady. If your fine tuner control does not seem to be bringing in as sharp a picture as in days gone by, it may be because of dirt or a film of oil and chemicals in the fine tuner mechanism. If some channels tune in fine but others don't, assuming most channels came in well before, that too may come from "noise" in the tuner section. Whenever a low key but nagging problem is detected in TV performance, it is a good idea to rule out tuner noise before digging into a set's workings.

"Noise" in all of these cases is TV jargon for the interference, static, or diminished performance caused by dirt, chemicals, or corrosion that accumulates on the very sensitive contacts inside the tuning section. When you twist the tuning knob from one channel to another, a complex set of contacts inside rotates to switch on or off the various circuits, which have to work properly if you are to pick up the desired channel.

You can cure noise with a simple spray can of cleaner and lubricant sold by most TV and radio supply shops. On most TV sets, if you pull off the tuning and fine tuning knobs, you expose the contacts underneath. In that case, simply spray the cleaner generously on all of the parts beneath the knobs, replace the knobs, and then rotate the channel selector through every position several times. This same cleaner works magic on other control headaches, particularly the volume controls that scratch or pop every time they are turned up or down. In case you are unable actually to expose the volume control mechanism—or even the TV tuner—sometimes by simply spraying enough of the cleaner on the sides and front of the covered-up part, you will force enough solvent inside to do the job anyway.

TROUBLE SHOOTING INSIDE

A look inside may be next on your troubleshooting trek. Absolutely everything said in the two preceding chapters can be adapted to televisions. One additional warning is called for, however. The voltages inside your television tuner can range upward of 20,000 volts in some areas—enough to curl your hair permanently at the very least. This warning should not be enough to stop you from looking inside the back cover of an ailing TV. But *do* disconnect the power plug from the wall. And *do,* as soon as you open the back, look to see where the power section is located. It will be close to where the power cord enters, and it should be enclosed in some kind of protective mesh, usually with a prominent warning sign. *Keep away from that area even after the set is disconnected.*

The power supply often contains large capacitors, which store electricity even when the plug has been pulled. To be doubly safe, *do not* use metal tools inside a TV set. Aside from adding a bit more to your own protection, this is to keep you from accidentally shorting some of the larger capacitors and possibly damaging them or nearby transistors. There is also the picture tube to be wary of. Its glass envelope is strong, but it's still glass and can be broken.

If your present TV difficulty is in the sound only, follow the leads from the loudspeaker backward to see where they take you. That should pretty well localize the sound portion of your particular TV chassis. Then use the various tricks and observations presented in Chapters 6 and 7 to fix your TV sound.

Should the problem lie in the picture only (sound remaining good), trace the wires from the picture tube to the various spots where they enter the electronic circuitry in the chassis. Once you have localized the site of possible trouble, run a visual check for broken wires or connections, overheated resistors, damaged capacitors, and the other clues that a sharp eye can pick out.

After a visual spot-check, apply your previously acquired electronic knowledge within the selected locations. And if you are sure that you have isolated the site of the trouble, but can't pinpoint exactly which individual component is to blame, you can resort to trial and error replacement. First, try replacing the capacitors, especially small electrolytic capacitors. Next come the resistors. Any small, localized potentiometers or similar controls should be next. Transistors are about last on your list, except for the big power transistors, which do need periodic replacement.

If your instincts have been well formed, letting you isolate the general area of trouble, even replacing a dozen small parts is cheaper by far than paying for the labor of a TV technician, who might end up doing just what you can do.

Only if the picture and sound both fail to operate *at all*—no buzz in the speakers, no sign of light in the picture tube—is it advisable to start running a check into the main power supply. In no event should you attempt to mess with the large electrolytic capacitors found in almost every high voltage power supply. On many well-made TVs, resistors have been included, which gradually drain off the huge amount of power stored in those capacitors. But some sets may not have such a feature. And those resistors themselves may become defective. If you've localized the headaches to that part of your set, turn it over to a pro unless you feel entirely safe and comfortable working in a potentially harmful area.

Calling in a professional TV fix-it person is inviting both extra expenses and less effective repairs. If it takes a technician half an hour to travel from a workshop to your living room, and another half hour to get back again, you are going to be charged for that hour of travel time, and rightfully so. On top of that, the technician may not have the best equipment in a travel bag for repairing or even diagnosing your particular ailment. Some of the more sophisticated instruments are too cumbersome or too delicate to lug into every living room in town.

Even a pro may have to improvise or guess while working on your carpet. In the cluttered confines of a well-equipped shop, however, an oscilloscope or signal generator might take away some of the guesswork.

Again there is a moral to this tale: take your troubles to your repair shop, if possible. Don't invite the repair person in to have a look. Even though that portable TV is not exactly as portable as you had hoped, carrying it yourself is an economical exercise.

Consoles are not exactly portable, of course, but the working parts in most of them come out with relative ease. Speakers, as a rule, unplug from the main chassis. Don't try to remove them. Your repair shop will have speakers that can be connected to your set. And when carting the TV or when repairing it, treat that picture tube as if it were made of very, very thin glass—because it is! Don't scratch it, bang it, shove it very hard, or even swear at it.

COLOR SECTIONS OF TV SETS

The color section of your TV is very easy to adjust, which is a good thing because it does need frequent adjustment. To maintain proper color balance and focus, it is still necessary to give your TV a routine tune-up periodically, generally once a year.

The picture tube of your color TV is cluttered with coils and magnets, which help to direct the beams of electrons to their proper locations on your viewing screen. Each of the three primary colors has its own beam and, consequently, its own set of adjustments. Fundamental strengths of all components change gradually, and the coils or magnets on color tubes are no exception. That is why, about once a year, a color TV should be retuned.

We said earlier that adjusting color balance and color focus is simple. It is. But the equipment required to accomplish such a tune-up can cost fully one fourth as much as a well-built television set itself. Your repair person can get a good return by investing in a color bar generator because it will be used maybe 100 times every year. You

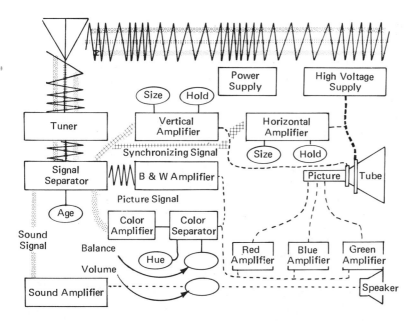

Figure 107 Block diagram of typical color TV set. Incoming signal contains picture, in black and white, plus auxilliary sub-signals which tell TV set how to color the picture.

might use it once a year. At that rate, it could take four years for your investment in a color bar generator to pay off.

There is one spectacular alternative to sending out your colored TV so often if you lack the tuning equipment. *Build your own color TV!* It's not so funny as it sounds. Since the power supplies and circuitry needed to build a color bar generator—the basic color tuning device—are already an integral part of a good transistorized color TV, it would seem highly expedient for manufacturers to spend a few extra dollars to build a color bar generator into every set. Trouble is, repairs are making as much money for some companies as building the sets in the first place.

You may have noticed that care has been taken so far to avoid all commercial endorsements, real or imagined, in this book. In this instance, however, there is little alternative but to name the one significant firm that does include a color bar generator in the circuitry of its TV sets; it is Heathkit. And their prices compare favorably with competitive sets, but they ought to because Heathkit gets its labor free—from you.

Heathkit includes test equipment within most of its TV kits, so once you have put together your own TV set, you will also be able to repair it yourself. Assembling a kit from Heathkit is not much more complicated than assembling some of the toys you buy in boxes at the dime store. The average person can assemble a complete TV set from Heathkit by spending evenings for about two weeks on the project. You need only two skills to assemble such a kit—reading and soldering. If you don't already know how to solder, look back to the first electronics chapter. Heathkit booklets also teach the art.

A book or set of books comes with every Heathkit kit. They help you to perform the various fine tuning chores that are necessary to get your new TV working at its optimum. And the books double as repair manuals as the various components inevitably begin to age. When your once-a-year tune-up is needed, dust off the auxillary test equipment you stored at the back of some closet, switch your color TV set to its test position, and tune away!

Heathkit has built its reputation on the fact that virtually anybody, once they overcome their mental hangups and buy that first kit, can follow the beautifully clear, step-by-step, pictorially clarified directions. But if something goes wrong along the way, Heathkit has centers scattered around the country to set things straight for you—generally without charge.

Color TV hit the market just about the time that people tired of supporting cars as their supersymbol of this age. And one of the reasons that cars lost of lot of their luster was one revelation after another about the questionable construction, questionable safety, questionable profits, questionable competitive practices in the automotive industry, including the auto repair field. People could not build their own cars as a way of both saving a dollar and making an important social point. But it appears that you can build and repair your own TV. Imagine the kind of changes that the color TV market would go through if thousands more people decided they had had enough of what the TV assembly lines and repair lines had to offer!

Plugs, Sockets, Switches, Cords, and Other Electrical Problems

9

The whole practical side of electricity is misunderstood by most people. But what you don't know about electricity can cost you some money and some unpleasant moments.

Unlike the plumbing codes, which in many parts of the country almost seem to stand in the way of technical progress, the National Electrical Code is quite a sound document. The most commonly used printed version of the code weighs in at two pounds and includes nearly 1000 pages of fine print and interpretations, even some pictures. The National Electrical Code (NEC) is revised every few years to keep it in line with current trends, discoveries, and developments.

Provisions of the NEC provide a fail-safe system for house, factory, and outdoor wiring. The engineers and corporations represented by the code formulators devise wiring schemes to make things work in a manner they hope will never go wrong. But, *when things do go wrong* with electrical equipment or with someone behind the switch—as they inevitably will—the code makes provisions for safe dissipation of the potentially lethal amounts of electrical power.

There is a saddening amount of literature on the market that openly flaunts the electrical code both in letter and spirit. One national womens' magazine, for example, gave readers step-by-step instructions on how to build a picturesque lighting device that ignored safe wiring practices. Manufacturers and retailers of window-mounted air-conditioners, as another example, may stick to the precise letter of the electrical code in their formal, written documents, but then advertise and advise salespeople to encourage unsafe installation of their equipment.

To be sure, formulations of the electrical code are not without some ax to grind. In part, the NEC is a document intended by insurance companies to reduce the number of fires and accidental deaths for which they pay millions of dollars annually. If insurance companies want to stop electrical fires and accidents to save money, perhaps we can all follow their lead and stop injury to ourselves and others.

If you have any questions about safe wiring practices, there are many local sources of authoritive information. Your local power company and fire department both are generally very free with safety information in the electrical area. A good insurance company writing fire coverage can arrange to discuss wiring safety with you. In fact, you should be wary of any company that writes a fire insurance policy on your house or apartment without making a thorough inspection. If they can afford the luxury of writing policies on both safe and unsafe homes, their rates may be terribly out of line.

Before any fire insurance policy goes into effect, the company's inspector should visit your home and make a brief tour. An inspector should look at obvious signs that reflect the wiring condition, watch your own practices that may contribute to fire or other electrical hazards, and look into the fuse box to see if somebody has been adding larger fuses over the years.

Tackling most wiring problems around a home, whether in the wall on in the plug of an iron, actually is one of the easiest repair situations you may encounter. Electrical devices are clean, they don't demand heavy pipe wrenches as do your bathroom repairs, there is almost nothing hidden about wiring circuits because the electrical code demands so. And repair or installation materials in the electrical field are very inexpensive. Considering both price and ease, there is no excuse to put off tackling any electrical annoyance you have been enduring.

When you go shopping for replacement or original electrical parts, or for equipment of any sort, look for the Underwriters Laboratory emblem indicating that the product has been tested and found to meet the requirements of the Chicago lab that is the guardian of electrical standards. And if you can't find the U/L label on some item,

204

*Plugs, Sockets,
Switches,
Cords, and
Other Electrical
Problems*

ask the hardware store or electrical supply house owner to find it for you.

Don't assume that because a plug or appliance looks good that it naturally has been tested or rated. If the U/L logo is not on the part or gadget itself, *it isn't approved*. You should not buy it! And simply because you find a U/L label wrapped around the *cord* of some gadget does not mean that the entire mechanism has been subjected to Underwriters Laboratory scrutiny. A favorite trick of some importers of cheap merchandise is to have a U/L rated cord included on their non-U/L rated item, hoping that the sight of a U/L label on the cord will fool you into thinking that the entire product meets the lab standards.

Unfortunately, almost no local ordinances require stores to sell only tested and approved electrical equipment and supplies. But on your way out of a store that sells unrated merchandise, you might exchange a few words with a salesperson or the manager. You can also contact local fire and electrical union officials or even an insurance association—but don't expect fast (or perhaps any) results.

PLUGS

Plugs are among the most frequently handled electrical part. Nearly every electrical gadget in the entire house, except for some battery-powered ones, have a plug of one kind of another. Most are the common two-prong variety. Plugs on factory-made equipment today are most often molded right onto the end of the service wire.

The common two-prong plug is being phased out of the electrical code for many applications. More and more appliances have a three-prong plug unless a particular appliance enclosure is designed to isolate the user even in times of severe electrical breakdown inside the appliance. This specially designed equipment can still safely use two prongs and bears a prominent label such as "Double-Insulated Construction."

Whenever you troubleshoot a balky appliance or gadget, the plug must be one of the first areas examined. Just because it is inserted into a wall outlet does not necessarily mean the plug is transmitting power. One barrier might be that the prongs are not making good contact with the conductors inside the outlet. Age and hard use often bend the main two prongs so that although you can insert the plug into the wall outlet, no useful electrical contact is made.

To check for faulty contact between outlet and plug, twist a suspected prong on the plug outward as far as it will go, still allowing

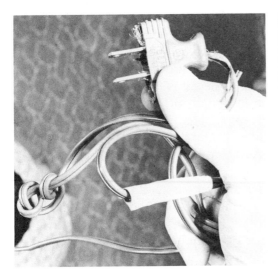

Figure 108 Plugs and cords like this one should be replaced. About the only thing right is that the plug has a Underwriters Laboratory (UL) logo. It has (1) bare wires showing on cord, (2) bare wires showing around prongs since cardboard cover is missing, (3) knots in cord, (4) tape (not electrical variety) wrapped around damaged spot.

Figure 109 Grounded outlets are advisable when operating power tools and other large items. Grounded type (3 wire) extension cord should be used with them for short times if needed. Where grounded outlets are not available, use adapter screwed carefully to center screw of ordinary outlet.

you to insert the plug into the outlet. If that fails to solve the power problem, try the opposite tack. Twist the two prongs together as far as possible. If that also fails, look deeper.

Wires come loose from the screws inside a plug, assuming it was not molded onto the cord at a factory. Pry off the cardboard protector, which should be over the plug, and examine the interior. The wires should be held firmly in place under the two (or three) screws. There should be no loose ends of wire hanging free of the screws like split ends of hair. To check further that the wires in the plug are sound, shove the cord farther into the plug opening, which ought to lift the knot a bit and at the same time let you watch for any wires that may have been snapped off.

Presumably by the time you check into the interior condition of a plug, you earlier had determined conclusively that the outlet itself was good. That can be checked quickly by plugging in some item that you know to be working. Toting a lamp or radio around to repair sites can be a drag, however, so you might want to invest in a very useful, very inexpensive bit of test equipment called a *neon glow tube circuit tester*. It is nothing more than a tiny neon tube connected to a large resistor, both of which are then enclosed in some kind of case, generally with a red and a black lead.

Installing a new electrical plug is a five-minute exercise. New plugs are sold anywhere from drugstores to grocery stores, and even at electrical suppliers. The easiest to install is the snap-on type, which doesn't require you to strip insulation off any wires or twist any screws. Such a simple replacement plug is fine for very low level applications, such as a small table lamp that doesn't get much abuse. But the snap-on plugs are often more headaches than they're worth if used in areas or on gadgets that get a lot of use. The tiny, sharp contacts inside the snap-on plugs and outlets tend to corrode or bend easily, leaving you with just one more troubleshooting situation some time in the maybe not-too-distant future.

A defective molded-in-place plug can be cut off with any number of implements: wire cutter, pliers with wire cutting edge, jack knife, kitchen knife, tin snips. The free end of the cord is then cut down the middle to separate the two individual wires (three for grounded cords) for about 2″, being careful not to remove insulation from either of the two halves (see Figure 110). About ½″ of copper wire has to be exposed at the end of each separate wire. Lay the blade of a sharp knife against the insulation about ½″ from the end of one wire and press the insulated wire firmly against the blade with your thumb. Maybe with some help from your other hand, rotate the wire so the pressure of your thumb has a chance to slice gently through the insulation all the way around the wire. Don't cut deeply, not at first anyway.

With most household cord insulation, if you simply break the surface only part of the way around, you've done enough for that part of the job. If you press too hard or cut too deeply, you will slice off some of the fine braids of wire beneath the insulation.

After the cut, pull firmly on the loose end of insulation. Hopefully it will just slip off, leaving you with a shiny bare wire. If not, put the knife blade back into the same slit and press a bit harder this time.

During your first several tries at stripping insulation, you may cut too deeply and remove all or a substantial chunk of the wire along with the insulation. In that case, simply cut off the whole wire once more; all you've really lost is ½″ of cord and a minute or two of time.

The wire inside almost all flexible cords is braided. It consists of hundreds of very fine wires twisted or braided together to form one larger, flexible, highly conductive line. If you have just stripped the insulation off a braided wire, twist the bare end firmly several times in the direction of the braiding. This will firm up the collection of tiny wires and keep them from developing "split ends."

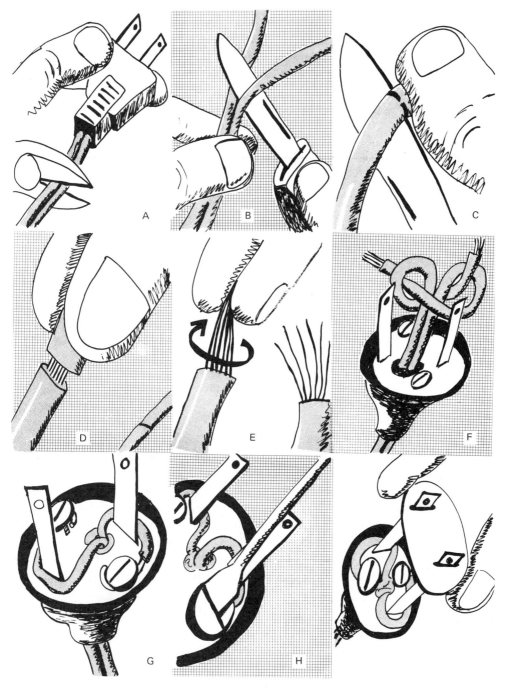

Figure 110   Here's how you can simply replace a faulty plug.

207

208

*Plugs, Sockets,
Switches,
Cords, and
Other Electrical
Problems*

After both (or all three) wires have been stripped, carefully slide them through the end of your new plug. To keep the connections from being jerked loose by people continually plugging and unplugging the gadget, learn how to tie a knot in the wire. Here's how: A knot holds the wires together as well as resists pressures that might pull the stripped ends loose from the plug contacts. Look at part ''f'' of Figure 110 to see how a professional Underwriters knot is made. It is simple if you think it is simple. But if you find it too much to follow, a simple square knot or a granny knot is better than no knot at all.

Before the knot is pulled down into the handle part of your plug, hook the two (or three) bared copper ends under the screws. The wire must be pointed *clockwise*, the same direction the screws will turn when you tighten them. If the wire twists in the other direction, pressure from the screw, instead of making a connection even tighter, might force all or some of the strands of bare wire out from underneath the screw head. In *every* electrical connection made with screw contacts, the wire must lie the same way as the screw, when it tightens, turns—clockwise.

Now tighten the screws. Tug the knot gently but firmly into the handle end of your new plug. But before you jam the plug into the outlet, there is one more step, a bit of safety sense too often overlooked.

The business end of the plug has to be covered with a cardboard shield, which should have come with the new plug when you bought it. If not, make one yourself with cardboard such as that found in shirt protectors or the backing on tablets of writing paper. The circular shield should slip into the inner curve of the plug and have a hole through which each prong can protrude.

The cardboard shield protects the inner wiring of a plug, which is not in the wall, so dirt and corrosive agents cannot easily get inside. It also helps to keep braids of wire from getting knocked loose. If just a few strands from both contacts work loose and touch each other, you are likely to experience a small but ferocious-sounding bolt of lightning the next time you shove an unshielded plug into the wall.

TERMINALS AND CORDS

At the end of your appliance cord *opposite* the plug, the cord goes through whatever kind of cabinet or housing may be present. That is the second common place where cords go awry from bending,

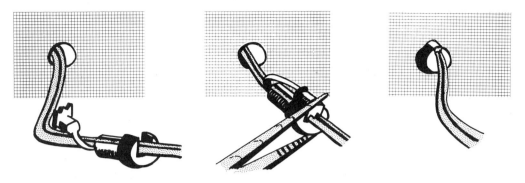

Figure 111 Cord strain relievers help cords on most electrical appliances resist the pulling and bending. Here's how you install or reinstall one.

jerking, plugging, unplugging, and other use or abuse. Some gadgets, electric irons in particular, suffer so frequently from trouble at the end of the cord that many manufacturers have a removable bit of decoration to let you examine the condition of the terminals without disassembling the entire iron.

Whether tool, toaster, toothbrush, or TV, the terminals that link the cord to the appliance are all basically similar. The wire passes through the cabinet via a *grommet* or *cord strain reliever*.

The grommet is nothing more than a rubber donut that grabs a cord fairly tightly and holds it in one place within a corresponding hole in the cabinet. The cord strain reliever is a bit more elaborate and gives more protection because it grabs the cord with considerably more pressure than a simple grommet (see Figure 152).

Some very simply made devices incorporate a substitute cord strain reliever molded right into the plastic body. If you have to repair the cord at its terminal end and no strain reliever or grommet is at hand, the Underwriters knot generally makes an adequate substitute.

Terminals, which make electrical connections to convenience cords in most appliances, are either screw type or solderless connectors. If something happens to the connection or to the cord itself, simply snip off the appliance end of the cord a bit below the trouble spot—with the plug pulled out of the wall, please. Then strip off ½ ″ of insulation and fit the renewed wire back into place either twisted under a solderless connector or curled clockwise under a screw terminal.

Some terminals, fortunately not many, are soldered. Generally in this case the ends of the convenience cord are simply soldered onto the terminals of some internal mechanism as a way of saving time and money on the assembly line. Chapter 6 gave you tips on soldering and

210

*Plugs, Sockets,
Switches,
Cords, and
Other Electrical
Problems*

the same techniques apply here. There is one exception to the soldered terminal question, however.

Electric waffle irons, clothes irons, and even a toaster may have soldered connections. Due to the great amount of heat present, ordinary solder cannot be used because it would melt about midway through the second waffle. If you encounter soldered connections in hot gadgets, suspect that silver solder has been used. It melts over 1000°F., and inexpensive home soldering equipment won't make a dent in it.

Silver solder and a chemical known as *flux* are easy to buy in many hardware stores and most electronic mail order houses. To apply it, you will need a torch, one of the common propane torches or one of the less common miniature welding gadgets with bubble-sized tanks of oxygen and butane. The torch, which uses approximately 16 ounce tanks of propane, is the least expensive and most versatile of the two.

It would probably be uneconomical to accumulate the necessary equipment and materials for a single silver soldering job. If you already have a torch, however, everything else you might need to know about elementary silver soldering is covered in the music-maker chapter except the temperature is substantially higher.

If terminals are corroded when you find them, it is important that you get rid of the foreign deposits, which can seriously hamper the flow of electric current. The fastest and probably surest way to lick corrosion, short of replacing the terminal itself, is to remove each screw from the terminal and soak it in vinegar or a proprietary metal cleaning agent. Rinse them well and dry thoroughly before reinstalling.

Cords themselves may need replacing if they have been subjected to a lot of heavy use or abuses, such as too many kicks, slams, bends, or if it happened to dangle across the stove while a burner was lit. Whenever the cord of a relatively new tool or appliance needs replacing, there are two things to do before rushing out to buy a new hunk of wire.

One, figure out what you or your family has been doing wrong. Cords that are habitually stretched across doorways, or put away so the cord can dangle into the hot part of a stove or radiator, or run under windows or through doorways are not only going to wear out prematurely, but are also apt to short out or get pulled apart while someone is holding on.

Two, figure out how big a wire you need. Do all wires look alike to you? They're not. There are many, many sizes of wire conductors and many types of insulation for the wires. Your best bet is to replace an appliance cord with exactly the same size wire and the same type of insulation. On really good cords, the insulation designation is

211

*Plugs, Sockets,
Switches,
Cords, and
Other Electrical
Problems*

stamped right on the side of the cord at short intervals. Unfortunately, it is very difficult to find a big selection of specialized cords in local stores so you may have to consult Figure 112 after first calculating how many watts of electrical power the appliance consumes.

Figure 112 assumes that your new cord will be the same length as your old one. If it would be convenient to have just a little more slack, you can add a foot or two. But if you decide to add substantially onto the length, select the next largest wire size for any length up to about double the length of the original convenience cord. Example: Your worn out cord was 8 ' long and ordinarily a number 16 size wire would be adequate. But you want to make the replacement 15 long, so you have to choose a number 14 wire.

Wire sizes are calculated inversely. In other words, a number 18 wire is *smaller* than a number 16 or 14 or 12. The numbering sequence goes much higher for very fine wires and beyond 0 to 00 for very hefty cables.

Fig. 112 How Many Watts of Power Can Safely Be Carried by Wires of Given Size and Insulation Properties (at 120 Volts)*

	WIRE SIZE			
Insulation Code Designation	*No. 18*	*No. 16*	*No. 14*	*No. 12*
Rubber & Plastic—Not for hard use: PO, C, PD, E, EO, EN, SRD, SV. SVO, SP, ET, ETT, ETLB, ETP, SRDT, SVT, SVTO, SPT	1000	1300	1800	2500
Rubber & Plastic—OK for hard use: SJ, SJO, SJT, SJTO	1000	1300	1800	2500
Rubber & Plastic—OK for very hard use: S, SO, ST, STO	1000	1300	1800	2500
Heat Resistant Cords: AFS, AFSJ, HC, HPD, HSJ, HSJO, HS, HSO, HPN, SVHT	1000	1500	2000	3000
Heat & Moisture Resistant Cords: AVPO, AVDP	1700	2200	2800	3600
Cotton Covered Heat Resistant Cord: CFPD	600	800	1700	2300
Asbestos Covered Heat Resistant Cord: AFC, AFPD	600	800	1700	2300

*Based on the 1971 National Electrical Code Table 400-9(b), "Amperacity of Flexible Cords." Amperage figures from the NEC have been multiplied by 100 to provide a very conservative wattage figure for the purposes of this chart.

SWITCHES

A very common ailment to all kinds of gadgets, lamps, appliances, tools, and toys is the switch that fails to work properly. (Wall light switches and similar house wiring devices are covered later.) Unlike the switches you replace in home music equipment and similar items, the somewhat larger switches you will install in lamps and other household electric applications are not often soldered into place.

The switches sold for household use come in so many varied sizes, shapes, and configurations that the only way you can be 100 percent sure of finding an exact replacement is to buy one from an authorized parts dealer for the manufacturer. This is seldom necessary, however, unless the switch is extremely specialized or wierd. If a replacement switch is similar to the old in several of the following basic areas, all other dissimilarities should be of little consequence:

1. Voltage. The replacement unit must have a voltage rating stamped on it showing that it can handle at least as many volts as the old. In most cases, that will be 120 V. If the replacement voltage rating is *higher*, the switch may be physically larger than the one it will replace, but electrically it is okay.

2. Amps. Sometimes expressed in watts, but usually in amps, the new switch must be built to cope with at least as much power as the old. Read the fine print because you will often see a rating such as 10 amps at 120 volts, 5 amps at 220 volts. If your lamp or tool is operated at 120 volts, you need consider only the 10 amps rating.

3. Poles. Replacements have to include at least as many poles as the old switch. In other words, there must be facilities for at least as many incoming lines on the new as on the old (see Chapter 6 for electronic part nomenclature, which gets into this area graphically).

4. Throws. A majority of switches for household uses are single throw. Each line is either "on" or "off." If each line fed into the switch is able to leave via one of two separate routes (double throw switch) or even into three separate outgoing circuits (triple throw), your replacement must do likewise. However, you can use a double throw switch to replace a single throw if you carefully disregard and isolate the unused set of output connections.

5. Mounting. In-line switches are fastened right into the wires they regulate. This is a common configuration for lamps and some tools. It is not a particularly satisfactory arrangement for anything that gets heavy use. *Panel switches* are fastened onto the panel or case of whatever items they serve. Wires are brought to the switch terminals,

213

*Plugs, Sockets,
Switches,
Cords, and
Other Electrical
Problems*

which are concealed behind the panel. Panel switches usually are held in place by a threaded retaining ring. A new retaining ring comes with a new switch, so it is not imperative that the threads of your replacement switch match threads of the old one. However, your new switch must fit into the hole vacated by an old one unless you plan to machine the opening to fit. Likewise, if the thread size of the new switch is substantially smaller than the old, you will probably have to add a couple of washers to keep the new switch from falling through the larger hole. Fortunately, there aren't more than two or three major thread sizes for panel switches.

6. Body size. All electrical properties aside, you have to give at least some thought to the physical size of the new switch. Will its body fit into the space left empty when you pulled out the faulty switch?

7. Switching configuration. If the old switch was a push-on and push-off type or push-on and pull-off, you might find an up-down flickering operation to be either a nuisance or a physical impossibility. This has to be considered when shopping for a replacement switch. Likewise, you have to duplicate whether the switch stayed on only as long as someone held it down with a finger or whether one flick or shove would turn the switch on until another flick or shove would turn it off.

8. Connections. If your old switch is hooked up by looping the wires under screws, you will probably want to find a replacement of the same type. The alternative is a switch that has pigtail leads already fastened into the switch and is hooked up by twisting the existing wires onto the new switch wires. In almost every case these types can be interchanged, space permitting.

Don't let these differences in switches throw you. All of these eight points are easy to keep track of and rather obvious once you hold any switch in your hand.

There are only two steps in installing most replacement switches. First, make the mechanical connection if you are working with a panel switch. The new switch is slipped into place and tightened there, generally by a screwed-on retainer ring.

Second, the electrical connection is made. Make sure the electricity is turned off before removing the old switch and before installing a new one. As double protection, you can carry a neon glow tube tester to check for "hot" wires before resuming a wiring job.

Solderless, screwless connections are made with a *pigtail splice.* The loose ends of bare wire, about ½" long, are simply twisted together and a solderless connector is twisted over the joint (see Figure 155).

Solderless connectors, mentioned earlier in the section on terminals, come in a variety of sizes to match the size wires being joined. If a connector is too large, the coiled spring inside will not grab at the wires firmly enough to provide a lasting and secure connection. Conversely, should the connector be too small, it will not fit over the two wires or will not extend far enough down the length of the splice to give good mechanical and electrical coverage.

Solderless connectors are a cheap enough accessory that if you have doubts about what size to buy, pick up several in varied sizes. They come in colors too.

Solderless connectors are not limited only to use in hooking up new appliances or lamp switches. You will find them a safe way to make almost any electrical connection where screw terminals are not already involved.

An older way of joining two wires was by splicing them together

Figure 113   Connecting two wires is done best with solderless connectors (A) by simply twisting the 2 wires together and then twisting on the connector. Otherwise, wrap first one wire around the other, then the remaining wire around first (B) Apply a double layer of electrical tape over the splice.

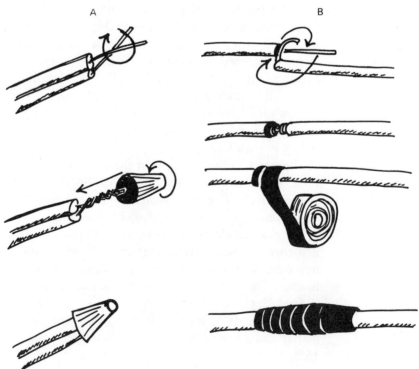

A   B

215

Plugs, Sockets,
Switches,
Cords, and
Other Electrical
Problems

and applying a layer or two of electrical tape. The solderless connectors are many times easier and probably even safer than the way many people wrap splices with tape. But if you insist on using tape, or if you have electrical tape in the toolbox but no solderless connectors when some electrical repair job comes up, the accompanying photos show how to do it. There are, however, some other things to remember.

Use *electrical* tape for *electrical* jobs. Other plastic tapes just are not safe enough to risk your life on. Use plenty of tape. *One* layer may do but *two* will add some worthwhile insurance. Cut the tape carefully with a scissors or knife. Don't break it into pieces with a jerk. Vinyl tapes have a memory for their shape. If you have stretched a piece of plastic electrical tape either while cutting it or applying it, the tape will start to creep back to its former shape the instant you let go. And the creeping can result in the end working loose.

LIGHT SOCKETS

Sockets need replacing too often. The most frequent reason is that the switch inside the socket wears out. With age, the screws that hold wires in place also may work loose and resist all of your efforts at tightening them. Likewise, the cardboard insulation around the internal contact points in sockets can deteriorate or get rubbed off, allowing the metal shell to touch the metal current-carrying parts. The result can be a shock to someone who turns the switch on or off.

The sockets that hold light bulbs in most lamps, whether floor lamps, pinup lamps, or desk lamps, can be replaced with one of the relatively few standard varieties most hardware stores stock. Take off your old socket and compare it with a new one if you feel unsure of choosing the right replacement. Most variations have to do with switches more than sockets.

The technique you learned for rewiring a new plug onto an ailing gadget holds true for sockets too. And for almost everything else of an electrical nature (see Figure 114).

It is important that you keep the cardboard insulator around the working parts of a socket to isolate the metal exterior with hot wires. And if the lamp or appliance wire is color coded—generally one black lead and one white—you should attach them to the same terminals from which they were removed. The light colored lead as a rule should be attached to the outside, socket terminal, usually silver colored. And the dark colored lead should attach to the contact, which touches the tip of the bulb, usually a brass colored terminal.

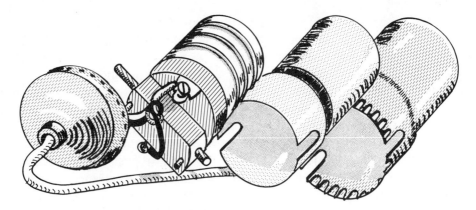

Figure 114 Exploded view of properly-wired lamp socket.

When in doubt, connect dark to dark and light to light, black to black or brass, white to white or silver. This procedure is in keeping with newer provisions of the electrical code aimed at bringing consistency even to simple wire setups. The consistency, in turn, will let you take advantage of the optimum protection from new electrical safety equipment being introduced for home use. By recalling that one simple rule, "dark to dark, light to light," you will not have to learn specifically how to tackle every individual electrical job. Instead, you will have a general knowledge of the whole field ready to lick any specific core intelligently.

LIGHTING FIXTURES

In many ways, lighting fixtures resemble the basic parts of a simple replacement light socket. However, the socket portions of many fixtures slung onto ceilings and walls are not replaceable. You should examine each lighting fixture individually to determine whether or not it is worth the labor and expense of trying to replace an individual socket or whether you might be better off junking the old fixture and installing an entirely new one.

When you examine a light fixture, don't depend on a wall light switch for protection against electrical shock. The switch probably connects to only one of the two or three leads. And in old houses or in installations done by electricians who didn't know or care about running consistently distinct "hot" and "ground" wires, you might accidentally grab a hot wire even with the switch off.

Chandeliers and common lighting fixtures of all sorts, whether hung from a ceiling or fastened to a wall, have many parts in common although most of them are concealed until the fixture is

216

217

*Plugs, Sockets,
Switches,
Cords, and
Other Electrical
Problems*

loosened from its moorings. At the base of such installations is a metal *outlet box* sunk into the ceiling or wall to protect the electrical connections made to the house cables. Such a box is required by the NEC whenever the cables are spliced or attached to any other wires.

You will generally find a metal *cross bar* attached to the outlet box. It is held to the box with an 8 × 32 bolt at each end. Some cross bars are flat. Others, known as *offset cross bars,* bulge in the middle to accommodate wires or canopies of varying sizes. The *canopy* is that part of a lighting fixture that fits right against the ceiling.

There is a hole in the center of a cross bar into which fits a short threaded piece of pipe called a *nipple.* On occasion, the nipple will not thread directly into the cross bar but is inserted through the cross bar hole and held by lock nuts on either side. In any event, at least one lock nut helps to hold the nipple in place when you turn the *loop,* that sometimes fancy piece of hardware that actually holds most canopies in place.

Nipples, being nothing more than ordinary pipe, are sized according to plumbing designations. The pipe nipple most often used in lighting installations is called ⅛-I.P., or ⅛" International Plumbing thread. But it isn't ⅛" in diameter at all; it is ⅜" on the outside.

A second common pipe size found in lighting installations, floor lamps in particular, is ¼-I.P., with an outside measurement of ½". You might even find a pipe nipple measuring ⅝" outside diameter, designated as ⅜-I.P.

There is yet one other threaded implement you might encounter, particularly when you take apart the threaded fittings that hold lamp shades in place. This item is designated ¼-27; it actually is ¼" in diameter and has a machine thread like bolts instead of a pipe thread. The "27" indicates there are 27 threads for every running inch. Figure 115 shows a generalized layout of a ceiling-mounted lighting fixture. Turn the drawing sideways if you want to understand a wall-mounted fixture.

Since the size of standard outlet boxes varies from 3" to about 5" depending on how many wires have to be crammed into the box and the personal preference of each electrician, the cross bars usually have a slotted space to accomodate the two 8 × 32 bolts that hold it onto the box.

Nipples come not only in various diameters but in various lengths. Since they are so inexpensive, if you have any doubt about what size to buy for a new fixture you plan to install, buy two or three different lengths. A really friendly hardware store will let you return the unused ones anyway.

This is how to calculate the approximate length for the nipple,

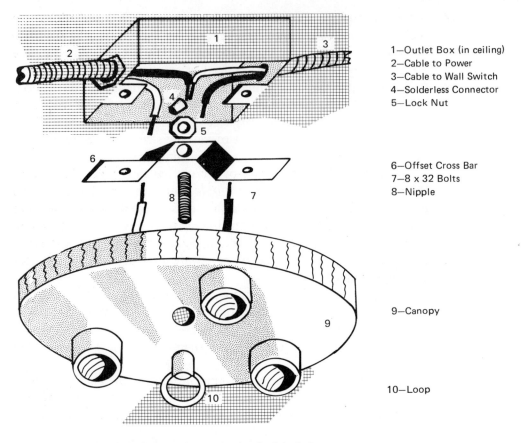

1—Outlet Box (in ceiling)
2—Cable to Power
3—Cable to Wall Switch
4—Solderless Connector
5—Lock Nut

6—Offset Cross Bar
7—8 x 32 Bolts
8—Nipple

9—Canopy

10—Loop

Figure 115 Ceiling light fixture, when properly wired, includes these elements. By laying this drawing on its side, you have the proper layout for a wall fixture.

which must bear much or all of the weight of your ceiling or wall fixture:

Thickness of the canopy to be installed,
PLUS ¼ " to thread the ornamental loop outside the canopy,
PLUS ¼ " to thread the lock nut inside the cross bar;
PLUS or MINUS the amount of offset in the cross bar (*plus* if the offset points into the ceiling or wall, *minus* if it points into the canopy) equals
TOTAL approximate length required for the nipple.

For particularly large or heavy canopies, mounting screws are often used to give support in addition to the loop. And on some fixtures there is no connection to the nipple at all. The entire weight is carried by the mounting screws, although this is not an ideal setup.

218   Since we are interested in spreading practical knowledge and confi-

219

*Plugs, Sockets,
Switches,
Cords, and
Other Electrical
Problems*

dence instead of "cookbook directions" about every object in a home, table lamps, and floor lamps, and similar electrical items will not be described here. From what we have already said, you should understand enough to tackle any kind of incandescent lighting hook-ups. (But Figure 116 will help too.)

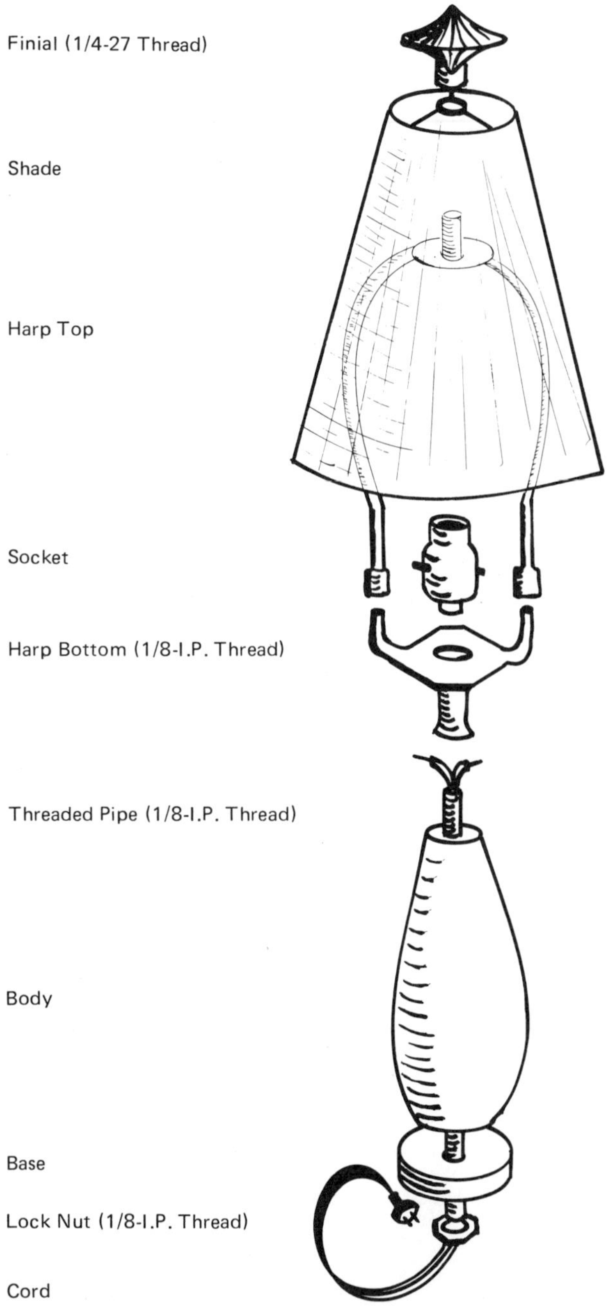

Finial (1/4-27 Thread)

Shade

Harp Top

Socket

Harp Bottom (1/8-I.P. Thread)

Threaded Pipe (1/8-I.P. Thread)

Body

Base

Lock Nut (1/8-I.P. Thread)

Cord

Figure 116   Table lamp exploded view.

220

*Plugs, Sockets,
Switches,
Cords, and
Other Electrical
Problems*

This seems to be the era of *hanging lamps,* which is a fine idea. Aside from their appearance and design possibilities, these lamps also can conserve power. Especially in older, highceiling buildings, it is often necessary to consume double the number of kilowatt hours compared with rooms built with 8 ′ ceilings just to provide enough light for reading. By dropping the lighting fixture on a chain or decorative cord, properly made to support the weight, the light is brought closer to the user. As a result, smaller bulbs can be used.

There are special canopies designed for hanging lamps. Generally the lamp is hung directly beneath the spot where a lighting fixture previously was ceiling mounted. Alternately, a chain extends from the site of the canopy to some new location and then drops down. In any event, the canopy for hanging fixtures is principally designed to cover the old outlet box, to provide a smooth hole for the wires to run through, and to give a secure mooring on which to anchor the chain. These canopies are installed exactly like any lighting fixture and according to techniques described above.

If the hanging lamp is going to hang anywhere but directly beneath the outlet box, an ornamental swag is called for. The swag is little more than a hook that you can fasten to the ceiling via its own long screw or a toggle bolt (see Figure 117). The screwed-in swag is best, assuming you can find the precise location of your ceiling beams and if a beam happens to pass almost exactly where you want to hang the lamp. But if not, a well-installed toggle bolt is the next best thing.

Swags, chains, cords, switches, cross bars, and virtually every other piece of hardware you will need to rehabilitate old fixtures or

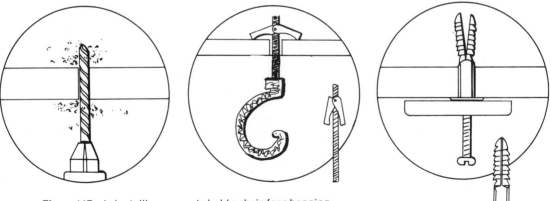

Figure 117   In installing a swag to hold a chain for a hanging lamp, first test whether there is an available wooden beam to screw the swag into directly. If not, drill a hole (A), then insert a toggle bolt while it is in its folded position (B) and attach the swag head to the bolt.

221

*Plugs, Sockets,
Switches,
Cords, and
Other Electrical
Problems*

install new ones are available from hardware stores, electrical and lamp supply stores. Even many paint and wallpaper stores are getting into the lamp scene. At least one company publishes an 80-page booklet about making and remaking lamps and lighting fixtures.

FLUORESCENT LAMPS

Fluorescent lamps are still a mystery to many people. But they shouldn't be. At each end of the common fluorescent tube is a filament that glows red hot during the starting operation. Each filament gives off a powerful electrical discharge of electrons. The discharge and the filament heat combine to strike an electrical arc through the length of the tube.

A fluorescent lamp is coated with chemical compounds called *phosphors,* and they are so activated by the radiation generated within the tube that they give off an intense glow. That *glow* is what we call the light.

Fluorescent lamps are noted for long life and economy of operation. A fluorescent light that consumes only 30 watts of electricity generates about as much light as a 100-watt incandescent lamp. The fluorescent lamp will also last from 10 to 20 times longer than the ordinary incandescent light bulb.

For the most part, fluorescent tubes and even circular fluorescent lamps have not exactly inspired beautiful lighting fixtures. But they are a highly utilitarian source of light wherever beauty is of secondary importance.

In many home modernization plans, fluorescent tubes are recessed into a lowered ceiling, then covered with translucent plastic. The combination makes a neat and relatively inexpensive-to-maintain installation. But the initial cost of fluorescent fixtures and tubes is worth thinking about.

For home use, fluorescent fixtures are generally purchased as a unit, ready to be installed just like the incandescent lighting gadgets and hardware. You must be certain, however, that the fluorescent tubes and fixtures you select are made for each other.

Instant start tubes and the more traditional *heater started* tubes are not interchangeable. Each requires its own type of switch and ballast. Fluorescent tubes are superconductors when they get started. They would simply draw more and more and more electric current until something burned out. To limit their appetite, and often to assist with the starting process, two pieces of seldom-noticed components are included in most fixtures.

A *ballast* is a variation of transformer and/or resistor depending upon the type of lamp, size, and manufacturer's preference. It limits

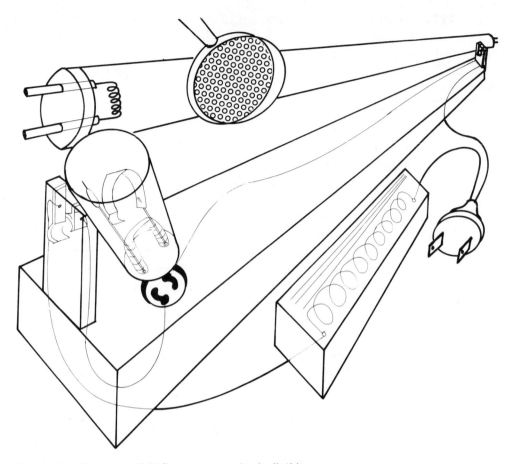

Figure 118 Fluorescent light fixtures operate basically this way. Power enters the ballast (similar to transformer), which regulates the flow of electricity to the tube. When starting (except in instant-start models), the starter (at left) short circuits the tube so that current flows through each filament, heating it. After a few seconds, the heater inside the starter moves a bimetal strip and opens the circuit. Then electricity flows through the tube between the filaments. That generates energy which excites the phosphors in the coating inside the tube (magnified view) and produces light.

the amount of current the tube can consume. The *starter* short-circuits the filaments to heat them up the instant you turn on the light switch. Once enough heat and electrical emission have built up to sustain the fluorescent operation, the starter contacts open, and instead of electricity flowing *through* each filament individually, electricity flows the length of the tube—via argon gas and mercury vapor—*between* the filaments.

Troubleshooting a fluorescent tube requires just a bit of understanding about the function of the various parts. Fluorescent systems

223

*Plugs, Sockets,
Switches,
Cords, and
Other Electrical
Problems*

are more sensitive to voltage fluctuations than are ordinary incandescent light bulbs. If they are operated for too long below 110 volts, such as during "brown outs," they may function erratically and their useful life-span can be shortened significantly. The more drastic the voltage cut, the more drastic will be their demise.

In cities or R.E.A. areas where the normal voltage is 120 volts, if the power company lowers the voltage by more than 8 percent during a power crisis, the actual current will drop below the 110 volt limit. (At 120 volts, an 8 percent cut leaves 110.4 volts.) And in areas served by a normal output of 115 volts, even a 5 percent drop in voltage brings the figure below 110 volts. At the outset of power difficulties, electric suppliers often lower the voltage by 5 percent. But if the over-demand continues, they consider reducing voltages by as much as 10 percent.

The active materials coating fluorescent tubes is consumed more quickly during starting operations. For the sake of obtaining the longest possible life-span for fluorescent tubes, continuous operation is ideal. That might not be ideal in terms of paying for the electricity required to run the light continuously, however. Manufacturers strongly recommend that fluorescent lamps not be turned off and on again more frequently than every three hours.

Temperature is a second environmental factor that affects the operation of fluorescent tubes, unlike incandescent light bulbs. At normal room temperatures, between 70° and 80° F., the fluorescent tube is actually warmed to 100° to 120° F. If the room temperature increases or decreases the lamps operate with less efficiency.

The cooling effect is particularly noticed when a draft of wind is also present. When the room temperature around a fluorescent tube has dropped to 50°, and the tube is in a draft as well, its light output is about 50 percent below normal. That doesn't do wonders for the life-span either.

As with so many other electrical or electronic gadgets, *loose connections* can plague fluorescent lights too. If a bulb will not start or if it flickers during operation, check to see that it is properly set into the fixture.

If there is *no sign of life at all* when the light switch is turned on, or the fluorescent light's own switch is activated, first go through the preliminary steps outlined in the troubleshooting chapter. As part of your troubleshooting ritual, replace the starter. That obscure little piece of inexpensive equipment is responsible for the greatest share of fluorescent repair chores.

Since fluorescent tubes almost never burn out suddenly unless they have been subjected to physical abuse, if a new starter fails to inject life into a fluorescent light, and if you have checked that electric

224

*Plugs, Sockets,
Switches,
Cords, and
Other Electrical
Problems*

power is ready to surge into the fixture, then get out your neon glow tube tester.

Loosen the fixture from its mooring on the ceiling or wall. Locate where the power enters and makes its connection to the ballast. Generally, one lead on the ballast is hooked up to one side of the house power and the second lead runs to one lamp socket.

With one lead of the tester touching the "hot" wire from the house current and the other lead touching the input side of the ballast, you should get a strong glow. What you are doing is no different than simply touching the tester to both sides of the house current. If there is no glow, there is no current reaching the fixture and you should backtrack in your troubleshooting procedure to the switch, plug (if any), fuses, and such.

If the input side of the ballast gives a glow, switch that lead of your neon tester to the output side. It also should glow. If not, try the switch in both the on and off positions to see if power is present at the output side under any conditions. If not, you are quite safe in assuming that some part of the ballast is defective.

It is very important that your new ballast be identical to the old one, assuming it worked well during its lifetime. Jot down the numbers printed on your old ballast before running downtown for a new one. If a replacement of the same model by the same maker is not readily available, a reputable electrical dealer should be able to supply one for you if you can give the type of fixture plus the size and number of bulbs used.

There is an alternate way to test for a defective ballast, one which does not require that you removed the fixture from its mount on the wall or ceiling. Except for the circular tubes, you will need a way to extend one lead of your neon glow tube tester. One of the simple alligator test leads would be ideal (See Figure 119). Two might be needed, one holding onto the other, for very long fluorescent lamps.

With the fluorescent tube removed, the test lead with alligator clip is fastened to one of the two terminals at either end of the fluorescent fixture. The loose end of the tester is then touched to one of the two terminals at the opposite end. If the tube fails to glow, touch the second terminal at the same end. If nothing happens, move the clipped end of the test lead to the second terminal at the same end that first had the clipped lead. Now you should get the tester to light up when the loose probe is touched to one of the two terminals. If not, the ballast apparently is not working or wires leading to it are disconnected.

In the case of a circular fluorescent tube, the alligator clip lead is unnecessary since all four terminal points are in one small area. Making sure that the power switch is turned on (as you should do with

Figure 119 Unless lamps, switches, cords, and similar electrical devices in your home are in proper working condition, you may be asking for trouble, serious and unexpected trouble. Most problems lie in switches, outlets, and similar places where a handy person can easily make repairs before it's too late.

the long tubular fixtures also), touch the leads to any two terminals. Keep trying different terminals until you either get a positive result between one pair or you are convinced that no power is present at any of the terminals.

Should you flip on the light switch for a fluorescent tube and see the ends light up but nothing else happen after a reasonable period of time, don't leave the switch turned on for very long. Likewise, if the tube lights up but the ends stay exceptionally bright and hot anyway, turn off the switch.

The filaments must be heated to a high temperature to get the electrical reaction within the tube started when you first turn it on. But if they remain permanently hot, the life of your tube will be greatly shortened. Most often the explanation for filaments that remain heated for too long is a shorted starter. Replace it.

A *starter* is little more than an automatic switch, which at the outset lets electric current flow through the fluorescent tube filaments to heat them and the gases inside. After a second or two of such heating, the starter's own internal heater should have bent the heat-sensitive switch contact enough to open up the filament line. When that happens, the electricity has no other alternative but to surge through the ballast and jump directly from one filament to the other.

If a fluorescent lamp blinks on and off, or if the ends of the tube keep getting darker and darker, it could be a sign that it has finally worn out and is ready to be replaced. The average life-span of a fluorescent tube ranges up to 15,000 and should never be less than 6,000 hours. If such a lamp is left on some 12 hours a day, even with a tube rated at 7,500 hours of normal life, replacement should be necessary about every 625 days, nearly two years. General Electric rates their T-

226

Plugs, Sockets,
Switches,
Cords, and
Other Electrical
Problems

12, 4 ' long tubes at 15,000 hours, which could mean about three and a half years between replacements.

Even routine replacement of worn out electrical components in your house, or updating of old ones, is certainly not beyond the skills and knowledge of anyone who has managed to read this far. Dangers are nil if you first disconnect the appropriate fuse or circuit breaker. And hazards to the house are wiped out by the same safety devices that will cut off the current almost immediately in case you really goof so badly that a short circuit occurs.

HOME LIGHT SWITCHES

Light switches that control the house lights or similar conveniences can last for years before their contacts, springs, or wires deteriorate. If a wall switch fails to turn on a light or other small appliance on the circuit any time the handle is thrown, the switch needs replacing. Or if it starts to hesitate when there was no hesitation before, replace it. Also put in a new switch if the tension on the old switch handle suddenly seems to have lost its snap.

For the most part, good switches are built with considerable fail-safe capacity. If something goes wrong, they just don't work. Seldom will a properly chosen, properly installed switch cause short circuits or other dangerous electrical faults. But you might consider that walking across a dark living room is dangerous on the night a switch finally fails for good.

Switches rated and tested according to Underwriters Laboratory standards are available at all electrical supply outlet and many hardware stores. Look for the U/L logo stamped on the switch, but *also* look to make sure that somewhere on the body it says the switch is rated to handle enough power—"125 V., 15 A." That means the switch can easily tolerate 125 volts at a load of 15 amps. Those figures were chosen because they match the rating for fuses and circuit breakers in most household branch circuits.

The electrical code recommends a system like this so that if a short circuit occurs inside any item plugged into an outlet or controlled by a switch, the switch or outlet will successfully handle the overload without catching fire, melting, or in any other way destroying itself before a 15 amp fuse or circuit breaker detects the excess current and shuts off the overloaded line. So even though a switch might never see more than one or two amps of power during its lifetime, *your* lifetime is protected by installing one rated at least 15 amps.

After you have shut off the circuit breaker or unscrewed *both* fuses protecting the line on which you need a new switch, unscrew the

227

*Plugs, Sockets,
Switches,
Cords, and
Other Electrical
Problems*

cover plate. There are generally two small brass screws holding the plate in place although on a few fancier models, the screw heads are hidden under adhesive covers that match the main body of the plate. Their location, however, is identical in common switch covers.

Beneath the cover plate you will find two screws that hold the switch itself into the outlet box. Unscrew them until you can pull the switch a bit free of the box. They do not have to come all the way out. *On new switches, they should not come all the way out* for fear that the screws will get lost. You should find a thin carboard washer on each of the screws to hold them in place during installation and repair.

If you have a neon tester handy, it is a good idea at this point to check that the power really is off before putting your hands into the box. Then you can reach in and gently pull the switch all the way out of the outlet box. The wires inside should be fairly stiff, so you may have to pull a little harder than you expect until the switch is just far enough out of the box so you can conveniently work on the screws that hold the wires in place, generally located on the side of the switch.

Before removing the wires, examine them to see if the insulation on

Figure 120 Here's all there is to that wall light switch that may need replacing. Shut off the house current first and the rest of job is easy.

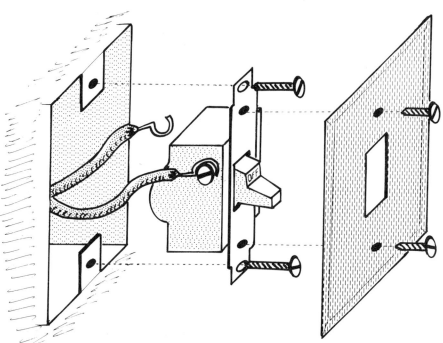

228

Plugs, Sockets,
Switches,
Cords, and
Other Electrical
Problems

one wire is white and the other black. You may have to wipe away some of the inevitable dust that accumulates inside these boxes. But if you do identify a white and a black wire, proceed to take off the wires.

If you are unable to tell whether one wire is or was white and the other black, look further to see whether the screws in the switch terminal are of different colors. Generally one set is brass colored, the other silver. If the wires cannot be identified by color, then attach an identifying tag before removing them from the screws.

Now take your new switch, and attach the black wire to the brass terminal, making certain the curved end curves clockwise. Then tighten down the screw. Do the same for the remaining wire.

Carefully return the switch and wires into the outlet box, reinstall the two screws that hold the switch in place, put back the cover plate, and then restore power to your renewed switch. That's it!

If you must replace some out-of-the-ordinary kind of switch, be sure to buy an out-of-the-ordinary replacement to match the important aspects of the original switch. For example, if the circuit involves what is called a *three-way switch,* by which a light can be turned on or turned off from two different locations, you must buy a switch plainly marked for that purpose. And in case your three-way wires get mixed up while you are installing the new three-way swtich, Figure 121 will help you to untangle them.

Figure 121 Three-way switches are installed this way. Pay attention to the position of black and white wires in particular. Gray ones are interchangeable as a rule (although they may be red or some other color).

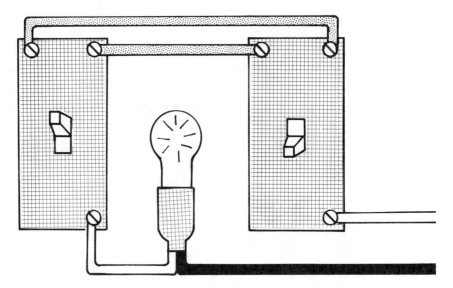

229

*Plugs, Sockets,
Switches,
Cords, and
Other Electrical
Problems*

It is important that only *one* of the two main current-carrying wires be connected even to a three-way switch. In all common household switching operations, in fact, only one of the two power lines is switched on and off. That is why, when you are working on a lighting fixture or some other switched implement, you first throw the circuit breaker or unplug *both* fuses, even if the fixture is controlled by a switch. The pair of wires that connect the paired terminals on the three-way switch can be interchanged without hazard or handicap since they are, in essence, just duplicate channels for the same "hot" lead to pass through.

The most common switch found in homes is called a *snap switch*, appropriately so because it makes a resounding snap every time somebody throws it on or off. If you would like something quieter or able to offer some other extra touch, there are several variations commonly on sale.

Mercury switches are great for a child's room or anywhere else that quiet is important. For areas that are often too dark for anyone to locate the light switch quickly, you can buy *illuminated switches* with tiny lights under the translucent handle. *Dimmer controls* allow you to turn a light fully on or fully off, and also provide an infinite variation between the light and dark.

No matter how glamorous, well-advertised, or impressive a particular switch may appear on the shelf, inspect it before paying to make sure that it bears the Underwriters Laboratory seal and is rated to withstand 15 amps, 125 volts. A great many of the dimmers sold by mail order *do not* meet the standard. If something goes wrong, the fireworks are likely to take place in your wall instead of in your fuse box.

Now that you are somewhat of an expert at installing a new switch in your house wiring system, a new *utility outlet* should come easy. The procedure is almost the same.

In newer houses, there will be a third, bare wire or green-insulated wire inside the outlet box. This is used to *ground* the fixture. In case the insulation or contacts break down inside the box or inside some appliance you may be touching, the potentially lethal surge of power should pass harmlessly through the grounding wire, and not through a human body, on its way to the ground (Figure 109).

In recent years, the National Electrical Code has insisted on progressively stricter grounding measures. In 1972 it became mandatory that all outdoor electrical outlets be grounded, and in 1974 all new indoor electrical installations were also covered.

Grounded utility outlets can accommodate both the traditional parallel two-prong plugs plus the grounded plugs, which have a third,

230

*Plugs, Sockets,
Switches,
Cords, and
Other Electrical
Problems*

rounded prong in addition to the traditional two flat ones. Household wiring installed prior to the deadlines need not be updated, although it would be a good idea. However, there is more to updating utility outlets than some new hardware. If an eager handyperson were to add outlets with grounding facilities to a very old outlet box, which was never adequately wired to a ground, the effect would be to build up confidence in a safety feature that actually isn't there.

The heart of most convenience power outlets is called the *duplex outlet*, named because it can accommodate two plugs at one time. Replacement convenience outlets must bear the U/L seal and be rated at 125 volts and 15 amps, as with switches. But outlets for some appliances and for some air conditioners may be greater than 125 volts or greater than 15 amps. Replace an old outlet with a new one rated at least as high but never less than the fuse or circuit breaker for the circuit involved.

If the old outlet was a grounded type, or if you find evidence of a grounding wire inside the outlet box, you should install a duplex outlet that has the third, grounding opening (see Figure 122). If your

Figure 122 Wall outlets should now, according to the National Electrical Code, be of the grounded variety. Aside from the normal two wires, a third is hooked up to ground to carry away possibly lethal current in case of failure or accident. Here is how the typical grounded wall outlet is installed. Black wire should go to brass colored screws. White wire goes to silver colored screws. Green or bare wire (the ground) goes to green screw.

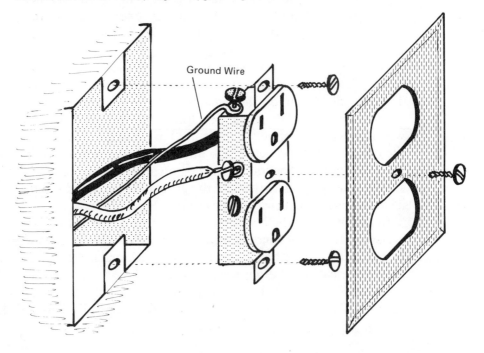

Ground Wire

231

*Plugs, Sockets,
Switches,
Cords, and
Other Electrical
Problems*

older house has ungrounded outlets now, you may want to change just one of them to the newer, grounded variety as a test. At the same time, make a modest but worthwhile investment in a Dearborn Circuit Monitor, which is designed to plug into grounded outlets and, via lights, inform you of the wiring condition—polarity reversed (white wire connected where black should be), properly grounded or improperly grounded, power lead connected to a terminal where the ground should be, and even whether or not power is reaching the outlet. If your research proves that the main wiring system of your home is grounded, you can proceed to install grounded outlets elsewhere, secure in the knowledge that they really will be grounded—assuming you use the monitor each time to double-check your own installation or the work of some earlier electrician.

BELLS AND BUZZERS

Actually, little can go wrong with a doorbell that you shouldn't already be equipped to find and fix. The beauty of bell and buzzer systems is that they operate well on low voltage.

At the heart of a doorbell system is a small, inexpensive transformer, which converts the 120 volt house current into 12 volts or some low voltage in that vicinity. It works just like the transformer on electric trains.

Because the National Electrical Code allows for low voltage systems to be wired and controlled differently than the usual 120 volt household power, doorbells, intercoms, and related small items do not have to be grounded, sheathed in metal, or even fused. These low voltage, low power systems are called *Class 2 low energy power systems*.

Class 2 systems do have a few restrictions to ensure your safety. Transformers used for low voltages have to be approved for Class 2 uses and must include some kind of protection against an overload. Many transformers use a thermal switch to cut off the electricity if the load becomes excessive. Wires used for Class 2 systems must not be run closer than 2″ from any 120 volt (or higher) power lines.

Earlier chapters have given leads on how the wiring network of a doorbell system can be tested for breaks or shorts. The pushbuttons can be tested best by removing them and shorting out the bare wires. If the wires buzz the buzzer but the pushbutton did not, you naturally would install a new pushbutton.

Buzzers that won't buzz simply may need cleaning or adjusting. Contacts on a buzzer or bell can accumulate dirt, oil, corrosion, and other detracting elements that should be cleaned off periodically—at

232

*Plugs, Sockets,
Switches,
Cords, and
Other Electrical
Problems*

least every time the thing gives you trouble. For your reference, Figure 123 presents several typical doorbell wiring systems. If you are stuck trying to make sense of an existing system or want to install a whole new one, the blueprints could save you hours of frustration.

Buzzers are simple electromagnetic devices. When someone pushes the doorbell button, a small set of contacts are closed and 12 volts of current are sent through the wires and then through the electromagnet windings. The *electromagnet* pulls on the iron *armature* of the buzzer. But as soon as the armature moves toward the electromagnet, the *movable contact*, which is fastened onto the armature, breaks away from the *stationary contact*, thus interrupting power to the magnet. With the magnet deactivated, a spring pulls the armature back again, causing contact so the magnet pulls the armature again. And on and on, some several hundred times a second.

The faster the make-and-break cycle occurs, the higher the pitch of a buzzer. To a limited extent, you can alter the pitch of a buzzer higher or lower by bending the armature strip gently with a pliers. With the armature closer to the electromagnet, higher frequencies should result.

A bell is little more than a buzzer that has a gonger attached to the armature and a bell for the gonger to gong. But chimes are something else again.

Figure 123 Bell circuits are simple once seen in graphic form like this.

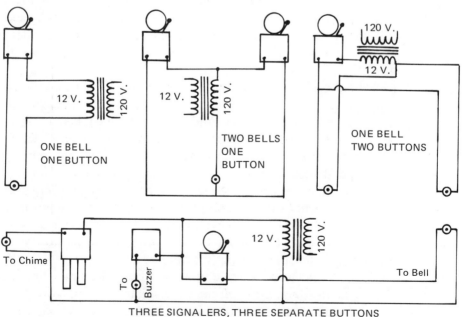

THREE SIGNALERS, THREE SEPARATE BUTTONS
(Each button activates a separate sound source.)

233

Plugs, Sockets,
Switches,
Cords, and
Other Electrical
Problems

Simple door chimes are little more than glorified buzzer electromagnets to which a chime column or two has been added and with the armature movable contact missing. When the button is pushed, the electric current usually activates an electromagnet, which bongs on a gong. When the button is released, the electromagnet springs back, often bonging a second gong. Those fancy multitoned chimes come in so many styles and with so many variations that you will have to draw upon your general skills and confidence to see you through. But they are easy to fix and easier to install.

THE EXTENSION CORD HAZARD

We will *not*, in this book, discuss repair of extension cords, the great American fix-everything item, and we have deliberately not even mentioned them until the end of this chapter. The reason is that the National Electrical Code is pretty explicit about extension cords—*there shouldn't be any* in use today, except for strictly *temporary* use with *portable* equipment. Extension cords should not be used to light up a floor lamp or to operate the air conditioner all summer.

The reason that the code bans so many of the popular uses of extension cords very well could be written from the fire statistics. An extension cord is used to operate a lamp that won't reach the wall outlet. Suzie trips on it two or three times, so Dad hides the extension cord under a rug. But Mom vacuums over the cord every week. The extension cord insulation gives out from the wear—it is designed for temporary, light, exposed use—and one day while the family is out, the two copper leads of the cord, with the insulation worn off, touch each other, generate enough heat before a fuse blows to ignite the rug, the rug ignites the curtains, and then the rest of the house goes.

Or, the baby has a stuffy nose, so Dad wants to run the vaporizer. He wants it closer to the crib than the cord plugged into a wall outlet will allow. So he plugs it into an extension cord. Then Dad drops plenty of salt into the vaporizer so the steam comes up fast. However, as the night wears on, the vaporizer is pulling 6 or 7 amps of current through a cheap lamp cord rated to handle at most 5 amps at room temperature. Heat from the vaporizer transmitted through the copper conductors and the overloaded wire combine to turn the apparently helpful little cord into an incendiary bomb.

The solution to extension cord bombs is obvious, but one that a great many households are bound to consider impractical. Toss away the extension cords? Maybe not, but at least they should be

234

Plugs, Sockets,
Switches,
Cords, and
Other Electrical
Problems

prominently labeled by their makers with a warning about their legal and practical limitations. Manufacturers have for years been selling millions of inexpensive extension cords in cities where local electrical codes all but forbid their use. And the *sale* of extension cords and other poor electrical material is *generally legal even if their use may not be*!

To avoid the extension cord hazard, new electrical codes require utility outlets within 6' of every part of a room. But new codes apply only to new homes, not ones built before existing code provisions. This is the same loophole that keeps most parts of the country from benefiting by code provisions requiring grounded outlets only in newly wired buildings.

As more and more, bigger and bigger electrical appliances, gadgets, novelties, and necessities are crowding into the kitchens, dens, basements, bedrooms, and living rooms of our homes, the electrical overload problem becomes more acute every year. There is no solution short of every household buying and using fewer electrical appliances or every home owner spending several hundred dollars per home or apartment to update existing wiring. That might mean buying a new color TV *next* year and spending that money on a new wiring job *this* year!

 # Hot Household Gadgets

When the can opener went electric, Grandmother was sure the end of the world was just around the corner. But it wasn't. What *was* just around the corner for everyone who rushed out to buy every new electric gadget was a headache every time one of them decided to stop running.

For the most part, electric gadgets for use around the house are relatively inexpensive. They are built with a small amount of parts and a generous amount of chrome. But it's the little things about them that can keep a person busy.

Toasters, coffee makers, waffle irons, irons, and most heated household gadgets may seem unique from the outside. But on the inside, their basic functions are very, very similar. Only the levers and rods and buttons that begin, end, or monitor the various functions are not identical in appearance.

To locate the light-dark setting on a toaster in what it considers the best location, one manufacturer might need a long, skinny rod connected to the control inside, but a competitor might choose a short, fat rod to accomplish the same chore. So when you read that the "hot adjustment" or the "cold adjustment" screw has to be adjusted, don't go looking for it with a preconceived notion about what it will look like. It might even be necessary to think a bit, at the very least to use some intuition.

TOASTERS

Reduced to its most simple design, a toaster consists of a set of wires or tapes, which become very hot when an electric current passes through them. To ensure that bread comes out toasted to the right degree of brownness, some kind of timing device has to control how long the bread will stay in the heat. And that's about all. The rest is chrome.

In practice, most toaster problems stem from two ailments, one internal affecting the timers and one external generating a general nuisance. If you stuff oversized slices of bread, rolls, bagels, or tarts into your toaster, some of the crumbs and goo are bound to stick onto the heating elements. But that is still an external kind of repair headache.

When your toaster starts smoking one morning, it probably is not suffering from electrical problems but from crumbs. The solution is fairly obvious—*unplug the toaster*, let it cool, remove the crumb tray (if any), and empty it. Then clean the crumbs and other accumulations of foreign matter from the heating wires or tapes. Be gentle because the heating elements are made of a very brittle alloy of the metals nickel and chromium, called *nichrome*. An old toothbrush makes an almost ideal tool for scrubbing away smoke-producing pieces of crumbs.

If your dry cleaning treatment with a toothbrush doesn't stop the smoking, the problem may well have come from sticky deposits on the heating wires—butter, margarine, jelly, and other gooey things people put into toasters. No harm will come to the toaster if you use the right kind of cleaning agent on the wires or tapes, assuming you unplug it first.

Finding the right kind of cleaner might be a problem these days. It has to evaporate completely without leaving traces of chemicals, soaps, detergents, or anything else. Any deposits will only add to your toaster problems.

Clear household ammonia is good, but none of the sudsing products are. A good cleaning fluid *should* be okay, but since none of them seem to be well labeled, you might get hold of one that contains some nonvolatile additives or impurities, which will leave a toxic or untasty residue for your toast to absorb. Safest of all, therefore, might be rubbing alcohol. After your wet cleaning operation, make sure that the toaster is thoroughly dry before you use it again.

If the toaster fails to toast at all, remember some of our trouble-shooting rituals. Since a toaster is such a simple electrical gadget, you should be able to go through a complete troubleshooting procedure in five minutes. Most often, a toaster that shows no sign of life at all—no heat, although the catch that holds the toast down inside the gadget is working—suffers from a broken connection either at the heating element or in the cord. Often such a problem can be traced to a snapped wire or deteriorated connection somewhere in the wall plug or where the cord connects to the toaster's inner wiring.

In Chapter 9 we covered all sorts of electrical repairs, including cords and connections such as the ones that keep your toaster toasting. You may have to open up the toaster to reach the internal electrical connections. Every toaster is individual when it comes to disassembly methods, even different models made by the same manufacturer. Most often, however, you will have to remove the crumb tray at the bottom and then look at how the chrome cover is fastened in place. It may be, if you're lucky, that the whole thing pulls off after loosening a few screws or wing nuts.

In some cases it may be necessary to remove the two large handles first, and then you will get down to the bolts that secure the cover. In any event, with practically every toaster, before the cover slides off, the handles of the light-dark knob and the toast-lowering knob have to come off first. Most simply pry off, but before prying too hard, take a quick look to make sure that there is no small hex nut holding the handle to the shaft.

As part of your opening physical examination, study the heating elements themselves. If they consist of simple uncoiled strands of nichrome wire, you will be able to spot a break in one of them easily. Since all of the wires in most toasters are wired in series—in other words, like the old-fashioned Christmas tree lights, if one wire breaks the heat stops on both sides of every toast slot—you will not have any physical clue as to which individual heating element may be the bad one. If you scrubbed out crumbs with a toothbrush, however, think back to which element may have received the roughest treatment. Unless a toaster is very old or very heavily used, the elements seldom snap without some kind of abuse—this assumes, of course, that it was put together properly in the first place. Keep in mind how delicate your toaster's heating elements can be the next time you're tempted to use a fork or knife to pry loose an oversized piece of toast.

A broken nichrome wire can be pieced back together without a great deal of trouble. Before doing that, however, consider what may have caused the break. If you just cleaned the heating element rather vigorously, and that could have led to the break, then patching the wire could be worth your time. The patch might endure almost as long as the rest of the heating wire.

If one of the elements broke without violence, however, then the entire series of heating wires or coils may be suffering from old age. Your efforts at splicing the one broken spot might just break another. In that event, your time would be better spent in replacing either the one faulty element or the entire set of heaters. If they have to be ordered by mail, however, you will probably want to risk a temporary repair rather than live a few weeks without toast.

Replacement elements for good toasters come in matched, tested sets. If you buy a matched set of heating elements, the manufacturer is supposed to have tested them to ensure that the heat output of each separate element is close to identical. In that way, every side of every slice of bread stands a good chance of coming out evenly browned.

If you're not a fanatic about evenly toasted bread, then it is perfectly fine for you to replace only one or two elements at a time. When replacing them, however, be sure to note more than just the model number. Also jot down the voltage and wattage ratings listed somewhere on the toaster, typically on the bottom. Some manufacturers may stock them for local voltrage conditions as low as 105 volts and as high as 130 volts, or 220 volts for export models.

Also check to find out whether your new elements have to be soldered into place. If they do, just go back to our discussion of silver soldering in Chapter 9. The heat of your toaster could very easily melt the soft solders that are fine inside TV sets and hi-fis.

Some toasters use one of the elements as part of the thermostat, which controls the on-off switch. In that case, if you want to order replacement elements, you must specify whether the new element is for the front or back, left or right position. Always note this information with the toaster up-and-down lever facing you.

Once you have accumulated all of the data necessary to obtain and install a new element, pause for a minute before buying it. What is the cost of the total repair job to you—elements, silver solder if that's required, the price of a new tool or two if needed? Then, what is the price of an entirely new toaster? If the repair costs come out favorably, take the repair materials home.

If you do decide to mend a broken toaster heating element, instead of replacing it, here is what to do. First, make sure the toaster is not plugged in. Then, with a tool such as a needlenosed pliers, pull a bit of the broken ends of wire toward each other until there is almost ½ " overlap. Gently twist the end of each wire into a hook, and hook the two hooked ends together. Squeeze the connection together with a pliers, although it may be difficult to squeeze very firmly if they are in an awkward location.

In case your repair is simply temporary, the heating element should do well enough in this makeshift condition. For a more lasting splice, however, invest in a soldering lug at an electronic or electrical supply store. You may even have one around from some earlier project. You want only the gripping end of the lug, so bend off the unnecessary portion (see Figure 124).

Slip the broken-off connector over your hooked repair job and crimp it into place with a pliers. The improvised connector is less for electrical protection than to keep the wire ends together even in heat. Nichrome wires can expand considerably when they heat, and contract when cooled. Such continuous motion might unhook the splice without the addition of the connector.

Figure 124   A toaster heating wire that snaps can be held together by simply crimping both broken ends, (top) although that can on occasion result in a worse break. In that case, the heating element is so old as to require replacing. An alternate method (bottom) is to improvise a coupling from such as a decapitated soldering lug.

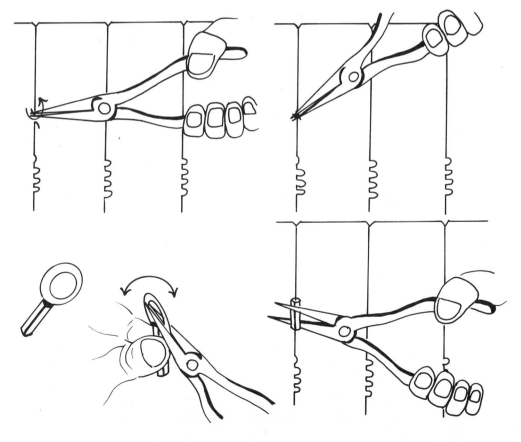

All of the elements may work, but even with the darkness setting all the way to "dark" the toast may be coming out too light. Or with the level pushed all the way to "light," the bread may come out nearly burned. Then you have to adjust the thermostat according to the following directions.

When you push down the toasting lever of your toaster, you lower the bread into position. You also force a *latch* to grab onto the *bread lowering arm* somewhere inside the toaster. At that same instant, a simple switch is closed so that electric current can flow through the heating elements.

Most of the latches are mechanical—a mere notch in the toast lowering arm catches in the latch or a notch in the latch catches in the arm. Some, however, are electromagnets. A coil of wire wrapped around a steel center piece called an armature holds the arm down until the toast is ready to pop up. Even those toasters that automatically lower the bread as soon as it is put into the toaster rely upon mechanisms exactly like these. The only difference is that in the apparently automatic bread-lowering models, the latches and arms have to be more delicately constructed, and consequently treated or repaired more delicately.

There are several basic devices for controlling how long the bread remains inside the hot part of a toaster. One is a simple *mechanical timer* very similar to those found on many nonelectric stoves. When the toast is pushed down, the spring of the timer is wound up. After the timer has passed through its proper time cycle, the spring releases the raising and lowering arm, allowing the toast to pop up.

Thermostats, or *bimetal strips* as technical manuals call them, control the timing cycle in some toaster designs. In some models (such as some Hoover and Proctor toasters), heat reflected off a slice of bread heats up the thermostat. Other toasters have a separate heating wire wrapped around the thermostat (such as models of General Electric and Knapp-Monarch). There are advantages and disadvantages to both systems, but none of them so great as to influence your choice of toasters.

Thermostatically controlled toasters, which are in the majority, are not actually simple. If the thermostat simply released the toast as soon as it got hot enough, the first set of slices would come out fine. But if you immediately put in a second set of bread, the thermostat might still be hot from its first job. Thus, the second and subsequent sets of bread slices might come out considerably too light. Therefore, toaster designers have included a heating and a cooling stage in the thermostat cycle.

When the bread is first lowered, the thermostat gets heated either by heat reflected from the toasting bread or from the heating wires wrapped around it. The bimetal thermostat strip bends under the heat and when it reaches a given point in its curl, the force of the bending thermostat strip turns off electricity to the heating wires of a wrapped thermostat.

As the bimetal strip cools down, it gradually bends back to its original shape during the cooling cycle. In some wrapped thermostat type toasters, as the bimetal strip approaches the maximum bend during the heating cycle, it contacts a relatively heavy magnet. As the strip straightens during its cooling cycle, the magnet is lifted. But an adjustable bolt or other device knocks the magnet loose from the bimetal strip at whatever point the engineers have decided to end the cooling cycle. The magnet drops onto whatever delicate latch was

Figure 125 Toaster timer mechanisms. Left, magnetic type that holds onto iron thermostat arm until enough pressure is generated on heated bimetal arm to force it loose from the magnet. To right, mechanical type in which latch is operated in two stages by moving a heated bimetal strip. (1) Toast lowering handle. (2) Toast lowering tray. (3) Toast tray latch. (4) Thermostat. (5) Thermostat adjustment—external. (6) Thermostat adjustment—internal (cool). (7) Thermostat adjustment—internal (hot). (8) Magnet. (9) Switch.

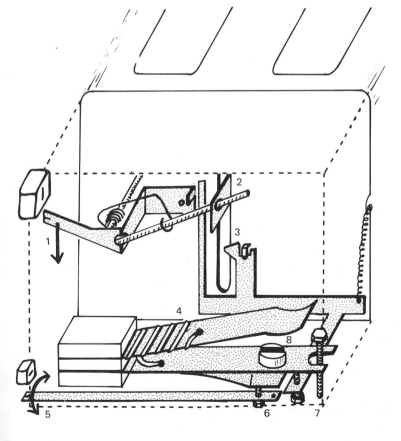

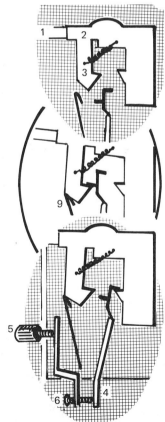

holding the toast lowering and lifting arm, knocks the latch loose, and allows a spring to send the toast upward.

Other engineers have worked out a way to send the toast up at the proper moment without magnets, both in the wrapped and unwrapped thermostat toasters. When the bimetal strip has reached its maximum degree of bend during the heating cycle, it trips a lever, which unlatches the latch that originally held the toast down since you first lowered the arm. However, the lever that releases the first latch has its own *second latch*, which keeps the toast from popping up while the thermostat is still hot. As the bimetal strip relaxes during its cooling cycle, the lever moves with it. And when the strip has just about reached the end of its cooling cycle, the lever lets go of the toast and allows the spring to pop up.

Now let's take a look at the several controls generally concealed inside the toaster. Some engineers have marked the one you want with a logo such as "light and dark control adjustment." Most have not, however.

There is only one control you should adjust if the lightness or darkness is off the mark—the adjustment bolt or nut, which can lengthen or shorten the distance that the thermostat bimetal strip travels during the heating cycle. Often it is the easiest adjustment to reach and change. But don't count on it always being that way.

If your toast fails to pop up consistently at the proper end of the thermostat heating and cooling cycles, you can tamper with whatever bolt or other device is connected to the latch for adjustment purposes. This adjustment is quite delicate, however. A quarter turn of the screw often can be too much. You will want to test the various adjustments you have made before reassembling the exterior again. On those models requiring reflected heat from a slice of bread to operate the bimetal strip, you must be sure to insert a slice of bread into one slot that traditionally is labeled with "one slice" or something similar.

Another cause of inconsistent or improper action on the up or down strokes of your toaster can come from faulty housekeeping. An accumulation of crumbs, butter, jellies, and anything else that gets into the sliding and springing mechanisms can interfere with good toast. As long as you have the toaster taken apart anyway, it is a good idea to clean it with a tasteless solvent such as alcohol and a gentle tool such as a toothbrush.

Moving parts such as the various levers, latches, springs, rods, and bars deserve lubrication every time you remove the toaster exterior. Use graphite for the lubrication because it can withstand the heat better than common oil or grease. Besides, in case you are overly generous with graphite, it doesn't taste half as bad as oil!

There are at least two electrical contacts inside most toasters that can stand some maintenance whenever the toaster isn't working well. The main switch, which is tripped when you lower the toast, and the contact, which turns the thermostat on or off, should be cleaned. A small, fine file is the preferred tool for polishing most electrical contacts. For emergencies, however, substitutes such as a nail file, sandpaper, steel wool, or similar abrasives can be used. Be sure to blow away the metal filings when the polishing job is completed.

Most replacement parts for toasters are simple to install but not always simple to buy. In larger cities, major manufacturers have reasonably well-stocked service outlets, which will sell parts to professional and nonprofessional repair people. In more remote areas, you will have to write or call the head office or regional supply center of the company.

WAFFLE IRONS

Having already solved the problems of the toaster, waffle irons seem very, very simple. Strung out inside the bottom and cover portions of the waffle iron, two identical heating elements heat the waffle from both top and bottom. A signal light is an integral part of most waffle irons, so you can sense visually instead of with your nose when the waffles are done. A simple thermostat controls the temperature of the baking surface.

Old age or abuse *can* snap the coiled heating element in a waffle iron, but rarely. If it happens, however, you will have to examine the whole coil both top and bottom since they are wired in series with each other and the light and the thermostat. The advice on how to make temporary repairs and permanent replacement of the heating coil in toasters applies to waffle irons too.

Since the signal light is such an integral part of the heating circuit in waffle irons (such as Sunbeam), replacement lamps and any attached resistors should come from the original manufacturer whenever possible to keep from upsetting the resistance of the circuit. In heating equipment, the greater the resistance, the lower the amount of heat generated. And vice versa.

Some waffle irons, or waffle bakers as many electrical people like to call them, have no signal lamp per se. Hoover, for example, puts a plastic lens inside of the chrome shell. When you think that you see the light begin to glow, what you actually are seeing is the glow from the heating element. In any event, it makes a perfectly satisfactory signal even if it is a bit dimmer than a well-designed lamp might be. And it eliminates just one or two more parts that can go bad.

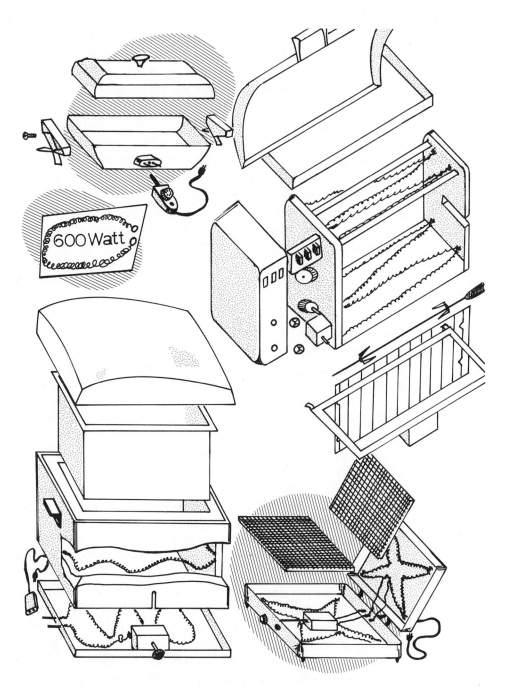

Figure 126 Heated kitchen gadgets all operate on a similar principle—a heating coil plus thermostat and possibly a heat regulating control. Heating elements are replaceable and often interchangeable.

If your darkest setting turns out waffles too light for your taste, or vice versa, the thermostat may need adjusting if all else seems to be well. Most often, you can reach the thermostat and heating elements simply by lifting out the bottom waffle grill, after disconnecting the cord. The thermostat itself in waffle irons generally can be turned a good deal farther in both directions than the light-dark control moves. Some sort of limiting arm or screw keeps the thermostat control rod from moving all the way clockwise or counterclockwise.

Pull off the light-dark knob, loosen the arm or cam or screw that limits the thermostat control rod motion, then turn the rod from ½ " to 1 " beyond its original end point in whichever direction you want to go—toward the low temperature or lighter side if waffles have been baking too fast, toward the high temperature or darker side if they have been baking too slowly.

Tighten up the limiting device, then move the thermostat control rod to its maximum or minimum setting, put the knob back in place, and tighten it with whatever hardware has been put there for that purpose. Before reassembling the waffle iron, however, clean the thermostat contacts with a file or similar delicate polishing device. Blow away the metal and corrosion filings.

You now should have restored your waffle iron to near perfect operation. If the adjustment wasn't enough, however, simply repeat all of the above steps except for cleaning the thermostat contacts.

If you ever have to replace a thermostat altogether, you may have to spend quite some time and some batter getting the thermostat control rod to its optimum position. Otherwise, replacing most waffle iron thermostats is a very simple matter, generally involving only a bolt or sheet metal screw, plus two screws for the wire contacts.

Leave off the waffle grill, which exposes the thermostat and elements, so you can adjust your new thermostat. Plug the waffle iron in and slowly turn the thermostat control rod until the elements start to light up for the first time. Then move the control rod another quarter turn. Assume that this point is your low temperature or light setting.

Set the control knob for a medium product, pour in some batter, and run a test—after replacing the grill first. If you are close to the mark, leave well enough alone for a meal or two. But if not, adjust the control rod upward or downward accordingly, then test again.

A lot of waffle headaches could be avoided by adhering to an old motto, the one about cleanliness being next to Godliness. First you will have to get the grills of your waffler back in shape. When the iron has cooled down completely, scour the grills gently—assuming it's not Teflon coated—with steel wool to remove all traces of burned-on past mistakes. Then wash the grill surfaces gently with soap or detergent and rinse thoroughly.

You should never hold the waffle iron itself in the running water since moisture can get beneath the grill surface. If you remove the grills, running water can be used. Otherwise sponge the rinse water on and off.

Dry the grills thoroughly. They have to be drier than mere paper towels can accomplish so you will probably have to set the waffle iron aside for half an hour or heat it up gradually by plugging it in for just a few minutes.

There are microscopic pores in the surface of waffle iron grills. And you want all of the moisture to be out of the pores before proceeding. Once the grill is thoroughly dry, apply a liberal dose of good cooking oil to the surface of both grills. Make sure that the oil splashes every part of the grill. Then blot the excess oil with paper towels. You should now have filled the grill pores with oil so they will act like miniature reservoirs for good cooking to come.

It should not be necessary to wash the waffle iron ever again unless it gets stored for long periods between use or if a particularly bad waffle got stuck or burned to the grill surface. After every successful use, simply wipe the heating surface with a dry towel. Avoid soaps, detergents, and water. If an accident fouls up a grill or if the waffle maker has been stored for months, you may have to go through the complete refurbishing routine again.

ELECTRIC COOKING EQUIPMENT

Electric frying pans, rotisseries, roasters, broilers, casseroles, and the dozen or so various small electric cooking gadgets are, with some exceptions, even simpler to repair than a waffle iron. An electric frying pan, for instance, aside from the pan itself, consists of a large heating element generally built into an insulated metal case. The element is replaceable by some manufacturers, not by others. In any event, with normal handling there should never be a need to replace the element if it was designed, built, and installed properly in the first place.

The thermostat in most frying pans is contained in the same control unit that selects the temperature. Some of these control units are sealed and have to be replaced entirely if anything inside goes awry. Even in those units that are not totally sealed, the internal parts are not often available since most manufacturers prefer to replace the control unit as a complete package—at your expense. Those electric frying pan control units that are not sealed can often benefit from a gentle cleaning of the thermostat contacts with a tool such as an ignition file.

If you have serious doubts about whether your frying pan thermostat is actually keeping the temperature at the specified setting, you can test it yourself. Fill the clean frying pan about half full of cooking oil. If you keep the pan and everything else clean during this test, the oil can be poured back into the bottle when it has cooled down.

Set the control at 300° and put the main body of an oven thermometer or other similar device into the oil. After the control light has cycled on and off half a dozen times, the thermometer should be within the range of 250 to 350°F. During the various on and off periods, the temperature may fluctuate by as much as 50° above or 50° below the 300° nominal reading. A span of only 25° up and 25° down is preferred.

On a relatively new electric frying pan, a serious discrepancy between what the control is set at and what the thermometer reads should be brought vigorously to the attention of the manufacturer's nearest representative. And if the representative doesn't give prompt satisfaction, write or call directly to the home office. Before that, however, be sure that your own thermometer is reasonably accurate. Borrow a neighbor's or in some other way verify that it is reading properly at the 300° part of its scale.

Dry cookers are calibrated by checking the air temperature inside. You can take the temperature of possibly ailing roasters, broilers, and rotisseries without using oil. Frying pans, kettles, and casseroles almost always are used with plenty of water or other liquids inside and their temperature controls are set accordingly. Incidentally, water is not used for checking wet temperatures because it boils at 212°F. No matter how much heat your pan turns out, the water will never rise above 212° at sea level except inside a pressure cooker.

Whenever you find an error of consequence in the temperature control of any cooking appliance, first look for a way to make an adjustment. In some cases, the temperature markers or the dial pointer can be raised or lowered by first loosening a set screw on the temperature control, as with many waffle irons. In a few other cases, the internal temperature regulator is moved in the appropriate direction, perhaps after first loosening some lock nuts, while the visible dial and pointer remain in the same place. This is how many toasters are adjusted. Still other controls have a screw or concealed knob just for making temperature adjustments. This is how many irons are designed.

However, if you cannot find any way to bring the real temperature and the temperature shown on the dial into line, ask yourself whether the amount of error is worth worrying about. Making do may be the sanest alternative in this case. Cooking is more of an art than many people care to admit. A frying pan might say that 325° is best for pancakes, 275° ideal for simmering pot roast, and 400° great for frying chops. But your preferences in food, your pancake batter, and your choice of meat might very well be better served at a substantially different setting.

Roasters and similar cooking gadgets typically have more than one heating element, and most of them can be repaired at least temporarily in the same way that toaster elements were mended. Almost all roaster and broiler elements are replaceable. But when ordering new ones, be certain that you specify whether the damaged one is on top, bottom, left side, or right. They often are not all the same.

In very simple roasters or horizontal toasters, the heating is often accomplished by simple coils of nichrome wire. A replacement might be handed or mailed to you as a coil or wire. Before you attempt to stretch the heating coil around the various insulators, first run a string or tape measure through the network. Compare the length of the measure to the length of the new coil. Before weaving the new wire into the old roaster, it should be stretched evenly to approximately the same length as the test string. Be careful not to stretch the springiness out of the new coil of nichrome wire, however.

Almost every thermostat in simple heating gadgets is very similar to the type of thermostat discussed for waffle irons and toasters. Adjustments are done in virtually the same manner, as are replacements. Not every hot gadget even has a thermostat.

Timers, whether mechanical or electric, are one piece units as a rule. And that limits your repair inclinations to simple contact polishing and cleaning. If the timer is not fully sealed—as it should be—it might benefit by a hearty squirt from a spray can of TV tuner spray cleaner. Most gadget timers are very inexpensive, which makes them very subject to breakdown but very easy and cheap to replace.

Some fancy gadgets, rotisseries in particular, have an elaborate looking set of colorful pushbuttons to set what is supposed to be the precise temperature for cooking a particular cut of meat. Most of these control units are hermetically sealed, and consequently you will not be able to clean even the contacts on any switches that give you trouble. Even on the unsealed switch units, you can clean the contacts and that's about all. They are designed to be replaced with distressing regularity.

It is not at all difficult to replace a switch or panel of switches in electric cooking utensils. You should first insist that the company replace the part free. However, when you do replace a switch, the most important thing to remember is that the wires—which are generally color coded—must be installed on the right terminals.

On a Hoover model 6611 rotisserie, for example, the "bake" button controls the lower element, the "grill" button turns the upper element on or off, and the "rotis" button regulates the small motor that turns the rotisserie spit. Either jot down the color of each wire alongside a sketch of the switch terminals or attach taped labels to the wires and terminals.

Those tiny motors that turn the rotisserie spit fairly ooze with troubles. When one starts getting temperamental, it could very well be because cooking fats have choked the windings and contacts inside. If there are enough exposed openings for fat to get inside, then TV tuner cleaner also can be sprayed inside perhaps to remedy the problem. You can forget about trying to disassemble most rotisserie motors. Putting some white grease on the gears is about as far as you can go. Beyond that, it is replacement all the way. The job is easy, however, and the new motor is quite cheap.

Don't become distressed even if the heating element portion of a simple electric frying pan quits on you. If you are unable to get the manufacturer to replace it, investigate the economics of buying a *replacement fry pan body*. Typically it will come minus all of the decorations, cover, handles, legs, cords, terminal guard, and similar items you pay for when you buy a new frying pan. You can pull the serviceable parts off the old frying pan and install them on the new, often at a good saving.

UNIVERSAL HEATING ELEMENT REPLACEMENTS

These replacements can be found at hardware and electrical stores. Suitable as substitutes for a manufacturer's replacement item when the manufacturer is out of business or far out of town, universal replacements come as lengths of coiled nichrome wire. Some are carded in a single length precut to produce a specified heat, generally 600 or 660 watts. Others are sold on a larger spool.

From the spool, a customer gets whatever length is required to produce the number of watts stirred up by the old heating element. Aside from locating the number of watts consumed by your appliance, you will also have to measure the diameter of the coiled heating element you want to replace so the new one will fit into the mounting brackets. Typical standard diameters are $\frac{9}{64}''$, $\frac{5}{32}''$, $\frac{7}{32}''$, $\frac{3}{16}''$, $\frac{1}{4}''$, and $\frac{5}{16}''$.

Nichrome wire is brittle, so handle it with care. If the ends of the element have not already been bent into a hook to fit under your mounting screws, make your own bend very cautiously. For the same wattage and the same diameters, you often can choose from coils of different gauge wire. Always pick the heaviest, which is of course usually the more expensive. Heaviest gauge has the lowest gauge number. A number 18 wire has a bigger diameter than number 20.

Toasters, roasters, rotisseries, broilers, waffle irons, and any other implement with a coiled heating element can be fitted with a universal replacement. They are even available for use in electric stoves, at least for those few older models with coiled elements. In the case of a stove, yours probably operates off 220 volt electricity, so be sure that the universal replacement is rated at 220 volts as well as the appropriate number of watts.

ELECTRIC TEA KETTLES

Electric tea kettles pretty much follow the pattern of other hot electric gadgets. Perhaps due to their enclosed appearance, many people get the feeling that they're untouchable. Not so.

The base, typically a smooth black color, is held in place by one or more nuts. And beneath the base is a thermostat, which can tolerate an occasional cleaning. Also, with an ignition file, gently hone the thermostat contacts.

Better electric tea kettles have two elements. The high powered one (maybe 500 watts) heats up the water very quickly. When the thermostat detects that the water temperature, or at least the temperature of the metal in contact with the thermostat, has reached the vicinity of 212°F., it switches off the high heating element. The water is kept warm for cup after cup by a lower powered element.

In electric tea kettles without double elements, the thermostat does not regulate the temperature of the water, which is heated about to boiling point and kept there by the one element. In this case, the thermostat protects the kettle from overheating in case somebody accidentally leaves it plugged in after the kettle has boiled dry.

If the old kettle seems to be getting slower, perhaps an overeager protective thermostat is opening prematurely, thus slowing down the boiling process. By removing the base, you should be able to adjust the thermostat toward a higher temperature, generally by moving the adjustment screw clockwise. Move it in increments of a quarter turn until you reach the point where the kettle does not turn off or slow down until the water is boiling briskly. Even with the water boiling, most of these thermostats should stay closed, opening only when the bottom of the kettle climbs to a temperature substantially above 212°, which it will do only after the water is all gone.

There are no test instruments, even for pros, that can set a tea kettle thermostat at its proper shutoff point for safe performance. The only method is trial and error.

Put just a small amount of water in the kettle and let it boil dry to make sure that the thermostat shuts off the heating element in a reasonably short period of time. As the kettle cools down, the thermostat will close again. *Before running such a test, make sure there is a thermostat in your particular tea kettle*! Not every manufacturer includes one.

Since the tank part on an electric tea kettle and the heating element are generally offered as a sealed unit, there is little economy in trying to replace any part beyond the cord and thermostat. And if you do replace a thermostat, the manufacturer should include some specific advisory data. If not, after the new thermostat has been installed, most often just a matter of three screws, turn the adjustment bolt clockwise until the thermostat just closes at *room temperature*. Then twist it an additional one and one-half clockwise turns. That should put the thermostat close to its proper setting.

ELECTRIC COFFEE POTS

A bit more complicated than tea kettles, electrical coffee pots are a mystery to most people. How, in fact, does a percolator work?

The gurgle gurgle of a healthy percolator at work is actually a small steam engine of sorts. The electric heating element features a compact round top, which sticks up into the bottom of the pot itself, called a *nose*. Surrounding the nose is the *pump chamber*, a broadened bottom part of the tube inside the coffee pot.

The nose gets so hot that water in the pump chamber boils and some of it turns to steam almost instantly. A simple valve inside the pump chamber prevents the steam from escaping down into the coffee pot, so it has to expand up the percolator tube. As the steam pushes upward, it moves a quantity of hot water ahead of it.

Once the steam and water have pushed their way out of the pump chamber, the pressure inside is lower than the water pressure outside. So a new supply of water forces past the pump valve and into the chamber, ready to get heated in a hurry by the nose, and then it gurgles up the tube.

If you never knew how the percolator worked, you're not alone. Recently, the Hoover Company found it necessary to issue a six-page theoretical discussion for its own repair people on the general theory and function of coffee pots!

Heat for the percolating process is generated by what companies call the *main heater*, the *main element*, or simply the *heater*. It is typically a heating element about 500 watts to over 1000 watts, depending on the size of the pot and how fast it is expected to brew. The thermostat in a percolator is situated most often against the bottom of the water tank itself so that its bimetal elements are affected by the overall temperature of the water, not the temperature of that tiny amount of water being heated in the pump chamber.

Once the thermostat has sensed that the water is at some agreed-upon temperature, it opens a switch and forces the electric current to pass through not only the main element but also what is labeled the *warming element*. You might think that the combination of *two* heating elements should generate *more* heat, but it doesn't. The resistance from both the main element and the warming elements in series combines to cut the flow of electric current to such a low level that the overall heating power during the warming cycle is about 100 watts.

When the thermostat trips the switch for the warming cycle, it also turns on a glow lamp in most percolators. And that light, of course, means the coffee is ready.

The little level along the side of your coffee pot, which reads "light-dark," is connected to the thermostat. The most times the

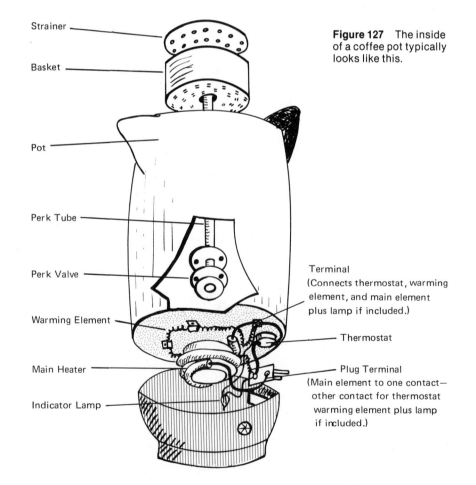

Strainer

Basket

Pot

Perk Tube

Perk Valve

Warming Element

Main Heater

Indicator Lamp

Terminal
(Connects thermostat, warming element, and main element plus lamp if included.)

Thermostat

Plug Terminal
(Main element to one contact—other contact for thermostat warming element plus lamp if included.)

Figure 127 The inside of a coffee pot typically looks like this.

water cycles through the pump chamber, the hotter the overall pot becomes. Consequently, manufacturers have calculated that a relatively cool pot of water indicates weakly brewed coffee whereas a hot pot of water should be strongly brewed.

Not many thermostats inside electric percolators are adjustable, but do look for an adjustment screw of some sort before proceeding too far in coffee pot repair. Adjustable thermostat or not, you can use a temperature test to help you evaluate whether your coffee pot is malfunctioning or your taste buds are reacting to a particular batch of coffee.

Use a good roasting, candy, or oven thermometer, or some other instrument capable of measuring temperatures up to 200°F. to put your coffee pot through a cycle either with or without coffee grounds. All of the parts should be in place, however. With the coffee strength setting at "weak," the temperature should be 155° to 175° when the perk cycle has just finished. For "strong," the thermometer should read from 190° to 205°. And after the warm cycle has been left on for maybe an hour, the temperature of the water inside the pot should be about 170°.

Replacing individual components inside the bottom of a coffee pot is not exactly an enjoyable task. Loose wires usually have to be silver soldered if they are to resist the high temperatures from the main heater. Terminals and screws often corrode together after some years without attention, especially with small amounts of moisture present so often. Even professional repair people have balked so frequently when asked to replace individual lamps, thermostats, and heating elements that manufacturers often supply a completely wired replacement heating unit, which includes all of the vital insides.

Removing the cover on the base of most coffee pots is not difficult. One bolt is about all that holds it in place on many percolators. However, if you own a pot that can be submerged in water, and if you want it to stay that way, don't open the base. You will never know for sure that the submersible pot has been properly sealed again unless you can apply about 15 pounds per square inch of air pressure through the bolt hole to test the seal after reassembly. The test is run with the pot in water. If air bubbles leak out through the sealed joints, the pot has failed the test and a new attempt has to be made at sealing and reassembling the bottom.

In nonsubmersible percolators, removing the bottom cover will allow you to inspect the thermostat and to clean its contacts. It will also let you look for visible signs of corrosion.

The one bolt and nut that holds the main element and all of its adjuncts in place extends through the bottom of the coffee pot. You will need a large socket for your socket wrench—if you own one—to

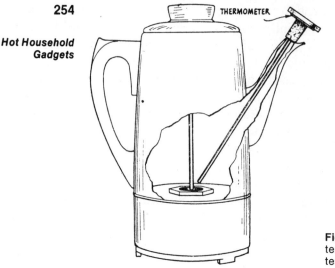

THERMOMETER

Figure 128 Taking your coffee pot's temperature, as shown, is one way to test if it is properly adjusted.

remove the working parts. If you don't have a socket, typically about 1-½ ″ in diameter, and if you don't feel the investment is worthwhile, then the job has to be turned over to a pro or factory repair center.

After the nut is loosened and the heating mechanisms replaced, the nut should be reinstalled with a new gasket under it. Order one at the same time you order the replacement heating unit. If you have to make do with a gasket, use silicone adhesive.

The nut has to be tightened very snugly, although not ferociously. There is more danger from overtightening the nut, thus bending the bottom or crippling the heating element, than there is from not tightening it enough. Once a replacement heating unit has been installed, operate the pot through at least one complete cycle, which you monitor with a thermometer, to make sure that the elements are working properly. Also make sure that there are no leaks through the bottom of the pot.

You might also want to consider some of the coffee making problems that stem from the pot user and not from the pot mechanism. Bad taste, for example, can come from bad coffee of course, but it also can come from a badly cleaned pot. Coffee is a complex and volatile chemical. It leaves a residue, which pros call *coffee coke.* Not only does this coke plug up the valve on your percolator mechanism, but it can lead to a nasty taste as well.

The easiest solution for cake problems is periodically to run through a coffee-making cycle with a baking soda solution. Toss a couple of tablespoons of ordinary baking soda into the pot, fill it to your customary level with cold water, mix up the baking soda solution by shaking the pot for a few seconds, put the percolator tubes and baskets into place, plug the pot in, and let it run through a "strong" coffee making cycle. Empty out the remains after the brew is finished, rinse the pot well, and go back to enjoying good coffee.

For those parts of the country with hard water, you might follow up the baking soda treatment with a second purging. Once the pot has cooled down a bit, fill it almost to your usual level with cold water, then add half a cup of ordinary vinegar. (Don't reverse the procedure for fear the full strength vinegar might injure some of the inner parts.) Again, run the coffee maker through a full cycle, discard the cleaning solution, and rinse well.

Baking soda helps to dissolve the coffee residues, which are quite alkaline soluble. And hard water deposits, if they are soluble at all, will most often be dissolved in acids such as vinegar.

Always start your coffee making with cold water. Hot water will speed up the process a bit, but it will also interfere with proper thermostatic control, all of which means you'll be getting weaker coffee than you should. And never, never plug in a coffee pot unless there is water in it. The main heater is very powerful and the heat is concentrated into a very small area. It can heat the metal pot severely enough to distort it permanently.

If the thermostat is working, if you've tried the acid and baking soda solutions, but the perking is giving you trouble, inspect the bulging pump chamber at the bottom of the percolator tube. Also look at the valve built into the chamber and at related surfaces. Long accumulations of hard-to-remove hard water or coffee deposits can block the valve or hold it open. If you cannot remove the deposits easily, invest in a new percolator tube from your dealer.

If you want an easy solution to the most annoying of coffee pot ailments—replacing the missing or broken glass percolator top—you're out of luck. Every manufacturer, or so it seems, has designed a coffee pot with a totally unique top. No two manufacturers apparently adopt a standard top. So, if you want to make an easy million dollars, invent a universal replacement percolator top!

ELECTRIC IRONS

Fortunately, there is very little inside a well-made iron that goes wrong. Most repairs are for faulty cords, damaged handles, and mineral deposits that hamper steam irons.

Handles are replaced by removing a couple of bolts, an operation that by now should seem fairly simple to you. We discussed faulty cords and related connections in Chapter 9. Just make certain that the cord you buy for a replacement is rated to handle the power and heat load an iron will give it.

Mineral deposits in a steam iron begin to make their presence known when steam stops escaping from some of the steam vents, when the spray nozzle stops spraying or sprays erratically, or often when steam comes and goes without warning. Deposits from hard water can be dissolved out in some cases with a vinegar solution, just as in the coffee pot.

Mix half a cup of vinegar with half a cup of water and pour some of the mixture into the steam iron water chamber. Run the entire one cup of acid solution through the steam and spray mechanism, but *do not* use it for ironing clothes at the time. The vinegar and mineral deposits would not do dresses or shirts any good.

Following the vinegar bath, rinse the iron chamber several times and run through one filling with clean water before ironing clothes again. Tough deposits near steam vents can be forced out with a fine wire handled discretely enough to avoid breaking it off inside any of the several steam openings.

Manufacturers' claims to the contrary, steam irons do best with distilled or mineral-free water in parts of the country with particularly hard water. Advertising offers steam irons that can be used on any kind of mineral-clogged water, but the one-year warranty usually expires before the deposits of calcium and other minerals begin to show up at repair stations.

The *sole plate* or *face plate* of an iron, the flat surface that actually flattens the wrinkles, can often become encrusted with tiny particles of dirt, burned-on starch, and such items. Roughness from the accumulations will make the iron harder to move. Fine steel wool should clean a rough sole plate. If you try household cleansers with the steel wool, be sure to keep them from getting into any steam openings.

Thermostats inside irons are generally very rugged, surprisingly so. But they do age and require some care. The adjusting screw on most thermostats is relatively easy to adjust. Finding it may require some persistence or imagination. It may be under the nameplate on the main body of the iron, which simply snaps out of place when pried loose with a screwdriver. It may be concealed beneath some decorative or temperature plate near the temperature control itself, such as on some Westinghouse irons. The thermostat adjustment on many Hoover irons is located on the thermostat itself and can be reached only by removing the hood, that streamlined cover over the main upper body of an iron. Removing the hood, however, usually requires loosening only one bolt.

To determine if a thermostat really does need adjusting, plug in your iron and set it at the lowest wash and wear temperature. Allow it to sit for at least five minutes before testing whether the actual temperature corresponds to what that setting should produce. Iron thermostats will very often overshoot their mark by a long margin during their first one or two on and off cycles of the day. Ths is one good reason why any iron should be allowed to warm up for 15 or 10 minutes before you start to iron.

After your iron has warmed up, lay it on a heat resistant surface such as Formica countertop. Put a cooking thermometer under it. A meat thermometer generally registers only to 200°F. and a candy thermometer to just above 220°, both of which are adequate for testing an iron set for wash and wear or synthetics. That setting should produce a temperature about 180° to 220°F.

Thermometers intended to measure the temperature inside an oven extend to 500°F. or beyond. They can be used to check the upper temperature ranges of an iron. An iron set at "wool" should produce a face plate temperature about 360° to 400°F. "Steam" settings, depending upon the particular iron manufacturer, may be from 250° to almost 400°F.

A particular temperature will not remain stable. It will move upward and downward. When the thermostat turns on the heating element, the temperature will soar by 10 or 20 degrees. And as the iron cools off gradually when the heating element is off, the temperature can progressively drop by the same margin. If the temperature range extends much beyond a span of 20 degrees, however, or if it moves erratically upward and downward, the thermostat may be defective.

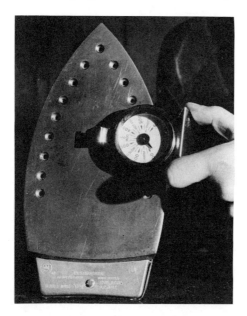

Figure 129 Taking the temperature of an iron, using oven thermometer or similar device, helps to determine if its thermostat is properly set.

Many thermostats can be replaced by simply unscrewing them and unscrewing the two wires connected to the thermostat terminals. Others, however, have to be cut loose and the wires on a new one silver soldered into the circuit.

When replacing or repairing any internal electrical connections in an iron, be very certain that the bare wires do not make contact with uninsulated metal parts, in which case the metal body of your iron may become "hot" and give you a shock. If the heating element is going, any shock would be very gentle, although annoying. And any kind of shock, unless it is caused by static electricity, is definitely a sign that you should disconnect the iron and look for some bare wire that is shorting out to the metal body.

If the thermostat in your iron is performing well at keeping the temperature spread close to 20 degrees, but if the overall temperature

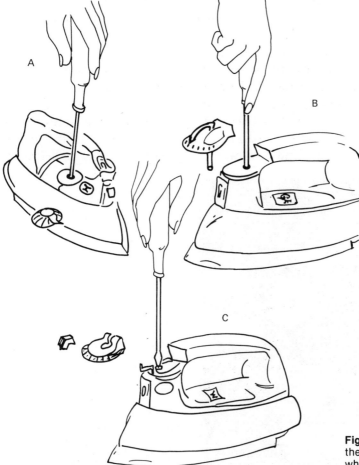

Figure 130 How to adjust an iron thermostat in its various positions where control is found.

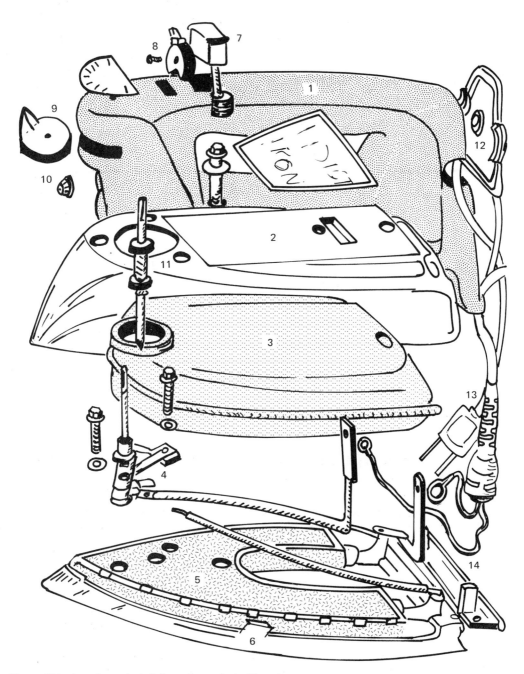

Figure 131   Iron, in exploded view, shows typical location
of major parts. (1) Handle. (2) Hood. (3) Water tank. (4) Thermostat. (5) Element. (6) Sole plate. (7) Spray control. (8) Steam
control. (9) Temperature regulator. (10) Spray orifice. (11) Water
valve stem. (12) Rear plate. (13) Cord. (14) Heel plate.

is hotter or cooler than that recommended for "wash and wear," "steam," and "wool" settings, it can be adjusted. If the adjusting screw is on the thermostat itself (such as with Hoover), it probably will be turned *counterclockwise to raise the temperature.* But on mechanical mechanisms that regulate a thermostat indirectly (such as Westinghouse), the *reverse* situation may hold true. In any event, you should find out conclusively which direction adds and which direction subtracts from the temperature after your first adjustment and subsequent test. One quarter turn is usually all the adjustment you should make at one time.

Surprisingly enough, the heating elements inside most irons are nearly identical. They are so identical, in fact, that if you cannot line up a factory replacement item when you need it, try shopping for a universal replacement at a good hardware or electrical supply store. One manufacturer of universal replacement iron elements says that its product "will fit over 90 percent of irons on the market."

Using the typical iron assembly in Figure 131, plus your ingenuity, tear apart the decorative and useful parts on your own brand of iron until you reach the defective element. If you have to silver solder it, do that *before* you lay the new element into place. Caution: the extra heat from your torch might be more than the fancy but cheap chrome case can withstand on some irons.

BABY FOOD WARMERS

The heating elements in food warmers are rugged enough to withstand most uses short of being dropped too often. Their cords, however, can require frequent attention.

Inside the G.E. baby food warming tray, a tiny light flickers on and off as the heating element does its job. But the lamp is supported solely by its two fragile wires. One knock too many and the lamp is out of service. You may be able to twist the leads together for a makeshift repair. Since G.E. does not consider the lamp a replaceable item, you have about three alternatives:

1. Let the company sell you the whole new cord set, which they do sell as a replacement item.
2. Do without the light altogether, not a bad idea once you get used to the change.
3. Replace the lamp with a tiny NE-2 neon glow lamp, which practically any electronic supply store should have available.

The next most frequently damaged item on the baby warming tray is the big suction cup bottom. It is a cheap item and one that most local parts supply shops stock. There are two odd bolts on the tray bottom, which hold the suction cup via an aluminum retainer plate. They have a square opening, which fits no standard tool exactly. Tackle the square opening with a common Phillips head screwdriver and you will be able to remove the bolts and reinstall them. But no G.E. repair person will be able to do it again with the square-headed tool.

The plastic exterior of the baby food tray is pretty rugged. However, one mother forgot about electric power one day and put the tray on a lighted gas burner. The food didn't get warm but the tray did, ruining the suction cup, which is easy to replace, and cracking the tray. After drying away the food and oil spilled out from inside, she filed down the cracked part of the tray, and smeared an epoxy resin onto the crack. When the patch was filed smooth and concealed with acrylic paints of the appropriate color, the warmer looked good again.

However, some oil had escaped. In these warming trays, the heating element warms a bath of baby oil, and that in turn warms the food. Since there was not way of telling exactly how much oil had escaped, a generous amount of baby oil was poured in by way of a tiny funnel slipped past the rubber plug beneath the suction cup. (If you have to jerk the plug out to get baby oil in, don't worry. It will still operate even though you won't be able to get the rubber plug back into the hole.)

For the next day or two, the tray was used over paper towels. The excess oil was forced out, then the suction cup was sealed to the plastic case with silicone sealant smeared generously around the rim of the suction cup. The tray hasn't leaked a drop or missed a day's feeding ever since.

This example should point out that no matter how straightforward all of the repair hints seem, the actual repair may require a bit more ingenuity than any step-by-step suggestions spell out. But the reward is in getting it to work.

11 *Motorized Household Gadgets*

If a gadget goes whirl, whirrr or buzzzzz it probably has a motor somewhere inside to turn gears or spin fans. And if it has a motor, it can start giving you trouble at any time.

ELECTRIC MOTORS

Almost every motorized household gadget is so similar that there is little need to divide this chapter into specific gadgets. An electric motor that spins around and around does so because of electricity and magnetism of one sort or another. A set of gears slows down the rate of rotation in the case of slower moving items such as food mixers, can openers, clocks, and floor polishers. Pulleys slow down the motions in many aquarium pumps. The motor directly couples onto a blower unit in items such as vacuum cleaners, electric brooms, fans, and hair dryers. And blender blades also fasten directly to the motor. In electric toothbrushes and electric knives, the apparatus is driven by eccentrics fastened to the electric motor.

Electric motors are driven by two sets of magnets as a rule. Some small motors in battery-driven gadgets have one set of electromagnets and one set of permanent steel magnets. Bigger motors usually have two sets of electromagnets. But if you remember that the opposite poles of a magnet attract and similar poles repel each other, you already understand the working principle of an electric motor.

Figure 132 shows a very simple motor, the kind that students in general science classes often try to make. The main electromagnet on the outside of the motor, often called the *field winding* by pros, generates one set of "N" and "S" magnetic poles. There is a set of *brushes,* which electricity feeds to the armature, however, and as the magnet in the armature rotates, the brushes keep reversing the direction in which current flows, which also reverses the "N" and "S" poles.

So, the motor starts out with the "N" pole of the field winding attracted to an "S" pole on the armature, making the armature spin by its powerful magnetic attraction. But by the time the "S" pole of the armature gets close to the field winding "N" pole, the brushes have reversed the polarity on the armature so that the "N" pole of the field winding is faced with an "N" pole on the armature. The two "N" poles repel, which adds even more power to the spinning armature. And on and on.

The simple motor in Figure 132 would have relatively little power as is. However, if we were to add four or more separate sets of electromagnet windings to the armature, and a like number to the field winding, the power would be multiplied by four or more. And if the amount of wire wrapped around the iron core for each of the magnetic poles was increased and we added a bigger battery, the power would increase almost proportionately to our winding and adding efforts.

Figure 132   A simple motor operates like this. More complicated motors operate by the same magnetic principles.

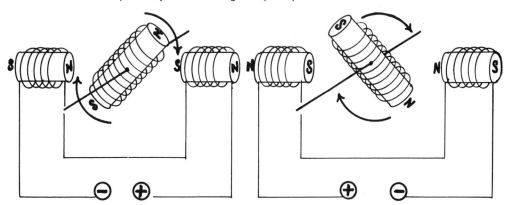

The electric motors in gadgets such as blenders and vacuum cleaners can have a half dozen or more separate sets of windings, forming a relatively powerful motor in a surprisingly compact amount of space. Instead of simple copper wires hanging loosely in contact with the armature, appliance motors employ stiff carbon *brushes,* which use springs to keep them in firm contact with copper contacts spaced around the armature. These motors are called *series* or *universal motors.* They can be used on either d-c or a-c power.

Since the universal motor will turn fastest when the poles of the field winding are at precisely the proper angle in relation to the newly changed "N" or "S" pole on the armature, the brushes can be slid clockwise or counterclockwise until the relative position of the poles is not at its optimum. The effect will be to slow down the motor. And that is exactly how the speed on some electric mixers is regulated, particulary on bigger, older models.

A second way to regulate the speed of small universal motors depends on internal wiring arrangements. When motor engineers design universal motors, they calculate how many windings of wire to wrap around the pole in the field winding to generate the maximum speed and power they want. This is generally a relatively small amount of wire and does not create much resistance. But the motor is not wound with just the amount of wire needed to drive it at top speed and power.

As the amount of fine wire wrapped around a field coil increases, so does the electrical resistance. As the resistance increases, the amount of electricity that can flow through the wire decreases. And as the flow of electric current decreases, so does the motor speed and power. Consequently, an engineer can calculate the amount of winding

Figure 133 Tapped winding as a speed control method is found on many common motorized gadgets. When wires for motor are wound, leads are spliced in periodically. In general, the longer the length of wire, the less electricity that can flow through the motor and the slower the motor will turn.

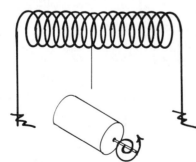
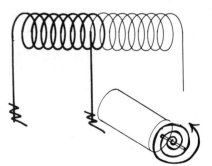

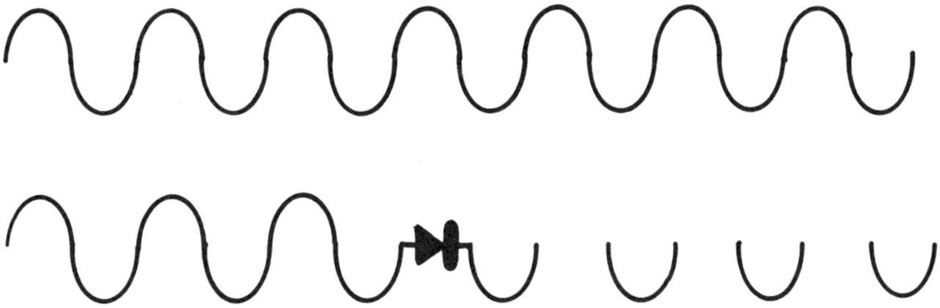

Figure 134 Diodes often are added to motorized gadgets to
regulate speed. Under operation with alternating current,
the motor runs full speed. With diode switched in, only half as
much (one side of the alternating current) electricity reaches
the motor, and it runs substantially more slowly.

needed to generate maximum speed and the amount needed for
minimum desired speed. In-between speeds are even feasible.

As the coil winding takes place, at two or more points along the
way, a connection is made to a terminal, being careful not to interrupt
the overall winding process. Each terminal connection is called a *tap*,
and a universal motor with taps is said by pros to have a *tapped
winding*.

As the makers wire a tapped motor into the gadget, the tap
connected to the shortest winding is labeled "high speed" or
something similar. And the tap leading to the longest wire—therefore
offering the greatest resistance to the flow of electricity—is labeled
"low speed." A tapped winding is used to regulate the speed on hand
food mixers, such as those made by Dormeyer, Hoover, and General
Electric.

A third speed control system has appeared, although for mass-produced gadgets it is often used in conjunction with tapped windings.
Since modern motors are designed to function well on common house
alternating current, a small rectifier called a diode (see Chapter 6) can
be switched into the motor circuit. The diode converts only half of the
alternating current into direct current and blocks the other half from
reaching the motor. In the process, it cuts the effective electric power
about in half, thus reducing the motor speed.

Used along with a tapped winding, the diode speed control system
can work in the following way. With the high speed winding tap
switched on and the diode switched out of the circuit, the motor would
reach its maximum speed. With the lower speed winding on and the
diode still off, the second fastest speed would occur. Now with the
diode cutting the electric current in half, the high speed winding would
produce the third fastest speed setting. And with the diode at work and

the low speed winding switched on, the motor would turn at its slowest possible rate.

A more sophisticated version of a diode speed control system is sometimes found on power tools and more expensive appliances. Instead of merely offering a choice of high or low speeds, a *silicon controlled rectifier* circuit can produce an almost continuously variable speed on universal motors. For a modest price you can buy this type of speed control equipment as a separate, self-contained unit and plug it between the 120 volt house current and your electric drill, food mixer, or similar tool.

Universal motors are often hooked up to a *governor* to regulate speed. A governor is a mechanical device that is sensitive to the amount of centrifugal force created by the spinning motor. The faster the motor turns, the more centrifugal force, and the farther away from the center the weights inside a governor are forced. Since the speed of universal motors can vary tremendously depending upon the type of load encountered, food mixers often use a governor to let the motor speed up when a sticky batch of batter grabs at the beater. And forces it to slow down if a cup of milk tossed into the batter suddenly lets the beater move quickly again.

Governor weights are generally attached to a set of electrical contacts in electric mixers using governors, Hobart's Kitchen Aid and Dormeyer's Mixmaster for example. The speed control knob, generally the entire back end of the mixer body, moves a second contact point closer to or farther away from the contact coupled to the governor's moving weights. Therefore, when you set a governor-controlled mixer at slow speed, the weights have to be moved only a small distance by contrifugal force before they open the set of contacts and shunt the electricity through a resistor, which lowers its voltage and results in a slower, less powerful motor performance. At a high speed setting, the governor weights have to move farther, hence have to rotate at a higher speed to gain more centrifugal force before they move the contacts apart and bring a resistor into the circuit.

With an eye always on simplicity, engineers have come up with a way to eliminate direct electrical connections to the armature windings altogether. Whenever electric current passes through a wire, it emits magnetic waves. If the wire is coiled, the magnetic waves are concentrated and the effect becomes much stronger. If an iron core is added to the winding of wire, the magnetism is still stronger.

By a lucky parallel, nature has decreed that when a changing magnetic field, such as from a moving coil of energized wire, passes over another wire, it actually generates an electric current in that second wire. And just as with magnets, if the receiving wire is coiled around an iron core, the amount of electricity formed in the second wire increases. The effect of one coil of wire-forming electricity or magnetism in a second unconnected coil is known as *induction.* And induction is used as the basis for another major type of motor found in small gadgets.

INDUCTION MOTORS

Induction motors have a field winding very much like that found in universal motors. There is no electrical connection to the rotating armature, however, and thus no need for carbon brushes. The windings in the armature, complete with an iron core, receive current enough to form alternating "N" and "S" poles through induction alone.

By developing induction motors, engineers have eliminated almost half of the parts that may ever have to be replaced. There are no brushes to wear out and the wire coils inside the armature are protected from burning out as they sometimes do in a universal motor subjected to a severe overload. Usually the field winding would burn out and thus stop inducing any current at all in the armature. And field winding easily can be replaced in small motors of many types.

The induction motor gives about the most power per pound of machine weight of any engineering accomplishment. And that makes the induction motor well suited for phonograph turntables, electric clocks, electric typewriters, electric can openers, and similar devices. The metal frame that incorporates the field winding in an induction motor is typically called the *stator,* after the Latin root for stationary. And the rotating armature can be called the *rotor.*

The speed of induction motors is established by the speed at which alternating current alternates. They cannot, therefore, be operated on d-c. In the United States, where most household electricity alternates through 60 cycles in a second (60 Hertz), an induction motor with two poles for the field winding would make one complete revolution for each + to − cycle. Hence, 60 cycles times 60 seconds per minute leaves such a motor with a speed of 3600 revolutions per minute.

If the induction motor is built with 4 poles, it would make only half a revolution every time the alternating current went through a complete + to − cycle; therefore, 1800 rpm. There are many 8-pole induction motors around also, having a speed of approximately 900 rpm.

Since the induction motor depends on 60 Hertz current for its speed, about the only way engineers have to build speed controls into a device using induction motors is by winding the various sets of opposed poles separately. In much the same way that a universal motor can have two or more tapped windings, an induction motor can operate at 900 rpm with 8 poles, then be switched over to 4-pole operation for a speed of 1800 rpm.

Variations of induction motors often have more specialized names, but the basic theory is the same. *Synchronous motors* are designed to rotate at very precise speeds through the induction motor's characteristic of rotating in time with the cyclical electric current. *Split-phase* or *capacitor motors* are generally larger induction motors, which have an auxiliary or starting winding in the field coil in addition to the usual 2-, 4-, or 8-pole windings. The capacitor induction motor uses a capacitor to direct current electrically through the starting winding when the motor first starts, whereas other forms of the split-phase motor may accomplish the same trick mechanically by using a centrifugal switch operated very much like a governor. In either type, it is the switch or capacitor that needs attention more often than the motor itself. Most capacitors are set apart from the motor, making troubleshooting or replacement quite easy. Centrifugal switches generally are located inside a motor and accessible through a removable plate at one end. The centrifugal switch should be closed when a motor starts but should open within a few seconds as motor speed increases toward the maximum.

The term "burned out," although popularly used when referring to items such as motors, actually can refer to a great many conditions. And it would be helpful if you would be precise.

A burned out field winding could result from a *short circuit* in the wires, a condition in which two bare spots of wire come together and let tremendous amounts of electricity flow through only part of the coil. This will generally cause the coil to overheat because a greater amount of current than normal will surge through the abbreviated length of wire, and more current causes more heat.

Overheating of the field coil could come from some other mishap, however. If a small electric beater, for example, were used to mix bread dough, the strain from the motor trying to keep up its speed under such a slowing influence could draw more current and cause overheating, perhaps burning the insulation in the process and eventually causing a short circuit, melting a wire, or blowing a fuse.

At exactly the opposite extreme, a burned out coil might draw no current at all. It might have what pros label an *open circuit,* a break in the wire. The condition could have come from a physical break caused if the gadget were dropped or if a careless fix-it person accidentally dragged a screwdriver through a connecting wire. It even might have developed during manufacturing.

You can spot a defective winding in a motor by simple troubleshooting tactics. Charred, bubbled-up enamel insulation on the winding will often provide a visible clue to an overheated motor. A more positive electrical test uses a neon glow tube tester while the motor is plugged in or a signal tracer (introduced in Chapter 6) when the motor is not plugged in.

The electrical drawings in Figures 132, 133 and 134 offer some step-by-step points to assist your troubleshooting endeavors. Especially if the motor is not turning, in no event should the power be turned on for more than a few seconds at a time when you use a neon tester. To do so might overheat portions of the motor and cause more damage.

If a motor does run but is obviously lacking in power or quickly heats up to a point where it is quite uncomfortable to lay your hand on it, the field coil can be suffering from an internal short circuit. Before replacing a hot field coil or the entire motor, be certain that the heating *really is new* and has not been present throughout the gadget's normal lifetime. Next time you use any motorized appliance, pay attention to how hot the motor becomes under normal operating conditions. Then you will know later on if a hot motor is just normally hot or overheating.

On an SCM electric portable typewriter, for example, the induction motor normally operates at a temperature that would be considered excessive if found in most electric can openers, blenders, or tape recorders. The owner of such a machine who had failed to observe the *normal* temperature might incorrectly assume that there was a shorted field coil at the first sign of mechanical troubles.

TROUBLESOME ITEMS IN MOTORS

A *control switch,* for example, might be dirty enough to interfere with motor performance, or shorted, or just plain broken. If a few speed settings work but one or several do not, you must find whether some contacts on the switch are defective, if the wires leading to the tapped windings are snapped, or if the internal wires of a coil are defective.

If a diode has been used as part of the speed control circuit, then some tapped windings could operate while others would not. A defective diode would put out of service only those settings that passed through the diode rectifier to lower the speed of one particular winding.

As an example, the Hoover model 8945/55 blender (and many others) has six speed settings, although there are only three separate tapped windings on the motor. Settings 1, 3, and 5 pass through the diode; 2, 4, and 6 do not. You could easily learn this for yourself by examining the internal wiring layout or an electrical schematic diagram of the blender's working parts. On this Hoover blender if only even-numbered settings work and the odd-numbered ones do not, the first place you should look is the diode or connections leading directly to it.

The equipment needed to test a diode is more expensive than the price of most household gadgets themselves. Diodes themselves are very inexpensive and easy to obtain. So replacement is most often the best test of all. Your nearest TV shop should be able to supply a useable substitute if you know the voltage and amperage or wattage ratings marked on the identification plate of your item. To be safe, try to buy a new diode with *double* the voltage and power rating required. Example: a 120 volt blender rated to consume 250 watts of power should use a diode able to handle 240 volts at 500 watts (approximately ½ amp).

Brushes need replacing periodically in any motor that uses the brush commutator system. Food mixers, power tools, some blenders, vacuum cleaners, and a good many older motors of all sorts should be given a new set of brushes occasionally. An experienced motor repair person can look at a set of brushes and know immediately if they need replacing. Your best bet is to order or buy a new set of brushes the first time you do any significant amount of work with a motor that has seen more than one year of frequent use or two years of occasional wear.

The following points will help you to look at brushes with a pro's eye:

1. The brush should look sleek and black, uniformly dull and uniformly colored. Signs of gloss on the edge that actually contacts the motor commutator indicate time for replacement.

2. There should be no signs of crumbling or deterioration in a good brush.

3. The springs that hold the brushes into position should have enough life in them that when you slide out the motor armature or unscrew the two brush retainers on the outside case, the brushes should immediately jump out of their slot.

4. If the brushes have worn away excessively, the spring may not be able to push them hard enough to make good contact. Different engineers use different relative lengths for motor brushes. As a rough rule of thumb, a good brush probably will occupy at least one third of the slot. Also, on a good brush, the carbon will usually be at least one third as long as the spring.

You must find a correct replacement brush. One that fits too loosely into the brush slot will hit the copper contacts at an angle, perhaps activating two windings at one time. One that fits too tightly will not move closer to the commutator as it wears away.

Ideally you should buy replacement brushes from a factory-authorized dealer for whomever made the gadget or whoever made the motor for the gadget. If that becomes a problem, however, many hardware stores, electrical suppliers, and motor shops sell standard replacement

Figure 135 Brushes supply electricity direct- ly to the motor in many power tools and other motorized gadgets. You can spot them by the screwed-in button, generally black in color, on opposite sides of the device. A healthy brush should spring out on its own.

brushes. Take your old ones with you to help pick out the correct width, depth, and spring size.

There are also plenty of mechanical ailments that can interfere with the smooth operation of a motor-driven gadget—*bearings* at both ends of every motor, for example. The trend for many years has been to build gadgets with what the industry calls *permanently lubricated bearings.* A genuinely permanently lubricated bearing is a mechanical treat for many household uses. But too often a company uses those words to disguise a cheaply constructed piece of something in which they have made no provision for lubrication. In that case they say, "lubricated for the life of the bearing." Of course—when the lubrica- tion wears off, the bearing wears out and that's the end of the life of the bearing!

In general, bearings should help a rotating shaft move accurately, smoothly, and with a minimum of friction. Electric motors on small gadgets generally have a simple *sleeve bearing,* which is little more than a soft metal or plastic hollow cylinder fitted over the harder metal shaft of the motor. There may be grooves in the bearing surface to retain oil; or there may be nothing—in which case you may have to squirt oil into the bearing area frequently.

Ball bearings protect motors in some gadgets, vacuum cleaners for example. In that case, the shaft rests against a series of metal balls, and the balls in turn rest against the outside sleeve, resulting in less overall friction than with a simple sleeve bearing. They also result in more noise. In general, ball bearings require grease for a lubricant; sleeves take oil. There are many other types of bearings too, but none of them common enough around the house to detail (see Figure 179).

You will most often have to begin removing the entire motor to check out what you suspect to be a faulty bearing. After each successive bolt or screw has been twisted loose, test how readily you can turn the motor shaft by hand. Before going through an entire disassembly routine, you may be lucky enough to uncover a bolt that has been too tight or too loose and led to pressures that distorted the motor shaft. In many small food mixers, the bearing can be removed without having to yank out the entire motor assembly.

Once you are ready to find out whether a bearing is doing its job or not, slide the shaft in and out of the bearing. It should move readily but not jerk around or bind. After a bearing has become too loose, it allows a rotor to drop out of position and bind or rub against portions of the stator. You may be able to spot signs of such binding by examining the rotor for scratches and worn patches.

At each step along the path to removing a possibly faulty bearing, be sure that you will be able to reassemble the apparatus in exactly the same way you found it. If electrical connections have to be removed, note the color of the leads and which terminal they belong to. Try to sense in advance how tight various bolts and screws had been turned in. Even though a strip of metal such as a bearing retainer or mounting support might seem, it may not be. With a marking pen of some sort, put an obvious dot or line at the top or left side of every item you must remove. Then, when you reassemble, reinstall everything with the mark pointed in its appropriate direction.

The bearings on many gadgets are replaceable items, and for good reason. On blenders, for example, the upper bearing is typically made a part of the motor-mounting bracket. Replace that and you've also replaced the bearing. On can openers, the rear bearing is often a part of the motor mounting brackets. Mixers tend to have separate bearings, which can be purchased one by one if the need arises. However, if both front and back or top and bottom bearings are equally easy to replace, replace both at the same time.

Some gadgets include their bearings within the motor case itself, electric knives and some vacuum cleaners, for example. Replace either the front or rear motor plate or motor case and you've installed a new bearing at the same time.

Some motors make no provision for bearing maintenance or replacement at all. You will see that most often on motors inside clocks, hair dryers, electric toothbrushes, electric knives, and similar very small items. In such gadgets, an entire motor has to be replaced.

At the other extreme, some heftier household gadgets do have bearings that require lubrication, most notably vacuum cleaners and fans. Many fans have some of the permanently lubricated bearings on one end and a bearing that requires periodic oiling at the other end of the motor shaft.

Ref. No.	Description
1	Lid Cap
2	Lid
3	Container
4	Cap Nut
5	Special Lock Washer
6	Cutter Blade - Upper
7	Cutter Blade - Lower
8	Metal Washer Cup
9	Rubber Thrust Washer
10	Washer
11	Drive Shaft
12	Container Gasket
13	Container Base
14	Washer
15	Top Coupling Assembly
16	Bottom Coupling
17	Spacer
18	Washer
19	Container Support - LH
20	Container Support - RH
21	Housing
22	Switch
23	Name Plate
24	Switch Nut
25	Switch Handle
26	Hex Nut
27	Motor Shield
28	Attachment Strap
29	Screw
30	Washer - Lock
31	Motor Assembly
32	Plug Bumper
33	Base
34	Base Screw
35	Base Screw - Front
36	Attachment Cord
37	Terminal
38	Snap Bushing
39	Bearing Assembly
40	Gasket
41	Washer
42	Nut - Hex
43	Exhaust Muffler
44	Liquid Container Base w/Bearing

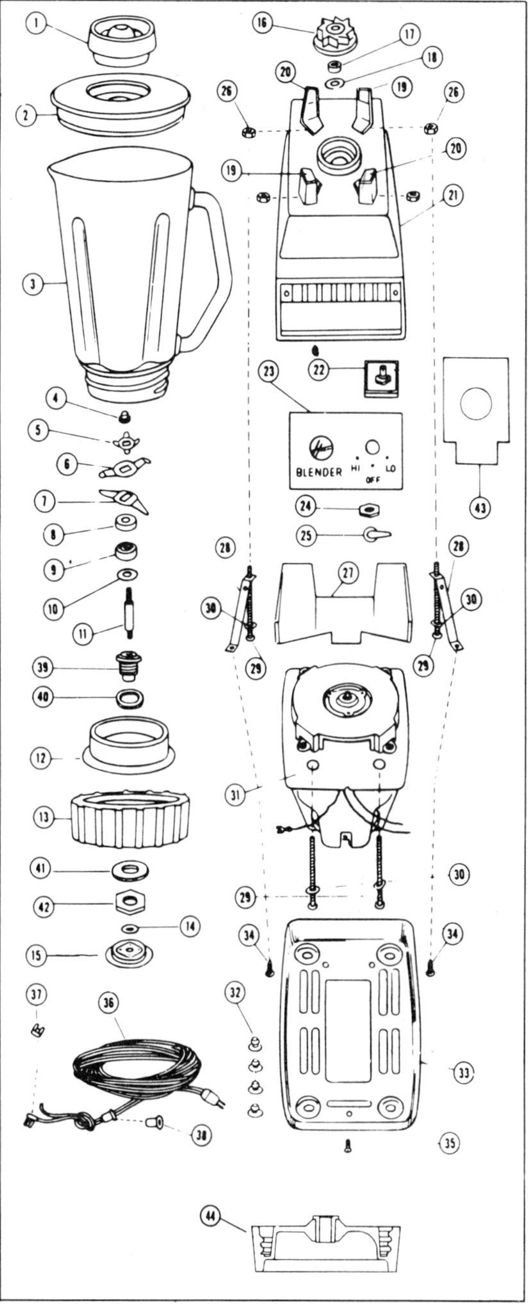

Figure 136 Blender, in exploded view, shows how many parts are involved but how few are likely to wear out. If you disassemble such a blender, you would be unlikely to touch more than a dozen or so of these parts separately. This is the actual manufacturer's (Hoover) drawing and parts description.

What distinguishes a bearing requiring oil from one that doesn't is not always clear. Hopefully, there will be an oil cup above the bearing that needs a periodic oil. Sometimes a felt wick is all the evidence you will find, the wick absorbing enough oil to keep a shaft and its bearing lubricated for a few months at a time.

Manufacturers should include lubricating instructions with every item sold across every counter. And customers ought to *insist*, first of all, that such instructions be given—in writing—and, second, should hold onto user manuals that deal with such details.

Many vacuum cleaners and large fans, unlike smaller gadgets, are significant investments. They can be dealt short life-spans if forced to spin at high speeds without lubrication. A good many vacuums require grease in at least one of their bearings, a fact that is not always pointed out in the user manuals.

If you do suspect that particular bearings on vacuum cleaners or other major pieces of equipment require lubrication, study the existing scene closely to see whether you can find any evidence of oil or grease. As a very rough rule, sleeve bearings are more and more being made "self-lubricating," whereas all other types commonly found in homes require lubrication as part of routine maintenance. If oil is sloshed onto a self-lubricating bearings, its self-lubricating feature is impeded and you will have to continue periodic oiling thereafter. So. when in serious doubt, you may be safer to oil a bearing if you promise to keep doing so. And if you find some oil or grease already on or in a bearing, you have nothing to lose by adding more.

Whenever a bearing has been unattended for a dusty period of time, always clean away the accumulation from the outside before adding fresh oil or grease. It's also not a bad idea to clean the inside of particularly dirty bearings. The easiest way to accomplish that is to squirt Liquid Wrench generously into the bearing, trying to catch as much of the fluid that runs through the bearing as possible, probably with a paper towel.

Sometimes there is a bit of an art to reinstalling specialized shafts and bearings once you have pulled them apart. At the bottom of some blender motors, Hoovers for example, there is a *thrust bearing ball*, a simple steel ball that acts as a very efficient albeit simple bearing. The ball is held in place by a bracket, which also holds the motor in place. Hoover recommends that its particular model be tightened while the blender is running at low speed but with the glass jar removed. Tighten the bracket until the motor begins to labor, in other words, slows down. Then back off the screws about one-fourth turn. This is a good procedure to adapt when reinstalling any bearings that have proven through balky performance to need some rather sensitive alignment.

Gears are found in the working mechanisms of household tools such as food mixers, oscillating fans, can openers, clocks, floor scrubbers, and many power tools. They do require lubrication beyond any doubt. Although clocks run for years with scarcely a drop of oil and can openers can clank through their occasional routine without obvious signs of deterioration even if nobody thinks to toss some grease into the gear box now and then, if the mixer gears cannot go ungreased for too long. This is especially true on those mixers with big gaps in their housing to allow air to circulate around and cool the undersized motor. The gaps also admit plenty of flour to form a thick paste in the gears and a heavy blanket of heat-holding dust over the wires.

Mixer gears should be depasted and greased about once a year no matter how often the item is used. After scraping away solid accumulations from the gears, they should be dry-cleaned with a solvent. Kerosene, cleaning fluids, lacquer solvent, and similar nonwater-based cleaners are dandy.

While working on the gears, you might also take a look at the bearings. If they are dried out or have accumulated some flour, bathe them in the same solvent. Add light oil to the bearings and a white grease or silicone grease to the gears *after* all of the solvent has evaporated.

TROUBLESHOOTING INDIVIDUAL MOTORIZED GADGETS

CAN OPENERS

The gears in electric can openers deserve much the same treatment as in the mixers discussed in the previous section, although you will probably never get around to such a chore until something seems wrong. At the very least, the *cutting wheel*, the wheel that actually cuts through the can cover, should be cleaned every few months. Detergent and water, aided by steel wool, is ideal. Then lubricate the cutting wheel with some cooking oil. Replacement cutting wheels are quite readily available and inexpensive. Most of them simply screw into place. At the first sign of a rounded or knicked edge, start planning for its replacement.

If a particularly bad run of cans jams up the can opener too often, perhaps overloading the gears each time, one of the small gears is likely to lose a few teeth, or in pro talk, *get stripped*. Some manufacturers have wisely added some plastic gears to their can opener gear train so that if any do strip, it will be relatively easy to replace a plastic one and not one metal gear picked almost at random, maybe near the bottom of the pile. Plastic gears are finding wide use in many gadgets and tools today, and not just for maintenance reserve. They are quieter than steel or brass gears.

When you first examine the gear train of a can opener, you might swear that some conspiracy on the part of its maker led engineers to lay out each big gear behind the next big gear, which means that to remove *any* gear you have to pull off the big gear just above it. And when you get to the last big gear, that one is often stamped onto the cutting shaft, unlike the others, which may be held onto their shafts with simple spring clips.

There is engineering sense in the arrangement of interlocking gears, however. The setup keeps the gears from pushing against their own spring clip hard enough to snap it out of place.

However, one or more of the other gears can suffer from some stripped-off teeth after too many sardine cans. The drive gear on many openers generally fits onto a squared-off shaft. At the factory, the gear is pressed on and the square end is struck with a punch, which

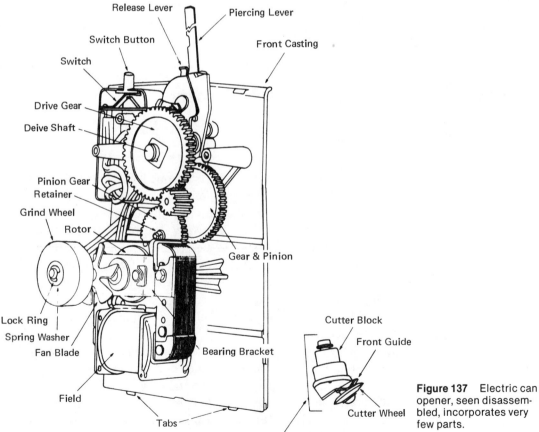

Figure 137 Electric can opener, seen disassembled, incorporates very few parts.

flattens each corner of the square just enough to hold the gear firmly onto the shaft.

It should take less than five minutes to file away the stamped edges on such gears. Then the drive gear can be pried off and each subsequent gear removed after its spring clip is snapped loose, being careful not to lose them.

Replacement gears for electric can openers are available at very small cost, although the repair service station may be very surprised when you ask for one. Very few people replace the gears. They replace the whole can opener instead.

After all of the gears are back in place, clean all traces of oil or grease off both the drive gear and the drive shaft. Slip the gear back onto the square shaft, push it firmly in as far as it will go, then cover the center with a blob of epoxy cement. One of the metal filled varieties such as Liquid Steel, Liquid Aluminum, or Smooth-On Metalset A4 work best. After the epoxy has fully hardened, your can opener should be in business again. Don't get overly generous with the epoxy, however, because if you ever strip another gear, you'll be filing away the mound of epoxy.

FANS

Since fans are often tucked away once a year, then dragged out again at the last minute when the sun hits its peak, you probably let maintenance go until dust, dirt, corrosion, or lack of lubrication slows the fan down enough to bother you. It may seem like a small matter, but if dust is allowed to clog the oscillating gear, it can slow down the overall speed of the fan and lead to deeper complications. Periodically, remove the mechanism that swings oscillating fans back and forth, clean it, and apply a liberal blob of grease.

Big window fans come in many sizes, shapes, controls, and motor types. Speeds are controlled by virtually every technique—diodes, resistors, tapped windings. Figure out what kind of motor your particular window fan employs, how the speed is regulated, look at the bearings to see if lubrication is required, and make sure the electrical contacts are tight and clean. The rest is pure enjoyment.

FLOOR POLISHERS AND SCRUBBERS

Polishers and scrubbers generally have a set of gears with a twofold purpose. Motors have to run at fairly high speeds to be efficient. So gears in floor scrubbers and polishers slow down the motor's high

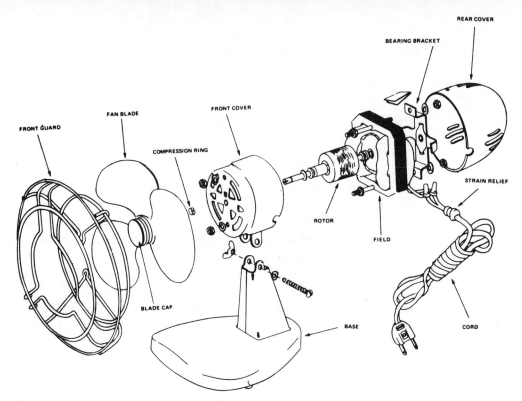

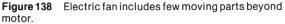

Figure 138 Electric fan includes few moving parts beyond motor.

speed and also change the direction of rotation so that the two brushes turn in opposite directions.

Your floor machines deserve care, periodic cleaning, and lubricating with silicone or white grease. The motor bearings in such devices are often the self-lubricating variety.

Replacement gears are available from reputable manufacturers. Many of them include two plastic gears in their scrubber's gear box, one for the right brush, one for the left.

Many of the more elaborate floor polishers and scrubbers, carpet shampooers as well, have a tank on them to hold suds or shampoo and a tube that squirts the cleaning agent onto the floor. Deluxe models even have a vacuum arrangement for sucking up much of the water and suds. In those deluxe models, a set of fan blades is attached to the electric motor to generate the vacuum.

The motor housing and gear box in any polisher, shampooer, or scrubber that has facilities for liquids must be sealed. Although the cements that hold the tank and hoses together are pretty good, leaks can happen. And you would not want to see what a few drops of water can do in a spinning motor.

Silicone sealant, the same kind of product sold for calking around bathtubs, is ideal for sealing or resealing the motor housing and gear box. Manufacturers recommend that their repair people install new hoses and new tanks (available at factory service stations) or repair old ones with a good, general purpose, plastic cement type of adhesive. But if you don't have a good collection of adhesives at home, buy only a tube of the silicone sealant and use that for repairing or installing new tanks and tubes.

VACUUM CLEANERS

The many shapes and configurations of vacuum cleaners all operate on the same basic principle. A motor spins at high speed, driving a fan that is most often connected directly to the motor shaft. The fan blows air out of the cannister, tank, or whatever kind of shape the cleaner is housed in, and the vacuum left behind by the fan action sucks air into the hose or bag. The rapidly moving air drags dirt, dust, and similar debris with it. Before the dirtied air is sucked into the fan and the

Figure 139 Exploded views of typical vacuum cleaners shows how few parts are involved.

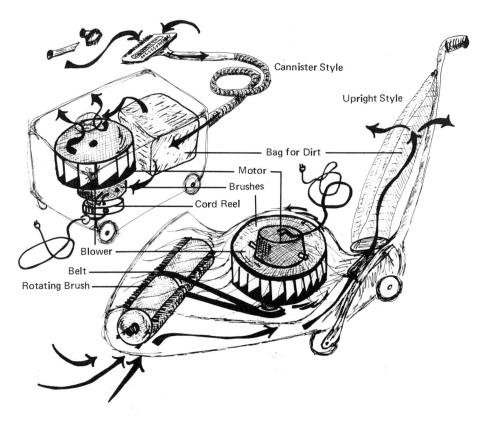

Cannister Style

Upright Style

Bag for Dirt

Motor

Brushes

Cord Reel

Blower

Belt

Rotating Brush

motor, however—which would ruin it instantly—the dirt is filtered out into a paper bag, paper filter, or cloth sack.

By far the greatest number of service difficulties with vacuum cleaners of all descriptions comes from too much dirt in the wrong places. Bags are replaced too infrequently, filters are torn or not installed properly, routine maintenance is postponed until the cleaner stops cleaning properly. By the time a handy person does take the vacuum apart, the rehabilitation may take an hour or more.

Assuming that your complaint is similar to most—the machine has started to make too much noise and pick up too little dirt—unplug the unit from the wall outlet and locate the particular set of screws or nuts that will let you take a look at the motor and fan unit. Chances are, you will find a sizeable collection of dust in every stage of disassembly. Brush the dirt carefully out of the way.

As you get closer and closer to the motor itself, you will eventually get to the fan blades. They are most often held onto the motor by a single nut. Some of them have a *left-handed thread* (turned clockwise to loosen instead of the other way around).

The space between a fan and its motor may be choked with dust, grit, and lint. Air passages can be blocked. As the threads and cushiony layers of dust build up, they gradually slow down the flow of air, which also slows down the cleaning process and maybe even the motor. The tangle of threads around bearings and shafts increases friction, slowing down the motor still more.

After all of the stray dirt has been whisked away, you can safely open the motor housing to inspect bearings, brushes, wire insulation, and all other internal components. You may find that one bearing is the self-lubricating type—this would most often be the one closest to the fan. And the opposite bearing, often a ball bearing, will require lubrication, generally grease. If your vacuum cleaner suffers from excessive noise, and you find no evidence of broken or bent fan blades, which will outscream even a happy two-year-old, examine the bearings for signs of excessive wear.

Here is a rough guide to use in locating noises. Bent fan blades should stir up considerable vibration as well as noise. Worn ball bearings generally rumble and have spurts of sound mixed in with the general din. Sleeve bearings, when they wear, put out a steady scraping sound.

Before you actually pull the motor loose from its mounts and bearings, try to jiggle the shaft or armature or fan from side to side. If it is free to move any noticeable amount, think about ordering replacement bearings. Just as we saw earlier with blenders, vacuum cleaner bearings are often an integral part of a mounting bracket or motor-mount plate. The replacement bearings are inexpensive enough and so easy to install that taking a chance on making do with the

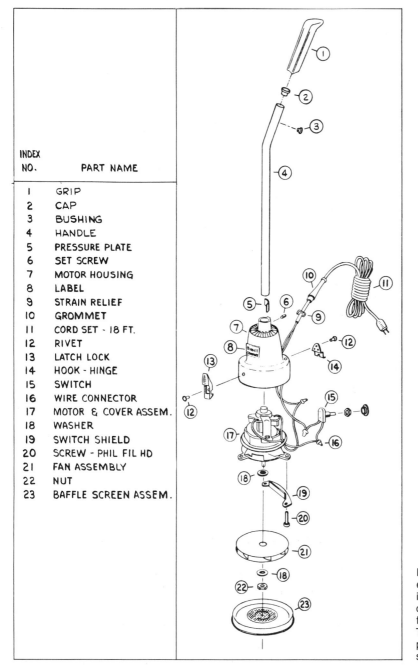

INDEX NO.	PART NAME
1	GRIP
2	CAP
3	BUSHING
4	HANDLE
5	PRESSURE PLATE
6	SET SCREW
7	MOTOR HOUSING
8	LABEL
9	STRAIN RELIEF
10	GROMMET
11	CORD SET - 18 FT.
12	RIVET
13	LATCH LOCK
14	HOOK - HINGE
15	SWITCH
16	WIRE CONNECTOR
17	MOTOR & COVER ASSEM.
18	WASHER
19	SWITCH SHIELD
20	SCREW - PHIL FIL HD
21	FAN ASSEMBLY
22	NUT
23	BAFFLE SCREEN ASSEM.

Figure 140 Compact electric vacuum (Bissell), in manufacturer's own drawing, shows that very few parts are involved. That means that very few problems in repair should be encountered.

possibly defective ones can only lead to complications such as burned out motor windings, which you will be unable to fix yourself.

Any sign of cracks, bends, or breaks in a fan should be ample reason to replace it. The fan moves at very high speeds, and if it gets out of balance, it will make short work of your motor bearings and perhaps the motor armature as well. If the fan appears to be in good physical shape, remove it from the motor shaft anyway and lay it on a perfectly

281

flat table. Every blade should be in an identical position. Either visually or with an accurate ruler, measure the distance from the table to the tip of every blade. Minor distortions can be corrected by gently bending any mispositioned blade. You should not attempt to realign badly distorted fan systems, however. Their replacement is a much surer remedy and not particularly costly.

If your machine has an automatic cord rewinder, take it apart only if you have tracked down some electrical or mechanical problems to that particular site. In general, don't let the relative size of your floor cleaners cause you to overlook the simple troubleshooting techniques we used on smaller tools.

Most automatic cord rewinding mechanisms consist of a reel, either open or closed, onto which the retracted cord is wound. When the eager cleaning person pulls the cord out, a ratchet keeps the mechanism from pulling it back immediately. At the same time the cord is being pulled out, a spring within the reel is being tensed, getting ready for the job of rewinding the reel. A tug on the cord releases the ratchet and the tight spring spins the reel, which in turn provides a snag-free home for the cord once more.

Electrical connections from the cord to the motor or any other controls that might be included are made at the bottom center of the cord reel. And it's there that any faulty terminals or wires are likely to be found. Use a good bit of care if you disassemble the spring-loaded reel. The spring may not be lethal, but it can be unpleasant if it gets out of hand.

First attempt to release all tension on the spring before opening the assembly. And then always point the mechanism away from your face as you prepare to open it.

Some of the cord rewinding mechanisms are held together with rivets, often used to attach various brackets or guards at the same time If you must enter a riveted reel assembly, drill out the rivets and replace them during reassembly with small nuts, washers, and bolts.

The ratchet typically is on top of the reel along with a small spring and catch known as a *pawl*. Beneath the reel is a commutator, a brass slip ring that transmits electric power from the end of the cord to the inner parts of the vacuum cleaner. You can imagine how hard it would be to design a way to solder the cord directly to the motor when the cord is on this reel, which keeps spinning around and around and around.

There is, in fact, a very early model of cord retracting reel you may find on some machines. It is totally enclosed; the layers of rolled up cord are not visible when you have disassembled your vacuum cleaner that far. And instead of a commutator, the end of the cord actually runs through a hole in the top (or bottom) of the reel and solders directly onto the various motor or switch terminals. The older, enclosed reels generally have to be replaced as a complete unit—reel, cord, ratchet, the works all in one ensemble.

Newer, open reels can be replaced piecemeal—cord, reel, ratchet, pawl—although there seldom is need to replace more than a worn ratchet or pawl. In ordering a new pawl or ratchet, be very specific about the model number of your vacuum cleaner, and describe the part you want. Some ratchets have gear teeth all around; some have teeth only part of the way around.

When it comes time to reassemble the cord retractor, just backtrack over the path you took in tearing it apart. The spring in the reel generally has to receive two complete turns to build up an initial reservoir of tension. However, if the cord does not snap back into the reel vigorously enough or far enough, you may have to move back to this step and experiment with more than two turns on the spring.

The commutator assembly should be treated to a stingy amount of grease or petroleum jelly when the time comes to put it back into place. But keep greasy fingers off the electrical contacts themselves.

Some vacuum cleaner models have a power switch at the end of the long vacuum cleaner hose. Since it would be dangerous, maybe even deadly to run 120 volt current through fine wires stretched around a coiled hose, somewhere inside the cannister portion of such a machine you will find a small transformer, which lowers the voltage to a safe level, often 24 volts. The 24 volt current passes through the wire in the hose, and when the switch is closed (turned "on"), the 24 volt current energizes the coil of a relay.

A *relay* is nothing more than an electrical switch operated by an electromagnet. The 24 volt coil tugs at a steel leve, which closes a small switch sending the separate 120 volt current down bigger wires to the motor.

Relay contacts need periodic cleaning with an ignition file or similar fine polishing tool. The coils of both the transformer and relay are wound with very fine wire and break or burn out on occasion. Your troubleshooting expertise from earlier chapters will help you easily to spot a relay or transformer that needs replacing. On the low voltage side of the transformer and relay, however, the neon glow tube tester will not be useful since the tube will not light up on currents below 50 or even 90 volts. A flashlight bulb or a continuity tester can be used.

Some upright cleaner models operate via a belt and pulley system. The belt, of course, wears out over a period of time and stretches or deteriorates. It is always more pleasant to replace one before it breaks entirely. Not only do you spare yourself the gamble of having to rush out for a new belt just as someone is expected at the front door, but if you put the new belt in while the old one is still in place, you will have no trouble installing the replacement correctly. You will be able to study the layout of the old belt.

The various uprights with belts generally use the belt to drive an *agitator*, which beats dirt out of rugs. The agitator itself is quite a finely engineered piece of machinery on better cleaners. Make certain to replace the agitator brushes with precisely the proper product. And always replace all of them at once, never one this month, one the next. The agitator moves at a relatively fast clip, and unbalanced brushes or roller can set up vibrations that will not only annoy you but will also damage the belt, pulley, and motor.

Bearings in the agitator must be lubricated with grease quite frequently. Several times a year would be ideal. And while you are greasing the cleaner, here are some other points to cover with a dab of lubrication:

Wheel bearings.

Switch mechanical parts (but not electrical contacts).

Handle bearings on uprights.

Any other moving parts such as hose couplings that you want to keep moving easily.

As various types of vacuum cleaners are used or abused, hinges can budge from their original location, spring clamps don't spring or clamp as firmly, hose connections get bent and distorted, and rubber seals become tattered or pushed out of shape or out of place. Although no one factor individually makes a vacuum cleaner obviously ineffective, all of them can contribute to a general sluggishness.

Ideally, air should enter the vacuum cleaner housing only through the hose opening or the nozzle. After your vacuum cleaner has given you several years of service, why not take a tube of silicone sealant and restore its youthful vigor. Spread a thin seal of silicone rubber around all of the openings through which air might be leaking—the entire opening area in cannister types, the various traps that open to permit cleaning or changing bags in both uprights or cannister models, and around the opening for your cleaner hose. What you're doing with the sealant is creating a set of flexible gaskets that will compensate for structural faults allowing air to leak in and dilute the vacuum cleaner power.

AIR PUMPS

Air pumps of the kind used to supply air to fish tanks or to small paint spraying equipment have a piston of natural or synthetic materials that forces air past a small valve and into plastic tubing, which carries air to the fish tank. In some designs the piston is little more than a flat diaphragm fastened in place at the edges; the motor lifts and lowers only the center. In other models, the piston moves up and down in a thin brass cylinder.

If there is a cylinder involved, the piston probably has leather washers. They dry out with time unless a drop or two of oil is allowed to slide down the inside cylinder walls periodically.

Almost inevitably, the motors and all of the moving parts require occasional doses of oil. Oil on the rubber belts, however, does *them* no good. Always inquire about the availability of replacement parts at the time you invest in the fish tank equipment or the paint sprayer. They are not always easy-to-come by commodity.

HAIR DRYERS

Another air-moving product, hair dryers are low priced, low quality, high chromed gadgets consisting of one elaborate case, one gaudy headpiece, a tiny motor, tiny heater, and sometimes even a thermostat. Switches barely qualify for that name. If you understood the heaters in toasters or waffle irons, and fans used in vacuum cleaners there is nothing you don't already know about hair dryers.

Many hair dryer component parts are made in so flimsy a fashion that you might think twice before trying to repair them. Switch contacts can be cleaned, thermostat contacts polished, and snapped wires or contacts mended. Beyond that, however, replace any parts that seem to be defective.

Make certain that all electrical connections are carefully insulated—they're not always in that kind of condition when they leave the factory! If you come across bare terminals or wires, the fastest and safest remedy is to coat the bare lead with silicone sealant.

TOOTH BRUSHES

Electric tooth brushes are simple little gadgets consisting of a rechargeable battery and a battery-powered motor in the handle. The base includes a small transformer and rectifier, which charges the battery between uses.

Parts for the toothbrushes generally come in preassembled units: the *base*, which is a fancy piece of plastic, the *charger assembly*, which is the key ingredient; and the *power handle*, which occasionally has a switch on it that can be replaced, and it often does need replacing. There are also various individual brushes and other parts. You will know if individual parts in any of the preassembled units

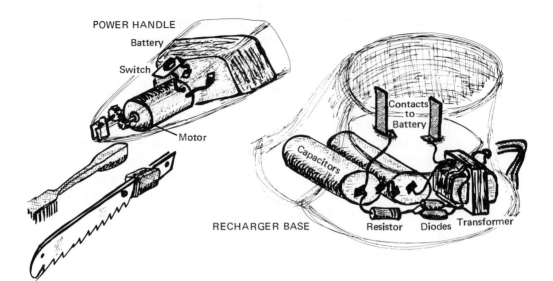

POWER HANDLE
Battery
Switch
Motor
RECHARGER BASE
Contacts to Battery
Capacitors
Resistor   Diodes   Transformer

Figure 141   Electric knife and electtric toothbrush, despite
size differences, operate on identical principle.

can be replaced by whether or not there are screws holding the walls together. If you go to all of the work of prying apart a plastic case, you might just find that the manufacturer doesn't sell separate parts.

ELECTRIC KNIVES

Your electric knife may be built just like your electric toothbrush. The d-c motor is bigger, however, because roast beef is a good deal tougher than teeth. And the battery inside the knife handle has to be bigger too. But in almost every basic way, the two are alike.

There are a few shortcuts you can use when troubleshooting almost all of the gadgets with separate battery charger base and handle loaded with battery and motor. You can see with a flashlight bulb if the transformer and rectifier circuits are working. Since units like this put out something in the vicinity of 6 or 12 volts, hold a lantern bulb (6 or 12 volt) between the two contacts of the base while the base is plugged in and turned on. Even the low voltage bulb from a so-called high intensity lamp could be useful. If you get light at the contact, you have power. And that means your headaches are in the handle motor, battery, switch, or wiring.

If the power supply unit tests out, put the handle unit on to charge for at least an hour. Then you should get the same test bulb to light up when touching the contacts on the handle through which the
286 battery is charged. If not, you can try leaving the battery on to

Ref. No.	Description
1	Blade Assembly Complete
2	Blade Guard - Left
3	Blade Guard - Right
4	Screw (Blade Guard)
5	Screw (Bottom Shell)
6	Name Plate
7	Top Shell
8	Bottom Shell
9	Screw (Support Guide)
10	Cover - Top (Support Guide)
11	Cover - Bottom (Support Guide)
12	Guide Assembly Complete
13	Screw
14	Screw
15	Fan
	Fan (Revised)
16	Snap Ring
	Snap Ring (Revised)
17	Screw
	Screw (Revised)
18	Rear Bearing Housing Assembly
	Rear Bearing Housing Assem. (Revised)
19	Washer
	Washer (Revised)
20	Rotor
	Rotor (Revised)
21	Stator
	Stator (Revised)
22	Holder Assembly
	Holder Assembly (Revised)
23	Carbon Brush
	Carbon Brush (Revised)
24	Front Bearing Assembly Complete
	Front Bearing Assem. Com. (Revised)
25	Bottom Gear Housing
27	Bushing
28	Gear Assembly
29	Cord Set
30	Body Screw
31	Switch
32	Roller

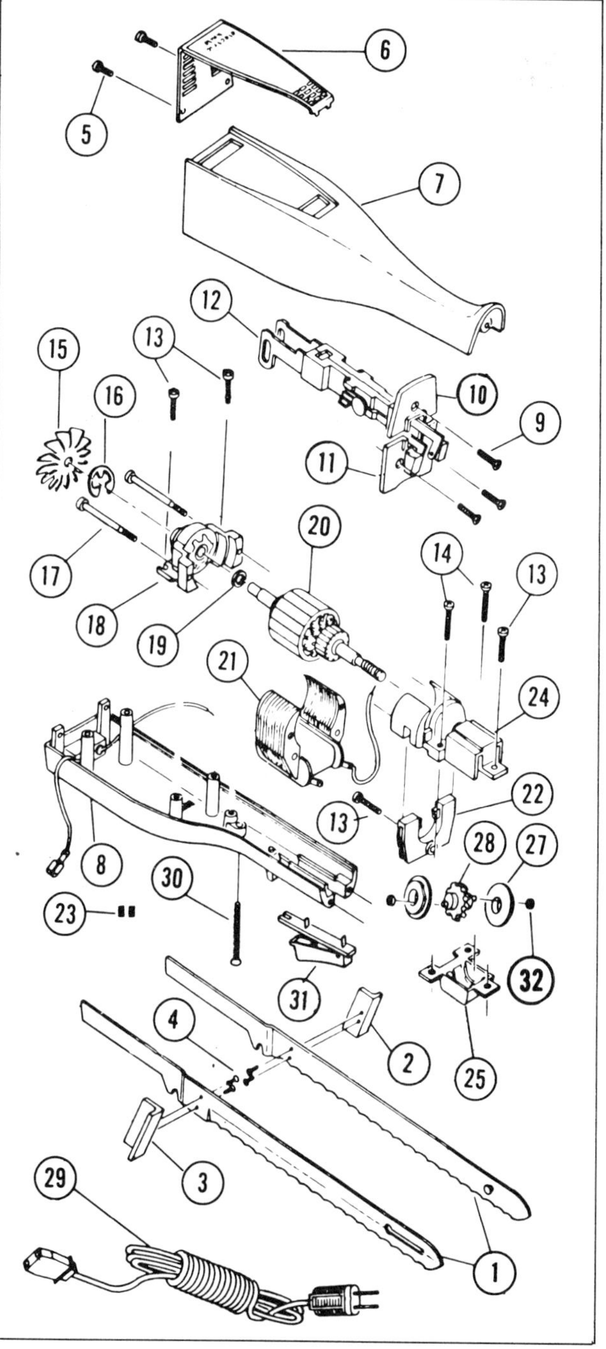

Figure 142 Exploded view of Hoover electric knife (in manufacturer's own repair diagram) which you can compare to simpler exploded view in Figure 141.

charge for the maximum recommended by the manufacturer, but never more than overnight. Then run the test again. Light means good battery, and look elsewhere in the handle for the fault.

Assuming you can get the handle apart, it will be quick work to short out the switch contacts with a wire or even with aluminum foil. If the switch is okay, or if the motor still doesn't run when the switch is shorted, then you have only the wires and motor to check. With an alligator clip, run power from the battery-charging contacts directly to the two motor leads and watch for any sign of life. If the motor spins, it is okay, and the wires must be at fault, unless the mechanism hooked onto the motor is somehow causing the headache. And if the case came apart easily, chances are good that you can buy replacement parts as needed from a factory service center and solder them or hook them into place very quickly.

WATER PICS

Oral hygiene devices, which have practically adopted the name of their major or earliest manufacturer, Water Pic, are not difficult to fix. The maker is willing to share repair manuals with lay people, but there is one important catch. To service almost any part of the device properly, you will need a pressure gauge to measure how much water pressure your Water Pic is putting out. The pressure can reach 75 pounds per square inch and *should* reach that much if the appliance is to do its job.

If you decide to invest in your own pressure gauge, spend additional change for the official repair manual. You can buy your own pressure gauge for a cost equal to about a third or half of what you paid for the whole Water Pic in the first place.

That isn't exactly a moral, but one important side of household repairs is "Let well enough alone."

When Major
Appliances Become
General Nuisances

12

Most used, most expensive, often most abused, and most difficult to get fixed—the washer, dryer, or other major household appliance doesn't seem so lowly when it decides not to work. In a vain effort to keep these most valuable of home workers in working condition, many people subscribe to so-called service contracts.

Most of the *contracting* in service contracts falls on your shoulders. The *service* end of the paper doesn't require the servicing company to serve you any faster than someone without the expensive form. In fact, if you have paid in advance for a service contract, your neighbor without the contract will probably get the first knock on the door from the repair person.

With a well-built, not too cheap, well-installed, and well-cared-for appliance, the parts that were defective when they came off the assembly line generally show up within the first year of use. That is when the original factory warranty is still in effect.

From the end of the first year until about the tenth, repair problems stem more from troubles caused by the machine *operator* than the machine *maker*. So, if you are in any way typical, by the time

289

290

**When
Major
Appliances
Become
General
Nuisances**

parts start going from wear and old age, you have already grown tired of paying money every year on a service contract you never seem to use.

If the financial aspects of appliance repair don't scare you, you may be moved by what seems to be a fact that such appliances generally break down when they are most needed. Are you content to sit around waiting for a repair person just because you've never looked at the back of a washer?

Earlier chapters emphasized the importance of little things as being capable of felling big gadgets. This is just as true with major appliances. Plugs, fuses, faucets, controls, and anything else that supplies electricity, water, or direction to the appliance should be checked before you even think of reaching for a screwdriver or a telephone. Also reach for the instruction manual before the toolbox. If you suddenly switch to a new method for washing clothes or send some different kind of food through the disposal unit, maybe you also have to push some different buttons on the machine. There is also the possibility of plain old lapse of memory, a situation that the original user booklet can overcome with only embarrassment, but which a repair person would charge plenty to overcome.

If you think that the manufacturer of your appliance is exaggerating when it says "empty the lint filter after every use," your washer or dryer may be choking to death. Lint that accumulates in the various filters slows down the water or air and interferes with proper cleaning or drying. Eventually it will stop the operation altogether.

The original installation of many appliances can account for later headaches. A dryer vent, for instance, should be as straight and uncluttered as possible. Otherwise lint will accumulate inside the vent pipes, eventually blocking the flow of air and leaving clothes wet after hours of tumbling. The remedy, of course, is first to clean out the pipe and next to find a better, more direct way of venting the dryer.

If a washer is permanently hooked into the sewer system via a rubber hose, the hose may have been too long at the time it was first installed. Age could cause it to droop and kink, forcing dirty water to stay inside the washing machine. At times, the pressure of a full tank of water being pumped out will force a passage through the kink, but the pressure of the relatively tiny amount of water being pumped out during the final spin cycle might not be able to penetrate the kink, leaving you holding an armful of clean but soaking wet clothes.

Almost every major appliance must be mounted exactly level—not level with the floor but level according to an imaginary line pointed toward the center of the earth's gravity. There is only one accurate way to ascertain that an appliance is level—with an inexpensive, easy-to-use tool known as a *level*. It is a small glass or plastic tube, usually several of them pointed in two or three different directions, mounted in a frame of wood or metal. The longer the frame, the more accurate the level.

For motor-driven appliances, the leveling process enhances the life of motor bearings. Gas stoves should be level so that the flames will not tilt to one side, heating pots unevenly, or pilot lights will soot up due to the flame touching cold metal surfaces nearby. Cakes will come out lopsided in an oven that is not level.

Wooden floors do not always stand as still as they appear to. It is wise periodically to check the level of major appliances. Many appliance legs have adjustment screws built in. If they don't, narrow pieces of wood, metal, plastic, or other solid materials can prop up the low side. By the time you discover that uneven legs caused bearing failure, the cure is several years too late.

Nobody seems ever to have told appliance users that one of the easiest ways to damage even some rugged parts in motor-driven appliances, such as automatic washers or dryers, is to twist their controls through changes while the appliance is running. Unless the user manual specifically says that quick changes in control settings are okay, exercise a little patience. On wash day, if you suddenly decide to set the washer at a different part of the timer dial, first pull out the knob or however else your machine gets switched off, so you can make the change while the motor is stopped and all parts disengaged. The same warning applies even to the water temperature selector.

WASHING MACHINES

Washing machines come in a staggering variety of sizes, shapes, makes, and models. So let's just concentrate on enough of the fundamentals—most of which are remarkably similar in all washers—that even a novice should be able to take on almost any washing machine repair effectively.

Don't worry if you can't tell what a solenoid looks like. The manufacturer assumes that *many professional repair people don't know either.* On the official washing machine chart, the matter is simplified for repair pros and amateurs. Uniquely colored wires are used throughout the apparatus. By finding out which color wire links the timer to the solenoid, you can find the solenoid simply by finding the appropriately colored wire. And you can locate nearly every individual part simply by studying the color of wires.

If you have never replaced a part on a major modern appliance,

When
Major
Appliances
Become
General
Nuisances

you may be in for a shock. It's easy! Take a look at Figure 143, and you're about all set. Since labor, both in manufacture and in repair, is the costliest ingredient, every conceivable shortcut is employed to keep from having to fasten wires to parts permanently.

The push-ons shown in Figure 143, or close variations, are used on most electrically operated parts, which means you can probably replace most replaceable parts in a washer and most other major appliances with little more than one screwdriver and one pliers. If any of the push-ons push off without a substantial effort on your part, they are too loose. Squeeze the terminal portion together enough so that the metal parts firmly grab their matching prongs.

At the control center of every automatic washer is a timer, which automatically turns on and off the various functions of the washer. The tiny electric motor inside resembles the rugged little version inside electric clocks. Such motors seldom require maintenance and almost never need replacing unless badly abused. The motor drives a set of irregularly shaped disks called *cams,* which turn tiny switches on and off.

Since slowly moving switch contacts would wear out very quickly because of electrical sparks and arcs between the two contact points, the timer motor drives a spring, and the spring couples to the disks. The spring advances the washer timer once about every half minute. That too is quite foolproof unless factory design or home tampering allows dirt into the mechanism. In that case, the fastest and surest cure is to douse the dirty or lagging timer with TV contact cleaner. It works magic on enclosed electrical contacts of all sorts. You may not be able to open the gadget to inspect whether sparking or air pollution has fouled the contacts. But if you spray TV contact cleaner

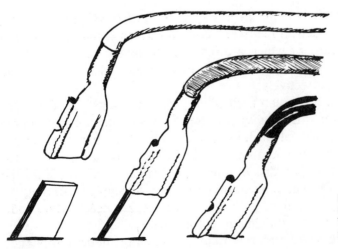

Figure 143 Push on connectors are used to wire appliances conveniently. The terminal receives the connector with a simple shove.

293

*When
Major
Appliances
Become
General
Nuisances*

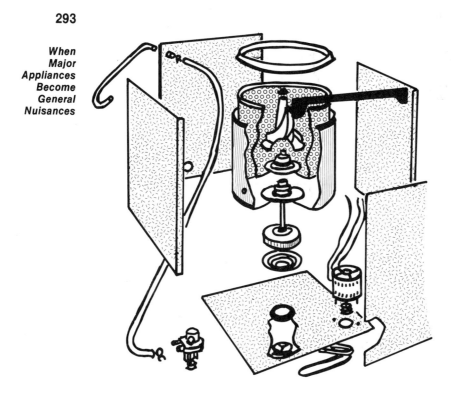

Figure 144   Washing machine chassis.

through every crack and crevice, and plenty of it, you'll know by the next day whether your problem has been solved. It sometimes takes that long for the cleaning to work.

Another way that an otherwise well-designed timer can be damaged is if someone tries to twist the timer knob backward. The timer is designed to move in one direction *only,* and for a very good reason. Don't try to change that.

Glued to the back of nearly every automatic washer is a diagram showing all kinds of valuable information, such as the layout and color of the wires that link the timer to the various solenoids and electric valves and a minute-by-minute chart of which parts should be on and which off during any part of the automatic washing, rinsing, spinning cycles. It's worth a few minutes to locate that chart.

A typical chart is shown in the accompanying Figure 146. If you look at the chart for this washer and then at the blown-up drawing of a washer, you can go through a dry run of which parts do what and when. Just keep in mind that everything in an automatic washer is controlled by electricity. The valves that admit hot and cold water

294

**When
Major
Appliances
Become
General
Nuisances**

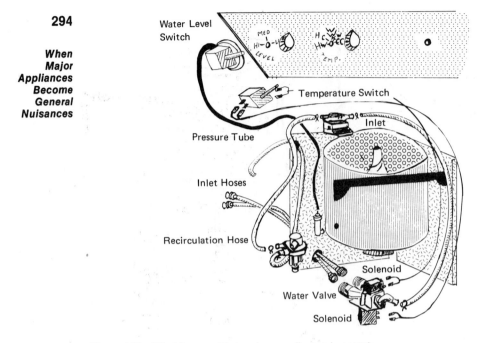

Figure 145   Washing machine water supplies and controls.

are run by electromagnets; the mechanical shift from agitate to spin is often done by a solenoid or two, which is nothing more than an electrical magnetic device; high speeds and low speeds are determined by which set of motor windings the timer activates; water is pumped out of the washer when the timer switch either turns on the pump motor, which can be separate from the agitator and spin motor, or, in those machines in which the pump is linked via a belt to the only motor, an electric valve is opened to the drain hose so the pump forces water to the drain instead of through the recirculating filter and hardware.

With your washing machine chart in hand, locate that portion of the chart that matches the ailing part of your washer cycle. For example, if the final spin cycle in the washer illustrated here is not getting the usual amount of water out of the clothes (assuming the load is normal sized and the clothes are normal ones for your family), the problem could be that the washer is not spinning at all. Or that it is spinning too slowly. Many automatics have two different speeds for spinning, a slow spin during the rinse cycles and a fast spin at the end to squeeze out as much water as possible through centrifugal force.

You can tell by ear whether the machine is spinning during its spin cycle. But it is hard to tell by sound alone whether it is moving at its usual high speed or substantially slower. And since there is generally a safety shutoff switch that turns off the whole machine if someone accidently lifts the washer cover during a spin cycle, how can you see for yourself what the speed actually is? By cheating.

Figure 146 Washing machine electrical controls.

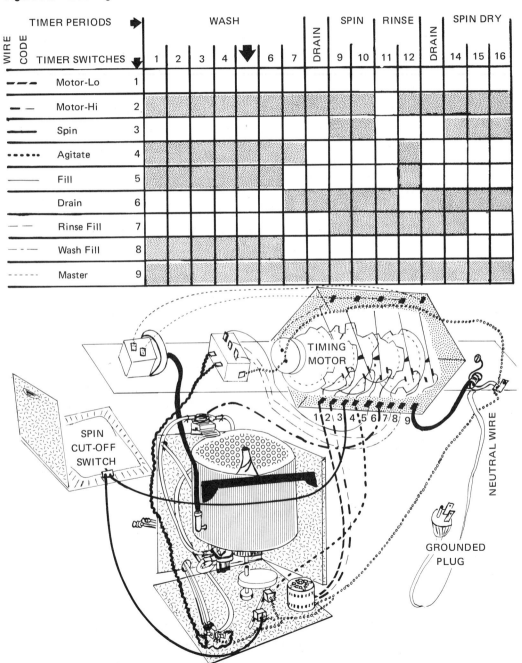

WIRE CODE	TIMER SWITCHES		WASH						DRAIN	SPIN		RINSE		DRAIN	SPIN DRY		
			1	2	3	4	▼	6	7		9	10	11	12		14	15	16
– – –	Motor-Lo	1																
– —	Motor-Hi	2																
—	Spin	3																
••••••	Agitate	4																
——	Fill	5																
	Drain	6																
— —	Rinse Fill	7																
— – —	Wash Fill	8																
- - - -	Master	9																

SPIN CUT-OFF SWITCH

TIMING MOTOR

1 2 3 4 5 6 7 8 9

NEUTRAL WIRE

GROUNDED PLUG

296

**When
Major
Appliances
Become
General
Nuisances**

Lift the lid and locate the safety shutoff switch. Depress it with one hand. With your other hand, turn the timer first to a rinse cycle so you can find out what the slower speed spin looks like. And then properly turn the dial to the final spin cycle to see whether the washer is spinning fast or at approximately the same "slow" speed as during rinse. *At all times keep one hand on the safety switch and one hand on the timer dial. In that way you will have no free hands to dangle into the washer!*

Once you have determined in our example whether the spinning speed is proper or not, the chart can help you proceed further. If the machine is too slow, the problem is probably mechanical rather than electrical.

The drum inside the washer should be *free wheeling* when most washers are turned off; try spinning it by hand to see if something is in the way. If the discharge hose is clogged or kinked, it could prevent water from being pumped out during a spin cycle and the extra load of water would slow down the spinning. Are you certain the washer is not overloaded with clothes? Look at the *belt* to see whether it might be frayed and worn or fits around the pulleys too loosely to transmit all of the power from the motor to the drum.

One of the least expensive and most versatile ways to incorporate two speeds into an appliance is with a motor that has two sets of internal wires, one for the high speed and one for low. Most washers (as well as air-conditioners and many smaller gadgets) use that type of technology. You can easily spot a high speed and low speed winding on the motor. You washer chart makes it obvious, for one thing. And there are three or four wires running from the motor instead of only two. In the case of a two speed motor, it is nearly impossible for the motor itself to run slow when it should be running fast. Since the change is made by a switch, usually within the timer mechanism, the motor is either on and on at the correct speed or it is off. There is little chance for the switch to be pointed in the wrong direction.

If your washer does not spin at all, look on the chart for those parts that should be on during the spin cycle. In the machine in Figure 146, the "on" parts include the spin solenoid, the drain valve, and the electric motor high speed winding.

While the washer timer is turned to "spin," you can get down on hands and knees, with flashlight, and see whether each of the appropriate items are on when they should be on. Likewise, make sure that the rest are off when they should be off. This is where togetherness is especially nice. If someone kneels and watches as you slowly turn the timer on and off, or help it through a complete wash cycle, the internal examination will be completed faster and with more certainty.

Once a faulty part has been isolated, don't immediately assume that the part itself is at fault. It might be the connected wires, especially if they pass through or are fastened onto moving parts, which unfortunately is too often the case in many machines.

By now, you should be somewhat of an expert at locating and patching errant wiring, so just a few specific words are needed here. With the machine disconnected from the electric current, try to pull off the various interchangeable connectors. If you can't pull them loose with gentle tugs, they are tight enough. Let well enough alone!

Follow all of the involved wires to both ends to make sure that all connections that should be connected *are* connected. Then, with the plug back into the wall outlet and the washer turned on at the ailing function, gently use a stick to bend all of the wires linking the malfunctioning parts to check for broken wires beneath unbroken insulation or loose wires your visual check did not spot. That condition will be signalled when the machine suddenly jumps into life but quits almost immediately after the stick is pulled out. Make sure that your hands are always out of the way so if the machine jumps to life, your hands won't jump with it.

If you have pretty definitely narrowed the problem down to a particular part—or maybe you're not really so sure, and it's narrowed down to a couple of possible parts—head for a supplier and buy new parts. Most washing machine parts are surprisingly inexpensive. All of the various levers and solenoids and valves and belts are dollar or few dollar items.

The pump and timers are somewhat more costly. About the only really budget-breaking parts on a washing machine are the transmission and the electric motor itself. Before deciding conclusively that a motor has burned out, first make sure that the various protective devices such as thermal overloads are okay. They should be marked on the machine diagram and come complete with distinctively colored wire leads too. See the chapters on motorized gadgets and power tools for more details on motors.

If you have conclusively narrowed down your washer's difficulties to a defective pump, you can take it apart to see if the soggy condition is caused by worn bearings, damaged impellers (those gearlike pieces inside that literally throw water through the pump) or just plain pileups of dirt, hair, lint, safety pins, and other debris (see Figure 185). Pumps vary, of course, from maker to maker. Some have a single chamber and set of impellers, some have two.

Replacement gaskets and impellers are cheap. Even an entirely new pump itself costs less than the hourly rate of a service person coming into your home. If you strip down the pump yourself (making sketches as you go if it deviates much from the model drawing shown here) and spend a few dollars for parts, you've saved a lot. If you strip down the

298

*When
Major
Appliances
Become
General
Nuisances*

pump and goof, you buy a new pump and still save some money. Plus you gain a lot of self-esteem and confidence enough to try an even more complex job next time.

You will have to disconnect the pump from its source of power, the motor. Then remove it from the washer chassis, a matter of a few bolts. Finally, the hose connections have to come loose. See Figure 147 for basic types of hose clamps.

The transmission on automatic washers is more complicated than a pump, but no more formidable. You will simply have to make a more elaborate sketch of where the parts are located. Most transmissions are filled with oil or grease, so spread papers beneath your work when resolving what you are certain from your complete troubleshooting procedure is an ailing transmission. At the same time, try to find out what caused the transmission failure:

> Steady overload of clothes?
>
> Someone who continually twists the timer control through several cycles with the switch in the "on" position?
>
> Just a gradual wearing out?

This condition will usually be announced by scraping, grinding, or rasping noises, which grow progressively louder with ensuing months, weeks, or days, depending upon how fast the gears are failing.

Figure 148 shows several manufacturers' transmission blueprints.

Figure 147   Hose clamps and how to loosen them. (reverse to tighten.)

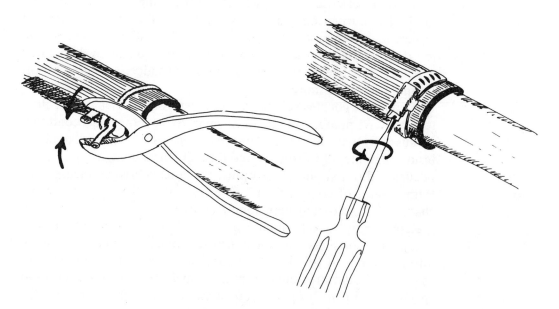

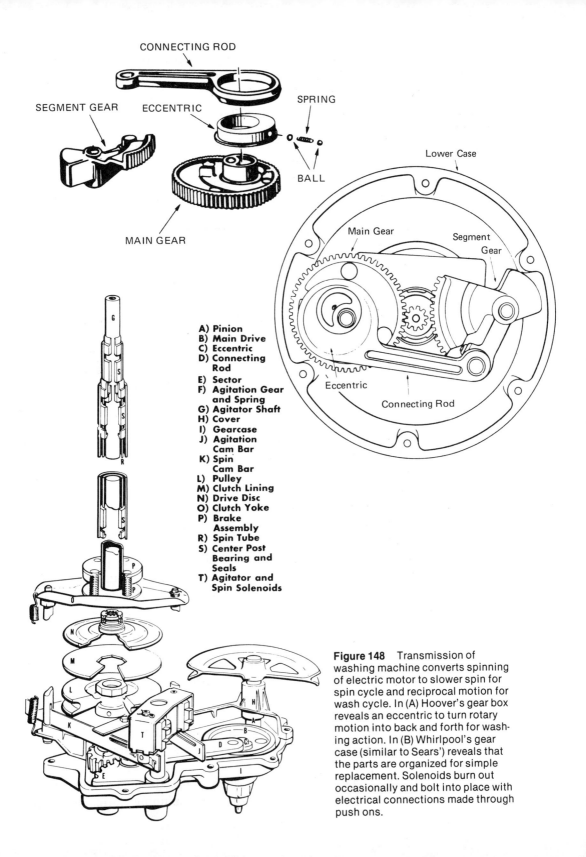

CONNECTING ROD

SEGMENT GEAR ECCENTRIC SPRING

BALL

MAIN GEAR

Lower Case

Main Gear

Segment Gear

Eccentric

Connecting Rod

A) Pinion
B) Main Drive
C) Eccentric
D) Connecting Rod
E) Sector
F) Agitation Gear and Spring
G) Agitator Shaft
H) Cover
I) Gearcase
J) Agitation Cam Bar
K) Spin Cam Bar
L) Pulley
M) Clutch Lining
N) Drive Disc
O) Clutch Yoke
P) Brake Assembly
R) Spin Tube
S) Center Post Bearing and Seals
T) Agitator and Spin Solenoids

Figure 148 Transmission of washing machine converts spinning of electric motor to slower spin for spin cycle and reciprocal motion for wash cycle. In (A) Hoover's gear box reveals an eccentric to turn rotary motion into back and forth for washing action. In (B) Whirlpool's gear case (similar to Sears') reveals that the parts are organized for simple replacement. Solenoids burn out occasionally and bolt into place with electrical connections made through push ons.

300

*When
Major
Appliances
Become
General
Nuisances*

Your sketches might look similar as you progressively remove one part after another. Many of the parts within a transmission are strictly nickel and dime items. Others are worth a dollar or two. But if you try to replace the entire transmission as a way to avoid tampering with what you think is a mysterious cast iron housing, you might just be better off starting over with a whole new machine. So with that economic reality in mind, what have you got to lose by tackling the thing?

Even the motor is not beyond household fix-it people whether or not you've ever tackled major appliance repairs before. Despite the fact that it is the largest, most expensive, perhaps even the most mysterious part of an appliance, it too fits into the logical troubleshooting scheme set up in Chapter 1.

For the motor's own protection, a thermal overload device is often hooked into series with the wires that supply electricity to the motor. Just like a thermostat, the thermal protector is sensitive to heat, in this case the heat of the motor itself. Under normal operating conditions, the protector's internal contacts allow electricity to flow to the motor, but should the going get rough and the motor windings start to overheat from internal overexersion or a mechanical breakdown elsewhere, the thermal overload device would open up and keep the motor from burning up.

As a rough test, a properly functioning washing machine motor should feel about as warm as toast freshly popped out of the toaster. If you find that the motor case is so hot that it is extremely uncomfortable to touch, the thermal overload device *may* have tripped. After that occurs, most modern devices will reset themselves automatically once the motor and thermal protector have cooled sufficiently. A few require manual resetting, but in that case a reset button should be quite obvious.

What should come to your mind about this point is *why did the thermal protector trip anyway?* An overloaded machine is the most obvious culprit. A household accustomed to laundering a lot of wash and wear or lightweight fabrics may toss in a few machines full of big towels after a summer at the beach. The towels soak up many times more water than synthetic blouses and shirts, and create a very heavy load, so the thermal protector snaps open. This may leave you and the wringing wet towels stranded temporarily, but be thankful it's only temporary. If the motor burns out, the repair takes plenty of muscle power and money.

If your motor does feel hot, wait for it to cool down to see if the washer works okay again. If so, remember the lesson. If not, look further.

Whatever couples directly or even indirectly to a motor can be jammed and preventing the motor from spinning normally. Some-

*When
Major
Appliances
Become
General
Nuisances*

times it is hard to tell a mechanical jam from an electrical malfunction, such as a defective condensor or a thermal overload.

To find out if mechanical problems are keeping the motor from starting, pry off the belt, assuming you are servicing a belt-driven appliance, and again try to start the motor. If it spins into renewed life, then you can almost eliminate the electrical malfunction possibility. Then trace the mechanical path from the belt, to the driven pulley, and through whatever mechanical gadgetry is driven by the motor, which has just proven to be healthy after all.

Assuming you already eliminated the basic troubleshooting matters such as fuses, plugs, and controls, and also assuming you eliminated the likelihood of mechanical jam-ups keeping a motor from starting, and assuming that you pretty well ruled out thermal overload as the cause, then the *condensor* is a likely item to explore.

It really is necessary to go in such a roundabout fashion up to the condensor because there is little that a household repair person can do to determine electronically if the little condensor is good or bad. If you have a neighborhood TV repair shop, he *might* be able to venture an opinion with the help of test instruments. Otherwise buy from the TV or electronic repair shop an electrolytic capacitor. In the electric motor field, this part is called a condensor and in the electronics or TV field it's known as a capacitor.

The TV shop probably will not have an exact replacement condensor since motor condensors and TV capacitors have substantial differences and slight electrical differences. The shop may not even have a close replacement. Always take a *higher voltage rating* in the replacement part. Try not to go more than 25 percent above or below the *original capacitance rating.* If necessary, buy two smaller capacitors and twist their matching leads together, positive to positive, negative to negative. Example: Your motor's condensor is rated at 40 mfg. 200 volts. The neighborhood TV repair shop has only 25 volt and 1000 volt capacitors. Take the 1000 volt size. Also, the shop has only 20, 25, and 100 mfd sizes. Take two of the 20 mfd size. Twisted together they will equal a 40 mfd. capacitor.

By all means don't spend a lot of money buying capacitors in your TV repair shop. This is only a test procedure, and the capacitors will be left in place only long enough to make sure whether or not a defective condensor is bugging your machine.

It is usually possible to bend the leads on your test capacitor to accommodate the motor push-on connectors. Make sure that none of the bare electrical wires will touch each other or other metal parts when you take your hands away. If necessary, wrap the temporary leads with electrical tape.

Once the makeshift new condensor is in place, try to start the motor

302

*When
Major
Appliances
Become
General
Nuisances*

once again. If it jumps into action, your test has proven its point. You can leave the test rig in place for a few days while you go out and buy an exact replacement for the obviously defective old motor condensor. It is not always necessary to buy replacement condensors from the maker of your appliance. Check the motor plate for the name of the motor manufacturer, and buy your replacement part from the nearest shop that handles parts for your brand of motor or appliance.

If all else has failed, then the motor may indeed have died on you. By the time you have conclusively reached that conclusion, the appliance is probably so well taken apart that you might just as well pull the motor out yourself. They often weigh 10 to 25 pounds but are not awkward to handle.

By dragging a sick motor into a repair shop, you certainly save paying for a repair person to drive to your home to dismantle the appliance for you. And you might save yourself a good deal of money and time at a motor repair shop.

Notice that the appliance manufacturer was not named as the place to take a burned out motor. Your choice in such a place is almost always limited to "We've got a new replacement motor. Take it or leave it." And you take it, paying full price of course, because the clothes need washing and drying or the furnace needs a blower. In a motor shop, the repair technician may be able to spot a relatively simple defect in your old motor and fix it inexpensively for you, and he'll be making a few well-deserved dollars in the process.

If your old motor is beyond immediate repair, a motor shop may be able to offer a variety of replacements. The case size and mounting facilities of most motors are quite well standardized. A new or rebuilt Westinghouse motor, for example, can replace a General Electric motor or vice versa.

Washing machine motors are a special breed in some ways. They are designed for the purpose of operating automatic washers and nothing else. Generally, a washer motor should be replaced only by another washer motor. And a washer motor should only be used in a washer, not a dryer or a blower. But you can switch around manufacturers and other features if a motor shop offers you a bargain. Just make sure that the replacement motor matches the old one in three ways: 1) the motor shaft and mounting holes match; 2) it has at least as many horsepower as the old; and 3) if the old motor was a two speed model, the new one should be also.

Most motors on washers or other appliances couple to mechanical devices via a pulley and belt system. One textbook estimates that 60 percent of all mechanical problems with washers stem from improperly adjusted belts. That figure is worth keeping in mind.

303

**When
Major
Appliances
Become
General
Nuisances**

Belts do break now and then. When that happens, take the old one to a hardware store or appliance dealer and get an exact replacement. They come in various lengths, widths, and materials. Figure 149 shows how to get belts on or off that last pulley.

Ordinary wear also gets to many belts. Look for signs of cracked rubber or frayed fabric cords on your belt. If the inner surface, the part that makes contact with the pulleys, is very shiny, your belt is ready to be retired. On most blowers, dryers, and on some washers, the belt can be replaced without having to remove half a dozen pieces

Figure 149 Prying belt off a pulley is a matter of one screw-driver and a bit of muscle power.

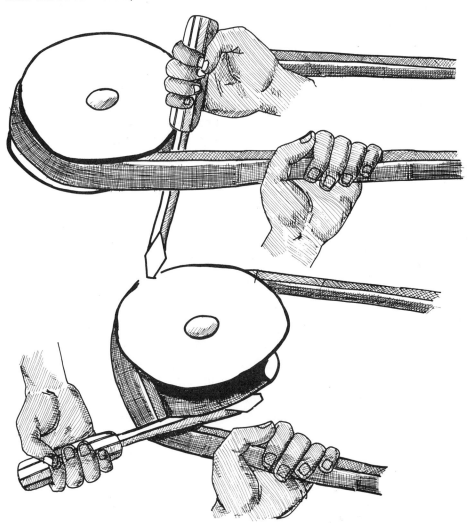

304

*When
Major
Appliances
Become
General
Nuisances*

of hardware such as springs, hoses, clamps, and couplings. Others will require a bit of patient logic to unscramble the belt from the washer insides.

The common tendency of lay people is to *want* to tighten the pulley *excessively* but find they are *unable* to tighten it *sufficiently.* In every appliance that uses a pulley, there should also be a simple adjustment, usually a screw or bolt that will tighten or loosen the pulley and belt system with the mere turn of a wrench or screwdriver. In the fortunate event that your machine has such an adjustment, the pulley you've tracked down—or at least suspect—as the cause of loss of power, erratic performance, and other maladies can be tightened to restore power, which otherwise would be lost to a slipping belt.

The advent of mysterious noises also could be caused by an overly tight pulley. A really overly tightened pulley might be able to keep an electric motor from starting, or at least slow down its ability to reach full speed quickly, and that causes extra heat. And *that* leads to a shortened life-span.

As a general rule, tighten a pulley with an adjustment screw only as far as you can comfortably turn the appropriate screwdriver or small wrench. The ritual is a bit less precise on those cheaply made machines in which the repair person has to force the pulley manually until the belt seems to be tight enough, and then try to find one spare hand to tighten a set of bolts hopefully somewhere nearby. In such a machine, you have to pry against the pulley with a small wrecking bar, tire iron, or similar tool. In a pinch, use a large screwdriver even though it's the wrong tool.

Pry as hard as you can when tightening a pulley. Then, assuming you have already laid out a wrench of the proper size, quickly tighten down the necessary bolts to hold the pulley in place before you relax your pressure.

Once you hope that the pulley is properly tightened, try out the machine to make sure it is working. If the belt is too tight, you will have to repeat the above ritual, but employ a little less muscle. Vice versa if the belt turns out to be too loose.

What is too tight and too loose? Most repair manuals duck the question altogether. A few offer a specific figure. Here is a general one you can use for a start: for every *foot of belt length*, the belt should be free to give ¼ " when you push sideways against it. Select a spot where the belt makes its longest jump between two pulleys to make the test (see Figure 150).

After tightening a belt as far as you think it should go, if slipping is still a problem and the belt shows no obvious signs of old age, buy a small tube of *belt dressing.* It is a sticky, abrasive kind of material that

Figure 150 On washers and dryers using pulley systems, the belt is probably too loose if there is more than a half inch of play (A) at mid-point of belt. There are several ways to tighten (or conversely, loosen) the belt. Some have a threaded adjustment (B) attached to the pulley shaft. Others require you to loosen the pulley and shove it into a tighter position (C) while you then tighten (D) the pulley's nut.

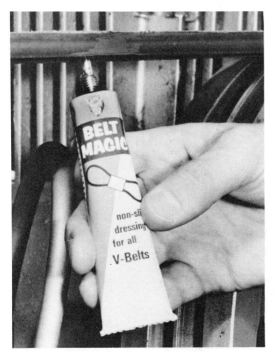

Figure 151 Pulleys that slip cause appliances to lose power. If you suspect a slipping pulley, you can cure the problem with sticky stuff known as belt dressing.

increases friction between belt and pulley. Belt dressing can eliminate most of the slippage that sometimes plagues an otherwise well-adjusted system (see Figure 151).

CLOTHES DRYER

A dryer is a deliciously simple piece of machinery for all its usefulness. Most of its vital parts are made of sheet metal, the drum, and air ducts. It turns at low speeds so bearings are not often a problem.

The electric motor is the principal moving part in every dryer. A pulley attached to one end of the motor slowly turns the drum and a blower attached directly to the other end, generally, sucks air through the drum and blows it out the vent.

With the exception of their source of heat, gas and electric dryers are identical in almost every detail. Your own brand no doubt varies from the sketch of parts in a typical dryer shown here, but the basic function of every part remains essentially the same.

Like the washing machine, a dryer cannot instantly do everything

Figure 152 Layout of a typical dryer, whether electric or gas. Arrows indicate flow of air.

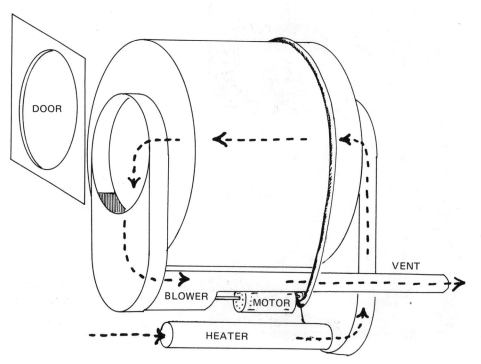

for every washable item. Most household dryers are designed to hold less than 10 pounds of clothes, *dry weight.* The drying capacity can generally remove about 9 or 10 pounds of water from wet clothes in an hour.

So, if you get the feeling that the appliance isn't doing its job well, maybe hasn't done its job well since installation, run a simple test. Take about 8 pounds of dry clothes, wet them until their weight totals nearly 18 pounds, and then run them in the dryer for an hour. In that time their weight should be back to the original 8 pounds by loss of the water.

In so many cases, what seems to be a dryer hangup really belongs to the owner. But if not, standard troubleshooting procedures, plus specific hints from this section, should enable you to locate one of the very few possible dryer maladies: a heater and its connections to the electric or gal lines; a thermostat to keep the heat near its proper level; a safety thermostat to keep the dryer from overheating in case the first thermostat fails; a timer, which controls how long the clothes tumble and which, in some dryers, doesn't measure time at all but operates off a sensor that turns the machine off when the moisture level of the vented air has dropped to a low enough level; and a safety interlock, which prevents the dryer from being turned on by simply closing the door, something which children could and would tragically do from the inside.

There is little that can go wrong with an electric heating element. Either it works or it doesn't. There is little chance for a heater to become only partly defective. But the *voltage* supplied to the heater can slip. If the dryer has never worked well, check the appliance name plate to see what voltage is specified. It should be 205, 220, or 230 volts, maybe even some other value. Then check with your local power company to find out what voltage actually is being supplied to the machine.

A 230 volt heater unit operated on a 205 volt supply line will do a very slow job or drying your clothes. Conversely, a 205 volt heater operated on 230 volts might make the thermostat turn the equipment on and off too frequently for efficient, long-lived operation. It is the responsibility of the dealer to make sure you are given a dryer with a correct heating element. But you will find replacement elements are surprisingly inexpensive if you have to do it or have it done yourself.

The 220 volt current in electric dryers is very dangerous if not treated with considerable respect. This is doubly true of dryers installed in damp basements. No repairs should be made while the dryer is connected. *None!* And any repairs or parts replacements you do make should be at least as well insulated and well grounded as what you found there.

308

*When
Major
Appliances
Become
General
Nuisances*

Replacing an aged or damaged heating element is generally a very simple matter: 1) disconnect the electricity; 2) locate the defective heater by following the heavy wires if necessary; 3) identify the size and model number of the heater to make sure you have an exact replacement; 4) remove the old heater, being careful to save all of the hardware; 5) install the new heating element, being careful that the black, white, and red wires (or whatever other colors the manufacturer used) go onto the same terminals they came from; and 6) test the new heater carefully at a bit of a distance after plugging the dryer back in.

A gas dryer's heating element is more complicated than its electric counterpart because it has to guard against the gas being turned on but not ignited. The safety arrangement in most gas dryers is identical to the one used in most gas ovens—a Baso Valve.

A Baso Valve keeps the main gas input line shut off unless it sensitive electromagnet is activated by a small electric current from a device known as a *thermocouple.* There is no need to understand *how* a thermocouple works, only that it does. In the presence of heat from the dryer's pilot light, a thermocouple internally generates a small electric current just like a battery. And that current is enough to power the Baso Valve's electromagnet, which in turn allows gas to flow into the main burner whenever the knob or thermostat chooses.

If the pilot light is not lit, there will be no heat. And without heat there will be no current from the thermocouple placed just over the

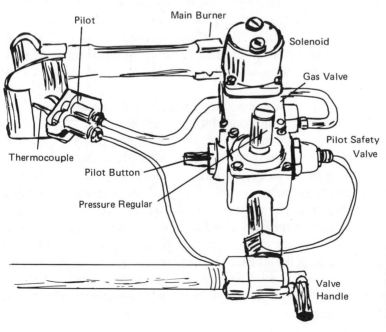

Pilot

Main Burner

Solenoid

Gas Valve

Pilot Safety
Valve

Thermocouple

Pilot Button

Pressure Regular

Valve
Handle

Figure 153 Ignition system of a typical gas dryer. Most parts are readily replaceable with standard gas valve fittings.

309

*When
Major
Appliances
Become
General
Nuisances*

pilot light. The Baso Valve's electromagnet keeps the gas shut off, and everybody will be happy because if the main gas valve opened without a pilot light to ignite it, the gas would accumulate and eventually reach explosive proportions (see Figure 153).

The Baso Valve actually doesn't figure prominently into the workings of your gas dryer or gas oven as long as everything is functioning well. Like the insurance policy tucked away, you're happiest when you don't have to use it. It is impossible to ignore the presence of a Baso Valve totally, however, since it is generally built into a single piece of hardware for use in gas ovens or gas dryers. Often repair manuals and schematic drawings give it another name. From that unit, tubes carry gas to the main burner and also to the pilot light, if any.

The pilot light, of course, is about the first place to check when a gas dryer stops drying. If it goes out too often, adjust it according to instructions in the section on gas stoves.

On gas dryers with pilot lights, the thermocouple senses whether or not the pilot is lit. If it is, the *pilot safety valve* opens electrically and allows gas to reach the solenoid, another electrical valve.

Pilot safety valves and thermocouples can be tested only with an electrical instrument called a millivoltmeter. If you do have one or can borrow one, hook one lead to the connection between the thermocouple and the pilot safety valve. The second lead hooks onto the body of the safety valve. The safety valve should always be closed when the voltage is less than 12 millivolts (12/1000ths of a volt) and should never be closed when the voltage is more than 16 millivolts.

If the thermocouple is putting out adequate voltage, it is okay. But if the safety valve is open or shut at the wrong voltages, it is not okay. The two gadgets can be replaced separately. Both items are inexpensive and simple to replace. The safety valve unscrews from the main gas valve body. And the thermocouple either unsnaps or unscrews from the burner assembly. In both cases, first disconnect the cable that joins the two. Close the gas shutoff valve before attempting repairs.

On any parts that control gas, it is very important that whenever you take threaded connectors apart or put in new threaded parts such as the pilot safety valve, you use plumber's dope, the sticky stuff sold in cans or tubes at hardware stores and most parts dealers. Threads do not contain liquids such as water very well without a generous application of dope to fill the gaps. And without dope, gas seeps through the threads with great ease.

After gas is allowed to pass through the open pilot safety valve, it next reaches the solenoid. The solenoid operates off normal house current as a rule, about 115 volts, and snaps open whenever the

When
Major
Appliances
Become
General
Nuisances

control thermostat calls for more heat. With the solenoid open, gas flows to the main burner and heats the dryer until the thermostat reaches its upper limit. Then current to the solenoid is shut off and it clicks shut.

You should be able to hear the solenoid clicking open and shut as a way of testing both the solenoid and the thermostat contacts. It's better to have a helper when you run this test. Someone works the thermostat control while someone else listens down underneath where the gas controls are located.

With the dryer turned on and at its lowest heat setting, twist the thermostat control to its highest setting. That should produce an audible click at the solenoid for someone else to hear. And gas should flow to the main burner almost instantly, there to be ignited by the pilot light. Also, going from the highest setting of a well-heated dryer to the lowest thermostat setting should produce a click as the solenoid shuts off the gas flow.

The presence of that telltale click indicates that both the solenoid and the control thermostat contacts are working well. If you don't get a click, you must figure out if the thermostat or the thermostat contacts or the timer contacts or the solenoid itself is haywire. Or a combination.

You can buy a new solenoid inexpensively, and it takes about 10 minutes to install one since the job usually involves little more than four screws and two push-on wire connectors. So if you know a parts distributor for your brand of dryer, one fast troubleshooting technique might be to stick in a new solenoid. And check the wiring while you're at it. Ironically, this is the same kind of "repair" technique used by many pros—replace parts until you find the one that was defective. But then it's your money they're spending. You might want to take a more patient approach with your dryer and your money.

Space is rather limited under a dryer, which is why the manufacturer mounted the entire gas burner and valve assembly with two or three easy-to-remove screws. If you shut off the gas valve, disconnect the gas line downstream from the shutoff valve, and remove the few mounting screws generally located under the main burner, you will have the whole burner assembly sitting on your kitchen table or basement workbench in 15 minutes.

The solenoid can be tested with 115 volt house current. To do so, you need a cord with a standard household electrical plug on one end and thin but bare wires on the other. If this is the first time you have used live 110 volt current for a test, you will no doubt feel more secure running this *cheater cord* through some sort of switch, whether it be on the wall, in a lamp, in the cord itself, or simply plugging and unplugging the cord from the wall in lieu of a more formal switch.

311

**When
Major
Appliances
Become
General
Nuisances**

Wrap the bare wires carefully around each of the two connector points on the solenoid. Then plug in the cheater cord and flick the switch. You should hear the click if the solenoid works. If not, replace it with a new one. (Needless to say, you should not grab the bare wires *after* you've plugged in the cord.)

Don't leave the power turned on to the solenoid for more than an instant. Someday some manufacturer may decide to use one that operates at voltages below 110. In that case, a very short exposure to 110 volts would still give you a valid test, but it should not harm the coils inside the solenoid either.

You can buy a replacement gas valve assembly that includes nearly everything we have been discussing—solenoid, pilot safety valve, the pilot button that lets gas bypass the safety valve only while you are lighting the pilot, and miscellaneous hardware. The price on such a gadget is about 20 percent what the whole dryer cost in the first place, a factor worth weighing before rushing out to perform lazy repairs.

More and more gas dryers, plus other gas appliances, are made without pilot lights these days. A transistorized circuit generates a spark very much as your car's ignition system feeds the sparkplugs. And that spark ignites the main gas burner whenever necessary.

The electronic ignition system needs a Baso Valve to protect the dryer or oven from escaping gas in case of a malfunction. It operates just like the pilot safety valve already discussed. This time the thermocouple senses heat at the main burner, however. And the electronic circuitry for the ignition system includes a delay system on the Baso Valve because when the start button is pushed or the thermostat says "more heat," obviously there will be no flame yet to activate the thermocouple, which opens the gas safety valve.

The circuits for an electronic ignitor are rugged but do need replacing at times. They have to be replaced as a unit. In fact, the diagrams included with most dryers featuring the electronic ignitor simply have a blank box where the circuit should be and say "transistorized circuit" or words to that effect.

Often the electronic circuit board and the electrode unit, which actually sends the sparks showering into the gas, can be replaced separately. If your troubleshooting has narrowed down the trouble definitely to the ignition system, it will be hard to test whether the circuit or the electrode is to blame. Assuming you find no physical damage on either unit, you will get somewhat better than 50-50 odds by replacing the electrode unit first. If that doesn't do the trick, you will have to buy the circuit board too.

Controls and thermostats cause much more trouble than the hidden items such as Baso Valves, solenoids, electronic ignitors, and thermocouples. (Now we are back to where gas and electric dryers are about identical. And much that is said here applies equally well to ovens, furnaces, and even air-conditioners.)

Electrical controls of all sorts generally have contacts built into them to transfer electricity from one piece of equipment to another. It's the machine way of talking in this electronic age. Just as you push a doorbell button to signal the fact that you are at somebody's door, your clothes dryer thermostat signals for more heat by closing a set of contacts, which allow electricity to start flowing again. However, other equipment may be part of the electrical signal too. In the case of a dryer, there is a safety thermostat that has to give its "okay" before electricity flows all the way through the circuit. And the timer also has a set of contacts that must "okay" until the time is up and the load of clothes is ready to stop tumbling.

Every one of these sets of contacts generates heat and corrosion as it works. General air pollution can often add extra layers of corrosion to the contact surfaces. As these layers of dirt build up, they stop the flow of electricity altogether. Sometimes the interruption is intermittent—the appliance works one day and not the next, works one minute and not the next. Other times the interruption is permanent or at least permanent until you get rid of the accumulated dirt. But since you usually cannot get inside the control without destroying its usefulness, you will have to use an indirect cleaning method.

Balky control or thermostat contacts often can be cured with a shot of TV contact cleaner. The aerosol reaches into the crevices of the control and timer boxes via openings at corners, terminals, the control knob, and wherever else you can find a crack through which the fine spray can be directed.

Whenever trouble befalls an appliance, keep the control contacts near the front of your mind, and especially if the trouble is intermittent. Be very wary about replacing some electrically triggered part until you have satisfied yourself about whether any controls in that same circuit are working well. On appliances such as dryers, simple timers and simple temperature controls often can be replaced at less expense than the heaters and gas mechanisms they regulate.

There are two basic types of thermostats in common use today. We looked at the bimetal ones in Chapter 10. A bimetal strip seldom needs attention. But the attached contacts do. Unless you can solve the problem with TV tuner spray, the usual repair procedure with such an ailing thermostat is to replace it with a new one.

Figure 154A shows the second major type of thermostat, the *capillary tube and diaphragm* version. Its liquid filled bulb is inserted somewhere along the air passageways in a dryer as well as an air conditioner, refrigerator, or oven. No matter what kind of appliance this thermostat is used in, the bulb must not touch the metal cabinet and parts or

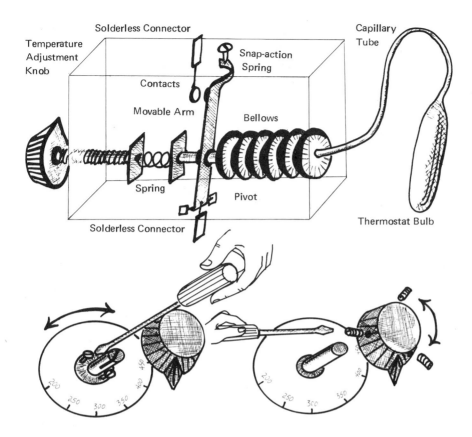

Figure 154 Operation of basic thermostat, whether for heating devices or cooling ones. There are two basic ways of adjusting a thermostat. One is by means of a movable number plate, another by means of a resettable knob. Others have internal adjustments.

the device will be sensitive not to the temperature of the heated (or chilled) air, but to the temperature of the cabinet. And that is often considerably different.

The bulb, tube, and diaphragm constitutes a single unit and must be replaced together. Some dealers call this a *bellows* type thermostat. On less expensive models, the switch contacts and setting knobs are incorporated into the essentially one-piece unit too, making total replacement easier but slightly more expensive.

Only two words of warning are really necessary for thermostat replacers. Treat the new capillary tube with loving care. Don't kink it, stretch it, or force it into place with sharp tools. And after installing the easy-to-replace thermostat, it is usually necessary to calibrate it. In other words, you have to twist the dial shaft until one of the "high," "medium" or "low" marks exactly matches the heat previously produced at the same setting.

313

In the case of your dryer, the air being blown out the vent, assuming your vents are not overly long, should be approximately 160°F. at its normal setting. You can easily measure the temperature with an oven or a laboratory thermometer.

Figure 154B shows how to set the new thermostat to its calibrated position. In case age has increased or decreased a dryer's heat, but in all other aspects a thermostat is still sound, simply follow the drawing to recalibrate the mechanism.

GAS AND ELECTRIC STOVES

Gas and electric stoves use a thermostat for regulating the oven in very much the same way that the thermostat regulated the dryer temperature. In fact, the capillary parts of both units are about identical.

The gas oven burner incorporates a Baso Valve like the dryer, and pilot lights or electronic ignitors are alike as well. (See how much you can learn by studying only the fundamentals of one appliance.)

Gas valves on the burners, usually covered with enamel or chrome handles, occasionally suffer from wear or lack of lubrication, or both. The usual single-action valve seldom can be replaced once parts wear out or get bent. They can, however, be lubricated if that is all that ails them. Use a good grease capable of withstanding 300°F. temperatures. Don't overdo a good thing, however, because too much grease can clog the small gas orifice. Modern ranges should not require additional grease in their lifetime. But if yours does, give it some grease but also give the matter some thought. You could be doing something to cause the situation yourself.

The double-action gas valve, used when a burner has a *simmer* setting, is a bit more complex than the single-action valve. But individual parts can be replaced, assuming that the original manufacturer can still supply them.

The tail nut on both valves is used to tighten the stem to prevent wobble and leaks in the valve. Overtightening however, makes the valve tough to turn on or off. Replace any valve that requires such a tight tail nut adjustment that turning the handle becomes a chore.

Figure 155 shows what burner flames look like when they get *too much* air, *too little* air, and *just the right amount* of air. To make a point, these photos go to a bit of an extreme, which you hopefully will not encounter in your own kitchen. In general, if a flame always has a distinct hissing sound like air escaping from a balloon, it probably is getting *too much air*. And if a flame usually has substantial amount of orange or yellow coloration, it probably is suffocating.

*When
Major
Appliances
Become
General
Nuisances*

Figure 155 Air-gas mixtures on stove. Top, too much air; center, just right, bottom, too little air. The air shutter is adjusted to reach an optimum flame.

Beneath the decorative top of your gas stove—the precise spot varies—is an opening that acts exactly like a shutter to admit more or less air depending upon how the repair person—you in this case— twists it. If your burner resembles some of the "before" shots, then locate the air opening for the particular badly behaving burner and spend a few minutes doing something constructive about it.

Pilot lights go out for reasons other than maladjustment. Fluctuating gas pressure in the line, even extreme changes in the outside air pressure, can force out delicate pilot lights. But they can stand adjust-

316

*When
Major
Appliances
Become
General
Nuisances*

ing if your pilot lights go out too often. Figure 156 also shows some typical locations where you can find various pilot light adjustment knobs or screws. The pilot flame itself should be big enough not to get extinguished frequently but small enough so that it consumes the minimum amount of gas. And it must always be small enough so that the pilot flame does not actually touch the metal cover usually placed over it. If that happens, large amounts of carbon develop and block the pilot.

In case you have doubts about which tubes are for pilot lights and which are for the burners, here is a rule of thumb. Pilot light gas supply tubes are about the size of common pencil lead. Supply tubes for gas burners are larger than soda straws.

Ideally, a pilot light works like this: You turn on the gas valve, which sends a mixture of gas and air to the burner. But nothing happens because there is no flame there yet. Some of the gas-air mixture moves through the flash tube, which is stuck close to the burner and ignites on the tiny pilot flame. The resulting flash ignites the gas accumulated above the burner, *unless* somebody has knocked the flash tube out of alignment with the pilot and the burner's flash holes. *And unless* somebody has spilled soup on the burner and clogged some of the fine holes pointing toward the flash tube.

The remedy for these situations should be obvious. But don't use toothpicks or broom straws to unplug the tiny holes. They will only plug them worse. A metal skewer, a stiff wire, or fine drills all work quickly and safely.

When you tamper with any gas installation, the problem of leaking gas must be kept in mind. But don't let it frighten you! You're

Figure 156   A gas stove valve and burner look similar to this in most kitchens. Arrows indicate adjustments for flame or pilot.

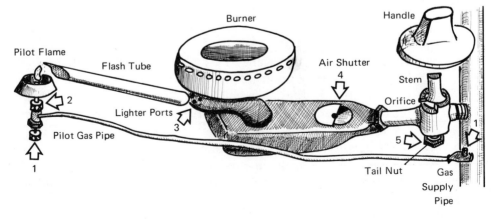

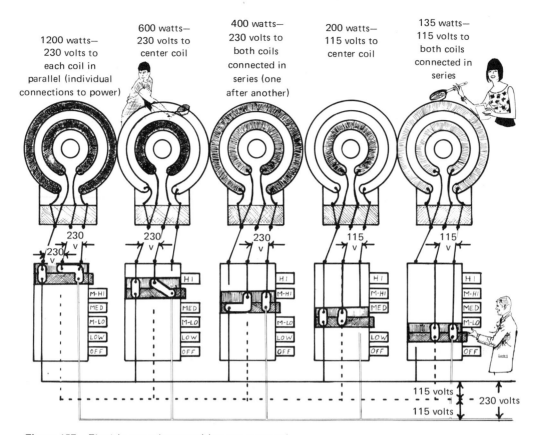

1200 watts— 230 volts to each coil in parallel (individual connections to power)

600 watts— 230 volts to center coil

400 watts— 230 volts to both coils connected in series (one after another)

200 watts— 115 volts to center coil

135 watts— 115 volts to both coils connected in series

Figure 157 Electric range burner wiring arrangement. Arrangements may vary considerably. This one has six different settings: some have more, some less. This one operates off 230 volts (3 wire) whereas others use different value. The purpose of this diagram, however, is to show the typical way in which burner switches distribute the three-wired electricity to the burners to generate differing amounts of heat. Remember, electricity that passes in a series through two coils creates less power than electricity that passes through two coils in parallel. Higher voltage creates more power than lower voltage.

probably safer making adjustments to your gas stove than you are driving downtown to a hardware store.

Once loosened, all pipes, valves, or any other gas-supplying vessels or tubes should be tightened to at least their original condition again and with a new coat of plumbers dope on the threads. Don't casually add new lengths of pipe to a gas installation. In many localities the normal gas is corrosive to iron pipe, and only copper or brass can be used.

It's been overdone as a joke, but houses have been blown up because a utility repair person used a match to look for a gas leak. Don't ever do that! Use soapy water instead. Smear it liberally along lengths of

317

318

When
Major
Appliances
Become
General
Nuisances

pipe where you have worked or where you suspect a gas leak. The leak, if any, will signal itself by blowing up a steady stream of soap bubbles.

Gas leaks are kept from becoming dangerous by ventilating the area thoroughly. Open a couple of doors or windows to blow away the gas. But remember, gas is heavier than air. Make sure it doesn't just settle into your basement through a kitchen archway. And then get busy to make the required repair.

Electric stoves, although far from foolproof, leave little room for home handy people to make repairs. They are powered by high voltage, and you must be certain that the range is fully disconnected from the electric power before tampering with switches, heating elements, or other internal parts.

Complicating the job is the fact that local power distribution varies so much that there are at least three entirely different ways your range could be connected to the utility lines. And voltages vary from 205 to 230. Even the stove top units are not standardized. They can have two, three, and even four internal elements.

Figure 157 offers a set of typical wiring diagrams to start you thinking about how switches and heating elements combine to provide the vast array of heat levels possible on a single electric stove element. You should fine a manufacturer's diagram for your specific range glued to it in some spot.

Armed with a basic blueprint or battle plan, you can refer back to Chapter 1 where continuity testing and testers were discussed. That technique can help you to track down burned-out heating elements, which can be replaced quite easily. Go to your parts distributor with your stove model and serial number since these will ensure that you go home with the right replacement element.

Defective switches can be isolated through signal tracing techniques too. Most are connected to the power and to the heating elements with simple push-on connectors. But before making the substantial investment in a new switch unit, be sure to try the TV tuner spray.

The electric range is really no more than an overgrown version of all these electric gadgets covered in Chapter 10. There you can find out why a long piece of heating element gives *less* heat than shorter lengths, what can go wrong with electrical switches used near heat and food, and how to clean heating elements. All of which goes to prove again, you can make a little knowledge go a long way.

Cooling It with Refrigerators and Air-Conditioners

13

ELECTRIC AND GAS REFRIGERATORS AND FREEZERS

One of the simplest of inventions ever was the icebox. But modern technology decided that the iceman and his horse-drawn wagon should be replaced by the power and light company. And so, we now have electric and gas refrigerators, freezers, and air-conditioners, which all depend on a very simple principle of physics that you probably learned in high school but no doubt have forgotten. Law A: When a gas is compressed, it liquifies and gives off heat. Law B: Conversely, when a liquid is changed into a gas, it absorbs heat in the process.

It would be convenient if refrigerator designers could rely only upon Law B. Alas, they would soon run out of liquid to change into gas, so they are forced to include an apparatus to keep changing the gas back into a liquid again. And that is only the first complication.

To simplify their problems but not necessarily yours, electric refrigerator designers use an extremely volatile liquid called Freon. The

319

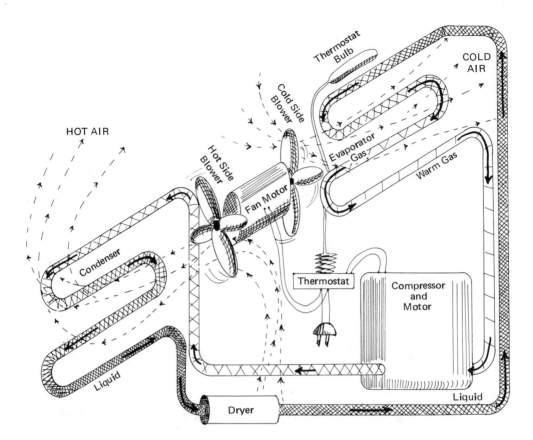

Figure 158 Schematic diagram of cooling mechanism used in refrigerators and air conditioners.

Labels in figure: HOT AIR, COLD AIR, Thermostat Bulb, Cold Side Blower, Hot Side Blower, Evaporator Gas, Warm Gas, Fan Motor, Condenser, Thermostat, Compressor and Motor, Liquid, Dryer, Liquid

trouble is that a liquid so active also escapes through the tiniest of openings. And that means that your entire air-conditioner system has to be sealed—the motor, the compressor, all the tubes, everything. One break in the seal and the whole thing needs an expensive overhaul.

The volatile liquid evaporates in copper tubes strung through the cooling chambers of your electric refrigerator. By doing so, it absorbs what little heat is present. Most of us think the refrigerator's insides are cold, but to a scientist, heat is present until −460°F. Therefore, the evaporating liquid absorbs what little heat there is.

The gas, once a volatile liquid, is drawn into a compressor by a vacuum. For a compressor to keep blowing compressed gas out of the output side, it has to draw gas in the input side. So, by attaching a pipe to the input side, a vacuum is obtained.

Once the gas is compressed in the compressor, it becomes very hot, **320** as Law A stated earlier. The compressed gas only needs to get rid of its excess heat to become a liquid again. By traversing another system of copper tubes, the hot gas gives off its heat, the same heat it acquired in the cooling chamber. And we are left with a volatile liquid once more, ready to begin the cycle all over again. And what becomes of the heat? That is transferred to the air in your kitchen. The condenser tubes are attached to the back of some refrigerators to dissipate the heat gently. On other models, the condensor tubes are strung out underneath and a fan blows the heat away.

Peculiar though it may sound, a refrigeration system works just fine by adding a gas flame and taking away the electric motor-compressor combination. The flame is to keep the gases circulating. Gas flame refrigeration systems have fewer moving parts—none—but must be more finely built and adjusted at the start. Therein lies the catch.

A bit of a flame bubbles water in an enclosed pot somewhere near the bottom of the gas refrigerator. The water bubbles rise, of course, and carry with them bubbles of ammonia gas. By the time the water vapor reaches the top of its percolator, just as in your coffee percolator, it enters a wider space so that the water bubbles fall back down into the pot.

The ammonia gas, however, because it is mixed with some very lightweight hydrogen gas, keeps rising to a condenser where it is cooled by the refrigeration chamber. The ammonia turns into a liquid again. The liquified ammonia is heavy enough so that it can carry the hydrogen gas with it and still flow, with the help of gravity, down the gently sloping tubes of the evaporator, which is located inside the refrigerator cooling chamber, just as it was in its electric counterpart.

While the droplets of ammonia meander through the refrigerator, they pick up heat. So, at the bottom of the maze of tubes, the ammonia is hot enough to become a gas again. Fortunately, there is a new supply of liquid ammonia forcing down from the top. That, added to the fact that falling water bubbles in the percolator create a gentle vacuum, pushes the hydrogen and ammonia gases back into the percolator to begin the cycle all over again.

With no moving parts to wear out, why doesn't the supersimple gas refrigerator replace the complicated electric models? For one thing, gas refrigerators require precision machine work, which is enough to make most manufacturers shudder. Besides that, the gas model would still have to be hooked up to electric power, and lots of it, because from one-fourth to one-half of all power consumed by a refrigerator is not spent on cooling but *on heating*.

People being people, they keep opening and closing refrigerator and freezer doors more often than manufacturers wish they would. And every time the door swings open, a cloud of moist air from the outside meets cold steel on the inside. The moisture quickly turns to ice. Consequently, doors on some early models had a habit of freezing shut. Today, the freezing problem is solved by adding a small strip heater to keep the edge of the door warm. When separate freezer doors were added, that meant one more heater.

Then came the days of *automatic defrosting.* Some engineers found a way to switch around the refrigeration process mechanically so that the liquids would temporarily warm the cooling coils to get rid of the accumulation of frost. Then they junked the mechanical defrosters in favor of another heater, a powerful one that gets turned on by a small electric clock twice a day to melt whatever frost has crystallized on the coils. But sometimes the defrosting cycle went awry because the water from the defrosting coils was supposed to run down a drain, and that opening at times had frozen shut. So—in some models there is one more heater at the defrost drain.

In years to come we may be living with heatless electric refrigerators, but in the meantime we have a lot of heaters to repair. Because it is the heaters and their equipment that go awry most often in refrigerators.

Since you now understand that your modern icebox runs more on heaters than on coolers, you can use the troubleshooting techniques learned in Chapter 1. You might also glance at your Yellow Pages under "refrigerator repair supplies." For most home repairs, that's a novel idea because it gives away some useful trade secrets. Shops who supply professional repair people advertise their most sought after supplies in biggest type. Defroster timers and thermostats are usually in the biggest type. These two parts are, in fact, the two most common headaches you are likely to encounter in refrigerator repair.

The Chapter 1 troubleshooting chart, leading you from the power source to the several powered items, works especially well for refrigerators. That, coupled with the schematic diagram on the back or inside a cover of your own model, can lead you systematically from the fuse or circuit breaker, to the plug, the cord, loose connections or broken wires, loose nuts on blower motors, and so on. From that you can move into replaceable items such as burned-out strip heaters, burned-out defroster timer, stuck or burned-out thermostat, faulty thermal overload or condenser on the main electric motor.

If you go looking for the compresser and its motor, you will find that they are in the same case. To ward off leaking refrigerant fluid, the two units are packaged in a single, hermetically sealed steel housing. If one burns out, they both must be replaced. And not only that, the replacement has to be added along with a new charge of refrigerant gas and the copper tubes resealed onto the new motor-compresser. That requires a highly skilled repair person, preferably a factory-trained one.

323

*Cooling It
with
Refrigerators
and Air-
Conditioners*

Since the defroster timer is so often replaced, let's find out why defrosting can be so vital. Today's machines sold for consumer use are very sensitive to slight changes, not necessarily because they are well constructed but also because the manufacturers want to get by with the smallest possible motor, smallest possible compresser, and shortest length of tubing. If the coils on your so-called frost free freezer or refrigerator frost over more than company engineers hoped for, the working mechanism has to work longer and harder to produce the same degree of cooling that the thermostat demands. Eventually, the compresser or its motor can overheat. And that can be the end of that. Unless a machine is very new, it is often more economical to replace the whole refrigerator then to pay for the costly compressor, motor, related parts, and labor.

Your first indication that you have defroster timer difficulties might be when the refrigerator seems to be warming up a bit. Once your suspicions have been confirmed, perhaps a day or two later, you might find that the evaporator coils are frosted over—if you knew how to find where they are hidden.

Figure 159 shows the insides of a simple refrigerator layout, similar to a Westinghouse or Coldspot. The *evaporator* coils cool the freezer portion directly. The *refrigerator* part of the box is cooled indirectly via a fan, which blows cold air from the freezer chamber into the refrigerator chamber. In this way a manufacturer needs to hook up only a single set of evaporator coils and a single defroster heater. With this design, if the coils frost over for whatever reason, the freezer generally stays at the correct temperature several days longer than the main refrigerator chamber.

An alternate scheme is to have two sets of evaporator coils, each one calibrated to keep their particular chamber at the prescribed temperatures. To keep the two sets of coils somewhat independent, additional equipment is added to the refrigeration system, such as a differential pressure control valve (D.P.C.). But the resulting unit does not lend the consumer any additional control over the relative temperatures between the freezer and the refrigerator compartments.

You might find that there are no coils and no condenser fan at the bottom of your refrigerator. Then they must be sticking out at the back of your model. And in that position, air circulates voluntarily around the warm coils to carry away the heat that the Freon gas extracted from the cool inside surfaces. No fan is used. General Electric, for one, favors this layout.

Refrigerator internal wiring, as is true with almost all appliances and many gadgets, is color coded. It matters very little whether or not you can recognize a defroster timer or a strip heater when you see one. If you can locate which item has the distinctly colored wire leads, you

324

**Cooling It
with
Refrigerators
and Air-
Conditioners**

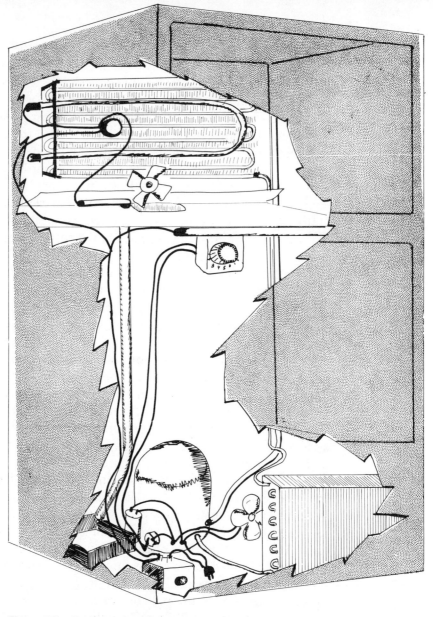

Figure 159 Exploded view of typical refrigerator with parts laid out in approximately correct positions. Compare them with Figure 158 to see their functions.

have made all the identification that is required. It's like a fingerprint. The schematic diagram also tells you in what part of the refrigerator the particular item is located.

Thermostat mechanisms are often concealed immediately behind the temperature control knobs, wherever they may be. "Mullion" is a term borrowed from architecture, which simply means the space built between the freezer cabinet and the refrigerator cabinet, a gap of some several inches on many refrigerators. Fans and evaporator coils are tucked into mullions along with maybe a dozen or so wires.

Most component parts of a refrigerator today are concealed behind plastic panels. And that includes many coils. If you spend a minute examining the edges of panels, particularly at the rear of each chamber, you will see that the panel is held in place by a handful of screws, generally with Phillips heads. Remove the screws, then the panel, and there is the coil, timer, heater, or terminal you seek.

To refresh your memory about push-on connectors and other appliance assembly tactics, go back to Chapter 12.

AIR-CONDITIONERS

An air-conditioner is little more than a refrigerator without a food box but with a bigger fan. A good many troubles with air-conditioners could be avoided in advance if you choose them well and install them with proper care.

Buying a home do-it-yourself air-conditioner became reasonable when manufacturers discovered a big market for what has become known as the *room air-conditioner.* It is a compact, self-contained fan and refrigeration unit with built-in thermostat that is said to be light-weight—actually 65 to 90 pounds. Most come complete with sliding side panels to facilitate quick window mounting—generally an hour or two of labor. They are advertised as "inexpensive to operate," about $5 to $10 a month during hot weather.

Unless your house qualifies as an antique, chances are you will be able to hook up at least one room air-conditioner to existing circuits. Before doing all of this choosing and fitting, however, you first should make certain that your house wiring is sound.

Buying and installing a room air-conditioner begins with a check of house wiring. If your fuse box has circuit breakers, the rated electrical load is printed on the handle, generally 15 or 20 amps for each individual circuit. If your house or apartment is protected by fuses, assume that 15 amps is the top load for each individual line. If you have to count fuses to check how many separate lines you have, screw them out so you can isolate which fuses serve which line. Most feeder lines are protected by *two* fuses, not one.

The National Electrical Code says that if an appliance draws more than 50 percent of a circuit's rated capacity, there should be nothing else on the same circuit. In other words, if you have an air-conditioner

326

*Cooling It
with
Refrigerators
and Air-
Conditioners*

that draws 8 amps, you should plug nothing else into that 15 amp circuit. The prevalence of 15 amp circuits is why manufacturers try so hard to keep their units rated at 7.5 amps. Another code requirement is that no more than 80 percent of a line's rated load should be used. That means a 15 amp circuit should not be loaded heavier than 12 amps. Starting up motors puts heavy demands on wiring, and that 20 percent leeway is necessary to prevent dangerous overloads and continually blowing fuses or tripping circuit breakers. And no matter how adequately wired your home may be, do not plug anything else into the same wall outlet as your air-conditioner.

Do not twist off that third prong that comes with the air-conditioner plug. The extra prong grounds the motor and controls to save you from a serious shock in case of malfunction. If your wall is not able to accept the third prong, see Chapter 9, which shows how to install a new wall outlet. And while you're at it, why not put in a grounded outlet controlled by a switch in the same unit.

Many air-conditioner headaches come from too many people adjusting the thermostat too often. Once you have set the thermostat to a comfortable level, pull the knob off if you have to. When people are home and hot, the switch goes on, otherwise, off.

Most room air-conditioners are rated at 6000 BTUs (British Thermal Units, a means to measure heating or cooling capacity), which is equivalent to ½ ton of cooling power under another system of measurement. You will get the widest selection and best prices if a unit near 6000 BTUs will cool the room you have in mind. But should your

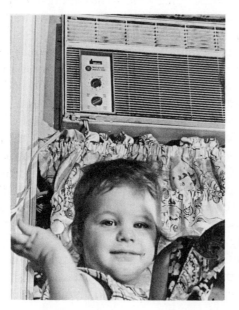

Figure 160 Air conditioner is ideally mounted at top of window and hooked up with grounded outlet to switch. That way it cools most efficiently and people are less likely to tamper with controls.

Customer _____ Estimate by _____ Date _____

HEAT GAIN FROM	QUANTITY	FACTORS					Btu/Hr (Quantity x Factor)
		NIGHT	DAY				
			No Shades*	Inside Shades*	Outside Awnings*	(Area x Factor)	
1. WINDOWS: Heat gain from sun.							
Northeast	___ sq ft	0	60	25	20		___
East	___ sq ft	0	80	40	25	Use	___
Southeast	___ sq ft	0	75	30	20	only	___
South	___ sq ft	0	75	35	20	the	___
Southwest	___ sq ft	0	110	45	30	largest	___
West	___ sq ft	0	150	65	45	load	___
Northwest	___ sq ft	0	120	50	35		___
North	___ sq ft	0	0	0	0		___

*These factors are for single glass only. For glass block, multiply the above factors by 0.5; for double-glass or storm windows, multiply the above factors by 0.8.

HEAT GAIN FROM	QUANTITY	NIGHT	DAY	Btu/Hr
2. WINDOWS: Heat gain by conduction. (Total of all windows.)				
Single glass	___ sq ft	14	. . . . 14	___
Double glass or glass block . .	___ sq ft	7	. . . . 7	___
3. WALLS: (Based on linear feet of wall.)			Light Construction Heavy Construction	
a. Outside walls				
North exposure	___ ft	30	. . . . . 30 . . . . 20	___
Other than North exposure. . . .	___ ft	30	. . . . . . 60 . . . . 30	___
b. Inside Walls (between conditioned and unconditioned spaces only)	___ ft	30	. . . . 30	___
4. ROOF OR CEILING: (Use one only.)				
a. Roof, uninsulated	___ sq ft	5	. . . . 19	___
b. Roof, 1 inch or more insulation.	___ sq ft	3	. . . . 8	___
c. Ceiling, occupied space above.	___ sq ft	3	. . . . 3	___
d. Ceiling, insulated with attic space above	___ sq ft	4	. . . . 5	___
e. Ceiling, uninsulated, with attic space above	___ sq ft	7	. . . . 12	___
5. FLOOR: (Disregard if floor is directly on ground or over basement.)	___ sq ft	3	. . . . 3	___
6. NUMBER OF PEOPLE:	___	600	. . . . 600	___
7. LIGHTS AND ELECTRICAL EQUIPMENT IN USE	___ watts	3	. . . . 3	___
8. DOORS AND ARCHES CONTINUOUSLY OPEN TO UNCONDITIONED SPACE: (Linear feet of width.)	___ ft	200	. . . . 300	___
9. SUB-TOTAL	x x x x x	x x x x x	x x x x x	___
10. TOTAL COOLING LOAD: (Btu per hour to be used for selection of room air-conditioner(s).)		___ (Item 9) X ___ (Factor from Map) = ___		

Figure 161 Use this chart to calculate how large a cooling capacity your new air conditioner should have. Too large, and you waste money as well as get inefficient cooling and dehumidifying. Too small, and the unit works overly hard to cool but doesn't last as long as it should.

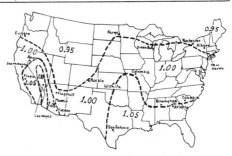

cooling requirements be considerably greater than 6000 BTUs, buying that size will be a waste of money.

A 6000 BTU air-conditioner is just about right for a 12 ′ × 15 ′ room with an insulated ceiling or lived-in rooms above, 2 average-sized windows facing other than west, well-insulated exterior walls, 2 or 3 people as the average occupants, and no more than 400 watts of lights and a TV or hi-fi going constantly. If you have doubts about whether your bedroom or living room qualifies for 6000 BTUs, go through the mathematics in Figure 161.

327

328

*Cooling It
with
Refrigerators
and Air-
Conditioners*

As the air-conditioning fad caught on, manufacturers also realized that they could package larger units very much like the so-called window air-conditioners. Now you can buy 12,000 BTU and even 20,000 BTU air-conditioners, which fit 120 volt 15 amp circuits and come with window-mounting hardware. So if you need a big one, or if you see a chance to cool two rooms at once, assuming both are used about the same times of the day, you might save some money on your initial investment and on monthly electric bills.

The mass-produced window air-conditioner is made to slip comfortably into the ordinary double-hung windows that are 2' to 3' wide. Some will go as narrow as 21", some expand to a width of 40". Although virtually all of the popularly advertised models are for 120 volts and 15 amp electric circuits, make sure that the specific item you pick out does fit your house wiring capabilities.

Select a cool spot to install your air-conditioner. If the sun beats down on a window all day, your unit there will have to work much harder to keep the room cool. The manufacturer's instructions will tell you simply to raise the window, put the air-conditioner into place, slide out the accordian-pleated side panels, and close the window. A few will include a mounting bracket for extra support. What the instructions fail to mention, however, is that such a two-minute installation job results in extra noise, extra work for the air-conditioner, and extra drafts, hot ones in the summer, cold ones in the winter.

A strip of 1" thick foam rubber should go beneath your air-conditioner to separate the noisy motor from the window sill, which will amplify the noise. A similar strip of insulation should go across the top before you close the window. Those sliding panels on each side of your window unit offer very little insulation. A piece of corrugated cardboard cut to the appropriate size and then painted or papered will be much better insulation. Plywood makes an even finer heat seal.

Any air-conditioner rugged enough to withstand a summer in the sun should also withstand a winter in the cold. Therefore, if you are cramped for storage space or tend to be a little lazy, or if you are really ambitious enough to want a nice-looking permanent installation, use pieces of ½" or ¾" plywood instead of the factory-built side panels. Such a technique is also a good way to get around having to buy a specially built model in case your windows are wider than the 40' standard size.

The possibility of mounting the whole unit at the top of your windows should not be overlooked either. It makes a beautiful way to keep little hands off the controls and often blocks less of your view through the window. An air-conditioner at the top of a window should perform more efficiently and also will keep some of the noise above ear level.

For added protection against drafts, squeeze some calking material around the entire permanent installation before you paint it. Remember, every draft that blows through the mount during winter also comes through in the summer and adds extra heat for your air-conditioner to struggle with.

Don't overlook the space between the bottom of your top window and top of your bottom window after mounting an air-conditioner. When the air-conditioner is in place, top or bottom mounted, a 2″ gap allows lots of wind to whistle in. Foam rubber makes a good, fast seal. But plywood *and* foam rubber is best for more permanent installations.

There is likely to be a drip from your window unit as it wrings moisture out of the sticky summer air. You want that drip to go outside, so tilt the unit slightly outward during installation. In New York City, among other places, allowing drips to fall onto the sidewalk is illegal. So a short length of rubber tubing often has to be stuffed into the drain hole to lead the water away, such as down the side of a building where it can evaporate before bouncing off someone's head.

All doors leading into the room being cooled should be closed. Archways may have to be fitted with inexpensive sliding doors. If the unit you have is significantly more powerful than the size and insulation of your room really requires, small open archways can be tolerated. But if the room and insulation factor keep your air-conditioner working close to its limit, you may have to check all doors and windows for fit. You can even nail weather stripping onto the bottoms of loose doors and windows to eliminate the loss of precious cool air.

Some neat people like to hang a plastic cover over the outside of their air-conditioner during winter. There's certainly no harm in doing that. What does help measurably is a generous coating of oil from an aerosol spray can so the blower and other exposed metal parts will be less likely to tarnish and to accumulate dirt or corrosion. If the user manual calls for periodic oiling and similar maintenance, the fall is a good time to do it.

You can be sure that any air-conditioner manufacturer who has included self-lubricating bearings *all around* will let you know it. Without that knowledge, assume that the blower motor can stand a few drops of oil. Compressor motors are sealed into an airtight box without oil holes.

Typically the oil holes on a blower motor are situated right above the bearings where the motor shafts leave the housing. Some oil holes are just dimpled slots in the side of a motor housing. Fancier ones look like teacups with a hinged saucer on top. Lift the "saucer" to add oil.

It is not always easy to reach oil openings on air-conditioner blower motors. At the very least you will have to slip off some part of the cab-

330

*Cooling It
with
Refrigerators
and Air-
Conditioners*

inet unless you can peek through the louvres from the *outside* and find a way to slip an oil can with an extralong, extraflexible spout into the vicinity of the motor's two bearings. Blower motors are mounted in the outer portions of air-conditioners to keep their noise and heat outside your living areas.

On some small General Electric models, for example, one of the bearings is mounted flush against the panel, which separates the inside from the outside. Your alternatives in such a case are limited. Either you unbolt the motor to reach the oil vent on that side or you squirt or spray oil directly on the little bit of bearing that is exposed. If you opt for the latter approach, apply oil several times during the cooling season. No blower motor, save for those few that do have genuinely self-lubricating bearings, will deliver efficient, quiet air circulation for more than a few years of use without some lubrication.

After maybe only two or three years without oil, a blower that needs regular lubrication will start to rattle, even grind, and the noise will get worse and worse until the motor is replaced. It would be economical if you could replace only the damaged bearings. But most air-conditioner blower motors do not offer that alternative. Keep this maintenance matter in mind when you select a new air-conditioner. Why not ask to see how easy it is to maintain the blower?

Replacing a fan motor requires that you buy the new motor from a dealer for the original air-conditioner manufacturer and at their price. The brand name makers who also turn out electric motors often design motors for their own air-conditioners that are so unique not even the best-equipped motor shop could duplicate them.

Many air-conditioner blower motors have very, very long shafts to handle a double set of blowers, one blowing outside air across the hot condenser coils and another blowing inside air across the cool evaporator coils. You have to handle them carefully or your efforts to unpack, inspect, and install such a motor might lead to its premature end.

It is generally worth your time to replace a worn or burned-out blower motor in any air-conditioner that has been in service for up to 10 years, assuming other parts are in decent working condition.

You might want to go back to Chapter 12 for the various simple techniques for analyzing and fixing whatever may ail a balky appliance motor. You can also reread the section concerning push-on terminals and related matters in that chapter.

About the only unique aspect of an air-conditioner motor is that the condensors for both the blower motor and the compressor motor are often built into a single container. If the ratings on each half of the unit are somewhat similar, the double condensor arrangement gives you a simple way to check whether a faulty motor is caused by a defec-

331

*Cooling It
with
Refrigerators
and Air-
Conditioners*

tive condensor. Simply switch the stopped motor leads over to the condensor terminals for the motor that does work (which means its condensor works too). Simple? Unfortunately, once you locate a bad condensor, you will probably have to go directly to a manufacturer's outlet to replace it, since they generally fit into a very precisely allocated amount of space.

Thermostats on air-conditioners are no different than what we have already discussed in the preceding chapter on clothes dryers. And the section on refrigerators covered how air-conditioners cool your air. The hermetically sealed motor-compressor combination used in air-conditioners is little different than the refrigerator unit.

What air-conditioners accomplish that refrigerators hopefully don't do is dehumidify the air. A properly designed air-conditioner passes the circulating air over the chilly evaporator coils to cool it, first of all, but also to wring out some of its humidity.

When air is cooled, it loses its ability to hold onto moisture. So the tiny drops of water that once were suspended in the air are helped to condense on the cold coils. The tiny drops merge into bigger ones and then slowly drip onto whatever the air-conditioner has beneath the coils. Hopefully the water will be able to flow smoothly out of a very large opening. In case your machine has a small opening, you may find water dripping out the front of your air-conditioner on a very hot and humid day.

That soggy spot on your carpet tells you that the time has come to get out whatever kind of makeshift tool will clean out the opening. Also, get out some implement such as a putty knife to scrape away the deposits that by then probably have gummed up the condensation tray. Third, get out your pen and write a nasty letter to whatever company manufactured the air conditioner.

Working with Power Tools

There are two areas of concern with power tools. How you can use or maintain them safely and intelligently is one. The other is how to fix them if they were used unintelligently or were made that way in the first place.

DRILLS

At the top of the power tool list is the inexpensive ¼″ electric drill. It is about the cheapest power tool a home can have, and one of the most versatile. Accessories are available to let you do a host of useful jobs, such as rough sanding, polishing, driving screws, drilling and countersinking holes in a single motion, mixing paint, carving or shaping, wire brushing, and it even drills holes!

For the simple job of drilling simple holes, an inexpensive set of drills for the electric drill do very nicely, assuming they are kept sharp. And the best way to keep them sharp is never to let them get dull in the first place. Rust dulls drills, so keep them out of damp drawers or

332

damp cellars if possible. If that is not possible, spray them with an aerosol oil can periodically, wrap them in an oily paper towel, and then in a plastic bag.

Heat also dulls a drill. When drilling through metal, you will have to use a little patience or the overheated tip of the drill will end up somewhat soft and round. (We will discuss this in more detail later.)

Precision is important if a drilled hole is to be useful. Measure the exact spot according to the measuring section in Chapter 4. A dot usually is not enough to mark the spot; use an X, one line to mark the precise horizontal location and the other for the precise vertical location.

Even before picking up the drill, make sure that the point of the drill will go down at exactly the proper point. Points can twist away as the drill spins around. Tap a little indentation into the wood or metal at the X. In wood, a gentle tap with a hammer and nail does well, but in metal a small *center punch* is much better. Since you are unlikely to buy one in advance, however, you may have to use a nail for the punch. Tap it hard enough with a hammer to dimple the metal surface (see Figure 162).

Try to stand as much above the work you are drilling as possible. This will help you to line up the drill so it will go squarely through the entire depth of the board or metal. If you keep aware of the fact that it is important to drill straight down through your work, you will probably be able to guide the drill on its true course with little mental or physical aggravation.

As the drill starts to penetrate the far side of the board or beam you are drilling, it usually will sliver the wood or bulge thin pieces of metal unless you plan ahead. You also might drill an unexpected and very unwanted hole into your best table, if that's where you decided to tackle some drilling project. If your work is laid securely atop a piece of scrap wood or even a small pile of corrugated cardboard, the drilled hole will end up neat and safe. For projects that involve a lot of drilling, a small vise will serve you well.

When drilling through metal, even small pieces, it is important that you put a drop of oil on the drill tip periodically. And if you are drilling through a deep piece of soft metal, the entire working length of the drill should be well lubricated. The oil lubricates the cutting edge and helps to keep it cool. Once the tip becomes very hot, it dulls very quickly and that lowers its cutting ability to practically zero. If the cutting goes on for more than five or ten seconds, add another drop or two of oil and continue to do this every five or ten seconds. Don't push too hard when cutting through metal because you will only generate excess heat but not extra cutting power. Drills actually cut toward the *side*. Study the tip of a large drill and you'll see why. So you

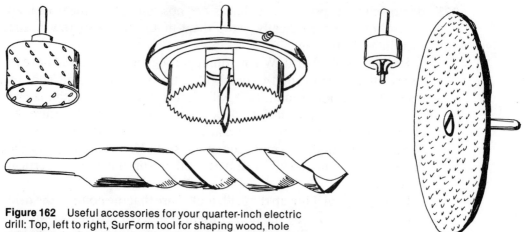

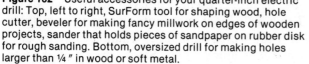

Figure 162 Useful accessories for your quarter-inch electric drill: Top, left to right, SurForm tool for shaping wood, hole cutter, beveler for making fancy millwork on edges of wooden projects, sander that holds pieces of sandpaper on rubber disk for rough sanding. Bottom, oversized drill for making holes larger than ¼ ″ in wood or soft metal.

need to apply only enough pressure to keep the drill firmly in contact with the metal.

The popular ¼″ drill actually can drill holes bigger than ¼″ in diameter. For holes in wood up to about 1″, cutting tools very similar to bits for a brace-and-bit are available. And for even larger holes, a sawlike hole-cutting tool reaches into the 3″ range. For cutting large holes in metal and plastic, a conventional metal drill is used except that the shank end is reduced by the manufacturer to ¼″ so that it will fit into that size of drill. (Larged-sized power drills are becoming popular enough so that their price is becoming reasonable.) The ¼″ drill gets its name from the fact that its chuck—the mechanical item into which the drills fit—will open up to ¼″ inch, which is a tool size that the motor in such a drill can generally handle with ease.

Also available are ⅜″ and ½″ drills, which not only have bigger chucks, but also bigger electric motors. Their motor is geared down to turn the chuck at a slower speed than the speedy ¼″ drill. The overall effect is that the slower, bigger drills bring considerably more power to the tool or drill stuck into the chuck. And they can take considerably more use or abuse.

SAWS

Sabre saws are probably the second most common power tool in homes. They are small, relatively inexpensive, and very versatile if you use your head at the same time you turn on the saw. Keep two things

334

away from the blade at all times—*your fingers* and *the cord*. Know where each of them is in relation to where the blade is going.

Beyond that, take it easy when you use a power saw. Don't shove on the blades too hard; be careful not to twist them sideways while cutting; don't let them overheat from excessive use; don't start the saw while the blade is touching something unless you do it deliberately and are ready for the rough and jerky start that will result.

Blades come in so many sizes and shapes that you can expect to get confused after your initial supply of blades runs out. Of crucial importance is the size of the blade shank; there are several basic sizes. Only one size will work well in your particular brand of saw. Find out what it is—if all else fails, try the user manual—and scratch it into the saw body or into your mind.

Beyond shank size, the blades basically come with teeth machined for ideal use in metal or ideal use in wood. For best results, always use a wood blade on wood, metal blade on metal. There is even a blade with a knife edge that is great for cutting linoleum, soft tile, and cardboard.

When cutting thin pieces of wood or metal, it is necessary to give them some added support if you don't want the sabre saw blades to pull the metal edges out of shape or sliver the wood. The most ideal solution is to package the thin materials, or at least the part of it that will be cut, in scrap pieces of lumber or cardboard. That means, however, that your accurate measuring will have to be drawn on the cardboard and not on the piece to be cut. If you are making a straight cut, common tape can be used to keep delicate materials from splintering.

Saw manufacturers advertise that the tool can cut through tremendous pieces of wood, not just thin plywood. And it will, but you will need patience. If you want to saw through lumber 6" thick, as at least one sabre saw seller promises, you will need a blade at least 6" long. And pulling that much steel through that much wood is hard work for the barely adequate motor in the saw. The blade heats up too, making it less sharp and less able to withstand as much twisting and jerking as a cool blade.

Therefore, cut accurately so as not to twist the blade when making corrections to your cutting path. And cut slowly so the blade and motor have a chance to cool off as you wade through a thick piece of wood.

Despite the best laid plans, a sabre saw blade may break before you take it out. And it will often snap off right at the saw shaft. Even if a $\frac{1}{16}$" piece stuck out, you could grab it with a pliers. But if none of the broken blade shows, what then?

Pick up the official size Allen wrench and loosen what is left of the blade. Plug in the saw, point the working end away from you and anything or anyone of value. And flick the switch on for a second or two.

The stub of your broken blade should pop right out. And unless you need a blade that is full sized, you can usually stick the broken blade into the saw and use it as is.

Circular saws are the answer for big jobs. Their motors are many times larger than sabre saw motors. And their blades are designed to handle straightforward sawing faster and better. The wider blade—a circle 7″ or bigger—cuts in a straight line better than the narrow sabre saw blade, which was originally intended to cut fancy circles and curves.

The way to use sabre saws applies to circular saws too—always know where your 10 fingers are when the saw is going and keep the cord away from the blade. It is very important that you use a three-wire grounded electrical outlet with power tools such as circular saws. In the first place, if an electrical malfunction takes place inside the saw, the electricity could use you as a wire unless the saw is properly grounded. Second, if you cut into the cord despite all precautions, the ground will draw off most of the hazardous short-circuited electricity.

Cutting through hard woods, wet woods, and even just cutting one large piece of wood after another heats up the blade enough to dull it. You will probably know when the blade has become dull just by the smoke that pours from your work then. The cutting also starts going very slowly and it will be very hard to stay on a straight line. A dull circular saw blade seems just to wobble up and down the line instead of toeing the mark. If you are planning to work on something important, it is a good idea to keep an extra blade handy. You can keep saw blades sharper longer by spraying them will silicone lubricant. Before every big cut, a quick squirt of silicone to each side of the blade works wonders.

Getting circular saw blades sharpened is not always easy. It requires someone with a good eye and a good feel for the use of a file or grinding machine. In many cities, the manufacturers of circular saws often have an office that, aside from selling tools and parts, swaps a sharpened blade for the dull one you turn in, for a fee. The price is generally right and it takes no more time than a walk or drive to the right office.

Cutting a straight line gets to be a problem for some people armed with either a circular or sabre saw. If you find your tool wavering off the line too often, add some sort of cutting aid. For cutting pieces not far from the edge of a board, metal cutting guides are available for most power saws, sabre or circular. Once you have adjusted the gadget for the proper width of board you want to cut off, all you have to do is keep the cutting guide firmly against the edge of your board and the cut will come out as straight as the edge of the board itself.

For cuts made farther away from the edge of a board, make your own cutting guide with a piece of straight lumber long enough to stretch the entire length of the cut. With C-clamps, fasten the cutting guide in place so that when you run the edge of your saw along the edge of the guide, the blade will fall exactly in the prescribed spot.

SANDERS

Once you have cut wood, you will probably want to smooth out the ridges left by the saw or put there by the weather that beat down on the wood while at the lumber yard. Unless you're more ambitious than most, you will want to use an electric sander to smooth out large wood surfaces.

Belt sanders are big and fast working. A relatively powerful motor spins the 2″, 3″, sometimes almost 4″ wide belt of sanding cloth at high speed to sand away the top surface of a board very quickly.

When using a belt sander or any other kind of power sander, it is important to let the sanding cloth do the sanding, not your muscles. In other words, don't push down on the sander very hard. It will only slow down the motor, which will heat it up and reduce the life-span of your tool. And by slowing down the sanding cloth, you may, in fact, slow down the sanding process.

Vibrating sanders are smaller and less expensive than belt sanders but not less useful in their place. Within this category is the *orbital sander,* which makes an arclike pattern. It is not as powerful as the belt sander but is cheaper to buy. And it can't be used for finishing sanding operations. The *line sander*, another vibrating tool, duplicates the back and forth motion of hand sanding, and that makes it valuable for finishing wood or paint jobs. When you read Chapter 19 on how to fix wood, you'll learn about specific kinds of sandpapers for specific kinds of problems.

MAINTENANCE OF POWER TOOLS

Power tool maintenance is simple but important. About once every year, more often if they are used frequently, each tool should be taken apart, cleaned, and relubricated. Generally a small handful of bolts, most of them with Phillips heads, holds the drill, sander, and saw together.

337   On a clean, uncluttered surface, remove each bolt and put it care-

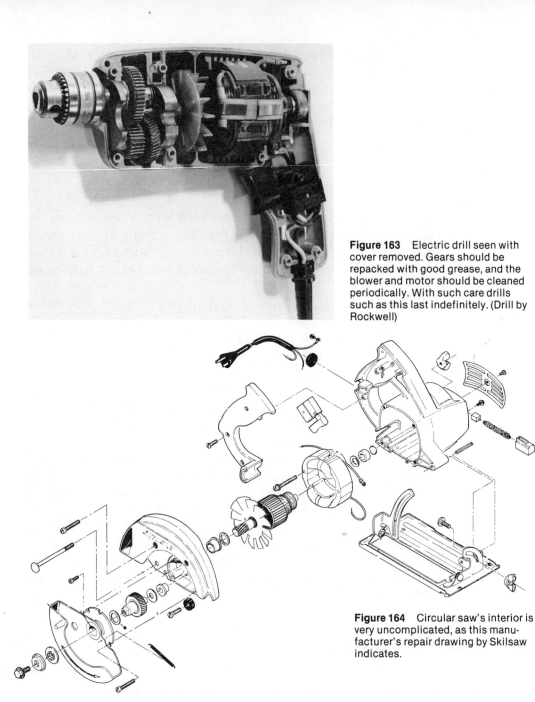

Figure 163 Electric drill seen with cover removed. Gears should be repacked with good grease, and the blower and motor should be cleaned periodically. With such care drills such as this last indefinitely. (Drill by Rockwell)

Figure 164 Circular saw's interior is very uncomplicated, as this manufacturer's repair drawing by Skilsaw indicates.

fully to one side. The top or side then can be pried gently loose to expose the insides. Most likely you will find a dark, sticky glob of old grease clinging to the gears and shafts.

338   Use a knife or small tool to scrape away as much of the grease as you

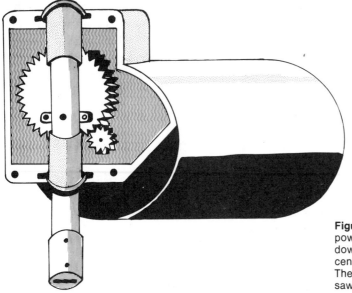

Figure 165 Typical sabre saw takes power from a small motor, gears it down, and then couples an off-centered bracket to the larger gear. The bracket raises and lowers the saw's main shaft.

can without prying against the gears and other inside surfaces. It is not vital that every scrap of used grease be removed because you are going to put so much new grease back inside the tool that the remaining dirt will be heavily diluted by clean grease.

Use the best grease you can find. A well-stocked hardware store will have a few silicone or lithium greases made specifically for packing the gearboxes of power tools. But the precise type of grease really is not critical. Grease intended for use in your car will do fine. And even the light, white Lubriplate grease you can buy in small tubes will do the job. Cover all the gears with fresh grease and loosely fill the inside cavities. Then put the tool back together again and reassemble with the bolts.

Circular saws have no gearbox to pack with grease since the blade couples directly to the electric motor shaft. And belt sanders generally use a small rubber belt to link the electric motor and the drive shaft. But both tools deserve a thorough cleaning inside and out at least once a year. Lubricate all moving parts such as motor bearings at the same time.

BRUSHES

There is one part that nearly every power tool has in common—*brushes*, a part of the electric motor. It is not important that you know

exactly what a brush does. Just keep in mind that it is responsible for distributing electricity to the dozen or so different power units within an electric motor. To accomplish that, the brushes rub against a set of copper contacts on a revolving drum. And that rubbing action gradually wears down the brushes. When the process goes too far, the electric motor loses power and your tool loses effectiveness.

Taking into account the kind of infrequent use most tools receive around a home, brushes should not require replacing more often than every two or three years. But they are cheap, so if you are looking for a reason why a particular tool is losing power, try replacing the brushes (see Figure 135).

Brushes, as a rule, are located one on each side of the motor at the end opposite from the shaft that drives the tool. A black plastic, slotted cover is the usually indicates their location. Put a screwdriver in the slot, unscrew the cover, and watch for the flying brush. It is connected to a spring, which should propel the brush at least part of the way out of its slot. If not, perhaps the brush is too short or the spring too weak. In any event, not springing is a sign that the brushes need to be replaced.

The new brush will be no more than a slab of carbon. You have to pull the spring and copper wire gently loose from the old brush and fit the new one onto the wire and into the spring. If the spring has lost its springiness or is distended, replace it. But that might be a longer process since few hardware stores stock replacement springs. You will have to get one from a parts distributor for your tool.

Whenever you check up on an old brush, put it back in so that the curve worn into the carbon edge curves in the same way the motor rotates. Most brushes are rectangular so that should be no doubt. But some are round or square, and then it's important to line up the brush curve with the motor curve.

New brushes sometimes are flat on their working end but wear into a curve very quickly, often with some smoke and sparking as the carbon is ground down. Don't be alarmed unless the condition continues.

You will be most certain to get an exact replacement if you buy a new set of brushes from whichever company manufactures your power tool. However, many hardware stores have a stock of sundry sizes and shapes of brushes. Don't hesitate to try such a replacement. If it works as well as the old one, you're in business. And if the hardware store replacement proves not to give the tool enough power—a rare situation indeed—no harm should be done if you dig up an exact replacement in the near future. In a pinch you might even buy a brush that is too big and file it down to size.

You will most likely find any spare parts you need at an authorized distributor. But items like belts and bolts and bushings on bearings can safely come right off your local hardware store itself.

Once a drill or sabre saw has seen a lot of use, or a little very hard abuse, the bronze bushings around the power shaft or shafts can get worn. Then you will be stuck with a wobbly shaft. The solution is simple—order a new set of bushings from the manufacturer. When they arrive, slip the old ones out and slip on the new ones after you generously lubricate them with grease. For about $1, the new bushings will give you years of new life for an otherwise tired, old tool.

If the various gears on a sabre saw or drill start to lose their crisp, sharp edges, or if parts of the teeth actually get broken off, that is a sign that you are either abusing the tool very badly or it never was big enough to handle the jobs for which you use it. In any event, if you decide to patch up the old tool instead of investing in a new one, the manufacturer will sell you a new set of replacement gears quite inexpensively. However, if any gear permanently attached to a motor shaft or drive shaft is over the hill, forget about salvaging the tool. Nothing short of a great machine shop would tackle that job. And if you have to pay the machine shop, you'd be money ahead to buy a new tool.

Assuming you buy a tool big enough to handle your usual jobs, assuming you choose a good manufacturer, and assuming you don't badly abuse them too often, power tools can last from 10 to 20 useful years.

 # Cameras and Projectors

Judging by the number of flashbulbs popping at weddings, circuses, and ballgames, there may be more cameras per square home than cars or tranquilizers. Most troubles with cameras stem not from use, abuse, or overuse but exactly the opposite—too little use.

Marketing studies have found that most families dig out their camera maybe three or four times a year. And in the interim, there is plenty of time to forget the instructions. So keep a special drawer, box, or shelf for instruction manuals of all sorts. And if all else fails, read the directions again. Inadequate though some may be, they're better than nothing at all.

FLASHES AND BATTERIES

Batteries are the single most common cause of mechanical problems in cameras. Light meters built into some more sophisticated cameras require a set of batteries as does the flash portion of most.

First, it would be a good idea for all of us to heed the camera and battery manufacturers' advice about not storing a camera or flash attachment with batteries inside. But since we don't always heed good advice, alternate strategy may be needed.

If your flash flashes only sporadically, or if the pictures taken with your battery-powered camera are not consistently good, batteries could be to blame. Chapter 1 gives some tips on how to keep batteries and battery contacts clean. That applies to cameras too.

On flashcube cameras that use battery power (some use mechanical force to create a flash), don't overlook the small contacts where the cube sits atop the box. They benefit from polishing or scraping just as much as the batteries. And flashcubes themselves can pick up oil, corrosion, and other deposits that prevent good contact.

Most batteries are held in place by springs of some sort. And in cameras, most of them are so cheaply built that they can cause as much grief as corroded batteries. Every time you polish or scrape corrosion off your camera's contact points, stretch the spring clips gently a little bit. And once the battery compartment is closed up again, if the batteries seem to jiggle about, they probably are not pushed tightly enough against the contacts. Pull on the springs or contact clips even more. Sam, the so-called camera maven of Prospect Photo in Brooklyn, New York, says that he keeps a small hammer under his counter. "Everytime I put batteries in an Instamatic that uses the AA size, I close the cover and then tap it with my hammer. Otherwise the cover seems to loosen up the batteries as it closes." That solves the battery contact problems for Sam's customers. It might do so for you too.

POLAROID PROBLEMS

The Polaroid-type of cameras have one rather important peculiarity. You have to keep cleaning the rollers inside them. Whenever you pull a sheet of film out of the Polaroid camera, a set of rubber or stainless steel rollers squeezes the film pack together, and in doing so squeezes the powerful developing chemicals over the surface of the film. Theoretically, since the film is inside a paper protective wrapping, chemicals never touch the rollers. But theory and practicality are two entirely different things here.

Fortunately, the Polaroid rollers are easy to clean. A tissue and a little water, plus elbow grease, will restore your camera's rollers to like-new condition. But unless you keep them that way, your pictures will come out streaked and uneven.

There is another bit of cleaning that all cameras—not only Polaroids—deserve. But judging by some of the results that roll out of processing shops and some of the complaints that roll into photo stores, snap shooters are not keeping the vital parts of their cameras cleaned. Since dust and other grime accumulate almost everywhere, regardless if you use a camera every week or only every major holiday, take a soft tissue and spend about one minute occasionally to clean the lens, the front of any electric eyes, and the viewfinder. Before rubbing with the tissue, however, give the lens a vigorous puff of air to blow away any solid particles of grit that may have lodged there. Rubbing the grit around, no matter how soft your tissue, might scratch the front surface of your lens.

INSTAMATICS

Instamatic cameras, and most simple cameras using the Instamatic type of easy loading film cartridges, generally have a steel finger that reaches through the perforations along the edge of the film. The finger pulls the film forward whenever you advance to the next picture. That finger quite often gets jammed in midpush. When that

Figure 166 The camera operator was shaky when this picture was snapped. The camera was probably OK.

Figure 167 The camera operator may not have set opening or shutter correctly. The battery on meter may not have been fresh. In some way, too little light entered camera.

happens, you will generally find that the film advance lever will move only part way forward and no more, no matter how hard or how persistently you push on it. If you shove too eagerly on the advance lever of Instamatic and similar type cameras, the lever will bend. Assuming you don't bend it too hard or too far, simply bend it back to where it should be.

To unjam a jammed Instamatic type camera, you must open up the back. That means one or two exposures of film will be ruined unless you can open it in a totally dark place such as a closet. Once the camera back is opened, simply shove the camera's finger with your own finger and you will almost always succeed in advancing the film, recocking the camera shutter mechanism (accomplished whenever that finger moves forward), and unjamming the whole thing. If you assume that such a jam is going to happen to you and if you practice how to go about unjamming it a few times with an empty camera, when it does strike, you'll be able to walk into a dark closet, successfully open the back, and unjam the mechanism without light, thus saving a picture or two.

When wedding bells are ready to ring, baby is about to take that first step, or some other once-in-a-lifetime-or-two event is expected and you want to capture it on film, test your camera in advance. Turn on any switches or other gadgets to make sure whatever lights or needles are supposed to do something, do indeed do something. And at the very least, put a flashcube into the socket and flash it. That may waste one quarter of a good flash cube, but it will save you from wasting much film and many nerves.

Figure 168 Too much light entered the camera. The meter may not have been functioning, the camera may have been pointed toward the sun, the battery may not have been fresh. Also, the lens may have been very dirty.

Figure 169 Blotches like these at end of the roll (or beginning) indicate that light leaked in when the film was being loaded or unloaded—perhaps in bright sunlight. Blotches along the rest of the film indicate a leaky camera body, or that the camera may have been left in a glove compartment (where temperatures are too high for film in summer), or that the film is badly outdated.

EXPENSIVE CAMERAS

So far, most of our photo fix-it words have been limited to less expensive cameras. Cleanliness, contact scraping, and fresh battery rules apply to costly cameras too.

The insides of an expensive camera are very delicate. Besides that, mechanisms vary tremendously from maker to maker and even from model to model from the same maker. If you think getting a copy of a refrigerator repair manual is difficult, try to get hold of a camera repair manual some day. In short, unless you feel very competent, major repairs should be turned over to a pro, expensive though that is. Two exceptions come immediately to mind, however.

Light meters built into costlier cameras are notorious for having bad connections and loose wires. If your meter starts acting up, locate the three or four tiny screws that probably hold the meter cover in place, unscrew them, and put them in a safe place. They vanish quickly. Now you can probe around inside the meter while it is turned on. If the meter springs into life when you push on one particular wire or one particular connection, you have probably spotted the trouble. Just the tiniest drop of solder should make the balky meter good as new again.

Anyone who buys a good camera should also buy a few good jeweler's screwdrivers. If you carry a camera around much, particularly in a car, some of the dozen or so tiny screws are bound to work loose. Periodically take screwdriver in hand and gently tighten all of the exposed bolts, nuts, screws, and such. Whenever one or two fall out and get lost, order replacements before the whole thing falls apart for want of a few nickel screws.

Avoid the temptation to add just a drop of oil on this part or that. It is fine on most moving equipment but deadly on cameras. Oil can ruin a good shutter. Many camera parts are lubricated with graphite, but

Figure 170 Pointing an automatic camera at a bright light source results in bright background but shadowy faces such as seen here.

Figure 171 Missing heads are usually not the camera's fault. Many people, especially those who wear glasses, have a tendency to point the camera too low.

even that, if used indiscriminately, could cause more harm than good. However, if you decide that a specific part has a specific problem that lubrication probably could fix, try the tiniest drop of oil.

Never put oil on a shutter or a shutter mechanism. Use only graphite there, and then run the mechanism through a couple dozen dry runs to work the lubricant into the parts where it will do the most good. Finally, be sure to blow away and wipe away all traces of excess graphite, or you will be finding mysterious spots on your film.

PROJECTORS

Both slide and movie projectors give most trouble by way of burned-out bulbs. If you are having people over some evening and plan to show off your prize collection of movies, you can almost count on the bulb burning out. So buy a spare next time you buy film.

As with cameras, cleanliness is a very rewarding virtue for projectors too. Little bits of paper slide mounts or scraps of torn film work their way into the mechanisms and eventually jam them, bend them slightly, or in some other way foul up the works. If a seldom used projector is blown clean with a vacuum cleaner or your own lungs, then dusted clean before or after every use, your problems will be solved in advance about as much as possible. Areas in and around those pesty self-threading movie film mechanisms are especially vulnerable to bits of scrap film.

Slide projectors needs straight, unbent, unruffled slide mounts for good performances. Not only will a bent slide jam in the mechanism, perhaps getting ruined in the process, but the jamming inevitably bends some of the barely adequate parts too. Given enough metal-bending jams, the troubles will begin showing up with greater and greater frequency. Then you'll be stuck with the headache of carefully examining all of the projector's moving parts until you locate which ones seem to be misaligned.

When working on a slide projector, due to the fact that irregular slide mounts begin the troubles, it may save time to reverse the troubleshooting procedures you learned earlier. Start more toward the *powered* end of things, where the slides meet the slide changing mechanism. Then work your way backward to the powering end.

Belts are the major mechanical bugaboo in movie projectors. They don't break often, which is why when one does break, it catches everyone by surprise. If the sprockets and reels won't turn at all, or if they turn only very slowly, or if sprockets turn but not reels, take a look at the belts. If one is not broken altogether, maybe it is worn out to the point where the belt slips so much that it no longer transmits power from the motor to the reels and sprockets.

In some slick-looking projectors, you have to remove a cover or two to reach the belt or belts. Inevitably there is one linking each reel to the motor or control center. And there are often belts linking the motor to the film sprocket mechanisms.

It is not always easy to reconstruct the exact path that a new belt must take if the old one is pulled out too quickly. Hopefully, the old belt will be still almost in its proper place by the time you unbolt enough covers and hardware to find it. Thoughtful manufacturers include a diagram of how a belt should loop. If yours doesn't, draw one now. If you have to install a new belt by trial and error, you'll be frustrated for days.

The easiest solution for a belt path is to buy a replacement belt made out of a metal spring. It is noticeably noisier than a rubber belt, but if noise doesn't bother you, the spring belt is simplicity itself. All you have to do is unhook the two ends, slip the loose ends under all of the obstructions and around the various pulleys, then hook the ends together again and turn on the switch. Unfortunately, simple trips such as this are not to be found in your user manual.

Bikes, Trikes, Strollers, and Other Wheeled Wonders

16

SNAP-CAPS AND COTTER PINS

A nickel piece of steel with a shiny plastic cover, the snap-cap *tries* to hold wheels onto the vast majority of inexpensive wheeled household devices sold today. It is a cheap, quick, colorful way to get wheels onto that narrow rod that passes for an axle. The springed fingers inside a snap-cap grab at the rod with amazing force. But the sideways force on wheels going around corners is even more amazing—and snap usually goes the snap-cap.

You can invest in new snap-caps at well-stocked hardware stores. And you'll have to if you simply want to snap a new one back on where an old one snapped off. Once a snap-cap has snapped off, it won't snap back in place with as much force as before. But once the original snap-cap has snapped, chances are good that it will do the same thing again. So why not reach a more permanent settlement with your wheels?

If you insist on using snap-caps, do what a few manufacturers do—snap the cap fingers into a *ridge*. Measure how far away from the

351

Bikes, Trikes,
Strollers,
and Other
Wheeled
Wonders

end of the rod-axle those fingers will grab. Then file a groove all around the rod at that point. Now the snap-cap will have some permanence.

More permanent than snap-caps are old fashioned *cotter pins*. You can still buy a handful of them for a few cents. First, you have to drill a small hole for the cotter pin into the axle rod close to the wheel. Mark the right spot accurately and slip the wheel off to give yourself some working room. A $\frac{3}{32}$" hole is about the biggest you could want. For most cotter pins, a $\frac{5}{64}$" drilled hole is plenty big.

Slip the wheel back into place, slip a small washer onto the rod, and shove the cotter pin through its new hole. With a pliers or screwdriver, twist the two cotter pin prongs in opposite directions, and the wheel is now about permanently in place—unless you deliberately want to remove it some day. In that event, simply straighten the cotter pin's two legs and jerk it out of the hole with a pliers. You can use the same pin for a new wheel if you have to. But it's safer to rely on a new cotter pin.

In case you like the cotter pin permanence but enjoy the beauty of a snap-cap, you can snap the plastic cap off a colored snap-cap, fill it with silicone cement, and shove the cap onto the exposed end of the axle.

WHEELS

Ironically, you may find that the toughest aspect in repairing a wheeled implement is finding replacement wheels when needed. They are not the sort of merchandise stocked by most of the department stores that sell strollers and trikes and carts and wagons, although they should be. Even manufacturers of strollers and such don't always have wheels readily available.

To replace a wheel, you may have to practice the fine art of making do. So it will help if you plan just a bit ahead. Here are some of the places to watch for wear and signs of coming destruction.

Many wheels are stamped out of two pieces of iron, often riveted together with a plastic hub and bearing in the middle. When the plastic starts to wear out or to distort, the wheel will start wobbling badly, a sign that you may have only a short time to locate replacements.

Some wheels have thick rubber treads cut from a long strip of rubber and literally stapled around the wheel. After a certain amount of wear, the rubber shifts or the staple weakens and the rubber begins to separate a bit from the metal part of the wheel. That is a sign that the rubber and metal soon may part completely.

Wire wheels with nonadjustable spokes will often bend enough to start rubbing against some part of the wagon or cart. You can bend them back into shape temporarily, but you should start looking for replacements as soon as the first realignment becomes necessary.

Some wheels are built like casters. The wheel axle connects to a bracket and the bracket ends in some sort of swivel, which in turn fits into a slot in the stroller. With age and wear, the bracket can bend and that weakens the metal further, a sign that replacement would be wise.

It is not always necessary to replace wheels with duplicates of exactly the same size. That's a blessing because you're not likely to find exact replacements. However, as long as you replace wheels by the pair, almost any size close to the original dimensions will do. Especially if an implement is used on rough pavement and ground, or off the smooth sidewalks, large wheels are less likely to get caught in potholes than small ones.

Try bicycle shops, hardware stores, department stores, stroller or

Figure 172 New axles and/or wheels for strollers and other small wheeled devices are simple with threaded rods (right) or steel rods and cotter pins (left).

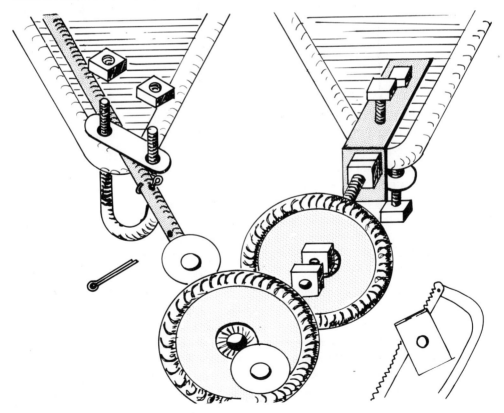

353

Bikes, Trikes,
Strollers,
and Other
Wheeled
Wonders

wagon dealers, and manufacturers in search of wheels. Maybe your local dime store will have some too.

Sometimes a hardware store that caters to the industrial set may stock some very good rubber tire replacement wheels, but the axle hole will be substantially larger than the one on your stroller, wagon, or other wheeler. Then you will have to look around the store until you accumulate some pipe or tubing with an *inside dimension* approximately the size of your old axle and an *outside dimension* approximately equal to the new wheel. Maybe two sets of these make-do bushings will be needed.

There is an alternative to going through a lot of trouble trying to match a set of replacement wheels to an original axle. You might get a good set of standard replacement wheels off a hardware store shelf and make a new axle at the same time. Figure 172 shows several alternative ways to accomplish that.

STROLLERS

Strollers suffer from torn seats and supporting fabric, as well as faltering wheels. But don't think that an entirely new stroller is called for when that happens.

Most manufacturers do sell replacement seats. Even if the fabric holding your old one in place is riveted around the frame, you may be able to cut off the old, buy a new set, and snap it over the old. Department stores and manufacturers seldom advertise replacement seat units, but the time it will take you to write directly to the manufacturer should be well worth the savings over the cost of investing in a new piece of baby equipment.

BICYCLES

Given the chance, nearly any boy or girl (and many adults) will pick up a pliers and try to fix a bike whether or not it needs fixing. *And that's what we ought to be encouraging.*

There really isn't much that a child can break on his or her first bike. Some of the bearings can get tightened up so badly that the rider will have to puff like the devil to make the thing go—but that's one way to learn not to tighten things up too tight. Or he or she might loosen everything up so the wheels wobble. But that can be fixed too.

Parents who are eager to see that their children don't assume that

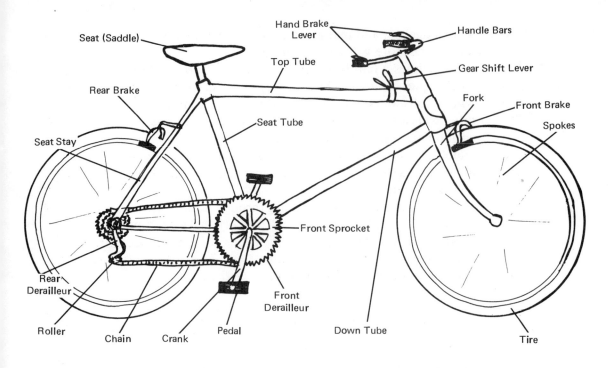

Figure 173 Bicycle nomenclature.

repairs are for professional, highly trained, factory authorized repair people only, should give the youngsters some appropriate bicycle accessories. How about a pair of pliers and a screwdriver, maybe a wrench or two also?

Let's get to the flat tire first. To patch a *tire*, you will first have to take the wheel off the bike. (We'll deal with specific kinds of wheels later if you don't already understand your own bike.) There is a wire bead around the inside of a rubber tire, often called a *balloon tire*, which fits snugly into the rim of your bicycle wheel. *Tubular tires*, found generally only on certain expensive racing bikes, are not widely used. We will assume that if you buy such a specialized piece of machinery, you will also be shown how to contend with patching tubular tires.

The secret of getting the tire off the rim is expressed in this way: you have to pry *very hard* against the tough wire bead of the tire while being careful *not to pry* against the delicate rubber inner tube. You can buy a handful of small tire irons from a bicycle shop, but with care, two or three screwdrivers work nicely. You can even use one screwdriver and several popsicle sticks.

At any point around the tire, except where the valve stem goes
354 through the wheel, force the screwdriver or tire iron blade between the

355

*Bikes, Trikes,
Strollers,
and Other
Wheeled
Wonders*

wheel rim and the tire bead. Then carefully pry the tire bead up and over the wheel rim. Leave something there—the screwdriver, the tire iron, or a stick—to keep the bead and rim separated. Then move two or three inches away and do the same thing. By the time you have pried the tire bead over the wheel rim in only two or three places, enough pressure will have been taken off the tire so that you can simply slide your tool along the rim and easily guide the rest of the tire off the wheel.

There is a bead on both sides of the tire. If you had to remove the tire from the wheel completely, you would have to go through the entire pry-and-hold-and-slide procedure a second time. However, if you're only interested in inspecting, patching, or replacing the inner tube, which is what actually contains the air, you can slip the inner tube out of the tire without prying both beads out of the rim (see Figure 174).

Once the inner tube is pulled free of the tire, you can start to locate the leak, if that's the problem. You will have to add some air to the tube first. And the way in which air is pumped into bicycle tires causes many people many headaches.

Your neighborhood gas station is a convenient source of free air. But, if not well controlled, the air pressure in the hose there can top 100 psi (pounds per square inch)—fully three times more pressure than most bicycle tires can handle.

Your best method for inflating bicycle tires is with a small hand pump. But if you use the gas station compressor, proceed with

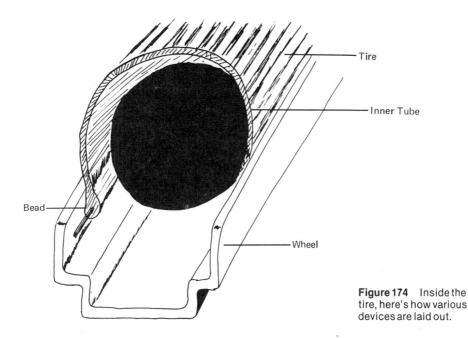

Tire

Inner Tube

Bead

Wheel

Figure 174 Inside the tire, here's how various devices are laid out.

caution, one tiny squirt of air at a time. And don't rely on the air pressure gauge built into such systems. It isn't even accurate enough to trust for car tires. Invest in your own small tire gauge, inexpensive but worthwhile for both bicycles and cars.

For those who never learned, here is how to fill a tire with air. Sticking out from the inner part of every inner tube is the *valve stem*, often shortened just to "valve." *Inside* the valve stem is an *air valve*, controlled by a tiny rod that you can easily see because the end extends almost to the top of the valve stem. When the valve rod is pushed in, air can flow either into or out of the inner tube. If you simply push on the rod with a tool or the tip of your air gauge, air goes out, which is what you should do if you have checked the air pressure and found it to be excessive.

When you put a source of compressed air over the valve stem when the rod is pushed in, air will flow into the tube. When you screw a hand tire pump onto the stem or simply shove a filling station's air hose connection over the stem, a rod inside the air connection automatically pushes down the valve rod. Generally, you should pump or squeeze until you think that you have just a bit too much air in the tire. Then take away the air hose, check the pressure, and let out enough air—checking pressure frequently—to bring the pressure down to the recommended level.

If all else fails, if you don't have a hand pump and if you don't have a gas station just around the corner, you can take out the tire valve by unscrewing it with a special valve cap on sale at bike shops. With the valve completely out and carefully tucked away in a clean, secure place, you can simply blow enough air into the tube to test it for leaks. You will have to keep one finger over the valve stem, however.

Hold your questionable tube under water. A bathtub works fine. If there is a leak in the rubber, you will see bubbles. Sometimes you will have to squeeze the tube to put more pressure on the air inside before enough bubbles pour out a tiny leak to make them easy to spot.

If you don't have easy access to a bathtub, simply rub soapy water over the surface of the inner tube. Escaping air will make soap bubbles. Be sure you mark where the leak or leaks are located before laying the tube down again. Dry off the spot and put a big X over the leak with a crayon.

Tire patches intended for bicycles are thinner than their automotive counterparts. So when buying a tire-patching kit, be sure to specify that it is for a bike and not a car. You can make do with car tire patches, but on very lightweight tires, the heftier patch could unbalance the wheel enough for you to feel the difference.

Tire patch kits generally have detailed instructions with them. In general, you have to clean the rubber around each hole. And they do mean *clean*, no matter how clean the tube may look to you. Then a rubber cement is applied to the tube, sometimes to both the patch and the tube. Finally, the patch is fitted into place and given a chance to dry. Before you put the tube back into the tire, it's a good idea to dust some talcum powder or cornstarch onto the area you cleaned. This will prevent the rubber tube from sticking to the rubber tire, making future removal very tough if not impossible.

Almost all air should be squeezed out of the tube when you begin to reinstall it into the tire still hanging by one bead on the rim. Reinsert the tube by starting with the valve stem. Be very careful that the tube is shoved toward the enclosed top of the tire so that the delicate tube will not be pinched by your tools as the tire bead is pried back onto the rim.

Wheels in the front simply can be slid out of the front fork. Some have quick-release fittings with a large handle, making wheel removal a quick operation. Other front wheels, however, require only a small wrench so that both nuts, one on each side of the wheel, can be loosened. Just about the same procedure holds true for the rear wheel on bicycles with derailleur gearshift equipment, except that the chain has to be removed first.

With only minor variations, the hubs on all front wheels (and rear wheels on derailleur bikes) are essentially alike internally (see Figure 175). And they seldom need attention. An annual cleaning and greasing is good preventive maintenance, and in those hubs that have an oil cup, a squirt or two of oil every month is wise. Beyond that, leave the inside of your wheels alone unless there is a definite reason to believe they are causing trouble. When you hear about internal troubles such as through scraping noises in the ball bearings, it is generally a sign

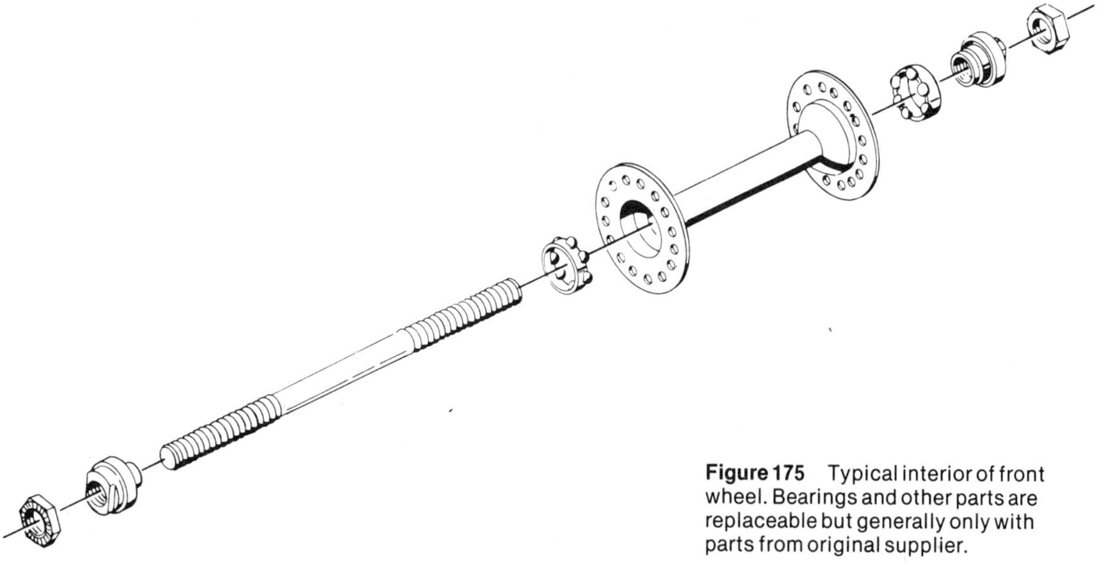

Figure 175 Typical interior of front wheel. Bearings and other parts are replaceable but generally only with parts from original supplier.

358

*Bikes, Trikes,
Strollers,
and Other
Wheeled
Wonders*

that dirt has worked its way beyond the dust cap and cone. Move quickly then, or the dirt will literally grind down the metal parts.

The balls in your wheel ball bearings are not always permanently held into place. That is about the sole complication to taking apart a wheel hub. Just expect that after the cone has been pulled up, you will be facing a handful of loose steel balls. Grab onto all of them, tuck them into a safe, closed container, and the rest is simple. Once a wheel hub has been disassembled, clean all of the parts with a good nonexplosive solvent such as kerosene or cleaning fluid.

As each part is cleaned, inspect it for broken and worn threads or gouges. Balls should be perfectly rounded; their surface should not be pitted; surface coloration should be uniformly glossy without spots of higher gloss or patches with an extremely dull complexion. If any part of the hub is worn or damaged, replace it with an exact duplicate. If any one ball in the bearing set needs replacing, replace the entire set of balls at the same time. Count the number of balls and make sure that the replacement set has the same number and that they appear to be the same diameter as the old ones. If too many hub parts are in a bad way, you would be wise to invest in an entire new hub assembly or even an entire new wheel. Apply a generous layer of grease to the ball bearing section before completing your hub reassembly.

The *cones* are the key to good front wheel performance. When you first reinstall them, turn each cone down firmly with a wrench and then back off about one-half turn. At this point, spin the wheel by hand. If it wobbles, the cones may be too loose. Tighten each cone slightly and see if that mellows the wobble. If it does, tighten each cone just a bit more and test for wobble again.

At the opposite extreme, if the cones are too tight the wheel will not spin freely. And that means you will have to peddle too hard when the bike is back together. In that case, loosen up each cone a bit and try to spin the wheel again. Assuming the cones and bearings are in good shape, you should reach one point where the wheel spins freely but there is no wobble to it. And this is generally not the kind of hair-trigger adjustment where a mere quarter turn will make a difference between tightness or wobble.

If a wobbly wheel is not caused by cones that are adjusted too loosely, the problem probably comes from a distorted wheel. This can be caused when a wheel hits a big rock or bounces over too many curbs. You may have twisted the wheel when tumbling off the bike. But it can also be caused by improperly adjusted spokes.

Regardless of why a wheel wobbles, it has to be taken care of. Aside from being a riding hazard, a wobbly wheel can damage a hub. A minor wobble can be straightened out by adjusting some spokes. This is usually done with a spoke wrench, but any small wrench or pliers can be pressed into action. If the top of a wheel wobbles toward the left, for example, try tightening two or three spokes that end on the right side of the wheel at the top.

It is generally unwise and uneconomical to try tightening more than two or three spokes without the proper equipment. In other words, if your early efforts at straightening a wheel with a slight wobble do not pay off with immediate dividends, you should take the ailing machine to a well-established bicycle dealer or bicycle repair shop, which has wheel-aligning and spoke-tightening equipment. Check out the cost of such a service in advance, however. You might find that buying an entire new wheel will come out cheaper. In any event, keep in mind that the narrow wheels on today's lightweight bicycles—unlike the older, fat-tired ones—require the kind of care and alignment you would expect to give all other precision machines.

Pedals require little maintenance except for a squirt of oil at each end every month or so. The exception is all-metal "rat-trap" pedals, which do not get oiled. Once or twice a year they are disassembled, cleaned, and repacked with grease. They very closely resemble a front wheel hub, right down to the cones. Assembly and adjustment is similar too.

If a pedal wears out or gets bent, it should be *replaced rather than repaired.* Pedals on the right side of a bike have left-handed threads; they loosen counterclockwise, the traditional way. Pedals on the left side have right-handed threads, which loosen clockwise.

Chains are really very simple, if you will accept a simple explanation for a chain and what it does. It transmits motion, period. Your bicycle's front sprocket gets turned by people power, your feet. But the motion has to reach the rear wheel somehow. So each link of the chain *pulls* on the link just behind it. And each link pulls a full one people-power worth of load. Since each individual link has to withstand the full force of your legs, the chain is quite a rugged piece of machinery. It should be treated that way too.

Ideally, a chain should be inspected periodically. Practically, however, you will probably not bother with the chain until something seems to be wrong. Before doing anything else to a questionable chain, assuming it is still on your bike, grab it firmly between the front and rear sprockets with your left hand. With your right fingers, try to pull the chain away from the front sprocket near the front-most part of the sprocket. If you *can* pull the chain a noticeable distance away from the sprocket, the chain seems to have stretched and probably must be replaced. Before junking the old chain, however, turn the pedals so you can make this test at several different points along the chain to make sure the whole chain has stretched and not just a few defective links in one place.

360

*Bikes, Trikes,
Strollers,
and Other
Wheeled
Wonders*

A stretched chain is not likely to cause immediate mayhem, unless it is stretched very badly. It is the sort of thing to take care of at some convenient moment, however, or it will soon start slipping over some cogs in your sprocket, perhaps causing more expensive damage in the process. And once the chain has stretched to a point where only a few chain links are taking the full load as you pedal, you may be stranded somewhere with a broken chain that should have been replaced months ago.

Many chains are fastened together with one link called a *master link*. They come in several basic shapes, but all of them are distinctly different in appearance from every other link in you chain. If your chain does have a master link, you need only pry its cover out and the entire chain can be gently removed from its sprockets.

Some chains have no master link. For them, you should have a *chain rivet remover tool.* The inexpensive tool slips over any link of chain. Its driving point is screwed against a chain rivet until the rivet has been forced *almost* out of the backside of the chain. Then, once the driving point has been screwed back out of the chain, the links separate easily and the chain can be removed.

A chain rivet remover is the sort of tool you probably will not have around the first time you need it. So substitute a hammer and thin nail. Lay the bicycle on its side and make sure the chain is well supported near the point you plan to hammer out a rivet or you may damage the chain and sprocket. Place the point of a nail against the chosen rivet and gently tap it until the rivet is not quite all the way out of the chain. When you are ready to put the chain link back together again, simply reverse all of the above directions. Use the rivet driver or the nail to force the loose rivet firmly back into place.

It is good preventive maintenance to clean a bike chain periodically. You don't even have to remove it from the sprockets. Kerosene or another safe solvent works well. Light motor oil can be used too. Even a pressurized can of cleaning fluid can be squirted onto the chain. After cleaning, oil the chain well, making sure every link is given a drop.

If you suspect that your chain may be causing trouble—you may get jerky or uneven rides while peddling—after you check to see whether the chain has stretched substantially, remove it and give it a link by link inspection. Flex the joint between every link. It should rotate freely without much exertion on your part. On the other hand, it should not be so loose as to wobble sideways. A wobbly link must be replaced. One that is too tight may simply suffer from bad lubrication or dirt. Squirt penetrating oil or a potent cleaning fluid into the tight joint and flex it repeatedly. If that cleans up the problem, finish the job with a dose of lubricating oil. If not, replace the links in question.

361

*Bikes, Trikes,
Strollers,
and Other
Wheeled
Wonders*

On chains that never had a master link, use the chain rivet remover tool to take out the bad links and put in new ones you can buy at a bike shop. If you have to replace only one or two scattered links on a chain that originally did have one master link, the quickest way is to buy more master links. Two master links should never be joined together, however. In that case, use the rivet remover tool to put in standard links.

Links you replace are seldom as strong as the ones assembled at the factory. We should hope they do a good job anyway! If you have to replace too many links in one part of a chain, it is possible that the patched chain will not perform as well as an entirely new one. If that proves to be the case, it will be cheaper and less frustrating in the long run to invest in a new chain at some convenient moment.

The rear wheel, especially on single speed bikes or those multispeed machines with only a single sprocket at the rear, determines how tight the chain tension will be. Most often you simply pull outward on the rear wheel until the chain looks about as tight as you think it should be. And then, while still holding tight to the wheel, you are supposed to tighten up the nuts that hold the wheel in place. Trying to accomplish such a feat by yourself is something else again. Some manufacturers include a set screw that lets you mechanically set the chain tension.

In any event, the chain on bikes with a single sprocket fore and aft should be loose enough so that you can push it up and down about ½ ' between that long expanse of chain between the tops of both sprockets. If you are going to make an error, do so in favor of a chain that is slightly too loose. But once you adjust a chain to what you suspect is a good setting, test ride the vehicle under varying conditions to make sure that it doesn't pedal harder than before (which may be a sign that the chain is too tight) or that it doesn't slip out of the sprocket when you pedal very hard (sign of a chain that is too loose).

Young cyclists reading this will by now be mumbling, "He doesn't even know how to take a chain off a bike!" True, there is yet another method for getting a chain off or on the sprockets. It's like slipping your foot into a tight shoe with a shoehorn. Not a gentle method, it does work well if you can master the shoehorn technique.

All you need is a screwdriver. Insert it between the chain and the top of the front sprocket. Then slowly turn the pedal as you twist the screwdriver enough to keep the next link from engaging the next sprocket point. Once you've done that, every successive link will miss the sprocket points, and with just a little more turning on the pedal, you will quickly have a pile of loose chain in your hand.

To put a chain back on with our alternate method, first string the chain over the rear sprocket in its normal position. Then hang one

362

Bikes, Trikes,
Strollers,
and Other
Wheeled
Wonders

chain link over a top point on the front sprocket. As you slowly turn the pedal, following links will automatically fall into place while you keep a firm grip on that first link so it will not come loose. The critical moment comes just as that leading link of chain finally reaches its lowest position on the turning sprocket. You will have to use a bit of extra pressure just then to get the chain moving smoothly on its proper way.

Rear wheels on single speed bikes contain a hub known as a *coaster* or *coaster brake.* When you're peddling frontward, the spocket engages a clutch deep inside the hub, which makes the rear wheel turn frontward too. But if you push the pedal backward, the clutch disengages and internal brake shoes rub against the hub to stop the bike.

In a well-made bike, there is little reason to take the coaster apart except in time of trouble. It would be a great idea to clean the thing out periodically, but unless you are fairly skilled in the mechanical arts—or very confident already—you might cause more trouble than you stand to prevent. Letting well enough alone seems to be the wisest kind of maintenance here.

When a coaster brake does cause trouble, the first place to look at the thin clamp that is supposed to hold onto the brake arm. If that is in place, check that all of the nuts that hold the coaster hub together and hold the rear wheel onto the frame are still in place and not too loose.

Next step logically would be to check that the hub bolts and nuts are not too tight. In general, the hub nuts should be as loose as possible without allowing the rear wheel to wobble noticeably. Some wobble can come from a poorly aligned wheel itself and have nothing to do with a loose nut in the hub.

Assuming you have checked that all appropriate hardware is tight but not too tight, and you still believe the problem lies somewhere inside the hub, think about this for a minute. If your major complaint is that the brakes do not seem to be working as well as before, new brake shoes could solve the problem. And if the hub slips when you peddle hard, a worn or broken clutch or drive screw could be to blame. If the bike is more than a few years old, however, you could very well find other worn parts inside the hub that will also need replacing. By the time you are finished, there is a chance that the bill may be close to what an entirely new back wheel would cost. Check it out, but if that does prove to be the case, what have you got to lose except some fear by tackling the insides of the coaster brake?

If you are really adventuresome or confident, or if you really want to conserve funds, take a long look at the drawing (Figure 176) of one popular coaster brake assembly, the Bendix RB and RB-2, and then reach for the tool-box. Other makes and models generally are very

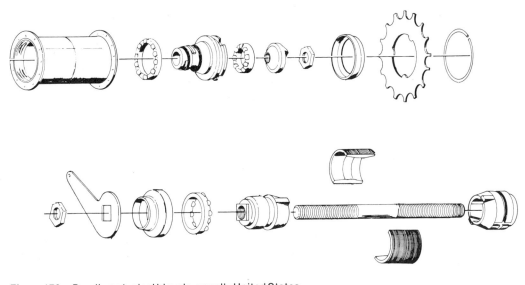

Figure 176 Bendix on typical bicycle, usually United States-made, which doesn't have gear shifts or has only a three-speed hub on rear. This device allows for braking (with backward motion of chain) and pedaling (with forward motion). Parts have to be replaced with similar ones from Bendix manufacturer.

similar to the one pictured here. The major variations are in the shape of the brake shoes and drive clutch or drive screw.

Hand brakes, which seem to be more popular than ever, come in a multitude of sizes, shapes, and styles. But the essential care of hand brakes is the same for every type.

The brake pads have to be replaced periodically, preferably before the rubber has worn thin. The rubber brake surface may also get especially shiny, soft, hard, or broken. You can buy replacement rubber brake pads separately for little money. But by the time most people get around to sticking new pads on, the entire brake shoe and adjoining nuts and threads are so corroded or damaged that you're probably best advised to invest a little more in four brand new brake shoes and pads.

Simply unbolt the old brake shoe and bolt in the new. Pads typically have a metal tab at only one of their two narrow ends. The metal covered end should point *forward.* If you should accidentally point the unprotected end toward the front, the direction your bike wheels turn, when you apply the brakes there is a good chance that the rubber will be pulled out of the brake assembly.

Brake pads should be parallel to the *rim,* not to the tire. Your rim probably is beveled. As part of your preventive maintenance routine, check that alignment periodically.

363

364

Bikes, Trikes,
Strollers,
and Other
Wheeled
Wonders

There are two basic types of hand brakes, the *center pull* type and the *side pull,* although it scarcely matters that you know about the two because there are so many makes and models within the center and side pull types that you will still have to shop very carefully if something goes wrong with a brake. And a more descriptive choice of words for the brakes might be *single pull* (for "side pull") and *double pull* (for "center pull").

In both brake styles, your hands pull a lever, and that in turn pulls on the brake cable, which runs from the handlebar to the general vicinity of a wheel. In the so-called side pull brake (or single pull), the wire attaches to a lever, which pulls the brake pad against the wheel rim. The pad on the opposite side is also attached to a lever but is stationary. Both of the brake pads rub against the rim on their respective sides because when the active pad is pulled hard enough, it forces the wheel out of line just a bit, and thus pushes it against the stationary pad.

In the center pull (or double pull) brakes, the brake wire attaches via a *cable carrier* to a *transverse cable.* That cable pulls on two levers attached to the brake shoes so pads on each side of the rim are pulled toward each other at the same time, a somewhat more sensitive and better-engineered system.

The cable, or cables in the case of a center pull brake, should be replaced occasionally or you run the risk of having one snap as you speed down hill. If your bike is given a lot of constant hard use, or if it sits outside frequently, you should think about putting in new brake cables at least every year. You can look for worn spots on the cables by working the hand lever back and forth as you examine the cable every place it passes through some sort of hole or is fastenend onto some piece of hardware. *Any detectable sign of wear* is too much.

At replacement time, you can estimate the size of your present brake cable by running a string alongside the cable housing. Then invest in a new cable at least several inches longer than the string. The cable end, which fastens to the hand lever, may be just an ordinary cable end or it may be threaded. If the latter, be sure that the new thread fits the old threads.

Lubricate the new cable with something like Lubriplate grease. Then snake it through the cable housing, twisting it periodically as you go. It should slide through with relative ease unless the housing itself has been distorted or bent. In that case, get a new housing too.

Fasten the new brake cable to the hand lever either with the threaded fitting or the mounting bracket and screw, whichever system your brake uses. The other end, after being properly fitted over, under, through, or around whatever gadgetry has been provided for

365

*Bikes, Trikes,
Strollers,
and Other
Wheeled
Wonders*

the cable and cable housing, is fastened to the *brake caliper lever* on a side pull system or to the cable carrier in a center pull hookup. In either event, the brake pads should be ⅛″ away from the rim when the cable is tightened into place.

The most precise way to end up with a ⅛″ space is to slip enough paper, cardboard, or plastic into the gap and tape the pad temporarily against it. Then tighten the *anchor bolts*. Loosen the tape, jerk the spacing material out of the way, and your brakes should be about ready to go. Don't cut off too much of that excess piece of cable too quickly, however. Try out the brakes first.

Does the cable slide smoothly inside its housing? Do all brake pads contact the rim about the same time? Are the brakes grabbing well before you have pulled the hand lever as far as it will go? If your brake job passes muster—when you can answer "yes" to those three questions—*then* clip off as much of the excess cable as you feel must be done away with.

During periodic checkups or tune-ups, it is not usually necessary to unbolt the cable to adjust the brake distances. Manufacturers as a rule have provided an adjusting barrel. First loosen up the adjusting nut, then twist the barrel in whichever direction the adjustment must be made. Finally, tighten up the nut again.

No matter what you do to the brakes, *test them* afterward. Hop onto the vehicle and take a spin, testing the brakes repeatedly.

MULTISPEED BIKES

Engineers have long known that by turning the biggest gear available and connecting it either directly or via a chain to the smallest gear available, maximum possible speed could be gained. That is what your bicycle accomplishes at its highest gear setting. The chain is on the front sprocket's largest gear and on the rear sprocket's smallest gear. Result—lots of speed.

You can't get something for nothing, however. When you *gain speed* by hooking a big gear to a little one, you also *lose power*. You may not notice the loss of power on your bike as long as you are cruising down a straight, hard, flat road. Add just a small incline, however, and watch how much more power you have to put into every push in a high gear than in a low one (see Figure 177).

When a smaller gear on the pedals is used to drive a bigger gear on the rear wheel, you *lose speed* but *gain power*. So, to help you get a bicycle over hills, engineers incorporate a setting that features a larger rear sprocket (gear) and, in 10-speed bikes, also a smaller front sprocket. Therefore, you may not be going as fast when the differ-

366

*Bikes, Trikes,
Strollers,
and Other
Wheeled
Wonders*

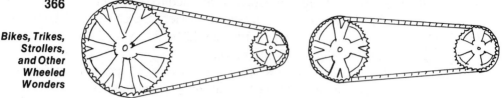

Figure 177 Speed vs. power in gear shift bicycle. At left, large front gear coupled to small rear gear leads to maximum speed, minimum power. At right, the front gear is not as large and is coupled to a rear gear not as small as that at left, so maximum power is produced but minimum speed.

ence in size between the front and rear sprockets has been cut down, but you won't be called on to put out as much power either.

On a single speed bike, you have one front and one rear sprocket, no change of gear ratio to select in favor of power or speed. On a three-speed, there is a single front sprocket and three different sizes of rear sprockets.

A five-speed model usually has one gear in front and five gears rearside. The 10-speed bike has two sprockets up front and five in back, providing a total of 10 different combinations of gear ratios.

If you think the available gear ratios are numerous, you should see a list of the variations in *gear shifting equipment* that is installed on today's bicycles. The gears themselves are relatively simple to maintain. Keep them clean and well lubricated. Barring an accident, they should not bend or wear out for years and years if the chain and derailleur are adjusted competently.

If you ever get the notion that one gear in a cluster needs replacing, look again. You are likely to find that more than one has been damaged by whatever led to the end of the first gear. And at that point, begin investigating the economics of replacement parts versus complete wheel replacement, gears included. Include in your cost analysis the price of a *freewheel removal tool,* since the cluster of gears are held onto a notched or slotted cluster body that you can damage without this tool. Once that cluster body has been removed from the rear wheel, the gears themselves simply screw off or slip off after a retaining ring has been removed. In the case of gears that screw off, the largest two generally have left-handed threads and they loosen in a clockwise direction.

The odd-shaped piece of hardware that encourages your chain to move from one gear to another when you move the gearshift lever is called a *derailleur,* a French word that Americans more likely pronounce "de-rail-er."

Figure 178 shows how the chain winds its way through the derail-

367

*Bikes, Trikes,
Strollers,
and Other
Wheeled
Wonders*

leur. On 10-speed bikes, there is a simple derailleur on the front sprocket and a more complicated one to the rear. With lesser gear ratios, normally there is only one derailleur, part of the rear sprocket assembly.

There are at least five different derailleurs installed on bikes of various makes, Simplex, Campagnolo, Huret Allvit, Shimano Lark, Sun Tour. It isn't so important that you know about the differences in case you want to make major repairs on your derailleur. It is generally more economical to replace a badly damaged derailleur than to try locating proper replacement parts. Besides, since most of them come from countries that have been on the metric system of measures for a long time, you would need some metric-sized tools to make internal repairs.

The derailleur differences become important and annoying when you have to adjust the chain and derailleur tension on your bike. If the chain is too tight, which is caused most often by a deraileur with too much tension, you will have trouble getting into a new gear. But with too little tension, you will have trouble keeping it in a new gear. Unfortunately, each system has its own way of adjusting tension. But if all else fails locate the bolt or spring that creates the derailleur tension and do what seems logical to make it tighter or looser.

If you have not already bought your first "modern" bike, when you do, insist that an adequate user manual accompany your purchase.

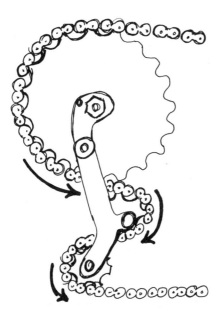

Figure 178 In derailer (or derailleur), chain threads through rear gears in this fashion.

Mowers, Blowers, Scooters and Other Engine-Driven Items

17

"Put-put" machines seem to drive many people into a state of shock even faster than electrically powered equipment. Probably the psychological reasons have to do with the feeling that gasoline-powered engines are too sophisticated and too complicated for lay people to meddle with—nonsense!

ROUTINE MAINTENANCE

Most of your attention on these items should be devoted to routine maintenance, so you will seldom really have to get into the greasy insides of a balky go-cart engine or lawn mower. Gasoline, oil, grease, and loving care are the major ingredients of enlightened maintenance. But even those simple items have been clouded by lack of information and much misinformation, which we will now try to clarify.

Gasoline should be *regular and no-lead.* Buy as little as you conveniently can. Like wine, gasoline ages too—but not well. As it sits around in even the best sealed cans, it forms gum and varnish,

368

369

*Mowers,
Blowers,
Scooters
and Other
Engine-Driven
Items*

which will make the carburetor and moving parts of your engine sticky. That's not good.

Do not store gasoline from one season to the next. And certainly do not try to keep it from one summer to the next. That is dangerous. Also, it will "spoil." Ads to the contrary, virtually all gasoline makers blend their products to handle best the seasonal changes peculiar to a certain part of the country. It is best, therefore, to buy winter-use gasoline in winter months and summer-use fuel during summer.

At least one lawn mower manufacturer recommends "white gasoline" for the product at the same time the company that made the engine mounted atop that same mower specifically says. "No white gasoline, please." White gasoline is almost like fuel oil or kerosene, not volatile enough to do a good job inside a gasoline engine. So don't use it.

Oil keeps moving parts moving smoothly Most people know *that*. In the more sophisticated engines, oil also *cools off* the fiercely heated metal surfaces. Gasoline burning inside an engine generates a couple thousand degrees temperature. And that kind of abuse could shorten the life of any metal part not cooled down well enough and often enough.

Your automobile, unless it is one of those small air-cooled machines, has a water-filled cooling system and radiator to carry away excess heat. A small one or two cylinder gasoline engine usually has only the outside air and the inside oil to do the job.

Here is the moral to all words on the importance of oil—buy the best, and buy it often! Oil comes in various quality ratings. The best for small engines (except those like outboards that have oil mixed directly with gasoline) is a *detergent oil* rated SC or SD. Oil also comes in several thicknesses, or viscosities. At room temperatures, SAE 5 oil is about as thin as water; SAE 40 compares well with dark molasses. (SAE, incidentally, stands for Society of Automotive Engineers.)

For summer time, the most often recommended type of oil is SAE 30. If you can't find it, the next best is SAE 10W/30 or SAE 10W/40. When the temperature falls to 40°F., switch to SAE 5W/20. Next best is SAE 5W/30 and then SAE 10W/30. When the mercury dips to zero, Briggs & Stratton recommends adding 10 percent kerosene to SAE 10W or SAE 10W/30 oil. That amounts to 3½ ounces of kerosene to a quart of motor oil.

Oil should be changed whenever the manufacturer recommends or sooner. Briggs & Stratton says, "Oil should be changed after each 25 hours of engine operation. More often under dirty operating conditions." Never allow more than a year to pass between oil changes no matter how few hours you spend with the engine.

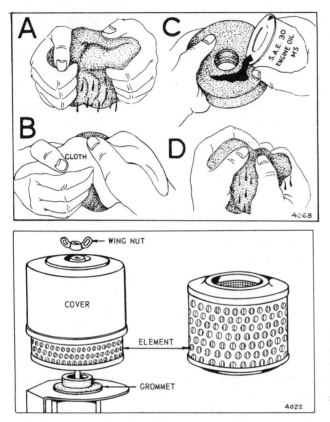

Figure 179 Various air cleaners on gasoline engines require different cleaning methods. Spongy ones are washed with soap and water. Solid elements are blown clean. Both should be replaced about once a year.

The engine *air cleaner* should be cleaned at the same time that oil is changed. If the engine gets dirty air or too little air due to a plugged air cleaner, you will begin to think that some drastic mechanical ailment has happened when actually only a good housecleaning is called for. Figure 179 shows how to clean various air cleaners.

Beyond using the proper gasoline and oil, there are many seasonal and periodic maintenance routines that will ensure both the ultimate in trouble-free operation and long life for your gasoline engine—which is the key ingredient of most lawn mowers, blowers, scooters, and similar noise makers. If you don't have to get your hands greasy, why should you? Here are several checklists to simplify and to systematize your maintenance routines. Doing everything on one of these lists should not take longer than 10 minutes.

BEFORE EVERY USE

1. Check the level of both gasoline and oil. If either is unusually low, check the ground where the machine last stood for wet spots caused by leaks. Then try to locate the leak based on the location of the wet spot.

371

*Mowers,
Blowers,
Scooters
and Other
Engine-Driven
Items*

2. Look for loose parts on the engine, such as air cleaner, oil drain plug, mounting bolts, spark plug wire, fuel line connections, gas tank mounting brackets, throttle, choke springs, levers on the carburetor.

3. Look for loose parts on the rest of your machine, such as seat mounting bolts, controls, brakes, lights.

4. Oil all of the principal moving parts.

AFTER EVERY USE

1. Clean away all grass, dirt, leaves, and other accumulated debris. This has a valid mechanical purpose.

2. Wipe the machine clean and dry. If it receives only sparing use, spray exposed metal parts with an aerosol oil.

3. Fill the gasoline tank (or empty it completely). A partially filled tank allows too much contact between gasoline and air. That leads to harmful deposits inside the tank, which eventually work into the engine's moving parts.

4. If your machine uses a nickel-cadmium battery, clip it onto the charger. They can be left almost permanently hooked up to the battery charger without harm *except in freezing weather.*

PERIODIC CARE (ABOUT EVERY 25 HOURS OF USE)

1. Charge the battery unless it has been taken care of under the "after every use" routine.

2. Unbolt the engine blower housing and clean away any debris. Do the same for any other parts that might obstruct the free flow of air to cool the engine.

3. Change the oil. Remove the oil drain bolt, normally at the bottom of the engine. It is usually near the blade on rotary lawn mowers. After all of the dirty oil has drained out, replace the drain bolt and add the recommended amount of oil through the oil filler cap.

4. Clean the air filter.

5. Clean and inspect the ignition points unless they are located beneath the flywheel (more about this later).

6. Gently clean the spark plug and set it to the proper gap (Figure 180).

7. Make sure that all pulleys, belts, chains, sprockets, and such are properly tightened and not wearing out (reread Chapter 11).

8. Oil or grease all moving parts on the engine.

9. Take care of items not on the engine, such as lawn mower blades, snow blower blowers, scooter tires, outboard motor lights and propellers. Many of these specific parts will be dealt with later in this chapter.

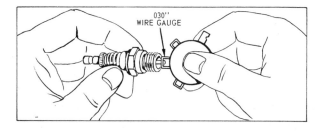

Figure 180 Setting a spark plug gap is important unless you plan to install a new plug. The 0.030 inch setting is standard on Briggs & Stratton engines.

Mowers,
Blowers,
Scooters
and Other
Engine-Driven
Items

1. Drain the gas tank and remove fuel from the engine by running it until the gas is all consumed.

2. Change the oil even if the engine has been operated very little since the last oil change. Moisture, acids, and metal filings accumulate in the oil and can cause subtle but serious damage during long seasonal layovers.

3. Remove the spark plug and add a tablespoon of clean motor oil through the spark plug hole. Be careful to clean away dirt before removing the spark plug so no dirt gets knocked into the cylinder cavity. Replace the spark plug and move the flywheel or activate the starter briefly to distribute the oil over all internal moving parts. This will shield pistons and cylinders from rust.

4. Dry and then oil other metal parts, moving or otherwise.

5. Charge any storage battery your machine may have. Disconnect it to prevent accidental discharge. Then clean the battery case.

6. Block up the axles so rubber tires sit off the flat ground during the off-season.

AT THE BEGINNING OF EVERY NEW SEASON

1. Take away the tire blocks and check the air pressure, if any.

2. Inspect snow blower blades, hone or sharpen lawn mower blades, check the operation of clutches, brakes, controls, and similar devices.

3. Oil or grease all moving parts.

4. Clean deposits off all electrical parts that are easy to reach, such as spark plug, ignition points, shorting terminal (for stopping the engine).

5. Drain the oil and replace with fresh.

6. Fill the gas tank with fresh fuel.

7. Start the engine and let the oil you placed into the spark plug hole burn away in a cloud of smoke before proceeding further.

8. Tune the engine by making sure that the carburetor and ignition settings are adjusted to create maximum engine performance (more about this later).

ENGINE TROUBLESHOOTING

Troubleshooting a troublesome engine can proceed exactly according to the plan presented in Chapter 1 no matter what kind of equipment your engine may be mounted onto. You will soon see that the noisy, greasy, mysterious gasoline engine is simple after all.

FOUR-STROKE ENGINES

A *four-stroke cycle engine*—known as just four cycle—is found on most gasoline-powered gadgets except outboards and some lawn mowers. It gets its name because the piston goes through four separate and distinct motions during every power cycle (see Figure 181). The cycle repeats some 25 times every second.

373

*Mowers,
Blowers,
Scooters
and Other
Engine-Driven
Items*

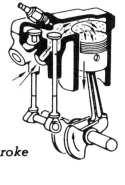

Intake Stroke

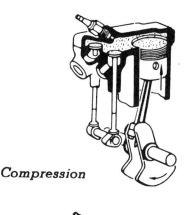

Compression

Power Stroke

Exhaust Stroke

Figure 181   Theory of four-cycle engine operation. Intake: gas
and air are drawn into the cylinder through the intake valve.
Compression: mixture is forced into a small space.
Power: spark plug ignites gasoline and air mixture to drive the
piston downward and give power to the crankshaft at bottom.
Exhaust: upwardly moving piston forces out burnt gasses
through the exhaust valve.

On the *intake stroke,* the falling piston sucks air through the air
cleaner, then through the *carburetor,* and finally through the open
intake valve. The properly adjusted carburetor has a supply of gasoline ready to be sucked along with the air, creating a mixture of
gas and air.

If air cannot pass freely through the air cleaner, the whole carbu-
retion procedure is slowed up or even stopped entirely. Dirt, wear,
vibration, and other gremlins can alter the carburetor adjustment
screws. Since most small engines do not directly regulate the amount
of air sucked through a carburetor, it is crucial that the carburetor
needle valve be precisely adjusted to allow close to the ideal amount
of gasoline to mix with the air being pulled into the cylinder. Both
too much and too little fuel makes for spotty engine performance.

The needle valve ought to be the most prominent adjustment on a
carburetor. Your user manual might assist you in locating it. In

374

*Mowers,
Blowers,
Scooters
and Other
Engine-Driven
Items*

general, the needle valve adjustment knob is the largest one; it requires a screwdriver and doesn't connect to any moving part outside the body of your carburetor. If your engine can be started, you will be able to prove to yourself both that you have discovered the right control and that you can't botch up the engine by fiddling around with it.

Turning a needle valve toward the right should make the engine hesitate, slow down, run rough, or in general show signs of losing power because of a shortage of gasoline in the air-fuel mixture reaching the cylinders. If you turn the needle valve toward the left, which increases the amount of gasoline in the mixture, the engine should speed up slightly, could send smoke out with the exhaust, and the engine will seem to lose power if the setting is changed far enough. This test should be done with the engine running well over half-speed.

On larger engines, those over about eight horsepower, your carburetor may have three or more adjustment screws. One should be a needle valve for *idle speed.* Idle is a low speed at which the engine sits around waiting for something to do. The other valve, the *high speed needle valve,* is for full power operation. As you might expect, the idle needle valve must be adjusted while the engine is idling and the high speed valve at close to full speed.

There is a throttle that controls the motor's speed, but on larger engines there is also an *idle speed control.* Generally, it is a simple although long-adjusting screw close to or even connected to the throttle or speed control mechanism. Turning the idle speed screw to the *right generally increases the idle speed* and vice versa. This is the reverse of most adjustment techniques. What the screw actually does is limit how far the throttle can move in the low speed setting.

A good speed for "idle" is the slowest that the engine can run smoothly. One good test of whether you have properly adjusted your engine to an appropriate idle speed is to let the machine stand at idle for at least several seconds. Then smoothly but quickly increase the speed control to "high." The engine should move up to full power quickly and without much hesitation. Don't be misled by the difference between idle speed and full speed in your car. On cars, idle is close to 10 percent of full speed. On small gasoline engines, idle speed is generally only *half* that of full speed.

If your engine won't start at all, and your troubleshooting leads you to suspect that lack of fuel moving through the carburetor may be at fault, turn the needle valve adjustment fully closed and then open it 1½ turns. Try to start the engine several times. If it still won't start, open the adjustment another ½ turn and try again. Keep

375

*Mowers,
Blowers,
Scooters
and Other
Engine-Driven
Items*

making ½ turn adjustments until the engine starts or until you are ready to move deeper.

The most logical step to take next is toward the choke. When an engine is first started or when it is presented with a sudden heavy load, a mixture richer in gasoline than normal works best. Instead of trying to flick the needle valve adjustment quickly back and forth, engine manufacturers have added a choke, which is little more than a metal disk that impedes the flow of air very much like the damper on those fine old wood or coal burning stoves. It does not impede the flow of gasoline, however, so the net effect is to create a fuel mixture that is richer in gasoline.

Manually operated chokes require only that you inspect the connection between the choke lever, wherever it is mounted, and the choke itself, which is located in the *throat* of your carburetor. The simplest machines of all advise you somewhere in a user manual to shove the choke lever to ''choke'' position prior to starting and then

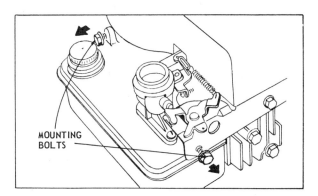

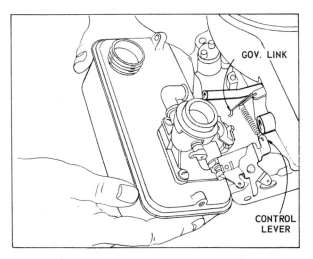

Figure 182 How to remove carburetor from typical small gasoline engine.

376

*Mowers,
Blowers,
Scooters
and Other
Engine-Driven
Items*

back to "open" once the machine gets underway. Other manual chokes are activated for starting by a lever somewhere on the control panel. Many lawn mowers, for example, include a "start" or "choke" position—the two are actually the same.

The simplest way to inspect any choke, manual or automatic, is to remove the air cleaner and peer down the throat of your carburetor. That metal disk should appear to be entirely blocking the throat. If it isn't in that position, find out why. Two reasons are most common: 1) The control lever or control cables are badly adjusted, in which case, adjust them until the choke falls into place; or 2) the pivots into which the choke plate fit are dirty, in which event, clean them. Often, squirting a generous dose of Liquid Wrench on each pivot will loosen the dirt enough to restore the choke to a full life again. Don't be tempted to squeeze oil onto the pivots. It will only burn at the high temperatures your engine endures and make matters worse.

Automatic chokes are operated by the same piston vacuum that sucks air through the carburetor. They are generally linked internally to a rubber diaphragm, which flexes from the vacuum and pulls the choke plate open once the engine is spinning enough to generate a steady, strong vacuum. Troubles often hit the linkage, and *that* means you have to disassemble the entire carburetor.

Tearing apart a carburetor is not as bad as one might think. Figure 183A gives a view of a typical small Briggs & Stratton carburetor. Before beginning such a job, however, it is wise first to have purchased a carburetor gasket set since you are asking for trouble every time you put old gaskets back into place. And before knocking down any carburetor, the outside exposures of all gaskets should be examined for signs of breaks. If air is leaking in or out of the carburetor through a leaky gasket, the repair job is simple indeed. Buy a new gasket from your nearest engine shop or (only when in dire straits) fashion one from some make-a-gasket materials available at hardware stores.

Most outlets that sell small engine parts should also stock extra copies of repair manuals or can order them. Look for these companies in the Yellow Pages under "Engines-Gasoline." Buy the repair manual for your particular engine if you want to tear apart a carburetor or any other major part because it will generally give step-by-step instructions.

The *compression stroke* stands alone. The *exhaust and intake valves* are both closed tightly, the carburetor and ignition systems are waiting for something to do, and only the piston is in motion. If the air and gasoline burned in the relatively large open space of the full cylinder, the result would be heat and little more. So the combustible

377

Mowers,
Blowers,
Scooters
and Other
Engine-Driven
Items

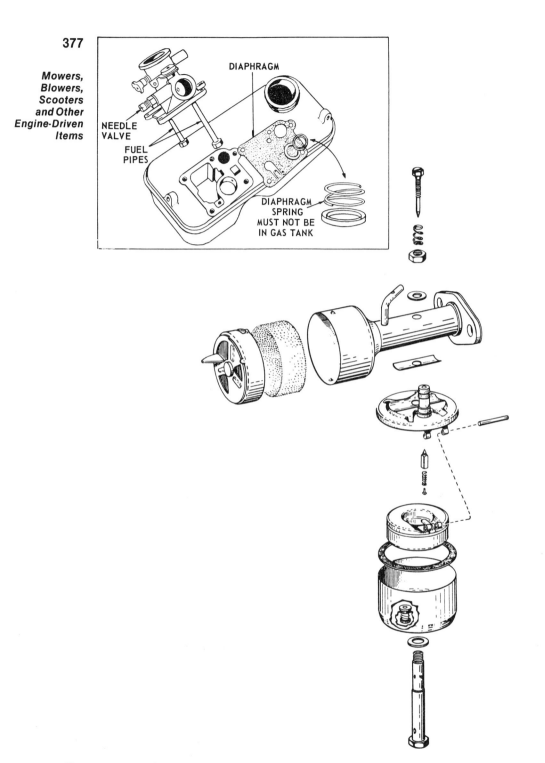

Figure 183 Exploded views of typical small carburetors.

378

*Mowers,
Blowers,
Scooters
and Other
Engine-Driven
Items*

mixture is forced into a tiny space at the top of the cylinder by the compression stroke.

Surprising as it may seem at first, it *is* possible to perform a rough test to see whether or not your small engine is developing enough compression. First, you must remove enough of the trim and other coverings to allow you to get a firm grip on the flywheel. That particular part, incidentally, is very important to the smooth operation of most engines. It is a heavy wheel that turns on the *crankshaft* to even out the roughness that otherwise would occur due to the fact that power is "on" during only one stroke and "off" during three.

Slowly turn the flywheel until the going suddenly gets very rough. That should be within two full turns. If you don't come upon a sudden increase in the amount of force you have to exert to make the flywheel turn, then try twisting it in the opposite direction. Some engines have an automatic valve that releases some of the cylinder pressure when the engine is stopped to make starting easier. On those engines, you will be countermanding the feature by turning the flywheel backward.

When you have reached the sudden hard spot that signals that the engine is ready to go through the compression stroke, both valves should be closed and the piston moving toward the top of the cylinder. At that point, give the flywheel a sharp twist in the same direction you have been turning. It should bounce smartly back in the opposite direction. If it does, the compression inside your engine appears to be okay. If not, look for troubles in the parts that affect compression.

1. A spark plug that is not turned in tightly enough can allow pressure to ooze out during the compression stroke. The same thing will happen if a spark plug has been reinstalled or even originally installed minus the gasket that ensures a pressure-tight seal.

2. Loose head bolts, which hold the top of your engine to the bottom—or in the case of vertical crankshaft engines, the side to the main body—can sometimes work loose due to vibration. More often they were not tightened properly in the first place. The ideal way to tighten loose head bolts is with a torque wrench, which, as we saw in Chapter 2, is a wrench with a dial on it to indicate how much muscle power is being applied to a bolt or nut. Since most junk drawers seldom have a torque wrench, the best way to handle the job is consciously to exert a uniform amount of pressure as you tighten each head bolt in turn, ending up by pulling about as hard as you can without jerking or hammering on the wrench handle.

3. A head gasket, the seal that helps hold in the cylinder pressure, can wear out from old age, abuse, excessive heat and vibration, or unevenly tightened head bolts. Often you can spot a break in it simply by examining the exposed gasket edges. In a bad break, you can even hear gas escaping at the gasket. Whenever head bolts are tightened, they must first be turned down by hand to approximately uniform tightness. Then, with wrench in hand, turn each bolt one full

379

*Mowers,
Blowers,
Scooters
and Other
Engine-Driven
Items*

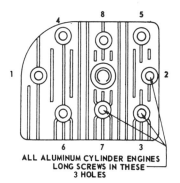

ALL ALUMINUM CYLINDER ENGINES
LONG SCREWS IN THESE
3 HOLES

Figure 184 Head bolts, which hold top of engine to block, must be tightened very carefully so as not to warp the head. Each bolt should be tightened slowly until pressure is felt. Then tighten a half turn at a time and in the order shown. (This is the order for the Briggs & Stratton aluminum engine. Other companies may have other orders. If you can't find your own instructions, take a chance on these.)

turn at a time, in the order shown in Figure 184. (If you have the official repair manual for your engine, follow whatever order is pictured there.) A staggered tightening procedure such as this puts as uniform a pressure on the gasket as possible so that you can get the cylinder head tightly back into place without injuring the important although fragile gasket in the process.

4. Dirt or carbon in the valve area can keep the valves from fitting tightly into their *valve seat*. Using leaded gasoline is one cause of this; lead from exhaust gases can accumulate at the exhaust valve, but does not always accumulate evenly. Just plain carbon, the result of the kind of incomplete combustion found in all gasoline engines, accumulates at the valves also. The easiest way to avoid loss of compression through such an occurrence is by preventive maintenance. Once a year, especially after a well-used engine has reached its second or third year, the cylinder head should be removed and all easy-to-reach carbon deposits scraped away.

A small knife makes a good tool for removing carbon deposits. Scrape with the knife edge, not the point, because the inside of your engine, although made from very tough steel, will not perform well with scratches in its precisely machined surfaces. Pay particular attention to carbon deposits at the upper edge of the cylinder and the piston, also around valves and valve seats.

If valves are to withstand 500 pounds pressure and 5000° temperatures successfully, they must fit into the seat precisely. Therefore, you cannot remove carbon from one side and not the other. And once you start to scrape away carbon, you have to continue until you have reached bare metal all around. That will ensure a uniform fit again.

Look at the *color* of your valves and valve seats. Should the metal surface look somewhat like wholewheat toast, perhaps even with a noticeable dullness to the metal, the hot exhaust gases slipping through accumulations of carbon seem to have burned the valve.

Both intake and exhaust valves can be replaced by unhandy people, but you will need a few hours, an authorized factory repair manual, a set of proper replacement valves, and just maybe a few specialized

380

*Mowers,
Blowers,
Scooters
and Other
Engine-Driven
Items*

but inexpensive tools recommended in the factory manual. While you're at it, invest in the best replacement valves possible. If you burned out one, chances are good the same thing can happen again. Buy a valve made for heavy duty applications (Stellite is Briggs & Stratton's trade name). If available, include a *rotator* on the exhaust valve to help ward off uneven carbon deposits, which so often are the cause of burned valves.

Comes the *power stroke* and the ignition system must do its job. An electric charge has already been generated by a *magneto* or *generator* and *spark coil.* A magneto and a generator are similar enough so that you do not have to worry about their theory. Just know that they can cause an electric charge of about 10,000 volts to be sent into the engine via a distributor and a spark plug.

As the compression stroke about reaches its peak, a sensitive switch called the *ignition points* is opened by the camshaft and sends about 10,000 volts to the spark plug. When the spark plug sparks, the gasoline ignites, causing so much hot gas that the pressure inside the little chamber at the end of the cylinder can reach 500 pounds per square inch. The piston is pushed back along the cylinder with so much force that the engine can coast through its three unproductive strokes and still keep something like a lawn mower turning at 3600 rpms.

The spark plug is the most obvious and easy-to-reach part of the ignition system to check both during preventive maintenance and troubleshooting. Although it is usually possible to take out and reinstall a spark plug without a special wrench, you won't regret a small investment in a deep-throated $^{13}\!/_{16}$" or ¾" wrench made especially for spark plugs. There are two standard sizes of spark plugs, and therefore, two standard sizes of spark plug wrenches. Find out which your machine takes.

A good spark plug, after you clean it up a bit, looks like a new one which has been sandpapered. It is perfectly all right to reinstall one that looks healthy. Most will not. Spark plugs are not at all expensive so don't be stingy about replacing one. But do buy the right kind for the right machine.

Spark plugs come in such a variety of sizes and electrical properties that if you were lucky after installing the *wrong* kind of spark plug, your engine just wouldn't run. If you weren't so lucky, you could damage or destroy the electrical system. Briggs & Stratton seems to be the only engine company with a unified spark plug system for their engines, .030". For other manufacturers, you will have to consult the user manual or take your old plug along with you.

If you plan to reinstall a used but good spark plug, check that the

381

*Mowers,
Blowers,
Scooters
and Other
Engine-Driven
Items*

terminal and electrode are the proper distance apart. This is known in the trade as "checking the spark plug gap." You accomplish this with a small, very cheap *spark plug gauge* or *wire gauge* as shown in Figure 180.

During troubleshooting, using expertise acquired in Chapter 1, if you think that you have tracked down the trouble to the ignition system, unscrew the spark plug. You can sniff for gas at the gaping spark plug hole to make sure the carburetor is working. No gas smell, no carburetor performance.

By this time, you should have invested in a new spark plug to make sure that the problem was not concealed somewhere inside the old plug. Just because a spark plug *looks* okay, doesn't eliminate the possibility that its internal connections may be faulty.

Hook up the spark plug wire to its usual place at the terminal atop the spark plug. And rest the threaded metal portion of the plug against the metal engine block. Turn the engine over several times with the starter. You should see a blue flame with orange fringes jump between the electrodes with a snapping sound. With a healthy, noisy blue flame present, you can pretty well assume that the magneto (generator or alternator in some larger engines) and spark coil are also healthy.

On almost all small Briggs & Stratton and Clinton engines, many others as well, you have to remove the flywheel to get at the ignition points and most other ignition equipment aside from the spark plug. This is a nuisance but a necessary one.

After removing whatever stands between you and the flywheel, you will probably still have to contend with the starter next. Its removal is a straightforward wrench and muscle job. On rewind and windup starters, the opened jaws of a pliers will help you loosen the *starter clutch,* a hollowed-out bit of hardware that holds the starter onto the crankshaft (see Figure 185).

Finally, you reach a naked flywheel, which may be held by one last nut around the crankshaft, the long steel shaft holding the flywheel. That nut may have left-handed threads (loosen clockwise).

The flywheel and crankshaft generally do not separate without a fight. The two parts are tapered to fit as snugly together as possible. That, coupled with corrosion, means you may have to pry gingerly at the bottom of the flywheel. But take your time. A flywheel, for all its weight, is quite a fragile item.

If your engine tinkering is not an emergency, it is wise to stock up on a few parts before exposing the inner parts of the ignition system. Especially if you have gone through the sweat of pulling off a flywheel, you may just as well install an inexpensive set of new ignition

382

Mowers,
Blowers,
Scooters
and Other
Engine-Driven
Items

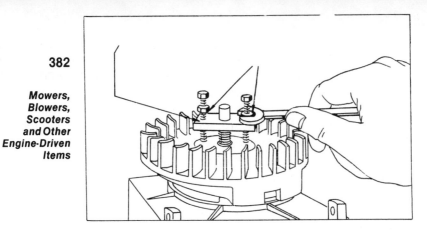

Figure 185 How to remove flywheel from Briggs & Stratton small engine.

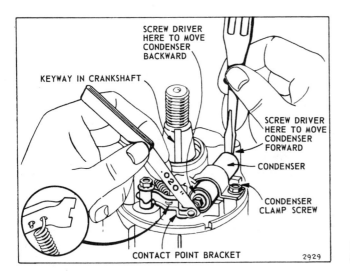

Figure 186 Ignition points on Briggs & Stratton engine are adjusted this way.

points and condensor. Buy a *feeler's gauge* too, a cheap tool that precisely measures minute distances with a set of metal leafs.

It is imperative that ignition points be meticulously clean and that the two contacts be precisely the proper distance apart when their cam, buried deep inside the engine on the camshaft, opens them to set off the ignition charge at the spark plug. On practically every Briggs & Stratton engine and other engines smaller than five horsepower, the setting is .020 inches. On larger engines the setting varies but seems to hover near .030 inches. It is wise to find the setting listed in your user manual, assuming you have it (see Figure 186).

If you replaced the spark plug and ignition points but your engine still is not working right, and you're still convinced that ignition

383

Mowers,
Blowers,
Scooters
and Other
Engine-Driven
Items

problems are to blame, then the magneto has to be checked out. This device consists simply of a series of permanent magnets mounted to the underside of the flywheel, which generate an electric charge in a coil contained within an *armature* fastened to the engine block but covered by the flywheel. As permanent magnets pass over the armature coil, they generate an electric current in the coil. Instead of a simple magneto, bigger engines have a generator or alternator driven by a pulley connected to the engine proper.

You can test the magneto magnets when the flywheel is off by holding a steel screwdriver blade on each magnet. It should take a substantial tug to pull the tool loose from every magnet. Permanent magnets will dissipate their magnetism with age, but it takes lots of age to remove a little magnetism. Beyond that, a sharp blow to the flywheel can sometimes muddle up the magnetism instantly. In any event, the only cure for a demagnetized flywheel is to invest in a new one, not a particularly expensive proposition.

The *armature legs,* there are two or three of them, should be adjusted so their tips are as close to the flywheel as possible without actually scraping against it. That will give you the strongest spark the magnets are capable of generating. On most mowers, every time you pull off the flywheel, you also have to adjust the armature. And if ignition problems have escaped solution, adjust the armature as part of your repair techniques.

There are subtly different recommended gaps between armature legs and flywheel for many popular small engines. If you don't know yours, try .010″ for a start. Figure 187 shows how a typical armature adjustment is accomplished, about a five-minute simple chore.

Unless you have a specialized tool for measuring armature gaps, look for a roll of ordinary Scotch brand Magic Tape, which is about .002″ thick. Therefore, if your armature gap must be .010″, if you put 5 layers of tape down, one on top of the other, when you finally tighten the armature screws, the gap should be very close to .010″.

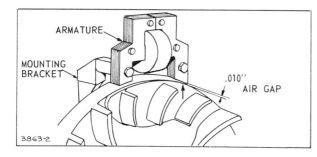

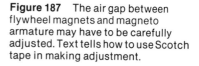

Figure 187 The air gap between flywheel magnets and magneto armature may have to be carefully adjusted. Text tells how to use Scotch tape in making adjustment.

384

*Mowers,
Blowers,
Scooters
and Other
Engine-Driven
Items*

If wires are frayed or maybe even pulled loose on the armature you find beneath your flywheel, the easiest and surest solution is to replace the unit. And be sure to adjust the air gap when you get the new one in place.

Briggs & Stratton has a magneto system known as Magna-Matic. You will probably hear the name from your engine sales person or user manual. The Magna-Matic armature air gap is permanently adjusted at the factory. Only severe damage to the engine should alter that setting. So don't try to tamper with the gap on such a magneto.

After putting your magneto in order, the flywheel is slid back onto the crankshaft and fastened into place exactly as you took it off. There is a *flywheel key* to contend with, however—a flat, often semicircular piece of soft metal that keeps the flywheel positioned accurately on the crankshaft. The key slips into matching slots in both the flywheel and the crankshaft. Without such an arrangement, the magneto magnets might not reach the armature coil at the proper instant. It is very important that the key be replaced, if need be, with one that is both the proper size and the proper metal. In the first place, your magneto might not work well if the wrong metal is used for the key. Second, having a soft metal key gives some protection. In case your rotary lawn mower hits a big rock, for example, instead of transmitting the shock to the entire engine, the key might bend or snap. It is bad enough having to replace the flywheel key, but if the soft key weren't soft, you might have to replace the whole engine!

Exhaust strokes come and go, and what happens is that the exhaust valve opens to let burned gases escape into the atmosphere. When that is out of the way, the engine is ready to begin the intake stroke all over again.

We discussed the exhaust valve, its care and replacement, at the same time intake valves were covered. That leaves us with the *muffler*. About all that can be said for muffler repair is that it unscrews in case it needs replacing. There are many styles and sizes of mufflers, so get one intended for your machine.

The four-cycle engine we have been discussing, assuming it is well designed and well built in the first place, is about as rugged a piece of machinery as anybody could ask for. Believe it or not, many of the small engines manufactured today are still almost as well built as the one put together in grandfather's time. Even hooked onto a rotary lawn mower, which is a really brutal application, a four-cycle engine should hold out for five years with minimum maintenance, another five if you're willing to tinker with it.

Mowers,
Blowers,
Scooters
and Other
Engine-Driven
Items

A *two-stroke cycle engine* (two cycle) is noted mainly for its scarcity of parts to tinker with. It has no camshaft or metal valves. That would seem like an economical, practical bit of design, and it actually is for some applications. But, in general, the two-cycle engine is not quite as efficient nor as long lasting as the four cycle.

Figure 188 shows how the two-cycle engine accomplishes in two strokes what the four cycle does in four strokes. The two-cycle engine is often called a boon for those who don't want to repair or even maintain an engine. That is because the two-cycle engine burns some oil along with its gasoline, which not only lubricates the moving parts but makes a terrible smell and some smoke as well. Ironically, the two-cycle engine is less able to tolerate lazy routine internal

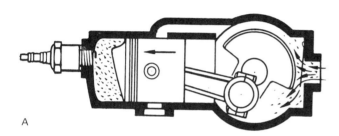

A

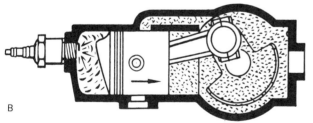

B

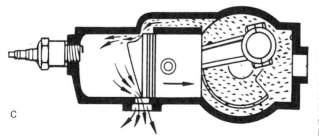

C

Figure 188   Theory of two-cycle engine operation. This type of engine is used on some lawn mowers, most outboard motors, and many chain saws or similar tools. (A) new mixture of air and gas is pulled into crankcase (at right) while earlier mixture is forced into top of cylinder (left). (B) spark plug ignite mixtures in cylinder, forcing piston downward in cylinder. This forces new mixture of gas and air into top of cylinder (C) as soon as intake port is uncovered. Rush of new mixture forces out burnt gasses through now open exhaust port at bottom of drawing.

cleaning, and, therefore, generally has a much shorter life-span than the four cycle.

On a *compression stroke* in a two-cycle engine, the piston moves upward to squeeze the gasoline and air mixture into a small space, just as in the four-cycle operation. And the bouncing flywheel test for good compression, outlined in the four-cycle section, is almost as effective for two-cycle as four-cycle engines.

In two-cycle engines, the vacuum that the compression stroke leaves behind in the *crankcase,* a chamber beneath the cylinder, is put to good purpose as well. It draws open a simple *reed valve,* and the vacuum then sucks air through the air cleaner and then through the carburetor, just as during the intake stroke of the four-cycle engine. In essence, then, the compression and intake strokes of a four-cycle engine are compressed onto one stroke, called the compression stroke in a two-cycle engine.

Carburetors in a two-cycle engine function the same as in a four-cycle one. Since the rest of the engine is so much simpler, however, some companies try to simplify the carburetor as much as possible too.

The reed valve is one of the most crucial parts on this engine. Visual inspection is about the only practical way to separate good reeds from bad. If they look broken, bent, distorted, or unevenly colored, replace them. New reed valves are cheap.

Replacement reed valves screw into place, often with a metal *reed stop* on top of them. The smooth side of a valve faces the engine cylinder and the rough side faces the carburetor.

The *power stroke* on a two-cycle engine also compresses several of the four-cycle functions into one stroke. The top side of the piston faces an electric charge from a spark plug. And the burning fuel-air mixture pushes on the piston. As the piston is shoved down the cylinder, however, it also builds up pressure beneath it. The pressure closes the reed valve and compresses the new batch of air and fuel, which had been sucked into the crankcase during the earlier compression stroke.

Midway through the power stroke, the descending piston uncovers the *exhaust port,* nothing more than a small hole in the cylinder wall. It has to be placed strategically so the fuel has enough time to burn before the piston uncovers the exhaust port and spills the burned gases into the atmosphere.

The exhaust port must be kept well cleaned. If carbon or other exhaust deposits are allowed to accumulate at the small opening, they can prevent exhaust gases from being expelled completely enough. As a result, there will be less room in the combustion chamber for fresh air and fresh fuel. And that will mean *less power* from your engine,

387

*Mowers,
Blowers,
Scooters
and Other
Engine-Driven
Items*

more heat for your engine, and a *shorter life-span* for your machinery.

Obviously, the muffler and exhaust pipe, if any, cover the exhaust port. They have to be removed after every 25 hours of use so you can clean out the exhaust port. Most manufacturers recommend that you locate a wooden dowel, which fits into the port. Turn the crankshaft until the piston fully covers the exhaust port and then gently ream away all carbon with the dowel.

On lawn mowers such as the Lawn-Boy, the exhaust from its two-cycle engine blows into the underside of the mower deck. That means you have to flop the machine gently over onto its fragile side when engine cleaning.

In the four-cycle section, you were advised periodically to remove the cylinder head for a thorough scraping away of all accumulated carbon and miscellaneous deposits. The same advice applies to these engines.

Still further along the two-cycle engine power stroke, the piston uncovers yet another opening, the *intake port.* The fresh mixture of air and gasoline being compressed by the bottom of the falling piston is then free to rush into the combustion chamber above the piston. In doing so, the fresh gasoline-air mixture helps to push out the exhaust fumes. Some two-cycle engines use pistons that slope on top better to regulate the distance between the exhaust port and the intake port. Others are able to accomplish the delicate maneuver with what you might say were normal, flat top pistons.

Up until now, you may have had a lingering doubt about whether your own engine is two cycle or four cycle. If oil is mixed with gasoline, it is two cycle. That is, if your user manual tells you to mix oil with the gasoline. You'd be surprised at how many people assume that all small engines, two cycle or four, require oil in the gas tank.

The proper mixture of gasoline and oil is important to two-cycle engine operation. In all events, follow the recommendations of the manufacturer. But if that information has been lost or forgotten, data suggest that you mix one-half pint of oil with every gallon of gasoline. And the oil should be of a quality rated MM or MS with a viscosity of SAE 30 or SAE 40. The product packaged as "outboard motor oil" should never be used for preparing gasoline-oil mixtures unless your user manual specifically recommends it.

OIL DISTRIBUTION

In four-cycle engines, oil distribution takes oil out of the crankcase and spreads it around all of the moving parts. In some large engines,

*Mowers,
Blowers,
Scooters
and Other
Engine-Driven
Items*

a pump is used. But most engines you are likely to encounter employ a *slinger*. It does exactly that too—it literally slings oil around the exposed insides of the engine.

Oil pumps and oil slingers vary in appearance from manufacturer to manufacturer, but in every instance the slinger must be able to move freely whenever the engine is in motion. It has to be kept clean so that accumulation will not reduce its oil-clinging capacity.

The slinger, called a *dipper* on some engines, is buried deep within the crankcase. To inspect one requires an hour or two of greasy work to tear apart such delicate moving parts as the crankshaft and camshaft. To avoid such mechanical exercises, you would be better advised to change oil frequently, use only the best grade of oil available, keep the air cleaner clean and in good repair, plus keep an eye on your engine's *breather*. All of this will keep the inside of your engine clean, including the oil slinger.

The breather on four-cycle engines is one of the most overlooked parts but one of the most important for long engine life and trouble-free operation. You can run a put-put machine for years without ever knowing about the breather. But during those years, the engine might be performing below peak efficiency and choking on dirt getting sucked in via the breather.

When the four-cycle engine is making a down stroke, either for intake or for power, the underside of the piston would build up pressure inside the crankcase if that were a sealed system. (In a two-cycle engine, that is the case. It is that pressure in two-cycle engines that pushes fresh fuel and air to the top of the piston.) The pressure would interfere with easy piston motion and also would force oil from the crankcase out through the various seals in a four-cycle engine. This is why a two-cycle engine has to rely on oil mixed with gasoline.

If oil leaks are a problem in your four-cycle engine, perhaps a breather problem is the reason. Breathers are very similar to a two-cycle reed valve. When there is pressure inside the crankcase, the breather valve—generally a simple thin metal or fiber disk—is pushed open to let the pressure escape. When the cylinder moves upward again, the valve is drawn shut and a slight vacuum is built up inside the crankcase.

Figure 189 shows what some typical breather assemblies look like. The portion built into or onto the engine cylinder block contains the breather valve and related parts. The tubes, if any, generally lead directly or indirectly to the air cleaner so that the air coming in contact with the breather is more likely to be free of dirt.

389

*Mowers,
Blowers,
Scooters
and Other
Engine-Driven
Items*

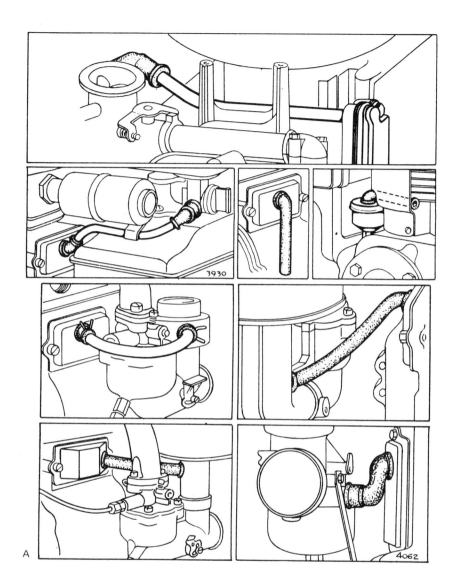

A

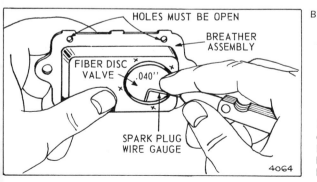

HOLES MUST BE OPEN

BREATHER
ASSEMBLY

FIBER DISC
VALVE

.040''

SPARK PLUG
WIRE GAUGE

4064

B

Figure 189 Breathers allow four-cycle engine to operate efficiently. Drawing (A) shows where typical breathers are located. And (B) shows how to test one. Replace if in doubt.

390

*Mowers,
Blowers,
Scooters
and Other
Engine-Driven
Items*

It is possible to inspect the breather valve for obstructions. But once you have reached it, why not replace it and be sure? Breather disk valves and gaskets for the breather enclosure are very inexpensive. If you change them every year or two, your small investment will be returned many times over.

Aside from knowing if you own a two-cycle or a four-cycle engine, you will also want to know the name of the company responsible for manufacturing it. So many different companies assemble items such as lawn mowers and go-carts and snowmobiles with parts they buy from original equipment manufacturers all over the country, that just because you invested in a Little Jiffy mower doesn't mean it has an engine manufactured by the Little Jiffy Company.

There are about half a dozen major engine manufacturers. Many of their products are fastened onto mowers and blowers and scooters with a label riveted or glued on. Here is an inside look at the engine makers' codes so you can spot the original manufacturer of your own engine. That way you can buy parts from a dealer most likely to have them in stock.

Briggs & Stratton marks their engines with a five-element code, which consists of either five or six digits. (The first code element can be a one- or two-digit number.) Once you crack the Briggs code, you not only know *who* made the engine but its authentic horsepower rating (the first code element) and every fundamental part Briggs hooked onto the engine.

Many equipment assemblers doctor up the Briggs & Stratton engine markings and try to conceal the code just a bit. But it is usually recognizable anyway. Sears & Roebuck, for example, is reported in the Briggs manual to tack a "500" in front of the Briggs code. A Sears model 500.20054 engine, consulting the code chart, would convert to a Briggs model 20054, an engine (8 horsepower) with gear reduction and a 12 volt electric starter.

Yardman's Model 2320-2 20″ lawn mower lists a part number "92905, engine." If your Yardman engine needed attention, you would be pretty sure that it was a Briggs & Stratton creation—a 3.5 horsepower engine with their Pulsa-Jet carburetor, a plain bearing, and a 12 volt electric starter. Instead of going to Yardman for engine parts, you could also go to a Briggs dealer.

The Kohler Company makes engines found on many larger machines. Their engines generally have a "K" in front of three digits. The numbers represent the engine size expressed in cubic inches times 10. Thus, if you found a "K241" on your engine, you would expect it

391

*Mowers,
Blowers,
Scooters
and Other
Engine-Driven
Items*

to be a Kohler engine with about a 24 cubic inch displacement, worth about 10 horsepower. Their K301 turns out 14 horsepower, the K321 about 14, and the K181 about 8.

Tecumseh engines are sent from the factory with a letter and number code. The letter "V" identifies a vertical crankshaft engine, the kind with a starter on top and the shaft on the bottom, such as on rotary lawn mowers. "H" signifies a horizontal crankshaft. Numbers are approximate horsepower ratings times 10. Therefore, an H50 engine would be a 5 horsepower model with horizontal crankshaft, popular for riding lawn mowers.

Tecumseh often adds extra letters to its code, but the "H" and "V" are the giveaways. Thus, an engine with part number "HH1000" should lead you to believe that it is a Tecumseh horizontal crankshaft engine with 10 horsepower. The Tecumseh LAV35 is a 3.5 horse-power vertical crankshaft engine commonly found on lawn mowers. The engines with vertical crankshafts are almost always used on rotary lawn mowers, although a very few make their way into small generating units.

Clinton identifies its engines with a 10-digit code without any pre-ceding letters. Briggs & Stratton's all-number code never stretches beyond 6 digits. Clinton's code leads off with a number "4" or "5". Briggs, fortunately, never begins with either number—not yet anyway. Clinton's opening "4" stands for a four-cycle engine and the "5" for a two-cycle engine. The third digit, if it is odd, represents a vertical crankshaft engine, and even numbers are reserved for horizontal crankshaft engines. The other parts of Clinton's 10-digit code identify various basic components in a manner similar to the Briggs system.

At the end of a *serial number,* not the model number, Clinton often adds a letter. This identifies a basic engineering change that occurred during the life-span of a particular model of engine. To obtain exact replacement parts, that letter must be given to the parts dealer along with your engine model number.

It is not practical to discuss every variation in every engine. Only the most widely used engines were emphasized. But armed with this knowledge, you should be able to tackle a good deal of what goes wrong with small engines. And if you want additional help, at least three engine makers sell their official repair manuals for a reasonable price. You can walk into any authorized distribution center for Briggs & Stratton, Clinton, or Outboard Marine (Lawn-Boy) and carry away a book full of blueprints and specific fix-it data.

You may not understand all the words, even all the pictures, in a

392

*Mowers,
Blowers,
Scooters
and Other
Engine-Driven
Items*

thick repair manual (the Briggs & Stratton manual weighs 10 pounds). Most repair pros don't either! But you can get some insights and some encouragement just knowing that it is all there whether you need it, want it, or can use it.

How to See Through Glass, Window, Door, and Lock Problems

18

It isn't really hard to see your way through window and glass problems—glass itself is wonderful to work with. It is easier to cut than wood; its surface cannot be marred with anything but a very sharp object; and a perfectly decent glass cutter is a very cheap tool.

WINDOW AND GLASS REPAIRS

Let's say that Junior steers his favorite model airplane through a bedroom window. You could call in a professional at a rather expensive cost. Assuming, of course, you find someone willing to make house calls. Or you can buy the glass at considerably less expense and install it yourself. Once you get the glass, the whole job of putting it into place should not take any longer than going through the phone book in search of a pro.

Measure the old window size precisely on the *outside*. What you see on the inside of a window is much different from what you will

394

*How to See
Through Glass,
Window, Door,
and Lock
Problems*

have to fit into the space outside. It is often a good idea to clean away at least part of the old window and its remaining putty to let your measuring tape rest right up against the frame, thereby ensuring an accurate fit. (Review Chapter 4 for measuring tips.)

Be sure to measure the height and the width at *several points*—let's say the two ends and the middle—to make sure you don't pick a misshaped spot by accident. Once you have jotted down the precise measurements of the old glass, subtract ⅛″ from both the horizontal and the vertical size. Example: You find the old window glass to be 18¾″ wide and 26¼″ high. Subtracting ⅛″ would leave 18⅝″ by 26⅛″. That missing ⅛″ allows for inaccuracies in the frame and in your measurements, and for expansion on hot days.

You can buy glass from many different places. Hardware stores often carry it, as do lumberyards. And window installation or repair outlets should sell it to you too. In every instance, ask that the glass be cut to your exact measurements. Most places will cut it for you, but, if not, buy the smallest stock piece that will fill your requirements and cut it yourself.

The secret to successful glass cutting is *confidence.* So pick up some scraps of glass to practice on, maybe a large piece or two of the broken window. Measure carefully and then lay a straight edge or rule *close* to (not on) your measured marks. The glass cutter itself takes up some space so you will have to take that into consideration or you will end up with a piece of glass perhaps ⅛″ or ¼″ too big or too small.

Run the cutting edge of the glass cutter *firmly* along the marked line. *But run it once and only once.* Press down hard enough to leave a sharply defined, unbroken line in the glass. Rather than actually cutting the glass, a glass cutter just penetrates the surface to set up a stress line. If you run the cutter back and forth, you will be contributing to *conflicting* lines of stress.

After making the scored line with your cutting edge, use the opposite end to tap firmly all along the line of cut. This increases the depth to which the stress line penetrates. Often the sheet of glass will snap cleanly apart at the appropriate line as you are tapping, which is a true mark of skill in making the scored line—or a true mark of luck.

Assuming the glass does not break in two during the tapping, move next to the snap phase. To this point, your new sheet of glass should be perfectly flat on a table or the floor. One way to execute the snap is to slide the glass over to a nicely squared off edge of a table. Lay the scored line facing upward and parallel to the table edge but hanging free about ⅛″ beyond the edge. Generally, the portion of the whole new piece to be used is kept on the table and the portion to be discarded is allowed to hang over the edge.

395

*How to See
Through Glass,
Window, Door,
and Lock
Problems*

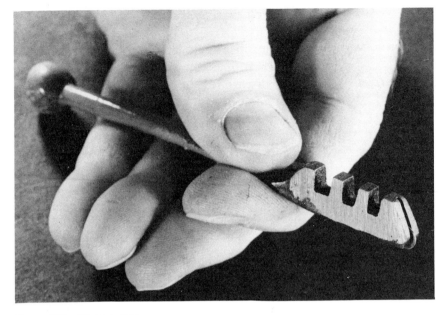

Figure 190   Glass cutter.

Lay your fingers against the end toward the center of the table. If that end is sharp, you may want to wear gloves or keep a rag between you and the glass. The purpose of your fingers is to form a hinge.

Now lift the hanging end of the glass a few inches, make sure the opposite edge has not slipped, and then snap the entire pane back down to the table. Hopefully you will be left holding the separate piece of glass in your hand. If not, repeat the process but snap somewhat more vigorously. If that does not break the glass neatly along your scored line, shift temporarily to a new tactic.

Turn the pane over and tap vigorously along the scored line *on the unscored side of the glass.* The object is to whack the glass as hard as possible without endangering the pane. Then repeat the snapping process as the scored line is pointed downward.

By this point you really should have successfully sheared the pane of glass into two neat portions. If not, the trouble more than likely is your lack of confidence, which in turn leads to a less than adequate pressure on the glass cutter, feeble tapping effort, and a hesitant snap. But here's what to do.

With the original scored line facing downward, line up your straight edge and glass cutter for a second attack. You want this new scored line to be exactly in line with the first. This time press on the cutting tool with the knowledge that all of your previous efforts really had not shattered what you thought was such a fragile pane of

396

*How to See
Through Glass,
Window, Door,
and Lock
Problems*

glass. Tap the new scored line—confidentially—and then proceed to snap it.

In case your measurements have failed and the new window pane doesn't fit the frame, you will probably be left with such a tiny bit of glass on the discard side of your next scored line that snapping it over the edge of a table is out of the question. In that case, go through all of the processes up to the snap. Then take a pliers and simply bend off the unwanted glass. The results will not be quite as neat as a snapped cut, but the edge is going to be covered up anyway.

Now, back to the window repair job. Clean away all the old glass and putty in the window frame. Better take out those broken pieces of glass with pliers or heavy gloves. Use a chisel or screwdriver to scrape the frame until it is quite smooth.

Smear putty generously into the frame where the glass will eventually rest. Putty has been the traditional glazing substance, but the newer caulking or sealant compounds in tubes work very nicely. Products in a tube are also easier to apply than putty in a can.

Set the new pane of glass into place and hold it there while you press *glazier points* into place near the corners. Glazier points are triangle-shaped bits of metal designed to hold glass into window frames. You can get the points started by pushing on them with your fingers. To set them firmly into their final resting place, lay the flat side of a screwdriver against the flat top of each point and pry down-

Figure 191   How to replace glass window. Get rid of broken glass (A) with pliers (B). Scrape out putty and glass (C) with screwdriver. Pull glazier points (D) out. Put in fresh putty (E) and window (F).

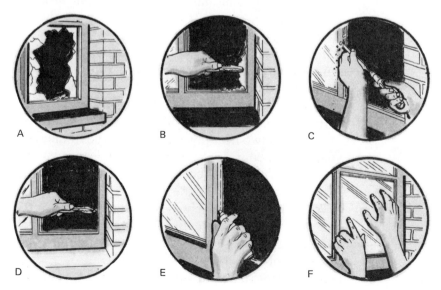

397

*How to See
Through Glass,
Window, Door,
and Lock
Problems*

ward vigorously. If the frame is tough or you aren't, tap gently on the screwdriver with a hammer to drive the point home.

After the glazier points are firmly in place at every corner, you can stop holding the pane of glass into place. Then add additional glazier points every 4″ or 6″.

Squeeze a wide bead of putty or caulking compound around the four outside edges of the window. If you keep the nozzle close to the corner formed by the wooden frame and the pane of glass, your compound will fill the corner more thoroughly and be smoothed down all in one motion. And then you have a well-finished, professional-looking job to your credit.

Windows in aluminum frames are generally even easier to fix than the wooden frame variety. A rubber gasket squeezed between frame and glass is about all you have to contend with. If the gasket is dried and cracked, replace it. And if that proves to be impossible or impractical, substitute a good tube of sealant for the gasket.

Most window glass for use around the home is called *single thickness,* which figures out to something close to ⅛″ thick. Larger windows or other specialized applications often call for double thickness, triple thickness, or beyond. They cost substantially more than single thickness and glass starts getting harder to cut at that thickness. You are generally well off to replace a window with the same kind of glass that was there originally unless there is a good reason for changing.

Plastic can also be used in place of glass windows. This is an especially fine idea if a window is in left field of the neighborhood ball park. A sheet of ⅛″ thick acrylic plastic such as Lucite or Plexiglas costs about double what you would pay for a sheet of glass the same size. But baseballs and even small caliber bullets bounce right off the plastic.

Ordinary plastic windows do have a couple of hangups. The surface scratches. Sharp toys can leave scratch marks, and vigorous cleaning with abrasive cleansers can dull the surface. Under most household circumstances, however, it will be many years before such blemishes become obvious. And if you want to install the plastic window good and proper, you can invest more money in a product coated specifically for use in industrial windows. Lexan or a similar product costs more than common plastic but its surface comes close to matching the durability of glass.

Sticking and falling windows develop gradually, as a rule. Wood that was not well cured and dried before becoming a window frame dries out over the years, and sometimes over the space of just a few months in a new home.

Drying wood shrinks. As the shrinking window pulls farther and

398

*How to See
Through Glass,
Window, Door,
and Lock
Problems*

farther away from the supporting pieces in the frame, there is less pressure against the window to support its weight. You lift the window one day, take away your hands, and, bang, it slides down with a thud.

Conversely, if a dried window works well but the weather becomes moist for a time, the moisture may swell the wood and you will have to exert yourself a good deal to raise it. Accumulated layers of paint or varnish, even dust and grime, can add extra thickness to the sliding areas of a window and make it stick.

To conquer a problem window, you first have to decide what kind of problem it has. Basically there are three ways in which a window is designed. Some go up and down inside a relatively loose fitting wooden track formed in part by decorative molding. A counterweight concealed behind the left and right sides of the window frame often is fastened to such windows, and they slide down or up as the window slides up or down. You will be able to recognize such a design because of the chain that fastens to each side of the window and disappears into a hole near the top of each frame.

If a counterweighted window will not stay up, it is because of the counterweight. More than likely the pulley over which the chain passes as it disappears through the hole in the frame is stuck. In that case, the chain itself often bunches up as you try to lift the window.

Try twisting a stuck pulley by hand. If that seems to be the problem, douse its bearing with Liquid Wrench to loosen the accumulated grime as quickly as possible. Then squirt or spray oil, grease, graphite, or silicone into the pulley bearing. A modest dose of graphite or silicone on the chain itself often helps.

Don't assume that a window pulley *has to turn.* Many of them have been stuck for years, but the chain slips easily over the unmoving curved surface. If that is the case in your home, leave well enough alone.

Old or defective counterweight systems can fall apart or get stuck on something. If that happens, you have about two choices, neither exactly pleasant. You can make do with what is left of the window system or take it apart. That means first removing all of the strips of molding on the inside window frame, and then sliding the window itself out of place. Finally, you can pry off the wooden piece of window frame that conceals the counterweight system. Next you will have to reattach the pulley, install a new chain (available at hardware stores), or get rid of whatever came out of place to block the free motion of the counterweight. Then you can reassemble the window frame. Inevitably it will also need to be repainted.

Some windows slide up and down in a fairly tight fitting frame. The window is held up by pressure put on it from side pieces in the

399

*How to See
Through Glass,
Window, Door,
and Lock
Problems*

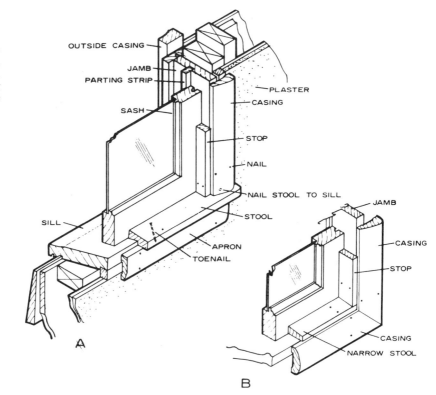

OUTSIDE CASING

JAMB

PARTING STRIP

SASH

PLASTER

CASING

STOP

NAIL

NAIL STOOL TO SILL

STOOL

SILL

APRON

TOENAIL

JAMB

CASING

STOP

CASING

NARROW STOOL

A

B

Figure 192   Here's an x-ray type view of typical window.

frame. A set of two or three, sometimes more, screws can be tightened to loosen the grip of the frame on a window. And vice versa.

Generally, the screws all up and down the adjustable piece should be adjusted uniformly. Theoretically, that should keep the window frame uniformly easy to deal with from top to bottom. However, the top window may get less use than the bottom and often gets exposed to less water and rain. You may have to tighten or loosen only *some* of the adjustment screws to arrive at the optimum overall performance.

Whenever the glass panes are dirty enough to require care, the track in which the window moves also should be wiped clean. The dirt and grime that lodges there is less obvious, but once it has accumulated for a time, its effect is more annoying and harder to deal with. Silicone lubricant, preferably the dry variety, keeps all kinds of window tracks slippery and helps windows to cope with changing weather and age.

The third basic type of window uses a piece of metal weather strip along the side of the window frame to fit snugly into a groove along the side of the window itself. The system works fine until

400

*How to See
Through Glass,
Window, Door,
and Lock
Problems*

weather dries out and shrinks any of the wood that was not dry enough when the window was manufactured. Or a moist spell swells the wood, especially those parts that don't get painted or varnished. The weatherstrip system is one of those engineering feats that requires almost "zero defect" precision. And life just isn't like that.

Keep the weather strip and its matching groove clean and slippery to make lifting and lowering the window easy. If a window consistently goes up too hard and goes down too hard, and you are sure it is not just a temporary problem caused by weather or dirt, a small metal chisel and hammer can offer relief.

Run the sharp edge of the chisel along the base of the metal strip right where the pointed "tongue" begins. Tap it sharply with your hammer as you move the chisel along. If the sticking problem occurs only near the top or only near the bottom, perhaps only midway, do most of your tapping right there at first. Don't imagine, however, that the problem is caused by the weather strip one foot from the bottom. There are a couple of feet of window groove to consider too. A problem *one foot* from the bottom, added to perhaps two feet of overlapping window groove, could very well be localized *three feet* from the bottom.

The weatherstrip style of window that doesn't stay up well enough presents an entirely different problem. One solution would be to take off the metal strip and put narrow shims behind it so the tongue extends deeper into the groove. But that is a lot of tedious work and by the time you are finished, it is likely that enough mechanical problems and misalignments would have crept in to complicate the problem more than fix it. If the lack of tension is not too severe, you could intentionally get the tongue and groove very dirty. For a job like this, the best kind of dirt is called *belt dressing,* a sticky, gooey substance that comes in a tube or can. Belt dressing is intended primarily for building up friction on a belt that slips over a pulley instead of moving it. The dressing contains sharp granules, which grab at the belt and the pulley. Or in the case of windows, the granules will grab both the window tongue and groove.

Winds, dust, and noise slip through whatever cracks they can find in a window system. That dust you find on windowsills every week doesn't *all* come from inside. Most, in fact, probably filters through from the soot and grime of the "fresh air" outside. Much the same goes for doorways leading to the outdoors.

People seem to notice the airways around a window most during cold winter days. If they paid as much attention to the air that comes through windows during the hot air conditioning season, their electric bills would be noticeably smaller.

Just what you do about leaky windows or doors depends upon

401

*How to See
Through Glass,
Window, Door,
and Lock
Problems*

how often they are used, what materials you find locally, and how ambitious you get over the issue of drafts.

The simplest way to tackle drafty windows is with a strip of foam rubber backed with an adhesive tape. Pull off the tape covering and stick it tightly against any of the areas where air leaks in. To avoid an unsightly job, work on the outside surfaces or actually between the window and the window frame. The foam rubber tape material is best suited for doorways. Properly placed, the weather seal is never seen when the door is closed, and that is also where it will do the most good.

Doors can be sealed tight with a tube or caulking gun full of a rubber sealant. Silicone products, although the most expensive, are best suited to this kind of work because they are durable, flexible under adverse weather, and set quickly. Simply run a generous bead along all of the framed-in pieces the door contacts—or is supposed to contact—when closed. Don't completely close the door until the new weather seal is set. Go over any spots that will leak after the seal is set and the door has been closed.

Used for windows, silicone rubber products go on just like the tape-backed foam strips. If you smear them onto the inside surfaces of windows, you will have to rough up the bead with coarse sandpaper before the silicone will take paint.

Some of the other sealants and caulking materials that come in tubes of various sizes can be used inside windows. But they better be used on windows you don't plan to open again very soon. If you think an accumulation of paint makes windows hard to open, wait until you try to open a window you caulked shut last winter! In an all-air-conditioned home, however, the use of a good sealant is an ideal way to make the windows look better (after repainting them) as well as to keep out drafts, dust, and noise.

You can get almost the degree of protection that inside caulking affords, without having to do a permanent job, by using a non-hardening putty, which comes in long narrow strips wrapped around a coil. The putty beads are pressed into any area where air might be leaking, and the pliable stuff just twists and oozes firmly into the spaces. But, as soon as you decide to open the window again, all you have to do is grab hold of one end of the bead and strip it right off. You can even wind it up for use next season.

SCREENS

If screens become full of holes, they can be patched or replaced. If some curious finger or a misdirected stick jabs a hole into an otherwise sound window screen, your best bet is to make a patch. If the

402

*How to See
Through Glass,
Window, Door,
and Lock
Problems*

screen gets holes due to age, you should consider replacing the entire piece of screen, assuming the wooden or metal frame is still sound.

Your local hardware store or dime store probably sells small packages of screen patches. But you can make your own if you have a spare piece of window screen around. The screen can be cut with a scissors, but use an old one. You might dull the scissor blades just enough so that you will have to sharpen them. Cut a screen patch considerably bigger than the hole. Then pull loose the last wire all the way around. Bend over the protruding ends of wire so that you can poke them into the mesh remaining around the hole in your screen. Finally, bend the loose wires toward the center of your patch until they are all flattened out (see Figure 193).

Screens in an aluminum frame are replaced just like the windows we discussed earlier. The rubber gasket is pulled loose, the new screen is fitted into place, and the gasket is tucked back between the screen and its frame.

Wooden frames generally have a quarter-round molding nailed into the outside perimeter of the screen. It is called "quarter-round molding" because its profile looks like one-quarter of a full circle. You will have to pry the molding out with a screwdriver or chisel to release the old screen. The most accurate time to measure for a new screen is when that molding has been completely removed. Some stores will cut screen to exactly the dimensions you provide. Others

Figure 193 Broken screen can be renewed with a bit of screen cut from another source or with patch bought at hardware store. Do-it-yourselfer pulls last wire all the way around small patch (left), then bends down all of the outside wire ends. The ends are shoved between wires around hole (center) and then bent over (right) to form tight patch.

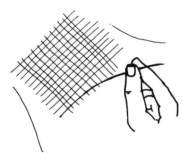
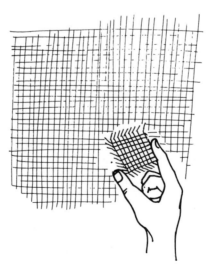
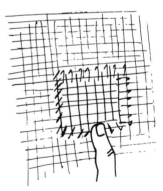

403

*How to See
Through Glass,
Window, Door,
and Lock
Problems*

sell "stock sizes," which you cut yourself. A tin snips is the ideal tool for cutting screen, but it hardly pays to invest in one for a single screen repair job. Use an old scissors in such a case.

After the new piece of screen has been laid carefully into place, nail the molding back to the frame. Use new nails and do not use the old nail holes.

WINDOW SHADES

Generally a very reliable window accessory, there is very little hardware to window shades.

In the center, shades are nothing but a wooden stick. The fabric or plastic is taped or stapled to the stick. Better shades have more "excess" shade material. If the shade for a 48″ window has just barely 48″ of material, the tape or staples are put under substantial stress every time the shade is lowered. If the manufacturer put perhaps 54″ or 56″ of material on the roll, the excess absorbs the stress instead of the staples or tape.

At one end of a shade is a simple metal pin. It gets hammered into the wooden center as a rule. That pin fits into a matching piece of hardware over or alongside the window, a bracket with a simple hole for the pin.

The working end of a shade fits into a slotted bracket. Although all you can see at that end of the shade is the rectangular piece of metal —the key, which fits into the slot—there is a bit more hardware concealed beneath the metal end.

There is a gear attached to the key. And the gear is held in place by a latch. Together the gear and latch form a *ratchet,* which lets you pull the shade down. But once you let go of the shade, the latch is resting in the pointed cogs of the gear to keep it from flapping back up again. To get the shade up, you of course first pull down just a bit. That releases the latch. And then you can let the shade go up, *but gently.*

There is a spring wrapped around all of the inner workings of a shade mechanism. It is tiny but powerful. When you pull the shade down, you are winding up that spring. And when you want the shade to go up again, the spring does the work of winding up the fabric.

If your shade doesn't wind up all the way anymore, the spring probably needs some attention. But don't think about prying loose the metal covering that hides it. Leave the shade in its mounting hardware and pull it down a couple of feet. Then take the shade out of its brackets and wind up the fabric by hand. When you wind up the shade yourself instead of letting the spring do it, you are actually

404

*How to See
Through Glass,
Window, Door,
and Lock
Problems*

increasing the tension that will be on the spring next time it is lowered. And that should make the whole thing work properly again. If not, repeat the process once or twice more.

Every time you rewind a shade by hand, assuming the spring has not found a way to ease up its own tension by tricking the latch into letting go, you should be increasing the tension on the rewind spring. You should detect a noticeable increase in how hard you have to pull on the shade. If that is not happening, the spring may have broken or the latch-gear combination either is broken or jammed. A jammed mechanism often can be fixed from the outside.

Squirt some lubricant into the working mechanism. Liquid Wrench is preferred because it actually cleans out whatever may be impeding the works. Aerosol cans of oil or silicone are second best. Move the key around by hand and tap vigorously on the top of the shade to let the lubricant do its job. But if this tactic doesn't solve your problem, a replacement is in order.

There is little percentage in trying to open up the working mechanism of a shade. Replacements are quite economical, and frustration is about all you can get by prying off the shade spring and gear enclosure. If the fabric or plastic part of your shade is still good, however, take that with you. Then all you need to buy is a replacement roller, something that most dime stores and hardware stores are equipped to supply.

Those little brackets that hold up the shades have a habit of bending with time. If you start having trouble with a shade, and if you can't pinpoint the reason right away, take a look at how well the brackets support the shade. If they just barely hold onto the key and the point, or if they grab both too tightly, the brackets and not the shade itself could be the culprits. Sometimes the trouble is the nails holding the brackets to your window moldings. If they come loose too frequently, replace them with narrow sheet metal screws about 1 ʺ long.

DRAPES

Drapes can have some of the same hardware problems as shades. If the tiny nails keep letting your drapes down, replace them with something bigger, preferably screws. But if age and abuse or use have taken their toll, don't forget that department stores, hardware stores, and dime stores generally stock a big selection of replacement drapery hardware at bargain prices.

Draw drapes have been the ruin of many a happy home. And needlessly. The instructions that come with many do-it-yourself setups are

405

*How to See
Through Glass,
Window, Door,
and Lock
Problems*

vague at best. And, anyway, the instructions are generally lost by the time a cord jumps its pulley or breaks.

There is one long cord inside a set of draw drapes, but it is wrapped around a main pulley at the end opposite from where you pull the cord. Think of it as a two-part rope. And the two parts always move in *opposite directions.*

The left drape is hooked onto the left rope. The right drape hooks onto the right rope. The main pulley divides the one long cord into two ropes and keeps them moving in opposite directions.

Assuming your pull cords are on the right side of the draw drapes, pull the right rope to open them. The right rope moves the right side of the drapes to the right. The left rope moves the left drapes to the left at the same time. You reverse the procedure to close the drapes (see Figure 194).

There is almost no reason for repairing a broken or worn cord on draw drapes. Except for a temporary repair, a patched cord will only cause more grief than it can cure. Go to a store that stocks drapery hardware and buy some new cord. Figure 259 should help you to estimate how much cord your set of drapes requires. If at all possible, don't jerk out the old cord until you are actually installing the new. That way you can follow the route exactly on the first try over and under and through the network of pulleys and fasteners.

If a cord breaks before it reasonably should, maybe the pulleys are sticking and causing premature wear. It is also possible that the cord has slipped out of a pulley and rubs against sharp metal. Also, the various moving parts can accumulate enough grit to slow them down. Whenever you have drape problems, check that none of the plastic drapery hangers or the two main moving drape pull pieces are bent, dirty, or out of their tracks.

Figure 194 Draw drapes operate this way.

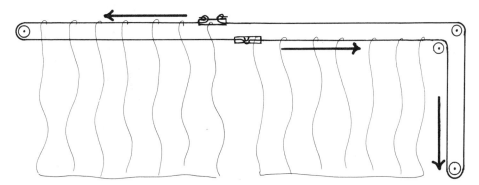

Venetian blinds are very simple mechanical gadgets. There are two separate cord and pulley systems in a venetian blind. They are separate from each other.

One pulley system *tilts* the blinds. At least it *seems* to tilt them. The cord you pull on actually moves a concealed pulley, which raises or lowers the *tape*. If the front of the tape is raised, the slats are tilted backward, and vice versa.

The second pulley system connects the heavy bottom slat to the cord, which you pull to raise or lower the entire blind. As you pull on the cord, it passes over several pulleys and then connects to the bottom slat. Therefore, the more cord you seem to pull out of the top of your venetian blind, the more cord is being lifted and the farther your blind system will be lifted (see Figure 195).

There really isn't much that can go wrong with a venetian blind. They need new cords and new tapes so seldom that you probably won't go through that procedure more than two or three times during your lifetime.

The use and cleaning of venetian blinds contributes more to their early end than anything else. Pull gently. And lower gently.

Figure 195   Venetian blinds operate this way. The sketch shows slats removed for easy viewing. At left, a tub on a cord rotates the pulley, which is attached to a long rod. The rod operates platforms fastened to blind's tape. The front of the tape can be raised, which tips slats backwards, or lowered, which tips them forward. To right, a tug on the double cord pulls indirectly on the heavy bottom slat of the blind to raise the entire bottom portion of unit.

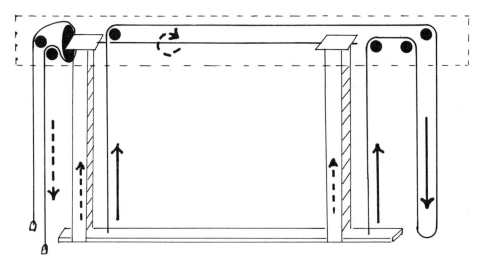

A slightly damp sponge is a wonderful venetian blind cleaner. It keeps the cotton of the tapes from getting soaked and weak. Don't use polishes. They *seem* to polish, but what they actually do is leave a film of something glossy over the surface. That film really attracts dirt, more dirt than an unpolished surface. Once you have built up a good collection of polish films and dirt, you will have to use heavier cleaners. And powerful cleaning agents have no business on venetian blinds. They soak into and disintegrate the fibers on the cord and the tape.

If you really feel the need for a thorough cleaning of venetian blinds, do it right. It will take no longer to disassemble the blinds than trying to hit the full surface of each slat with a soaking sponge, then rinsing the powerful chemicals away.

At the bottom of most blinds, you can unknot the cords. Once that is done, the cord slips up and out of the way as you slide each of the slats out of its place on the tape. Clean them with whatever kind of powerful chemical you like. Just be sure to rinse it away. Dry the blind slats well before sticking them back onto the tapes. Don't use abrasive cleansers such as scouring powder. The slats are usually beautified with little more than a few coats of paint, which will wear away quickly with harsh powders.

If you clean your slats in this manner, it isn't necessary to take the blinds off their hardware in the window. In fact, if you *don't* go to that extra trouble, you'll be adding some years of life to the blinds.

After years of service, the blind cord and tapes will probably look shabby. What then? Buy new tape and cord of the appropriate length. Better add a few extra inches to the length of tape and a foot or two extra to the cord.

With help from Figure 195, disassemble your own blinds beginning with the cord. Then pull out the slats, and finally the tape. If your blinds have a hinged opening on top, it may not even be necessary to remove them from the window.

If your tapes are fastened with small metal hardware such as staples, reinforce the tape at that point with a strip of fabric or plastic adhesive tape. Matching the length of the new tape with the old is the hard way. You are better off to disregard the length of old venetian blind tape and let the weight of the bottom piece pull the tape down to indicate where the top should go.

Don't be in too big a hurry to snip off what seems to be excess tape or cord. If you can, let the blinds hang a few days with the extra material. If you discover a way to make the blind work smoother after all the fabric has smoothed out, you won't have the problem of trying to stretch an unstretchable tape or cord.

Doors that *stick* are caused by much the same malady as windows that stick. The door may be too big or the frame too small. They may be the right size but fitted together poorly.

Study a sticky door as you open and close it slowly. If the top pulls out first and the bottom resists moving, then the bottom frame or bottom door probably is at fault. And vice versa.

Keep pulling the door open and shut. If the bottom is the general problem-causing area, is it the actual bottom of the door or the side of the door nearest the bottom? Before you assume that the door or the frame is too big at that point, make sure that everything fits properly.

If there are some loose screws that hold your hinges to the door or to the doorway, the hinge can pull part of the way out of its proper location and let the door get twisted against the doorway. Here is a quick test for loose hinges.

Stand with the door between your feet but as fully closed as it will go without trapping you between the door and the doorway. Take hold of the door. It would be easier to hold the door knob instead of the door itself, but some of them shake so much that you might not know whether the door or the knob was loose. Now lift on the door. Ideally, it should not budge at all. If you do find that the door moves up more than about $\frac{1}{4}$", some hinges seem to be loose.

Keep your eye on one hinge at a time as you lift and lower a wobbly door. See which hinge or which of several hinges are to blame. Usually the top screws in any hinge will be the faulty ones during a door test such as this. But look to make sure.

One solution for loose hinge screws is to invest in bigger screws. Take out one of the loose old ones and buy some new ones at least $\frac{1}{4}$" longer and two sizes wider. Screw thickness is identified by numbers that follow the actual measurement of screw length. Example: You find that the old door screws were $1\frac{1}{4}$ x 6. So you would want to buy replacements at least $1\frac{1}{2}$ x 8. Screws are so cheap that you can afford to buy a selection including some as big as $1\frac{3}{4}$ x 12. Use the biggest screws that will fit in the door.

There is a chance that the very wide screws will not fit into the hole left in the hinge by the old screws. And if you add only onto the length of hinge screws, at least $\frac{1}{2}$" or $\frac{3}{4}$" is needed. That can get to be hard to screw into place. In such a case, there is an alternative method that doesn't bother with new screws (see Figure 196).

Locate a few wooden matches or toothpicks. Break them off so the sticks are just a bit shorter than the hole left vacant by the loose

409

*How to See
Through Glass,
Window, Door,
and Lock
Problems*

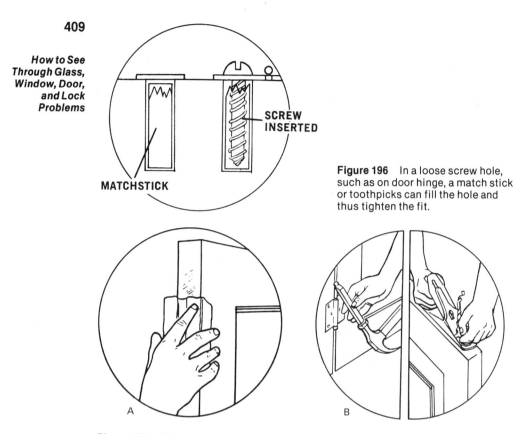

SCREW
INSERTED

MATCHSTICK

Figure 196 In a loose screw hole,
such as on door hinge, a match stick
or toothpicks can fill the hole and
thus tighten the fit.

A

B

Figure 197 When a door sticks, try rubbing soap on the
sticking part or spraying it with silicone dry lubricant. If that
fails, a bit of rubbing with sandpaper or SurForm tool (A) will
probably do the job, but if not, remove the hinge pins (B) and
then SurForm, sand, or plane the door as much as needed.

screw. One matchstick or a dozen toothpicks is about right for most
screw holes. You can also partially fill the old hole with a plastic
wood compound.

Put the old screw back into place, unless the slot has been chewed
up. In that case, put in a new one and twist it back into place. The
extra wood you stuffed into the loose hole generally tightens it up
well enough to keep the hinge from sagging.

Once all of the loose hinge screws have been tightened, that should
solve the sticking door problem unless the loose hinges only complicated the matter. There is still a chance that a swollen or misshaped
door or frame is causing some sticking.

Once you have localized the sticking problem, study the edge of
the door for glossy areas, scratch marks, or patches where paint has

410

*How to See
Through Glass,
Window, Door,
and Lock
Problems*

been worn away. That is probably where the swelling has occurred. Sandpaper the spot until your door opens and closes as well as you would like. Then sand it some more. You will want to repaint or revarnish the area. And if you don't sand away enough door to allow for the thickness of a new coat of paint, your sticky problem will be right back again.

Heavy problems call for heavier tools. If the frame or door is badly out of shape, or if a long area is slightly bulged, you will probably want to use a heavy rasp, a wood plane, or an electric sander to get the job done promptly (see Figure 197).

HINGES

Occasionally, hinges can make a door stick. If you have failed to locate a tight spot on the door or door frame, listen to the hinges. If they squeak or make raspy sounds when the door swings open or shut, they probably need oil. Squirt a few drops at the top of each hinge pin and work the door open and shut until the oil has had a chance to penetrate to the dry insides. If that doesn't do the trick, tap the hinge pin partway out. Assuming the pin looks clean, put some oil directly onto the pin and tap it back into place. Use steel wool or emory cloth to polish a tarnished hinge pin.

Sometimes the pin gets bent when loose screws have been unattended for a long time, if the door has served as a swing for kids, or if the hinges were not big enough to hold the weight of the door in the first place. Although it is possible to straighten a hinge pin, the best solution is to put in a new hinge. And this time, try a bigger one.

Hinges come in hundreds of widths and lengths. More than likely you will have to find a replacement of the same width as your old one. But it can be longer and built better. If the faulty hinge had spaces for only two screws on each side, get one that holds at least three. And if the original had three screws, get a replacement that has space for at least four.

You will need a wood chisel to expand the size of the recession into which the hinge fits if you buy a bigger set of hinges. Set the new hinge into place so the top lines up with the top of the old space. Carefully draw a line around that part of the hinge that does not fit into the old hole. Then chisel away the excess wood within your line, plus about $\frac{1}{16}$" extra for good measure.

Fill in the old screw holes with plastic wood. That will add strength to the weakened area and give you a chance to start over with completely fresh work instead of trying to move the new hinge around to fit one or two of the old screw holes.

411

*How to See
Through Glass,
Window, Door,
and Lock
Problems*

If you own an electric drill, make a small hole where each of the new screws is going. If not, make a pilot hole with a nail or a punch. Simply drive a nail into the wood about ½", then pull it out with a pliers. The hole will give the wood screw a good start, as well as making it easier for you to turn the screw into place.

Screw the new hinge to the door first. Then set the door into the doorway to make certain that the other half of the hinge matches the space for it quite precisely. If not, correct the matter before moving to the following step.

Next pull out the hinge pin so you can screw the second half of the hinges to the door frame. Assuming you have worked with a reasonable amount of precision, you can set the door into place and slip in the hinge pins.

KNOBS AND LOCKS

Despite the many lock and knob styles, the insides are remarkably similar. The knob mechanism is nothing more than a very simple mechanical lever designed to turn the *rotary motion* of the knob into the *linear (straight line) motion* needed to pull back the latch. The *latch* is the piece of metal that holds an unlocked door closed.

A *bolt* is added to door sets that use a key. The bolt keeps the door from opening even if the knob is turned. A mechanism hooked onto the bolt turns the rotary motion of the key into the linear motion needed to close or open the bolt, just like the knob and latch setup. A key closes the bolt and a key must open the bolt in some locks. In others, a key works the bolt on the outside and a *bolt handle* on the inside.

In effect, the difference between a latch and a bolt is small. Their shapes are usually different, and the latch has a spring to hold the catch closed except when somebody twists on the knob. But in their simplest forms, both the latch and the bolt are merely levers that convert rotary motion (from either the knob or the key) into linear motion.

If something goes wrong with a knob or a lock, there is no reason why amateurs should not tackle it. First, take off the knob. Usually there are one or two set screws holding the knob onto a threaded shaft. With the set screws loosened (you don't have to screw them all the way out), you can unscrew one knob from the threaded shaft that joins the two knobs. It is not usually necessary to take off both knobs on an interior door. Doors with locks built into them, however, often have a two-piece threaded shaft with a small rod protruding in the middle where the two pieces join. In that case, you usually have to

412

*How to See
Through Glass,
Window, Door,
and Lock
Problems*

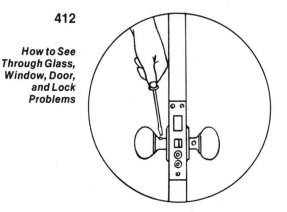

Figure 198   Door knobs are held in place by a screw, as shown here. Often they're turned onto threaded rod inside the door as well.

unscrew both knobs from the shaft or unscrew the two pieces while the knobs are still attached (see Figure 198).

Most doors, except those using a simple skeleton key, require yet a bit more work to get them fully disassembled. In many cases, the decorative inside plate, called the *escutcheon* in the trade, has to be removed. The outside one can often be left intact. The inside one comes off to allow you to pull the bolt handle out of the lock set itself.

The lock *cylinder* has to be removed in many cases. That is the round, heavy metal case into which the key actually fits. There are at least two basic styles of cylinder. One, a round variety often called the National or Yale type, is held in place by two brass screws located at the narrow edge of the door. The other, a shaped cylinder often called a Segal type, is held in place by two brass screws that you can reach from inside the lock set on the side of the door opposite the keyhole.

Once the two brass screws are removed from the Segal type (they lay parallel to the key), the cylinder simply pulls out. With the National type, once the two brass screws are loosened perhaps a dozen turns, you then have to unscrew the cylinder itself.

When all other hardware has been unattached, it is time to take out the two screws at the edge of the lock set. They are generally all that is holding the set into the door by that stage of disassembly. Remove them and you can slip the lock out of its slot in your door.

One side of the lock set serves as a cover. One small screw is often all that holds the cover on. Take off the screw and you can see the inside of the lock.

You should leave the inside of a cylinder to pros. Once you have taken an ailing lock cylinder out of the door, however, you are spared the considerable expense of having a locksmith travel to your house.

A lot of people have bothered with two or three sets of keys for years because they never realized that most cylinders can be changed to accept a new key. In other words, if you take three cylinders to a good locksmith and tell him to fix it so they will all operate off the same key, he will probably be able to do it for you, and it will cost very little.

Likewise, if some family member loses a set of keys and you feel it is time to put in new locks, don't. Just take the cylinders to a competent locksmith and have a new set of keys and pins filed for the old ones, for perhaps 10 percent of the cost of new locks. The cylinders do not even have to be by the same manufacturer or in the same style to get identical keys.

Little can go wrong with locks except:

1. *They can get dirty.* Clean off each part separately with a solvent. Don't try to clean all the parts at once. If you take one part off its pivot, clean it, and put it back onto the pivot, you have almost no chance of forgetting how to reassemble it. If you own a Polaroid camera with a closeup lens, you can be double safe and snap a picture of the lock before you start to disassemble it.

2. *They need lubrication.* All moving parts need lubrication, even the slow moving levers inside a lock set. Clean the insides first and then squeeze in a very generous amount of grease or graphite. Grease has the advantage of buffering some of the sound. Grease does not belong inside the cylinder, however. Graphite is all you should squirt into that narrow opening.

3. *Parts get worn out or bent.* Springs are especially prone to flattening out over the years. The best remedy is a replacement spring, of course, but that isn't always practical. While you are waiting for a new one to arrive, however, you should be able to bend the original one carefully back toward its intended shape with a pliers.

   A few lock manufacturers change systems so often that you may have trouble finding replacement parts. Then you will have to find a whole replacement lock set that will fit the knobs, cylinder, and hole in the door you own. But if you decide you would like something a little different, take heart in the fact that most locks can be fitted into most doors with only simple hand tools, such as a brace and bit, small saw, or chisel. The new lock set should come with instructions and blueprints.

4. *Parts just get loose.* A lock sometimes just gets balky. For no reason you are able to find, something may pop out of place. Put it back into place, or what you think is its proper place. If it works, forget it.

19 If You Would Fix Wood

Fixing wood, wooden furniture, or wood paneling is just like everything else. All you need is knowledge about the right materials, access to the right materials on the market, and the will to use them.

There are at least four levels of repairs when working with wood, depending upon how critical the situation is: 1) simple cleaning, 2) cosmetic repairs to the original finish, 3) refinishing or recovering, and 4) structural repairs to the actual pieces of wood.

CLEANING WOOD

To clean wood successfully, which also means to most people not expending much energy in the process, you have to understand the anatomy of a piece of finished wood. The wood itself was once alive, and its cell structure is still intact. It can still absorb or give up water. And in doing so, the wood cells will swell (with more water) or shrink (with less).

If you douse the surface of wood with water, as you might do when cleaning it, the upper layers of wood cells can swell and make the surface rough—called "raising the grain." Not only does it detract from the appearance of a piece of furniture, unless it was designed to be rough in the first place, but dirt can get into the swollen grain, to remain until the upper layer is sanded away.

Water that seeps into the joints of some glued furniture can break down certain kinds of glue. That will leave you with a wobbly table leg or other piece of furniture.

Some wood finishes *blush* when exposed to water or excess moisture, meaning they take on a cloudy, chalky surface appearance. Good finishes will not blush. Once a blush does appear, it will sometimes go away after the surface has dried out thoroughly. But if it doesn't, you're stuck with the job of sanding away the old surface covering and applying new.

All of this goes to show why you should choose your furniture cleaners with more care than a mere glance at a commercial. There must be a couple of hundred different cleaning or polishing preparations on the market for use on wood. Some contain a lot of water. A general rule is hard to draw up, but if the cleaner comes in a big container for a reasonable price, it is likely to contain a large percentage of water. That is no good for wood.

The safest approach to cleaners and cleaning is to test first. Try a dab of the polish on some out-of-the-way part of the wooden furniture or panel. Then wait. It would be a good idea to wait a day. If the test area still looks shiny, new, unblushing, unstained, and just as smooth as before, use the polish all over.

There is another good reason for testing new cleaners on old wood, or old cleaners on new wood. It might not be wood at all. There are many wood look alikes used on all sorts of furniture. And they are not found only on inexpensive things.

Figure 199 An X-ray view of finished wood.

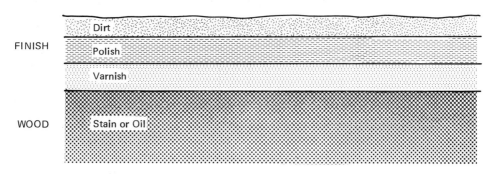

The Formica hard plastics are impervious to nearly everything. But some softer vinyls and other plastics can swell up, smear, stretch, or disintegrate with potent organic solvents, which might not bother natural wood and wood finishes.

Here is another easy-to-remember general rule. Wood should be cleaned as little as possible. A weekly once over lightly with a cloth treated with a gentle cleaner or polish is fine. But if you clean a particular piece of wood with really strong cleaners and elbow grease more than once or twice a year, *it has the wrong kind of finish for you and your household.* Better give it a new and better surface treatment before it's too late.

COSMETIC REPAIRS

Cosmetic attention is necessary whenever scratches, knicks, dents, stains, and other relatively minor physical calamities befall your wooden objects. The easiest treatment is simply to cover them over so they match the rest of the finish. If you have invested in a small set of acrylic paints (see Chapter 4), you can mix up a dab of appropriately colored acrylics and simply paint right over the damaged spot with a fine brush.

Owning a set of acrylics has the advantage of letting you choose a color as you are looking at the wood in question and under the same kind of light as you always see it. Your living room, for example, probably has incandescent lights, and the store where you try to pick out a matching stick or bottle of repair materials probably has fluorescent lighting. There is one further complication. The color of wood is rather unscientific. It's that individual quality that makes wood so great to work with. Even a fine craftsperson can't predict in advance exactly what color a particular piece of wood will take on or what contrasting color its grain will have. So if you pick up one stick of mahogany wood putty that you think resembles your damaged table, don't be shocked if the putty hardly looks like the table at home.

The solution to color hangups, if your store cooperates, is to buy at least three colors with the understanding that the unused two can be returned for credit. Select the color you think most closely matches the wood in question. Pick another a bit redder or a bit darker. Pick a third with less red or a bit lighter. At home, study the wood's color closely and pick the one closest to it.

Sticks of colored putty and sticks of colored lacquer are available for patching small blemishes in furniture and other wood items. The putty sticks are most widely available and easiest to use. They are also the least durable. Hopefully, you will not need a strong repair job. If scratches, dents, knicks, or other damage keep hitting a particular spot, you don't need a new repair substance but a new and tougher wood finish altogether, or a glass top cut to fit the size and shape of the heavy traffic area.

According to advertisements and even many instructions, the putty stick is applied to your damaged spot by simply rubbing it over the wood like a crayon. Life is not always that simple, however. You might be happier by applying the colored putty with a small, thin knife if you have to squeeze the stiff, waxy "putty" into narrow scratches.

Lacquer sticks are exactly what their name would lead you to believe. They are sticks of lacquer colored to resemble particular types of wood. Unlike putty sticks, you have no choice but to use a knifelike instrument when applying lacquer sticks. And the tool has to be heated. The hot knife melts a bit of the colored lacquer. And you try to smear the melted plastic over the scratch before the knife and the lacquer cool.

Figure 200   Small wood defects can be patched up with Plastic Wood (A), which may then have to be colored, or with a putty stick (B) of color that matches the wood. The latter is simpler but not as rugged.

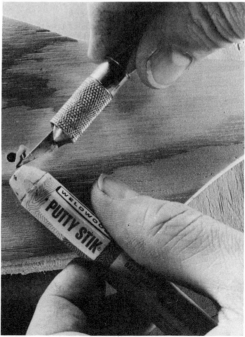

Figure 200 illustrates the art of crack patching. Perhaps the most important thing to remember is that you are not trying to restore the wood *exactly* to its original condition. You are only trying to *camouflage* the spot.

Other points to remember:

> *You do not have to make the repair material level with the existing wood or wood substitute.* It only has to *look* level. Or more to the point, it should not look unlevel. If you put enough putty or lacquer into a deep rut to level off the blemish, you may end up smearing it all over.
>
> *The color doesn't have to match exactly.* If you try to do that, you may become very frustrated and botch the job. If the repair is *close* to the original in color and texture, nobody is going to notice unless you point it out.
>
> With camouflage in mind, *you may not even have to invest in hardware store remedies for damaged or make-believe wood.* In a big set of crayons, you might find a surprisingly close match. Yellow for pine and light oak, red-violet for mahogany, brown for walnut and dark oak, yellow-green for pickled pine, white for ash, and so on.

REFINISHING OR RECOVERING

Chips knocked out of your wooden items are a bit more involved to fix than mere scratches. Simply adding color to the bottom of a ½″ pit is not going to camouflage it.

If you can find the missing chip, the best solution generally is to glue it back into place. Any good adhesive is okay, the faster drying the better. Just keep the top surface of both the chip and the furniture surrounding the mend from getting smeared with glue, or your next project will be a refinishing job.

Hold the chip in place while the glue dries, being sure to wipe away any excess glue that oozes out. Give the patch plenty of time to harden before working on the next step.

Once the knocked-out chip has been glued in again, assuming you preserved the surface, about all that should be visible is a line where the original wood meets the chip. Putty stick, lacquer stick, crayons, acrylic paints, or similar camouflaging agents should take care of that.

If the chip does not fit neatly into its old hole, or if its surface finish was damaged, you will have to refinish the area immediately around the glued-in chip. With very fine sandpaper, smooth off the juncture. You are only worried about the edges of the chip. Don't try to level off the whole thing or you may make matters worse.

Depending on how deep the original finish penetrated the wood, you may then be able to fix it with just a bit of putty stick or similar camouflage material. However, it may be necessary to add some surface finishing material so the texture of the repaired spot matches the surrounding surface. First, try some wax or furniture polish on the tip of your finger or a cotton swab or small rag. If the original finish had a very high gloss, however, you may have to use something like varnish or even clear fingernail polish to match its gleam.

When working with materials like fingernail polish, varnish, lacquer, or such, try just the tiniest bit first. Give it time to dry well before deciding if it really does the job you want. Some hair sprays may even match the texture. Spray some onto your finger and rub your finger across the patch.

Don't go out and buy fingernail polish or hair spray just to try matching the finish of some furniture. If you already have some in the house, fine. But your hardware or paint store have small cans or bottles of varnish, lacquer, waxes, and polishes at bargain prices.

For those nasty repair jobs in which the chip is missing or won't fit back into place, you will have to invest in a small can or tube of a plastic wood product. Stuff the moist plastic wood firmly into the gap. If it is a really big space, don't fill in more than ¼ " at a time. Wait until the lowest layer dries before adding the next batch.

Make the top of the plastic wood patch as level as possible, especially at the edge where the repair meets the original wood. A putty knife, butter knife, or any other flat, smooth tool wet with alcohol or other solvent can be used to smooth over the plastic wood surface before it starts to dry. When the patch is thoroughly dry, sand it lightly until the patch and original surfaces blend together again. Then you will want to color the patch.

Putty sticks or lacquer may accomplish the coloring job, as will small oil colors. Acrylic paints definitely will do the job, and they have the added advantage that you can blend enough matte or glossy medium into the color to match the flat or glistening original surface texture. Plastic wood comes in a variety of colors that should blend with any wood color known.

Stains, burns, and similar discolored spots on wood should be sanded away. There have been many articles in newspapers and magazines giving all sorts of chemicals for bleaching dark stains, chemicals for darkening light stains, chemicals for unsweetening sweet stains, and so on. But you may not know who-dropped-what-or-when.

For all things vaguely resembling stains and burns, just sand away the uppermost impression. First, sanding will remove the foreign substance, which can interfere with your efforts to match the texture of the original wood. Beyond that, you will be peeling away just enough wood that your covering colors will probably be very level with the wood already there. Besides, if you sand carefully on a blemish that is only skin deep, you might not have to add any extra colors to camouflage the spot. If the stain was trapped in the upper layer of varnish, for example, sanding will remove it. Then all you have to do is replace the varnish layer in that one spot.

For stains that go deeper into the wood, you will have to add colors to undo the damage. Most of the camouflage agents we have discussed so far are relatively opaque—putty sticks, lacquer sticks, crayons. Even the liquid penetrating oil stains have some covering ability. These helpers will cover right over a stain unless it differs radically from the original color of the wood. Iodine spilled on a blonde table or chlorine bleach on exposed mahogany are not so easy to cover. In such extreme cases, you first have to cover the sanded spot with a light paint in the case of light wood or dark paint for dark wood. Then you can cover over the paint with putty stick, crayon, oil stains, or whatever else will help you to match the appearance of the original wood. But if you are going to the trouble of using paints, such a crisis might be the right time for you to make that investment in a set of acrylics. They are opaque enough to cover over any stain the first time out.

Refinishing a wooden table, panel, or other item is a time-consuming alternative, but it might prove enjoyable. Taking a scratched up, peeled, dirtied, or damaged table or chair and stripping it down to bare, clean wood, then sanding, staining, finishing, and polishing it back to like-new-or-better condition can be very rewarding.

The upper layer of almost every piece of wood around the home is a coat of some wood-finishing product such as varnish or wax. To refinish, you will have to get rid of the old finish.

A good chemical paint and varnish remover not only saves you considerable elbow grease, but also removes the finish from delicate or complex ornamental woodworking details. And if the job is going to end up with a professional look (or better), it is important that you start completely anew with uncovered wood. The paint and varnish removers are powerful enough so that they also help to soak out layers of dirt and grime, which often get imbedded in the grain of wood. This type of chemical is very powerful, so follow the manufacturer's warnings and advice carefully.

Figure 199 shows the surface of a piece of old wood. You can see why the color of furniture often seems to change as you start to peel away those upper millimeters of the surface. In the forest, very few woods have a natural color resembling the tones we see on our walls and furniture. Oils and stains that soak into the porous wood contribute to the final coloration. But those coloring agents do not soak completely through a piece of wood. They start at the surface and work inward maybe only ⅛", tapering off gradually. So, as you sand the surface during a refinishing job, do not be surprised if you see gradual changes in color.

Scratches, gouges, nicks, chips, and similar imperfections should be taken care of after you have soaked and sanded the original wood finish. In that way you will be putting your patches on the wood itself and not on something like varnish, which the paint remover will try to strip away for you.

Sandpaper is the basic refinishing tool, combined with plenty of elbow grease. There are many types of sandpaper, but you will more than likely have to settle for whatever your hardware store stocks. Try to buy an aluminum oxide product and avoid flint products if possible. But what the sanding particles are made of is less important than their size.

After you have patched any deep surface imperfections, start sanding your project with "fine" grade sandpaper. Keep going until the surface looks and feels smooth. Then switch to "very fine" grade.

You will not be able to sand inside any of the elaborate millwork ornaments around the piece you are refinishing. But treat such places to a good scrubbing with fine steel wool. You might have better luck looking for this grade of steel wool in a hardware store instead of a grocery store. Your grocer's products often are coarse enough to scrub dirty pots and they sometimes contain soap, neither of which is good for fine woodworking.

Use sandpaper and steel wool *with the grain.* Move parallel to the length of the grain lines and not across them. If you sand across wood grain, you will be generating as many small scratches as you hope to get rid of.

Flat surfaces should always be sanded with a flat sanding surface. Therefore, wrap your sheet of sandpaper around a *sanding block.* You can buy one, but you can also improvise one by finding a scrap of lumber about 3½" by 5". Even a dry, stiff kitchen sponge works nicely. Sanding blocks are used with a quarter sheet of sandpaper. Tear the full 9" by 11" sheets in half both ways to make quarter sheets.

Sandpaper is a tool and should be treated that way. While you are sanding, occasionally pound the sanding block against your hand to knock loose the accumulation of sawdust. That will make the sandpaper last longer and sand more evenly. When you are finished or almost finished sanding, wipe the wood surface with a rag dampened in turpentine or lacquer thinner. You should have one or the other solvent on hand for the finishing step anyway.

If you were working on virgin wood, at this stage you should apply *wood filler* to hardwoods such as mahogany, oak, or walnut. Pine or maple, the kinds or wood generally used for unfinished furniture, do not require a wood filler. Hardwood grain has very coarse pores. It would soak up too much stain and make for irregular-looking finishes. Also it would pick up a lot of dirt later on. To avoid such problems, the sticky wood filler plugs up the grain.

Assuming you did all of your sanding by hand during a refinishing job, there is probably no need for a filler. If you used an electric sander, you may have removed enough wood so that you should apply filler to hardwoods just to be safe. Manufacturer's instructions vary, although invariably they will recommend applying the filler *after* you stain the wood. Make life a bit easier and fill the wood *before* staining it. Otherwise you will have to find some way to color the filler.

Even on a refinishing job, you may want to stain the wood before adding the finishing touches. By sanding away the upper layer of wood, you may have noticeably lightened the tone.

It is easy to add a darker hue to whatever color is on the wood already during a refinishing project. Going the other way around gets rough. You can add some reddish overtones to whatever is there by using a can of rosewood or redwood stain. The yellowish strains of maple or birch can be added to modify the original color. Don't expect that your finished furniture will in any way resemble the colored lid or label of the stain. In fact, even if you smeared the color onto a virgin piece of wood, there is no chance that it would look like the advertisements.

Brush or wipe on stain in the direction of the grain. Generally, manufacturer's directions call for you to wipe off excess stain after 10 or 15 minutes. You can add a bit of distinguished character to your furniture by wiping off the stain creatively.

On the front of drawers, along table legs, side panels, and similar boxed-in kinds of places, wipe a bit harder toward the center and softer toward the edges. By doing that, you will make the center a little lighter, creating what pros call a *framing effect.* You can also use a selective hard or soft wiping process to reduce unwanted irregularities in surface coloration, which may have been put there by nature or by you somewhere along the finishing or refinishing process.

You may suffer a psychological letdown when you first step back and gaze upon your almost finished work of furniture art. What you have built up in your mind and what the pictures in the hardware store built up for you may not in any way resemble what you first see in the furniture you are refinishing. That doesn't mean that what you have done is not good. It doesn't even mean that the pictured or imagined version is better than your real wood. It's different—that's all.

Choose a finishing coat with care. Take into account what went wrong with the old finish. If a table, for example, needed refinishing after only a year or two of use, the original finish was not equal to the job you gave it. Select something tougher this time.

Figure 201 lists major wood finishing products. They are on sale under diverse names and with infinite variations. The chart lists them roughly according to how tough they are.

In general, the least durable finishes bring out the greatest beauty from the natural wood and the tougher ones bring out less beauty. But the transition from great beauty to less-than-great beauty is much more subtle than the transition in toughness. You will gain much more toughness in moving from oil or shellac to polyurethane than you will lose in beauty.

One layer of any finish is *never* enough. The very first coat of a finish is used to *seal* the wood and its grain. It is like a base for all other layers of the finish. Therefore, it has to penetrate into the wood as deeply as possible. And to accomplish that, the initial coat is generally diluted with turpentine in the case of a varnish product, alcohol in the case of shellac, lacquer thinner in a lacquer type of product, or some other suitable solvent.

To get a good wood seal, many amateurs and pros use one of the wood sealers for their first coat or two. Then they switch to whatever finishing product they have chosen for the final coats.

Brush on a generous amount of finishing material with the grain. Then, while your brush is still well soaked, brush over the same area across the grain. Finally, as the brush is almost stripped of all shellac or varnish, brush very lightly with the grain again, letting just the tip of your brush smooth out the wet surface.

In between every dry coat, smooth out the brush strokes and bubbles with very fine sandpaper. This step is more important than many putterers realize. Even the final coat of finish gets sanded on professional jobs, something you can do too.

Pick up a few sheets of extra fine *wet grade* sandpaper or "000" grade steel wool. If you want a bright, almost glossy finish, try to locate super fine wet grade sandpaper. In this final polishing procedure, the sandpaper is used wet with some lubricant such as furniture polish, furniture oil, or almost any kind of noncleansing furniture preparation. Even cooking oil can be used in a pinch. The oil keeps the sandpaper from digging too deeply into your new surface.

This final buffing with wet sandpaper or wet steel wool takes off those few last imperfections caused by dust, brush strokes, or bubbles. It also eliminates the shiny effect that leaves your piece of furniture looking like it has been varnished. The whole secret to wood finishing is to end up with a piece of wood finished so carefully that nobody notices the finish at all, only the wood.

The more you rub, the more shine you will remove. A gentle once-

Figure 201 This chart can help you to select the best wood-finishing product for your needs. In general, you probably will have to reach a compromise between the product that emphasizes beauty the most, and the one that provides the toughest surface. Decide which is most important to you, then study the advantages or disadvantages of the products offering that type of finish.

Finish	Good Points	Weak Points	Relative Cost	Preliminaries for Finishing
Light-weight Vinyl	Easy to apply. Resists dirt. Easy to clean. Wood and non-wood (marble, burlap, prints, etc.) easy to obtain.	Cuts easily. Won't resist many common solvents. Heat spoils it. Moisture & temperature extremes loosen adhesive. Won't fit on 3-dimensional design surfaces.	Moderate.	Smooth surfaces with no large blemishes are required. Surface must be clean.
Heavy-weight Vinyl	Very rugged. Wood "grain" is embossed into surface for added realism. Easy to clean. Available in prints, marble, etc.	Heat spoils it. Sensitive to a few volatile solvents.	Expensive.	Smooth surfaces with no large blemishes are required. Surface must be clean.
"Formica" type plastics.	Extremely rugged. Very easy to clean. Resist heat and solvents. Available in wood. marble, prints, etc.	Brittle during installation. Not recommended for covering small areas.	Expensive.	Smooth surface with no large blemishes are required. Surface must be clean.
Paint				
Enamel	Rugged. Easy to clean. Resist many common solvents.	Looks childish or cheap in some uses. Brushes require cleaning in turpentine or benzine.	Inexpensive.	Smooth surfaces, well-sanded. Primer coat of paint is important. Sandpaper paint between successive layers.
Water-based.	Resists many common solvents.	Brushes clean in water. Looks childish or cheap in some uses.	Inexpensive.	Smooth surfaces, well-sanded and well-cleaned.
Colored lacquer	Rugged. Easy to clean. Resists many solvents. Looks elegant on modern furniture.	Brushes require solvents for cleaning. Flamable until dry.	Inexpensive.	Smooth surfaces, well-sanded. Sandpaper between successive layers.
Antique	Rugged. Easy to clean. Resists many common solvents. Looks elegant if well applied.	Takes time to apply. Brushes require solvents to clean in most applications.	Modest.	Surfaces, well-sanded. Primer is important on bare wood. Can be used on already-painted wood and in some cases to conceal surface defects.
Varnish	Protects natural appearance of real wood. Easy to clean. Relatively rugged.	Brushes requires solvent to clean. Doesn't resist water. or alcohol well. Dries relatively slowly. Won't stand up under heavy use.	Inexpensive.	Smooth surfaces, well-sanded. Hardwoods must be treated with filler. Fir plywood requires sealer. Sandpaper or steelwool between successive layers.

Finish	Good Points	Weak Points	Relative Cost	Preliminaries for Finishing
Clear Lacquer	Rugged. Easy to clean. Resists many common solvents. Looks elegant where clear, shiny look is appropriate. Dries quickly.	Requires solvents to clean brush. Flamable until dry.	Inexpensive.	(Same as above)
Clear Wood Sealer	Very rugged. Easy to clean. Protects wood very deeply. Resists most household hazards except cigarettes. Brings out grain well.	Requires turpentine to clean brush.	Inexpensive.	(Same as above) (Often used for several first coats and then another type of finish such as urethane or varnish is applied.)
Urethane	Very rugged. Protects against almost all household hazards. Easy to clean.	Requires solvent to clean brush.	Modest.	Smooth surfaces, well-sanded. Hardwoods must be treated with filler. Fir plywood requires sealer. Sandpaper or steelwood between successive layers.
Decoupage finish	Each coat is very, very thick and smooth. Provides a smooth covering over rough or uneven areas.	Requires solvent to clean brush. Not as rugged or easy to keep clean as more conventional finishes.	Moderate.	Surface does not have to be smooth but natural woods should be well sanded to show off their grain. A clear wood sealer should be used for one or more preliminary coats to bring out wood grain.
Furniture Oil	Beautiful grain and wood. Luxurious "unvarnished" appearance.	Gives wood very little protection. against wear or solvents.	Inexpensive.	Smooth surfaces, well sanded. Several coats of oil are usually rubbed in with a lot of buffing.
Wax	Easy to apply. Natural, "unvarnished" appearance.	(Same as above)	Inexpensive.	(Same as above.)
Shellac	Preserves natural look of wood well. Easy to apply.	Requires alcohol to dilute shellac and clean brush. Minimum resistance to wear, abuse and solvents or water.	Inexpensive.	Smooth surfaces, well-sanded. Hardwoods must be treated with filler. Fir plywood must be treated with sealer. Sandpaper or steelwool between coats.
Orange Shellac	Often used to provide an instant old-pine look. This effect works best on pine and on fir plywood.	(Same as above)	Inexpensive.	(Same as above.)

over-lightly with wet super fine sandpaper results in a *bright satin* type of finish. If you keep at it for a while, you will end up with a *dull satin* finish. Don't overdo it, however, or you will end up with *no* finish.

As a final touch, many people are inclined to polish the new surface with wax. Adding wax on top of lacquer, wood sealer, and polyurethane finishes is redundant. If you have gone to the trouble of carefully wet polishing a final finish, why should you want to add an extra coat of anything? If you feel that your finish needs the extra protection of wax, then you have probably selected the wrong finishing material in the first place. As a final finish over oiled or sealed wood, wax can be a beautifying ingredient. In that case, choose a good paste wax and use plenty of elbow grease to rub it as well as you rubbed the wood and finishes before it.

Until now, our wood finishing and refinishing has concentrated on methods that leave the wood showing through the finish. Sometimes the fine old wood is so badly scarred that it hardly pays to fix it. Or the old wood never was so fine in the first place. Or you just don't feel like spending all the time it might take to strip off the old finish, patch up the wood so the blemishes match the original natural wood, and then build up many layers of transparent finishes.

So, *opaque finishes to the rescue!* Paints cover right over whatever grain, stain, and color was on the wood. All you have to do is fill in the holes with something like plastic wood, forgetting about whether the patch color matches the wood color. Sanding, however, is just as important to a fine painted finish as to a fine varnished finish.

Most furniture is painted with a semigloss product. For some reason, you may want to choose a high gloss or flat finish. If the piece gets used by children with sticky, dirty hands, high gloss can be a practical choice.

Paint goes on just like the transparent finishes discussed earlier. *That includes a sealer too.* Diluting ordinary paint does not work as well for sealing purposes as it did with varnish and such. If there is still an obvious layer of varnish on the old wood by the time you are through scrubbing it with cleaning agents and sanding away the rough spots, you may be able to skip the *primer*—the paint version of what we called ''sealer'' when varnishing. If in doubt, start with a first coat of primer. And make sure that the primer goes with the type of paint you have chosen for your new finish, latex primer for latex paint, enamel primer for enamel paint, and so on.

High gloss finishes are often left that way on the final coat. Even then, a small amount of polishing with wet sandpaper or steel wool often enhances the gloss.

Semigloss finishes are given a final sanding just as if they were varnish. It is hard to convince many people that it is not only okay to use sandpaper or steel wool after the final coat of paint is dry, but it is preferred. That is how a good pro gets that satiny finishing touch you admire.

Professionally painted furniture is often treated to more than one color. If the main piece is painted cream, the final step is to wipe or to spray on a contrasting color, maybe tan or brown. And just as you learned about *framing* when staining wood was discussed, the overcoat likewise is framed, rubbed harder in the center of every area and softer at the edges. You are left with more of the contrasting color around the outside. Also more of the contrasting overcoat remains in the grooves of whatever kind of decorations were carved into the furniture.

Except for very dark base hues, the best choice in a contrasting overcoat is a darker shade of the same color. If you have chosen cranberry red as your main color, for example, you could choose deep crimson to rub on. However, if you have painted the furniture a deep shade of brown, dark grey, black, or some other dark color, the contrast is best met with light grey, tan, cream, and such.

Don't overdo the overcoat. A little bit of color goes a long way. And if you look at the job tomorrow wishing you had done the overcolor a little heavier, just do it again, but wipe off less color this time. It is much harder to go the other way around.

Rubbing a second color over an already well-painted surface is sometimes called *antiquing.* There must be hundreds of kits on the market that contain little more than two cans of paint chosen to get exactly the effect just described under the name of overcoating. About the only difference is that the directions included in the antique kits advise you to leave more of the overcoating on than we do here. If that's what you like, leave it on.

Wood grained self-adhesive papers and plastics can get you out of a lot of messy situations. These items simply cover up everything and create their own printed colors and grain for whatever "wood" you choose. You can even change to "marble," "tile," or dozens of other patterns. Paper-thin contact paper and vinyl are on sale at most variety and hardware stores. But for fine furniture or areas that receive substantial use or abuse, you would be more pleased with some heavyweight vinyl, also self-adhesive, which is known as *MacTac,* by Morgan Adhesives. You will have better luck looking for this product at lumberyards than dime stores and even hardware stores.

MacTac and similar products are heavy enough to avoid some of the wrinkling problems you may have with lightweight contact papers. And its thickness allows the company to build three-dimensional effects, such as wood grain and fabric textures, into their product.

Once you cover the top of a desk or table with wood-grained MacTac or a similar product, you can buy a roll of matching wood-grained tape to take care of those narrow edges. If you want to take care of a door, there is a kit for that. Before MacTac was sold at local stores, it was widely accepted for use by furniture makers, trailer makers, and the like.

Heavy vinyl films are rugged enough so that you do not have to fill in small imperfections in the surface of whatever you are covering. Just make sure that you thoroughly clean the area first.

STRUCTURAL REPAIRS

Structural breaks cannot be taken care of with peel-and-stick vinyls, although they can be concealed with it once you have mended the broken leg or other wooden support.

Loose joints are a common problem in wooden furniture. Often the wood dries out and shrinks, leaving the various pegs or fitted joints rattling around with nothing for the glue to hold onto. At other times, daily wear and tear simply destroy the glue's hold on the joined pieces of wood (see Figure 202).

All joints that hold pieces of furniture together should fit together tightly enough so that you cannot just slip them in or out. You should have to force them in with at least a solid bang from the butt of your hand. If not, build up their thickness. Apply a layer of glue to both parts of the joint, being careful not to let the glue accumulate somewhere to jam up the joint altogether. (If that happens, however, just pry the lump loose with a knife or chisel.) Then let the glue dry thoroughly.

Fit the joint together. If it is tight now, proceed with the gluing and joining. But if not, try a second layer of glue. Going beyond two glue treatments is more trouble than it's worth. Glue starts to get weak itself when it is glued onto nothing more than other layers of glue.

If your joints are so loose that even two thin layers of ordinary wood glue won't tighten them up, use one of the metal-filled epoxy products, which will not only grab tightly onto the two halves of wood but will also fill in the gaps. (Otherwise choose any good wood glue mentioned in Chapter 2).

Often one or two wooden joints get loose even though others nearby hold tight. If you try to pull out the loose ones, you may risk

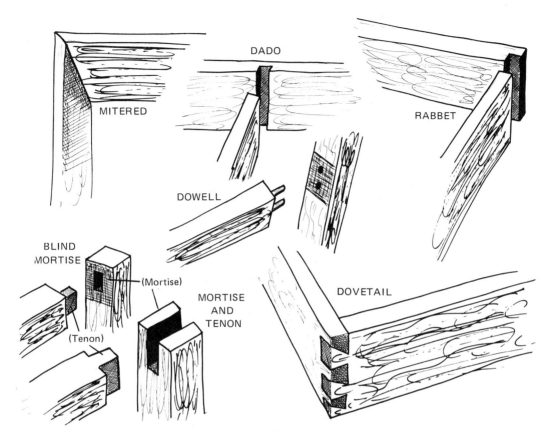

Figure 202 Major wood joints by name.

damaging some of the ones still glued together tightly. In such a case, your most practical solution is to get a handful of toothpicks and a container of wood glue. Liberally smear each toothpick in turn with glue and fit it into that little space around the joint that is causing trouble.

After you cannot force any more gluey toothpicks into the gap, gently use a sharp knife to trim off the exposed ends of the toothpicks. Then wipe away any glue that may have run out of the newly reinforced joint. After the whole collection dries, you may have to sand the toothpick ends a bit and camouflage them with putty stick or anything else that comes close to matching the color of the furniture.

One broken part on something like a dovetail joint with five or six "tails" in all can be ignored. Simply glue the remaining joint back together and, after the adhesive has set, fill in the broken spot with plastic wood or filled epoxy.

429

On a mortised or pegged joint, so much of the strength rests on just one or two appendages that you have little choice but to replace it with something strong (see Figure 202). In a mortise and tenon joint, if no more than a third of the tenon is broken off, but the missing piece remains firmly glued inside the mortise, leave well enough alone. Use a good wood glue to fasten what is left back together, as if you were simply faced with an unbroken joint that had pulled apart (Figure 203).

When all or most of a shaped wooden joint has broken off, you will have to add some extra supports of your own. If you own an electric drill or a brace and bit, bore a hole into both sides of the

Figure 203 How to repair common wood joints. If major piece of joint is left intact (A), simply glue it back into place. But if a major part is missing (B), glue first and then patch the opening (C) with Plastic Wood both for strength and appearance. Broken dowels (D) should be drilled out. New pegs or dowels are fitted carefully into the new holes (E) and then glued into place (F) for a joint as good as the original.

broken joint, making sure to measure carefully enough that the holes match up. You are going to slip a peg into those holes.

Drill up to 1″ deep into the wood, but never closer than ¼″ to the opposite side of the wood. Example: If your broken chair leg is 1½″ wide, you can drill a 1″ deep hole. But if the leg is only 1″ wide to begin with, drill a ¾″ deep hole.

Pegs for a repair project such as this are cutoff dowel sticks, which are on sale at most hardware and many variety stores. Unless you are patching something miniature, select a dowel at least ¼″ in diameter, larger if the size of the broken joint warrants it. The larger the dowel, the greater the strength as a rule, but never use a peg that is bigger than one third the size of the wooden piece you are working on. Example: If the legs and supports of a broken chair are all 1½″, you could use a ½″ peg. But if the furniture peices are as big as 2¼″ (which converts to ¾″), you could use a ¾″ dowel stick.

Cut off a peg about ⅛″ shorter than the combined depth of the two holes into which the peg has to fit. That allows room for the glue and for inaccurate measurements.

Speaking of measurements, your ruler might not fit into the peg hole, but your peg will. Slip the dowel into one hole, mark it with a pencil. Then slip it into the matching hole and mark again. Add the two measured lengths together, subtract the ⅛″, and that is how long your peg should be. *Measure each hole and cut each peg individually.* You may not be able to drill the holes to identical depths.

In a pinch, you can use a wood pencil for the peg. But you will have to scrape off all that yellow paint first.

When a joint is long and narrow—as most are—drill two sets of holes at least ½″ apart. That will give you two pegs and twice as much strength. In case you have not already caught on, what we are doing in this repair procedure is to turn whatever joint was broken into a dowel type joint. Generally, a break at a joint will leave both parts of the joint glued firmly in place. But if that is not the case, pull out any loose wood and firmly pack the hole with plastic wood or filled epoxy glue before drilling holes. Yes, you can drill holes even in metal-filled epoxy cements. For those without drills or brace and bits, buy some *corrugated metal wood fasteners* and find the hammer.

Make sure that the broken-off joint pieces are sound. If not, pull out the loose pieces and fill the spaces with plastic wood. Apply a liberal coat of glue to the two sides of the broken joint, and then force one of the wood fasteners just deep enough into one side of the joint so that it stays there unassisted.

Carefully line up the two pieces to be joined and start forcing them together with your hands. After the fastener is firmly squeezed into both sides, you will probably have to switch to heavier equipment.

Pad the nicely finished parts of the wood with cardboard, cloth, or scrap lumber. And then bang the joint with the hammer until the fastener is firmly fastened to both sides of the joint and the two pieces of wood are together tightly enough so that the glue will have a chance to assist the fastener in holding everything together.

By rights, you ought to clamp furniture together while the glue is drying. It is a fairly safe assumption, however, that the average home does not have a set of furniture clamps. Therefore, locate a spare length of clothesline rope or drapery sash cord and fashion a makeshift clamp out of rope. Loop the cord around the legs or arms on one side of the glued joint and draw it tight with a slip knot. Now do the same at the other side of the joint.

Replacement parts are available for a surprising number of wooden objects around your home. Those fancy-shaped wooden spindles that grace the coffee tables, end tables, headboards, knickknack racks, and other items are often selected from a standard set of patterns on sale at many hardware stores and lumberyards. If you shop around a bit, you may be lucky enough to find one that exactly matches the broken piece. More than likely you can find one that matches closely enough so that only you will ever know, assuming you take the time to stain or paint the replacement to match the original finish.

Should all else fail, you will certainly find some "ready to wear" spindles or legs that match the originals closely enough so that you can replace a whole set of four and finish the new ones to match the old. Even the wrought iron legs found on some furniture are on sale in do-it-yourself kits.

The same advice goes for broken knobs and handles. Replace the broken one with a new version that matches the old style as closely as possible. If you cannot find an almost exact replacement, consider replacing the entire set of knobs. But if you are dealing with some kind of heirloom and are reluctant to part with an unmatchable knob or other accessory, it really is not so difficult to *manufacture* your own duplicate.

The easiest way to make a duplicate of a broken knob is to invest in some latex rubber mold-making material at a local hobby store. After you have made a rubber mold of an unbroken sample of the knob or other doodad, fill the mold with a casting plastic available at the same hobby shop. You may not have such a store nearby, however, and you might very well wonder whether that new knob is really worth such an investment in time and money, modest though both really are. So here is an alternate scheme.

If you have patching plaster or plaster of Paris in the house, mix up a batch. Melted paraffin can be used too, but it is not as safe as wet plaster.

Spray an unbroken specimen of the knob with silicone, oil, "calorie-free" cooking spray, or anything else slippery. Fasten a piece of tape to one side of the knob and slowly sink the other side into the plastery material until exactly half of the object is in plaster. Use the tape to support the knob while your plaster casting dries. You should then be able to slip out the specimen and be left with an exact plaster (or paraffin) mold of half the knob to make your own duplicates.

If you need a natural wood for the new object, work with plastic wood. Otherwise you can use any material such as plastic wood, metal-filled epoxy resins. Fill up your mold with the modeling material. The plastic wood has to be done in several ¼″ layers to ensure good drying conditions.

Once the first half of your new knob is dry, slip it carefully out of the mold. Spray the mold with oil or silicone again, fill it a second time, and carefully press the dry half against the wet half. When the last half is fully dry, the two halves of the new knob should be firmly cemented together too. And then you can slip the entire knob loose.

Decorative moldings are glued into place. Knobs usually have to be treated to a new hole before they are screwed onto the door or drawer that awaits them. A lick or two with sandpaper, some stain or paint, whatever other creative finishing touches are required, and you have just accomplished a simple repair job that even most pros would not have known how to tackle. Maybe now you can believe that it really is possible for you to know "how to fix damn near everything."

20 Upholstery Work

The old stuffed chair losing its insides in one corner of your living room needs to be reupholstered, but you're afraid it would cost a fortune to sent out—and it probably would. You're probably afraid to tackle the job yourself too.

It's strange how threatening an old chair can become when it needs mending or renovation. There aren't any moving parts, as a rule. What holds furniture together, why the fabric fits the way it does, how those stylish lumps and bumps and buttons got there are all surprisingly straightforward and easy to figure out.

There is a skeleton under every chair and sofa. It is made out of wood. Legs, arms, and parts of the back or bottom, those parts of the skeleton that show, are made of fine woods. Hidden parts are made of tough woods, but they don't have to be sanded, stained, and varnished. However, hidden or showing, whatever can go wrong with wood has been covered by the last chapter.

Dirty fabric is reason enough for many people to get rid of a piece of furniture or to spend a handsome sum on having it covered or reupholstered. There are so many cleaning products on the market today that are intended for cleaning tough fabric stains that it is well worth the small investment in at least one box, can, or bottle to give it a chance. Some of them work! You might be surprised at the kind of life a one-hour cleaning job can give a dingy chair.

Some cleaning agents are intended for fabrics, some for plastics. There are even a few for natural leather. Buy yours from a reputable store and follow directions to the letter.

If cleaning doesn't get rid of that dirty look, there is another way to beat the cost or the time of putting on new fabric. If the old fabric is sound, just dirty, invest in a can or two of spray-on coloring agents. Again, some are for natural or synthetic fibers, others for vinyl plastic.

Do not plan on being able to dye the dirt away. The colors simply

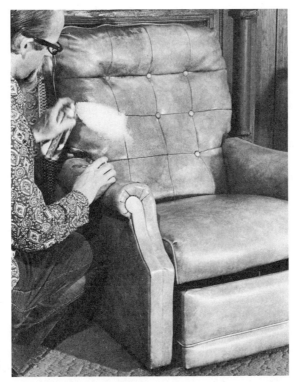

Figure 204 Fabric or vinyl furniture can be cleaned or colored with inexpensive spray cans. It's often a useful trick to try before launching a more ambitious repair.

435

cover it over. There is one small catch to this method—in most cases you will have to change the color of the fabric to something a shade or two darker than the original. And nobody has come up with a plaid spray just yet. Solid colors are it.

Patching a hole in cloth or vinyl can save many otherwise good pieces of furniture. In fabric-covered chairs and sofas, a needle and thread should come to mind first when a tear develops. Trouble is, it is hard to conceal a sewn patch. The stitches may show, and you often have to bunch up the fabric to have something solid for the stitches to catch on.

There are several kinds of adhesives that can help you mend torn fabric. The iron-on clothes patches work nicely if the padding behind the tear is solid enough to support the patch as you iron on it. Slip the patch through the tear so that the adhesive side touches the backside of the torn fabric. Carefully iron one side of the tear until the patch sticks firmly to the back of the cloth there.

Now line up the second half of the torn spot so any loose threads or fibers in the two pieces overlap a bit. Iron the second half into place by moving your hot iron *toward the tear* for the first few strokes in case the cloth slips.

To be doubly sure, reinforce the fibers on the outside of the patch with an extra dose of adhesive. Wet your finger with water, then smear it with a dab of watery white polyvinyl glue such as Elmer's Glue. Wipe the gluey finger across the patched spot several times, always trying to press down the loose threads just as you would do with unruly hair.

If the patched area gets quite a bit of use, repeat the water and glue treatment several times. When the polyvinyl glue dries, it becomes transparent, so if you don't end up with a big blob of it in one place, your camouflage job should be nearly invisible.

Before using an iron-on patch, always test whether your chair fabric can withstand heat. Touch the hot iron to some out-of-the-way place first. The same advice goes for any chemicals you use to color, clean, or polish furniture. You may think you know what the chair is made of and what chemicals it can withstand—until you see that rayon cloth start to disintegrate before your eyes seconds after you touch it with a hot iron or spray it with a dye.

There is a powdered fabric adhesive on the market that bonds torn pieces of upholstery together very nicely. Since it is a powder, however, you have to position your chair so the torn area is perfectly flat, or the powder will spill away from your working area.

To use the powder, simply slip a piece of heavy cloth through the tear and position it so that the patch extends at least ½" beyond the rip in every direction. Sprinkle the powder around the inside of the area and melt it into place with a hot iron according to instructions.

There are some liquid fabric glues on the market that work surprisingly well. Use them just like the powder. But you can also use a couple of the very common liquid general-purpose adhesives too. The water white polyvinyl glues and silicone adhesives are flexible enough when dry to patch a torn spot in your chair. In fact, they have an advantage over the two heated materials. You can use common glue on vinyl upholstery materials that would melt from the heat of your iron.

Although most glues won't stick well on most vinyl plastics, the vinyl materials used for upholstery are often backed with some kind of natural fiber fabric. So even if the glue will not grab to the vinyl, it will hold onto the cotton backing very well. Omit the finger full of glue on the face of the patch when you work with vinyls.

A *hole* burned, dug, cut, or worn into cloth or vinyl upholstery material presents a different kind of camouflage problem. You have to fill the gap with something that matches the surrounding cloth. Scout around the hidden undersides of your chair until you find a spot where you can cut off enough upholstery material to fill the size of the hole. Cut off more than you will actually need, however. Then carefully trim the patch until it exactly matches the hole. It must match not only the size but the pattern that may surround the hole.

Now glue a heavy scrap of cloth or an iron-on patch to the back of the area. When the backing is securely in place, glue or iron the patch itself into the hole. Again use the watered down polyvinyl glue to stick the loose threads around the edge into place permanently.

Even when *the fabric itself needs to be replaced,* don't get the idea that you need hundreds of dollars worth of tools and years of special education. If you spend 15 minutes reading the rest of this chapter and shop carefully for fabric, you should be able to reupholster any chair in your house during a weekend.

You may not have to strip away the *old fabric* before putting the new into place. *You don't need a sewing machine.* You probably won't even need a *needle and thread* to make this technique work for you.

As we know, there is a wooden skeleton that provides support and lends the basic shape to a piece of furniture. Over the skeleton, a layer of cotton or foam rubber padding gives the chair its detailed shape and body. If the padding gets flabby, the shape begins to sag.

Cotton padding inevitably loses its character over years of use. Good foam rubber costs more to start with but is easier to work on and holds its shape better if properly installed.

Finally, the "skin" of the chair, whatever natural or synthetic fabric you choose, holds the padding into its desired shape. At the same time, it has to be tough enough to withstand the rigors of the outside world.

Measure for your new chair fabric with generosity. Having an extra foot or even an extra yard will definitely help you to turn out a neat, professional looking job even on your first reupholstery project.

Pick your upholstery fabric carefully. It isn't necessary to shop only in the upholstery fabric section of a store, where your choices often are limited. But upholstery material has to be considerably heavier and more rugged than anything you would use in making a dress. Even slipcover materials are sometimes not heavy enough.

Corduroy, denim, and heavy synthetics are great for furniture that gets rugged use. For families with grown or no children, velvets, brocades, satins, and softer textures are fine. Even fabric-backed vinyls are within the range of amateur upholsterers.

Most upholstery fabrics are cut from rolls that are 54″ wide. You will save money by not buying much too much fabric and you will save headaches by not buying too little if you sketch out a rough pattern. Figure 205 shows how your sketch might look.

If you can figure a way to lay out the new cloth so all of the back and sides can be cut in a single piece, you will save some work and end up with a stronger job too. In Figure 205, the chair is so nicely squared off that even the inner pieces on the back and sides actually could have been included in one piece along with the big, outer back and sides. It was not sketched that way, however, because most chairs are not that simple. They have odd shapes, curves, or angles somewhere, which makes a complete one-piece job too complicated. Be content to get the back and sides on one piece along with anything else that naturally falls into place.

Now take a good look at the shape of your chair or sofa before you begin the operation. Does the padding still hold a good, firm shape, a shape you enjoy looking at, one with smooth and even contours that don't remain depressed for more than a minute after somebody leans on one spot?

How about the *springs* inside the chair? Do they creak or complain when somebody sits down or stands up? Maybe they stick out a bit in some places. Is the chair or sofa getting less and less comfortable as the years go by?

If you can answer "yes" to the padding questions and "no" to most of the spring questions, don't even bother to cut away the old fabric. Reupholster right over it.

You do have to perform a bit of surgery before reupholstering most furniture. There are probably some rounded bits of cord and fabric called *welts* at many corners or edges. Slice them off carefully

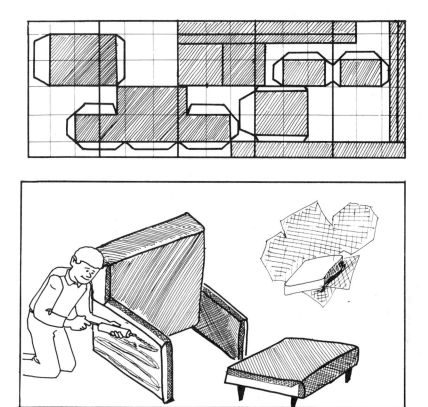

Figure 205 Putting fabric on an old chair isn't hard. Start (A) by laying out chair measurements into a pattern for economical use of material. Use adhesive (discussed in text) to glue inner pieces in place first (B) and then outer pieces (C). Finally tackle edges (D), which often need welts that can be made simply (E). Then cover loose pillows (F).

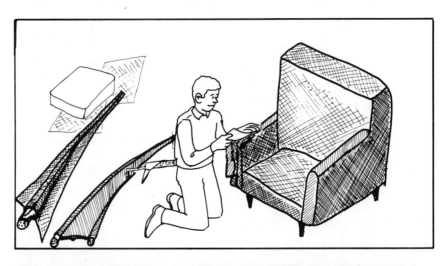

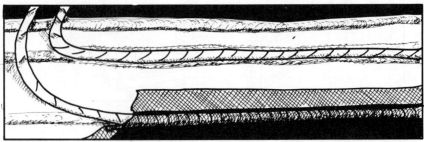

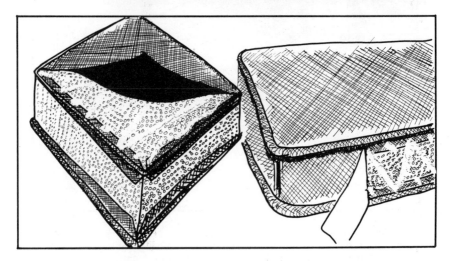

Figure 205 Continued.

so that your knife cuts off the welt's fabric wrapping but leaves the main cloth untouched underneath. Also get rid of any other decorations such as fringes, flounces, or pleats. When that is done, you should have a neat, smooth, uninterrupted skin over the old chair.

You will save many a banged knuckle and bruised ego if you remove the seat from whatever chair you are working on. Usually you can accomplish that by standing the chair upside down and removing about four long screws. They generally go from each corner through the wooden frame of the seat, and into the wooden frame that forms the side of your chair.

If you want to transfer your layout sketch to your goods before cutting, chalk is best. Magic markers can do the sketching too if you are careful not to let the ink soak through where it will show on the finished product. But don't cut up your whole piece of fabric all at once. You might change your mind about how best to stretch the cloth over the old skeleton. So cut out each piece as you need it.

Also invest in a big supply of glue before starting the reupholstery job. *Glue is what holds this project together.*

The most useful substance is silicone rubber adhesive. It sticks very well and remains flexible for life. One of the caulking gun-sized tubes holds enough for a full-sized chair. And if you do buy that size, you will save enough cash compared with the price of several small tubes so that you can even afford the caulking gun too.

Rubbery panel adhesive is sticky enough and flexible enough to tackle a reupholstery job too. And a quart size of polyvinyl glue will also grab onto fabrics well enough for a job like this. The trouble with the polyvinyls is that they are not as tacky as silicones as they come out of the bottle, so you will have to spend more of your time holding seams in place until the glue sets.

Apply a generous covering of glue to the old fabric as you go along. Don't try to scrimp by gluing only the edges. If you do that, the center portions of some areas may flap or wrinkle when people sit down.

Now let's start to glue the new layer of upholstery fabric into place. If you are following the approach of Figure 205 closely, you can worry about small areas later. At first, concentrate on the large backs and sides in the approximate order shown in the sketches.

The back piece, and maybe even the sides, has to be cut about 1″ bigger than the actual chair dimensions. To create a neat edge where the top meets the back, fold over the excess cloth. As any seamstress could tell you, you are creating a hem. Only in this case, you squirt a ribbon of glue under the hem instead of stitching it.

Position the edge of the hem so that it falls perhaps ⅛″ short of any sharp edges, such as where the top meets the back. And hold it there with glue. Since every other piece near the back laps over onto the back, there will be no bare spots.

Big areas go fast. They also go smoothly. Then you get to the corners, the edges, wherever the cloth meets wood or one piece of cloth meets another. Your best bet there is to let the old upholstery be your guide. If a particular corner was made by folding cloth from one side under cloth from another side, do the same. Often the cloth from two adjoining areas is fastened together a bit roughly and the joint is then covered over with a narrow strip of cloth, which hides the joint.

The backbone of many professional upholstery jobs is the welt. It amounts to little more than a piece of cord wrapped in some of the chosen fabric. Pros insist on stitching the cord in place. If you are even the least bit handy with a needle and thread, it is a good idea to do some stitching on your own welts too. This is not done so much for strength as for the fact that it helps to shape the welt better than glue alone.

Figure 205 shows how to make and use a welt. They are fairly useful on the edge of loose padding, such as when you cover a seat cushion. But on the solid narrow edges of a chair, they are as much decorative as utilitarian. Fortunately, the welt is going out of style except where it serves a purpose beyond pure decoration. Welts are almost never used with fluffy fabrics such as velvet or shags.

Figure 206 (A) That beat up old high-chair is a good example of how to reupholster. (B) First strip away fabric until you're down to bare padding and frame. (C) Wrap easy parts in fabric first and hold with staples, glue, or some thread. (D) Blind tacking or glueing conceals your work when you add finishing pieces. (E) Baby and others are delighted with job.

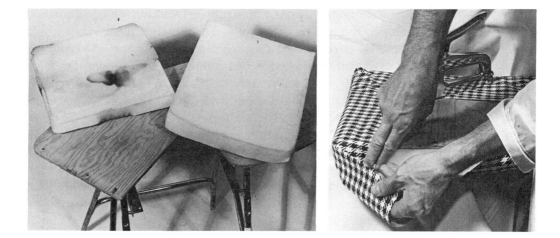

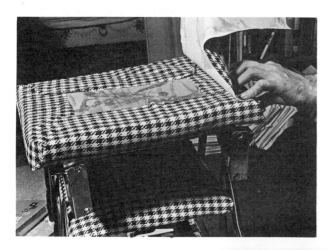

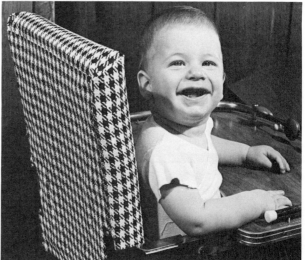

If you were doing the chair in Figure 205 without welts, you would put pieces 2, 3, and 5 on differently. The top side of each arm would be completely covered by a flap reaching up from the side. And the front of each arm would be covered completely by a similar flap from pieces 2 and 3. If you tried to use cloth from the same piece to cover both the top and the front of the arm, you would be forced to execute an awkward fold at the corner with plenty of bunched up fabric to contend with. By drawing on flaps from *two* nearby pieces, you can work with simple hems.

When all else fails, upholsterers use *upholstery tacks* to hold their work neatly in place at the same time concealing overlapped cloth. Tacks come in a rainbow of colors; if you shop in a well-stocked hardware store you will be able to find some that match your choice of fabric very closely. Consider the tack heads to be a part of your finished appearance. For children's furniture or mod adult pieces, you can even use upholstery tacks in colors that contrast with the fabric.

You will probably have to use quite a few tacks when you work with vinyl plastic coverings. Modern science has yet to come up with a glue that is worth anything on the surface of vinyl plastic. You can glue the fabric backing of vinyl into place nicely. And it stretches well enough so that you can create smooth-looking, almost one-piece jobs even if the original fabric had been stitched in many places. But wherever the vinyl has to be hemmed and then put in place or folded over, you will have to rely on tacks for holding power.

Ruffles and pleats are not beyond the capabilities of glued reupholstery jobs. The fastest way to make them is by copying exactly what used to be on the chair or sofa. You might have to rip the old decoration apart somewhat before you discover the very simple way such things are put together.

Figure 207 shows a generalized method for making pleats. Pins hold individual pleats in place until you have stitched or glued the

Figure 207   Pleats for upholstery work are formed this way.
Pins hold them in place until you can install them with stitching
or glue.

top. The niftiest method of all, however, is to buy a long, narrow strip of iron-on patching material and iron the pleats permanently into place. You have to iron the pleats anyway so they hold their shape once you pull out the pins. The color of your iron-on patch is not important since it goes on the back of the set of pleats.

Tassels and strips of fuzzy, frilly decorations of all sorts are best bought, not made. You may not find what you are looking for in the upholstery fabrics section of a department store. But you should find plenty of intriguing do-dads in the drapery section. Drapes are considered to be more in the do-it-yourself realm than reupholstering.

Padding inside a chair or sofa sometimes needs attention as badly as the fabric. On a piece of furniture that still has a solid frame and springs, but the padding is losing its smooth curvy shape, your best bet might be to leave the old padding and old fabric in place. Add an additional layer of thin foam rubber. Then install the new fabric. You will change the shape of the chair slightly—less than you would expect—but you will also save several hours of tedious and perhaps messy work.

Keep the number of separate pieces of auxiliary padding to a minimum. If you can make one large piece fit over several surfaces by bending it and cutting slits into the foam at a corner or two, you will save both the bother and the possible troubles inherent in installing several smaller pieces. In general, the wider the rolls of fabric or padding you buy, the more costly it will be per square foot. For that reason, you may want to use three separate pieces cut from a 24″ roll of foam instead of two pieces cut from a roll 48″ wide.

There are several fundamental types of foam rubber materials available, in sundry thicknesses. Only if you live in a large city can you expect to have much real choice over which material in which thickness you will buy. In general, try for the most rigid upholstering foam possible.

Foam rubber for an auxiliary layer of padding should be about 1″ thick. As with fabric coverings, work from the biggest sections to the smallest as much as possible. And try to do as much final cutting as you can right in place instead of measuring and then cutting. Padding stretches when you work with it. You will have to tape each portion of the pad in place until the glue sets.

It is a good idea to buy a completely new pad for the seat, which gets more wear than any other part of the chair, of course. A 4″ or 6″ thick pad of polyurethane will fix your chair seat nicely.

After you have applied an auxiliary layer of foam over an old chair, you can cover it with your choice of fabric just as we did earlier. This time, however, you should allow more fabric for overlap. The chair covering will be tougher if the cloth at intersections is glued primarily to *other cloth* instead of only to the *very pliable padding.*

Stripping a chair or sofa may be necessary if the old padding is really shot or if the springs underneath need attention. And stripping means exactly what the name implies. You take a hammer and a knife, a chisel and a screwdriver, and take off everything that no longer serves a useful purpose. Cut away the frills and pleats and welts first, always keeping your eye open for clues to how the original fabric and padding were put together. It is a good idea to make a sketch of the clues as you proceed.

Older chairs, and some new ones, were padded with a cotton material. That in turn was covered with muslin or burlap, sometimes both. You can dispense with such undercoverings unless you have metal springs. In that case, a layer of coarse fabric such as burlap is needed to keep the springs from tearing up the pads.

There is no need for a long discussion about various kinds of *coil springs.* If you have them now and really want to replace them with the same kind, you will simply have to make some phone calls or shopping trips around town until you find an outlet that has them or can get them for you. They come in various diameters and lengths, so measure your old ones first.

To install new coil springs, study the old ones and duplicate the method used to install them. In many cases, however, if you look closely enough, you will find that new coil springs are not needed at all. You can often just sit down and patiently tie the individual coils back to the wires that originally held them in place.

There is another kind of metal spring frequently found inside many pieces of furniture—flat, squiggly things. *Flat springs* have become popular largely because they lend themselves to mass production techniques. But they are difficult for amateurs to buy, let alone try to install. So the best advice when encountering a set of ailing flat springs is to replace them with webbing.

Webbing is used as the spring material in many original upholstery jobs. Strips of jute, canvas, rubber, or even thin steel form the seat back or sides of padded chairs and sofas, as well as providing that cushiony spring effect.

You may have trouble locating jute, rubber, or steel webbing, but you should find plenty of plastic webbing in hardware, novelty, and department stores because it is sold for repairing lawn furniture. If the plastic webbing you buy just about matches whatever other kind of webbing was on your chair, lay out the new just about like the old and fasten it down. If not, here is what to do:

Measure the width of the new webbing plus the width and length of the area to be webbed. Make a sketch of how you might lay out the webbing, starting with one piece right in the very center. You want to leave a space of about ½″ between each of the webs but no less than ¼″ and no more than ¾″. If you are not able to end up with one strip right down the middle in your sketch, you will have to place that imaginary center line between two webs. Example: The chair seat measures 23″ wide, 19″ deep. You have bought a roll of plastic webbing material 2½″ wide.

$$2\tfrac{1}{2} \overline{)23} \quad \begin{array}{c} 8\ R3 \end{array}$$

So you will have 8 pieces of webbing on the seat with 3″ (the remainder in your division) to be divided up for the space in between. That is tentative, anyway. Now let's multiply that 3″ by 16 so we will get an answer that reads directly in ¹⁄₁₆″ units on a ruler. (You don't have a ruler that measures in decimals, do you?)

$$3 \times 16 = 48$$

That means we will have ⁴⁸⁄₁₆″ to divide up into the 9 spaces at each side and in between the 8 pieces of webbing.

$$9 \overline{)48} \quad \begin{array}{c} 5\ R3 \end{array}$$

Therefore, we would use a space of ⁵⁄₁₆″ between each piece of webbing. Since there was a remainder of 3 in our division, which is ³⁄₁₆ left over, put an extra ¹⁄₁₆″ between the frame and the first web and an extra ²⁄₁₆″ between the frame and the last web. Since we want at least ¼″ between webs but not more than ¾″, our spacing of ⁵⁄₁₆″ is okay.

However, since ½″ spacing is closer to an ideal, we should try one more step in this example. If 8 separate pieces of webbing result in a ⁵⁄₁₆″ space, how much space would we have if we put in only 7 webs? Remembering that the webs are 2½″ wide:

$$7 \times 2\tfrac{1}{2} = 17\tfrac{1}{2}$$

Subtracting the space that 7 webs would occupy from the 23″ width of the chair seat:

$$23 - 17\tfrac{1}{2} = 5\tfrac{1}{2}$$

That 5½″ space left over gets put into ⅟₁₆″ units and then divided up into the 8 spaces between and at the ends of the 7 webs:

$$5\tfrac{1}{2} \times 16 = 88 \qquad\qquad 8\overline{)\,88\,}^{\,11}$$

That ⅟₁₆″ figure is just as far away from ½″ as the ⁵⁄₁₆″ mark. So you would be best off to work with 7 webs, since one right down the middle offers just a bit more strength.

A *staple gun* makes for a fast, neat job when installing plastic webs. If you don't have one, invest in a couple of boxes of #12 *barbed webbing tacks.* Since you may not find such an item on hardware store shelves, settle for the next best thing, #12 carpet tacks.

There are pieces of equipment made for putting in webbing. They help you get the proper tension in the spring. But you would be looking all over town to find such a thing, so try this method:

Don't start out by cutting all of the webbing into pieces. Cut it only after you have tacked or stapled it into place. That will give you the maximum amount of material to grab onto so you can pull good and hard on the new web. First, put two tacks or staples into the webbing on one side of the seat. Then fold the end of the web over on that same side so the two tacks or staples are covered up. Then put three more staples or tacks into the folded end of the web. At this point you will have a total of five staples or tacks holding the doubled-over web to one side of your chair seat.

Now stretch the webbing over the opposite end of the chair seat. Hold it there—or have someone hold it—while you put two tacks or staples into place to keep the web tight. Cut off the web and fold over the loose end. Stick three more tacks or staples into place.

After you have successfully installed new webs in one direction, you have to go through the same arithmetic, the same stretching, and the same tacking procedure in the opposite direction. This time, however, each new piece of webbing material is woven through the perpendicular strips already tacked into place.

The new plastic web job makes a fine base for whatever went on top of the springs originally, generally a pad. In some cases, webbing was tacked to the bottom part of a chair seat, then coil springs sat on top of the webbing. Finally, some padding rested atop the springs. You can dispense with such an arrangement if you want, by figuring out a way to tack the webs to the *top* of the seat. Then let the pad rest directly on the webs.

Buttons, channels, tufts, and similar upholstering devices may look so complicated that you would rather not even try a job involving them. With just a bit of ingenuity, however, they are no harder than any other part of the reupholstery process.

Buttons are little more than a plastic or wooden disk covered with a bit of padding and then fabric to match the material. They are held in place by a cord, a tack, or a sharp pin that looks very much like a cotter pin.

With luck, you can buy upholstery buttons. That is what the trade calls them. They come in many sizes and colors to match most basic upholstery materials. But you can make your own in about the same amount of time it would take you to track them down.

If you buy a wooden dowel of some appropriate size, you can saw your own thin wooden button blanks. You will have to drill a small hole or two through each blank. You can even use large coat buttons on sale at most sewing and novelty stores.

When a button pops off a well-upholstered piece of furniture and gets lost, you may have to hunt around to find something about the right size to use as a blank. Then you will have to scout around the chair until you find some spot where you can trim off enough spare fabric to cover your new button. You may not want to strip off enough fabric to fasten the replacement upholstered button into place the same way as the original. But even if you only glue the new button into the hole, it will look many times better than nothing at all.

During a major chair or sofa reupholstering job, you may have to do quite a bit more than simply stick a button into place after the fabric is glued down. Buttons are generally used to help form what the trade calls *tufts,* regular peaks and valleys that the buttons help to put into the surface of a piece of furniture. The peaks and valleys usually form either squares or diamonds, depending upon whether successive horizontal rows of the buttons are lined up with each other (to form squares) or spaced into alternating rows (to form diamonds).

Assuming you are not adding new pads to a chair, only covering the old fabric with new, all you have to do is pull out the old buttons, recover them with the new material, and then put the buttons back into the old holes again. Do the tufted sections at the start of your reupholstery procedure.

During tufting, the fabric has to be held firmly in place *but not rigidly.* Lay the new fabric in place and tape it down. Locate where one of the central buttons should go and stick it or tie it into the cushion. Smooth down the fabric as you move on to each successive button. Work your way from the center toward the outside, and you should wind up with a smooth, even, and professional-looking set of tufts.

Those who put on new pads but want to preserve the tufts of the

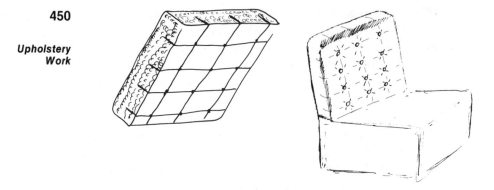

Figure 208   Tufting is simple when done according to the text.

old chair or sofa, and those who want to create a tufted look anew, have just a bit more to do than shove buttons into place. If the indentation that forms a tuft is deeper than about 1″, the fabric will bunch up and wrinkle near the button unless you plan ahead. On some informal furniture, sometimes on leather or vinyl, the wrinkles are fine. But when in doubt, get rid of them.

Actually, deep tufts are designed to get rid of small wrinkles near the button by forming *big wrinkles*. On the new furniture pad, measure and sketch the square or diamond-shaped tufting pattern with a marking pen. Poke a hole where each button will go (see Figure 208).

Now, with a sharp knife or razor blade, slice about halfway through the pad on the tufting pattern. If you are using a 4″ thick pad, cut about 2″ deep.

After the sliced pad is put into place, stretch your new fabric over it. Shove the tufting buttons through the fabric and through the hole in the pad with a long needle or crochet hook. If there is webbing on the chair or sofa, tie each button cord to the web. And if there is a wooden backing, you could use long tacks through the button blank instead of cord. Without webs or wood, simply slip the button cord through the pad and then into a 2″ square of corrugated cardboard, which will hold the cord securely without jabbing into the back of the pad.

As each tufting button is pulled into place, working from the center toward the outside, fabric between the buttons should slip into the sliced grooves, forming one neat wrinkle instead of countless unmanageable ones. Then lay your new fabric into place around the sides, top, and bottom.

As you begin to stretch the upholstery fabric around the shape of your chair or sofa edges, the excess bunches of cloth quite naturally slip into the slots, which extend to the edge of the pad. If you then fasten the fabric uniformly all the way around, you will end up with a well-shaped, professional-looking job. The fact that tufts are present in no way alters how you proceed with other aspects of reupholstery already presented.

Channels are just a variation on tufting. Those straight vertical rows of rounded mounds of padding and fabric, generally across the back of more expensive chairs and sofas, have traditionally been formed by a combination of stitching and drawstrings. If you were to do it that way, you would still be sewing a week from Tuesday. So here's another way:

If you are only adding a new skin to an old chair, all you have to do is be sure that your new fabric gets tucked deeply enough into the valleys of the existing channels so that your new glued-on cover exactly duplicates the contours of the old. Give the glue plenty of time to dry in the channels before you stretch the fabric around to the sides, top, and bottom. Otherwise you will end up with no channels.

For those who plan to install new padding over an old chair or sofa, sketch channel lines into the pad just as with tufts. Then slice three-quarters of the way through the pad along each channel line. On a 4″ pad, in other words, you would cut 3″ deep with a knife or razor blade (see Figure 209).

Lay your new fabric in place but put glue down only for the center channel. Slip your cloth into that channel slit and pull hard enough

Figure 209   Fancy channels are simple when done according to the text.

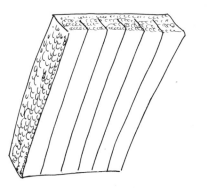

so that the padding forms a nicely rounded mound. You might want to practice this technique a few times before doing it for real with glue.

Let each channel dry thoroughly before going on to the next one down the line. You can hold the creased fabric firmly into its slit as the glue sets if you will lay the edge of some thin plywood into the groove and weight the plywood with books.

Once your center channel is dry, you can do one more channel on each side of it. Let those two dry and then move on to the next two.

Make sure that there is plenty of extra fabric on hand when you decide to make channels. And don't cut off what seems to be excess pieces until all of the channels have been successfully created.

You might want to add some additional strength to the channels, and at the same time eliminate the need to wait for one set of mounds to dry before forming the next. Roughly stitch through the fabric at the bottom of each slit, through the uncut 1″ or so of padding, and then through a thin cardboard strip put on the back of the pad. The cardboard will keep your thread from pulling through the soft foam rubber.

After all of the channels are formed, set the pad into place and stretch the fabric carefully around the sides, top, and bottom. Finish off the job according to the simple techniques discussed earlier. Then celebrate, because you will have completed one of the most sophisticated types of upholstering jobs.

21 It's a Plastic Life After All

In this chapter, we'll be concerned with new ways of putting old techniques into practice—specifically as applied to broken plastics and toys.

It would be possible, to draw up a chart that would list all of the plastic materials in a column, and then describe how to identify each plastic type. Then we would, of course, include information about which glues are specifically made for each variety of plastic. Trouble is, who would want to read it?

As we have stressed throughout the book, the simplest way is usually the best way. That applies to plastics too.

Materials made for gluing a specific plastic are usually expensive, hard to use, hard to find, and often dangerous to boot. Some of the common, simple, and safe materials you may already have will probably provide as good a repair job as you could hope for anyway.

Slippery plastics fall into two categories generally. One expensive type is *vinyl,* tough and flexible. And you will almost never see transparent vinyl items. Vinyls today are most often used as thin films for furniture coverings, inflatable toys, and the like.

453

The other slippery plastic is known as *polyethylene.* You probably first saw this in plastic squeeze bottles. Tupperware plastic storage containers traditionally have been made of white, almost translucent polyethylene materials. Some toys are now made of brightly colored polyethylene.

Because their surface is so slippery, vinyl and polyethylene provide home fix-it people with a few problems. Epoxy products might work well except for the fact that vinyl and polyethylene are generally used where flexibility is important. And epoxies just don't have enough flexibility to withstand the kind of bending these two materials get.

So look at the glue chart in Chapter 3 for silicone adhesives. Rough up the surface of your broken piece of polyethylene and the silicone adhesives will grab hold of the plastic and remain flexible too. If flexibility is really important, make your silicone patch as thin as possible.

Vinyl does not respond as well to silicone adhesives as polyethylene does. Vinyl, in fact, does not respond well to much of any kind of glue. Even though technicians for a company that makes a vinyl version of its superglue would not give a blanket endorsement of own product as a general purpose vinyl adhesive, you will find several packages on counters labeled "Vinyl Repair Kits."

If you are ready to try anything, try a vinyl repair kit if it's cheap. Make sure the area to be patched is spotlessly clean, rough up the plastic with coarse sandpaper, and give the glue plenty of time to dry.

You might be able to use silicone adhesives to create a patch even though you can't use the product for a complete reupholstery job. A smooth slippery vinyl surface does not give the silicone much to adhere to. But if there is a pattern embossed in the vinyl and the backing is embossed too, your silicone could probably find enough nooks and crannies to grab onto so that a decent patch would result. So if there is not already a rough surface, create one whether you are using silicones or vinyl cement.

Ironically, you may be able to make your own tape that will hold onto vinyl well enough to extend the useful life of some vinyl items. Buy a small piece of self-adhesive vinyl (contact paper) that matches the color and pattern of whatever you have to fix. Clean the damaged area well and carefully press the adhesive side of the contact paper into place.

Do you know why the contact paper patch works? *Chemical bonds* do not stick well to the surface of vinyl, but dry adhesives such as tape and contact paper rely on a *physical bond.* The company who makes contact paper figured out a way to make the sticky stuff cling

to one side of its vinyl product. It will also cling to one side of
your repair job.

Make-do vinyl repair jobs may not last forever, or as long as you
would like them to. But they will last longer than no patch at all.

Acrylic, styrene, and polycarbonate plastics are tough, rigid, and
very clear. The acrylics and polycarbonates are rather expensive so
they are used most often when their transparent properties or
strength are needed. Parson tables, plastic lamps, rigid shiny plastic
chairs, most of the accessories for modern plastic living, are acrylics.
Where economy is a factor, styrene plastics are usually used.

If you look at the index, you will find "acrylic plastic," "plastic,"
and "styrene plastic" mentioned several times. In Chapter 2, model
airplane cement, or Duco Cement, was said to repair broken plastics
of many sorts, these materials included. *You do not even have to be
sure which is which.* There are differences in the cements themselves,
however. Since a good blend of quality solvents is important, buy
the best your local store sells.

Curious people browsing around the shelves of hobby and hardware stores may encounter mysterious bottles of colorless chemicals.
Labels say they are for bonding various plastics. One bottle is for
acrylics. Another may be for styrenes. Use them if you like. They
will actually work a shade better than general purpose cements. They
are more expensive and considerably more dangerous to use. Chemicals like these are very volatile, flammable, and toxic to breathe or
ingest. But like any chemical or tool designed for a specific job, it
does that job better than something that tries to cover the field.

Styrene and urethane plastics are often molded into plaques,
statues, and furniture ornaments. Often you cannot tell whether all
of the fancy "wood work" on a piece of furniture is really wood
or molded styrene or urethane. Ironically, it may not make much
difference.

If you chip or break or knock a piece out of some ornamental
furniture, you can use plastic wood to fill in the gap. It will hold
well to wood and to styrene. It will not hold as well to urethane
unless the shape of the blemish helps to secure the patch to the
original furniture.

Epoxy adhesives will grab onto all three of the furniture-making
materials. In every instance, however, the epoxy or plastic wood
will have to be camouflaged. Acrylic paints, described in Chapter 4,
cover a multitude of such sins.

Fiberglass, to homemakers, is material for drapes. But to chemists,
it is a plastic. Both are correct. The soft, durable fiberglass material
is saturated with epoxy resins, or other tough chemicals, and molded

into various shapes to form a plastic that is generally called fiberglass too. The plastic fiberglass is valuable for molded kitchen chairs, shrouds on lawn mowers, fenders or hoods on cars, the hull of lightweight boats, and wherever else tough but thin and shapely products are wanted.

Whenever fiberglass needs patching, your first stop should be an auto supply store that sells fender-unbending kits with pieces of white fiberglass material and cans of epoxy resins and hardener. Boatyards stock similar kits.

The epoxy resin gets smeared onto the broken area. Then a patch of fiberglass is pressed into the resin. Additional coats of epoxy add strength and smooth out the patch. For really rugged jobs, you can add additional layers of fiberglass after the initial patch has set. Each new layer should be slightly *larger* than the one beneath so the epoxy and fiberglass grab onto the original material and not only onto the patch itself.

When the final layer of fiberglass and epoxy has dried, you can *feather* the edges, which means to sand the perimeter of a patch until the surface of the patch and the surface of the patched item seem to blend together. Then you can repaint the patched area.

Patches made with fiberglass need not be limited to items made of fiberglass to begin with. Since epoxy resins stick well to nearly everything, a patch like this can be used over metal, plastic, wood, glass, plaster, and so on. Now there's a fiberglass patch available which works without adding extra epoxy. "Sun-Set" patches have resins pre-applied and they set on exposure to sunlight.

Thermosetting plastics encompass many different materials, but we will lump them all together. *Melamine* dishes, *Bakelite* handles on kettles or pots, *Formica* countertops, and similar very rigid, *very* heat-resistant plastics are virtually untouched by common chemicals and adhesives. The best glue for this class is epoxy, and even that is a bit chancy.

In the index, "Formica" is listed in several places. You will find a way to cover over chips and other Formica blemishes with acrylic paints. You could use the same technique for melamine dishes, but none of the glues and paints available for home use are rated by health authorities. In other words, you would never know if you were unwittingly endangering your health with a patch in a broken dish.

Toys can be repaired despite the contrary intentions and designs of toy manufacturers. You have to decide first whether or not a particular toy is really worth patching up. If it is, all of the basic laws of physics, chemistry, and engineering apply to toys as much as they do to everything else, except on a smaller scale.

Figure 210 "Sun Set" patch repairs boats, cars, and so on
with fiberglas and resin that cure permanently in sunlight.

Cheaper toys are generally made of styrenes, more expensive ones
of polyethylene or molded urethane. Batteries and the battery contacts on toys cause many headaches, but these items are covered in
earlier chapters. The transformers that power electric trains are not
much different than the transformers that help to power hi fi sets
and similar gadgets, so see Chapters 6 and 7.

Electric motors that drive the trains, cars, robots, and other
motorized toys are basically the same as the electric motors that
power adult items, electric knives, electric toothbrushes, and so on.

Check in the index under "electric motor," or reread the chapter on Motorized Household Gadgets.

You can replace burned out electric motors used in toys. The manufacturer, after all, did buy them somewhere. And they were probably "off the shelf" items. Mail order electronics supply houses usually offer a small selection of battery-powered electric motors suitable for toys. The popular scientific supply outlets generally have a bigger stock. And a well-stocked hobby store is probably the best stop of all when you are shopping for new toy motors.

Here are some of the important things to watch for in a replacement motor: It should operate at a voltage close to what the batteries put out. The AA, C, and D batteries all produce 1½ volts. So if your toy uses 2 batteries, the motor receives 3 volts. If the toy has 4 batteries, the motor gets 6 volts. You can miss the voltage mark by 25 percent easily. In general, a motor operating at a higher voltage gives you longer motor and battery life. With a motor rated for lower voltages, you get more speed and less life out of the motor and batteries.

Motors are often geared down to some appropriate speed. Replace-

Figure 211 Even books can be patched with all-purpose glue such as silicone adhesive.

ment motors can have gears already mounted to their shaft, a convenient arrangement. Not all gears are alike, however. When in doubt, make sure that the new gears will mesh with the existing set of gears inside the toy.

Your new motor must have at least as much power as the old. In toy-sized motors, if the new motor is about as big as the old one, it will probably be able to handle the job.

To reach the inner workings of a toy, you may have to engage in a little detective work. The assembly line often stuffs the various parts into place and then cements a plastic case around them. The cement is not durable, however. You can gently pry the case apart at its seam, fix the insides, and then apply your own cement to complete the job.

Missing wheels and other parts ruin hundreds of otherwise good toys. In the woodworking chapter, we discussed how to mold new handles to replace broken or lost ones. The same modeling techniques will work for toy wheels. Squirt a silicone rubber product into the mold you make according to details presented in Chapter 19.

Speaking of wheels, there are some timely techniques for replacing wheels, axles, and other mobilizing gadgets in Chapter 17. Toy wheels may be smaller than stroller and shopping cart wheels, but wheels are wheels.

The molding approach for new handles and new wheels can work for other missing toy parts too. Arms and legs of dolls can be molded. So can those abstract people in educational toys. Puzzles are especially prone to ruin after just one piece gets lost. Spray some lubricant into the empty spot to protect the existing pieces, squeeze some plastic wood into the cavity, sandpaper the new wooden piece when dry, paint it, and the puzzle is as good as new again.

A few tools, some hardware, or some chemicals, and this book, are about all you will ever need to keep your home in good shape. Those things, and plenty of confidence that men and women can fix damn near everything.

Index

461